Introduction

Ken Green and Ken Hardman

This reader in physical education is the outcome of a configuration of ideas and aims. In the first instance, the process of developing "introductory" and "issues" modules in physical education at undergraduate level provoked the search for a core text combining coverage of persistent themes and key issues in physical education with a wide range of suitable seminar papers. Whilst there have been a number of substantial additions to the literature on physical education in recent years, what we take to be evidently lacking is a collection of contributions from eminent authors on a breadth of enduring themes and contemporary issues in physical education.

The attempt to identify *one* core text was also a response to the pressure of circumstances created by wider developments in higher education. The ever-increasing numbers of students following physical education and sports science related under- and post-graduate degrees appears to have brought with it a similar growth in modules that engage in some way with physical education. Pressure on student pockets and on the budgets of libraries and physical education/sports science departments is focusing minds, ever more sharply, on the search for the ultimate all-singing, all-dancing core text that does everything except sit exams and produce assignments! Many lecturers have felt quite keenly in recent years the relative dearth of texts bringing together potential seminar or background readings into one affordable and accessible volume. Libraries, in turn, face immense difficulties ensuring that institutions meet their side of the educational bargain. This book is intended, therefore, to meet the demands of students and tutors alike by providing a core text utilising suitable articles that illustrate key themes or issues in physical education.

In 1994, the *Physical Education Review* was succeeded by the *European Physical Education Review.* The idea for the reader provided a particularly suitable means of celebrating the *Review's* contribution to the study of physical education and sport over the last twenty or so years. We believe that there are a number of articles, previously published in either the *Physical Education Review* or its *European* successor, that provide the kind of thought-provoking, rigorous and enduring material for such a text. We are aware that many pertinent articles remain hidden from the academic and professional gaze in back issues of the *Review*. At the same time, the continued purchasing of back issues, as well as what we are led to believe by librarians is the tendency for issues to "disappear", convinces us that this collection will be "popular"!

The study of physical education has increasingly become a multi-disciplinary and occasionally inter-disciplinary undertaking. The reader attempts to reflect the multi- and inter-disciplinary approach that continues to mark the *European Physical Education Review* out as a distinct periodical in much the same way as its predecessor, the *Physical Education Review*. Thus, the reader includes philosophical, physiological, psychological, sociological and pedagogical perspectives on central issues and enduring themes in the academic and professional study of physical education. It is hoped, then, that the multi-disciplinary nature of the book will offer readers ample opportunity to gain insight into, not only the world of physical education but, also, the contributions to be made to the field from a range of disciplinary perspectives.

We are very aware of the relatively brief shelf-life of some empirical studies. To this end we have attempted to incorporate articles related to ongoing conceptual issues as well as empirical studies that may continue to be of relevance and interest to under-graduate and post-graduate students. The seven parts each represent a theme and each of the chapters within the parts picks out, broadly speaking, an issue within or dimension of that theme.

Ken Green/Ken Hardman (eds.)

Physical Education
A Reader

Meyer & Meyer Sport

British Library Cataloguing in Publication Data
A catalogue record for this book is available from the British Library

Green/Hardman (eds.):
Physical Education : A Reader/Green/Hardman (eds.).
- Oxford : Meyer & Meyer Sport (UK) Ltd., 2000
ISBN 1-84126-027-4

© 1998 by Meyer & Meyer Sport (UK) Ltd. Oxford,
Aachen, Olten (CH), Vienna, Québec, Lansing/Michigan, Adelaide,
Auckland, Johannesburg, Budapest
Member of the World
Sportpublishers Association
Cover Design: Walter J. Neumann, N&N Design-Studio, Aachen
Cover exposure: frw, Reiner Wahlen, Aachen
Typesetting: Angela Bell, University College Chester
Printed and bound in Germany by Firma Mennicken, Aachen
ISBN 1-84126-027-4
email: verlag@meyer-meyer-sports.com

Physical Education: A Reader

This book was published in collaboration with the
North West Counties Physical Education Association

Of course, any attempt to satisfy several aims runs the risk of satisfying none! As a celebration of the *Physical Education Review* we have sought wherever possible to utilise what we considered to be significant contributions from well-known authors in the field. We are happy that we have achieved this. At the same time, however, we are aware that there are a number of papers and authors we have not included. For this we can only apologise whilst accepting that the responsibility for this particular attempt to achieve a balance in selection is entirely ours.

The vast majority of the contributions have been amended and/or updated, as and where appropriate, and for this we thank the authors concerned for their kind co-operation. We hope the book provides a service for tutors and students alike. All that remains is to point out that any revenues generated by the reader will be used to meet the costs of publication in the first instance. Any additional income would be used, in accordance with the constitution and practices of North Western Counties Physical Education Association as a non-profit organisation, in the furtherance of physical education.

PART 1

THE NATURE AND PURPOSES OF PHYSICAL EDUCATION

Chapter 1

Knowledge, Practice and Theory
in Physical Education

Andrew Reid

Introduction: Propositional Knowledge and the Academic Standpoint

There are many issues of educational interest which must be regarded as controversial, but this cannot be said of the proposition that education involves some engagement with, or acquisition of, knowledge. For whatever else the use of the word "education" may be thought to imply, it cannot find significant employment except with reference to contexts in which learners and their characteristic experiences and activities are involved. The characteristic experiences and activities of learners are, needless to say, experiences and activities of learning; and the concept of learning, whatever its complications, must necessarily include the idea of acquiring or engaging with knowledge, in at least some recognisable sense of that term.

In this chapter, I aim to explore some of the philosophical issues relating to knowledge in physical education. What follows, then, is an essay in the philosophy of physical education. It is reasonable to ask what the expression "philosophy of physical education" might mean, and why it should be considered a worthwhile undertaking; one widely accepted type of response runs along the following lines. The practices, traditions, professional judgements and intuitions of physical educators, and the policy initiatives and developments to which they are called upon to respond, can be said to express, presuppose or imply certain assumptions and beliefs about the nature, aims, values, content and procedures of physical education. It is a worthwhile undertaking, for both theoretical and practical purposes, to reflect upon, and attempt to articulate as clearly as we can, these presuppositions, implicit beliefs and so on. In the course of this enterprise, we may find that the presuppositions which concern us, once explicitly articulated, stand in need of careful examination, rigorous justification, critical analysis, and modification or reconsideration. This task of reflection, articulation, elucidation and analysis is the characteristic business of philosophical inquiry, and I would argue that it is an unavoidable task for anyone seriously or professionally concerned with physical education.

Philosophy of education as a distinct, analytically-oriented and rigorous discipline of the kind outlined above came to prominence in the 1960s as a result of the pioneering works of writers such as PETERS (1966) and HIRST (1974). While it would be accurate to say that the best-known writings of these philosophers deal primarily with the analysis of educational concepts and issues in general, a great deal of valuable work has nonetheless been done specifically in the philosophy of *physical education* in the last twenty or thirty years. The range of issues examined has been wide, but much of this work has focused on the topic of how the concept of physical education might be accommodated within the general framework of ideas about curriculum, teaching, learning and educational significance developed by analytical philosophers of education, and indeed about the adequacy of that conceptual framework in relation to ideas concerning the nature and aims of physical education. The essay which follows can be placed within this tradition. It attempts to examine some of the ways in which the philosophically important concept of knowledge comes into play in our thinking about physical education.

On the general question of the relation between knowledge and education, many philosophers and their followers have adopted a position which derives in essence from the view developed some thirty years ago by HIRST. According to HIRST (1974), the content of education is to be determined by the concept of "forms of knowledge": this provides the differentiated framework within which the learning activities and experiences of the pupil are to be systematically located, and which thus determines the mandatory core of knowledge to be experienced by all pupils. Ideas such as these about the epistemological basis of curriculum content and structure have some bearing (and, over the years, have generated much critical discussion) on the question of knowledge in physical education. But what is perhaps of particular significance is the concept of knowledge itself which, in general, plays the dominant role in this kind of curriculum philosophy, and which continues to exercise an influence. For writers such as the early HIRST, knowledge is what is expressed by true *propositions* or statements. It consists in the possession of true beliefs which can be justified or validated by the exercise of a range of rational procedures; empirical procedures of observation and experiment in the case of the natural sciences, logical procedures of deductive inference in the case of mathematics, and so on. The procedures which test, verify, and validate knowledge-claims are the methodological strategies of inquiry or investigation by which knowledge is generated. The crucial characteristic of the propositional or theoretical knowledge generated in these ways is that it is expressed in the statements of a language, which may be the ordinary language of everyday discourse or the technical language of the specialised subject. An obvious test of such knowledge is, therefore, the capacity to produce spoken or written material. This means, given the dominance of propositional knowledge in the context of education, that the standard form of assessment is the written or oral examination. The assumption that knowledge in education is essentially propositional (HAMM, 1989), then, is one which consorts easily with the idea of education as essentially *academic*.

Physical Education from the Academic Standpoint

Acceptance of this conventional assumption, with regard to physical education, leaves us with two options. These are, first, to acknowledge its traditionally non-academic, and therefore non-educational (or, at best, marginal), status; or, secondly, to argue that, despite appearances, the physical activities which comprise the familiar physical education curriculum can somehow be shown to have academic significance and thus educational worth.

There is strong and growing evidence to support the contention that the second of these options is rapidly acquiring the status of a new orthodoxy in physical education (see REID, 1996). On the understandable view that the marginal or extracurricular position is not tenable (if it ever was), it has been widely concluded that physical education must claim and justify a place within the educational mainstream. And if the possession of academic credentials is a condition of entry to the mainstream, then physical education must fulfil this requirement by making increasing demands of pupils in terms of the mastery of forms of propositional knowledge; thus, the familiar idea of physical education as the teaching and learning of practical physical activities comes to be regarded as problematic or unsatisfactory. The assessment of knowledge in physical education will, moreover, tend to be focused on the mastery of theoretical content and its expression in written form. A distinction is thus made between the practical performance of physical activities and the propositional or theoretical knowledge which is related to them. But what is to be the character of the knowledge promoted within physical education? An answer widely given to this question, within the new orthodoxy, is that the forms of propositional or theoretical knowledge most apt for its purposes are to be found in the physical and human *sciences* which can be directed to the study of physical activity and human movement. This emphasis on the scientific analysis of physical activity is given further reinforcement by assumptions about the relationship between theory and practice; in particular, the belief that practical skills and techniques in physical education are to be developed and improved through the application of scientific principles. Much of the discussion which follows is devoted to a critical examination of these claims.

If we are resistant to the conventional assumptions outlined earlier, and the academic picture of education for which they seem to provide some form of philosophical legitimation, however, then a third option becomes available. This third position maintains that physical education, in the familiar sense of the expression, can indeed satisfy the knowledge requirements of education; but it does so without making claims to academic significance on the basis of the propositional or theoretical knowledge with which it is held to be associated. It is this third position which is adopted here. Very little of what I say, however, can lay any claim to originality (see CARR, 1978, 1979, 1981). This makes the persistence of what I would regard as mistaken views all the more remarkable, since the instruments for exposing their weaknesses and confusions have been available to theorists of physical education for many years.

Practical Knowledge and Physical Education

I have noted the conceptual principle that education involves some engagement with or acquisition of knowledge; and I have suggested that the "academic" tradition in education is that which defines this knowledge in terms of the mastery of material and procedures which are expressed in verbal or linguistic or propositional form. If physical education is not concerned with such mastery or material or forms, then it is, according to this tradition, non-academic and, therefore, non-educational. Now I maintain that physical education is, in the familiar sense which I take to be satisfactory, not so concerned, but I also maintain that it is simply an error to define "knowledge" exclusively in terms of propositional contents or the procedures for generating them. Knowledge, in short, is not exclusively or even primarily propositional or theoretical. It is expressed not only in words or symbols, but also in actions; it takes practical, and not merely theoretical, form; it is expressed in terms of "knowing how" as well as "knowing that". If (as I would maintain) the activities which comprise the familiar curriculum of physical education are to be regarded essentially as expressions of practical knowledge or knowing-how, it follows that physical education thus satisfies the knowledge requirement of education, and that the attitude which consigns it, as non-academic, to the extra-curricular margins of mainstream education is simply mistaken. It is not the status of physical education which is problematic, then, but rather the academic view of education. This argument seems to me to be irrefutable (see CARR, 1978, 1979, 1981), but it clearly calls for some elaboration, particularly with regard to the claim that the activities in the familiar physical education curriculum are to be seen as forms of practical, rather than propositional, knowledge. It is to this issue that I now turn.

The idea that knowledge (or, more generally, human rationality) is capable of expression in practical ways, and not merely in the formulation of propositions has, at first glance, the air of platitude about it. Of course, we may say, we *know how* to do many things, as well as *knowing that* many things are the case. Our knowledge is not merely theoretical or contemplative or spectatorial; it is not confined to our attempts to develop a true description or valid explanation of the world; it comes into play in our interactions with the world, in our attempts to shape or change things, and not simply in our reports about them. Human beings are not merely detached and passive recorders of the scene, but agents, players involved actively in the events and processes which comprise it. We are endowed not only with intellect, but with will, and our rational powers are exhibited in both types of capacity. It is one thing, though, to recognise the reality, indeed the inescapable everydayness, of practical knowledge in human life; it is another to give a precise analysis of its character. In particular, it is important to be clear both about its analogies with propositional knowledge and, on the other hand, about the ways in which the two kinds of knowledge need to be distinguished.

A number of deeply insightful and valuable studies have been made by philosophers of the logical character of discourse about practical knowledge and related concepts (such as the concepts of action, ability and skill). The earliest discussions are to be found in the writings of ARISTOTLE, but it is only in the second half of the twentieth century that the investigation of these topics has received the attention which it deserves. The philosophical study of action, practice, ability and so on, indeed, can be traced in modern times to the pioneering works of RYLE (1949) and WITTGENSTEIN (1968), and subsequently to ANSCOMBE (1957), KENNY(1975), DAVIDSON (1980), VON WRIGHT (1983), and many others. This historical observation is of some significance for it helps to show how deep-rooted is the convention which sees epistemology, in the great tradition of modern philosophy which runs from DESCARTES through LOCKE, HUME and KANT to more recent times, as the theory which examines and defines the nature and limits of human knowledge. Epistemology, in this sense, has been concerned essentially with the conditions of *propositional* knowledge (see LEHRER, 1990; EVERITT and FISHER, 1995; PORTY, 1980; TAYLOR, 1995), with our attempts to say truly how things are. Where practical knowledge has been recognised, it has often been supposed that it must represent a subordinate or derivative form; that is, that knowing how can be dismissed as mere "knack", or the kind of "physical ability" which calls for little if any exercise of rationality. Alternatively, it is sometimes held that if rationality is exercised in practical contexts, then this is to be accounted for in terms of "application" of theory to practice; that is, through the operation of propositional or theoretical knowledge in ways which "inform" or "underpin" practical ability; so it may be concluded that practical knowledge "reduces", in some sense, to propositional knowledge. All of these ideas are important in relation to the analysis of the activities which comprise the physical education curriculum, and thus to the question of the educational status of physical education. I propose, therefore, to examine them rather more closely.

The suggestion that practical knowledge represents an inferior expression of human rational powers is easily disposed of, since it rests on a simple error, a confusion of two sets of distinctions. We can distinguish theoretical and practical knowledge; and we can also distinguish, in general, between simple (or easy, or undemanding) and complex (or difficult, or demanding) examples of each of these. Now to suppose that depth or complexity or difficulty is characteristic of theoretical knowledge as such, and simplicity likewise of knowing how, is to commit just this error, and it is surprising and significant to see how this is done in the writings of at least one distinguished philosopher of education (PETERS, 1966). The profoundly complex kinds of practical knowledge which are required in order, say, to fly an aeroplane or play Tchaikovsky's Piano Concerto No.1, and which call for learning of a particularly lengthy, deep and demanding kind, are not to be dismissed as "mere knack". Similarly, the intellectual disciplines which comprise the traditional academic curriculum afford countless opportunities for the acquisition of simple and undemanding examples of theoretical knowledge. This is just as well, perhaps, since otherwise it is hard to see how learners could ever get started on the road to mastery of these forms of discourse.

Practical Knowledge, Ability and Performance: Some Problems

Again, the idea that practical knowledge can be identified simply with physical ability needs to be considered carefully. As CARR (1978, 1979, 1981) has shown, in a number of papers which are of great importance for physical educationists, it is a mistake to suppose that the relation between these concepts is one of identity. "Ability" is a notoriously slippery idea, capable of being used in a large number of quite different ways. Nevertheless there is at least one sense in which we can say that we know how to perform a given action, yet are unable (perhaps through injury) to do so, and that, conversely, we are able (perhaps through luck or chance) to perform a given action, without knowing how we managed it. CARR (1978), then, insists that we distinguish between practical knowledge and ability. There is, perhaps, some risk in pressing too hard at this point, since it may tempt us into the mistaken, indeed paradoxical conclusion that practical knowledge can be identified without reference to any kind of performative criterion. We may thus be led to the view which features in some recent official policy documents in physical education, that is, that "practical performance" must be distinguished from "knowledge and understanding". It is just this move which lies behind the idea which is the main object of criticism in this paper; that is, the idea that the knowledge-component of curricular physical activities is to be understood as essentially propositional or theoretical knowledge; knowledge, in short, of the kind which conforms to the requirements of the academic tradition in education.

The solution to this problem would seem to lie in the distinctions to be drawn between the different senses of the word "ability", and perhaps, as KENNY (1989) has shown, between an ability and its *exercise*. In the latter case, we would say that a lack of opportunity, or a disabling impediment to the exercise or demonstration of ability (which, in one of its many senses, KENNY identifies with practical knowledge), does not allow us to conclude that the ability is not present. It is fairly clear, however, that in normal cases the criteria of practical knowledge would have to include some reference to performance, that is, to what is to be done (since otherwise it could not intelligibly be characterised as practical knowledge). A complete specification of these criteria would probably refer to consistency and flexibility of performance, in order to enable a distinction to be drawn between the achievement which we attribute to chance and that which we see as testifying to skill. Practical knowledge, then, is not to be identified with or reduced to "mere" ability (in KENNY's terms: ability is not to be identified with or reduced to its exercise), but we must nevertheless have criteria for the meaningful attribution of such knowledge, and in standard cases these criteria will include reference to performance. Where CARR is surely correct, though, is in his analysis of practical inference as the "logic of knowing how". If propositional knowledge can be analysed (with some reservations) in terms of the inferential procedures we adopt in order to verify or validate our beliefs, then practical knowledge can be seen, analogously, in terms of the inferential procedures we adopt in order to achieve or effect our purposes, intentions, wants, decisions and the like. The key idea here is "inferential procedures"; practical knowledge, unlike simple physical ability, calls for the exercise of our rational powers. The question is, how is this exercise of rationality to be described?

Theory and Practice in Physical Activities (I): Technical Knowledge

For CARR (1978), the exercise of reason in the context of practical activity cannot be explained in terms which would reduce it to a form of propositional knowledge or inference. Just as it is a mistake to suppose that practical knowledge can be reduced to mere physical ability (which seems to dispense with the need to refer to reasoning), so it is a mistake to suppose that "knowing how" reduces to "knowing that", or that practical inference reduces to propositional inference (which seems to dispense with the performative criterion of practical knowledge). It is precisely because practical inference concludes in action, and propositional inferences conclude in propositions, that their logical character has to be sharply distinguished. It is not difficult to show, for example, that there are patterns of valid inference in practical reasoning which are not valid in standard propositional logic (see KENNY, 1975). CARR's position is that it will not do, therefore, to hold what may seem to be the common-sense view, that is, that rational practice is to be regarded simply as physical ability which is informed by, or underpinned by, or based on, theoretical knowledge or reasoning. If practical knowledge is not to be identified with ability, then it cannot, given the distinction between theoretical and practical inference, be identified with "ability plus theory" either.

Nevertheless, it would seem that propositional knowledge must play *some* role in practical reasoning. An important case would be the way in which it features in the role of minor premiss in what AUDI (1989) calls the "basic schema of practical reasoning". According to this schema, practical reasoning starts from (i) a major or motivational premiss which expresses some end, purpose, want or intention, and proceeds via (ii) a minor or cognitive premiss setting out what should be done (that is, the means or method to be adopted) if this purpose is to be achieved, to (iii) the practical conclusion of embarking upon this course of action. We might say, since propositional knowledge operates in this schema in relation to one's grasp of methods, techniques or strategies for achieving one's purposes, that propositional or theoretical knowledge typically functions as *technical* knowledge or as the technical component of practical knowledge. There are two features, then, of this propositional component of practical discourse which call for particular emphasis. The first is its hypothetical character: it typically specifies the conditions which have to be met or the means to be adopted if a given effect or end is to be achieved. The second is its reference to human action; it typically specifies what the agent must do. The propositional or theoretical component of practical knowledge, then, when it is employed in its technical role, functions as a hypothetical imperative, which presupposes the possibility of human action. It is in this technical role, arguably, that we see the most familiar example of "theory" in its relation to "practice".

Where the assessment of this technical knowledge, however, is conducted in abstraction from its use in physical education contexts by means of written examinations and the like, then it is assessment not of knowledge and understanding as such, but of *theoretical* knowledge and understanding. Some philosophers (for example, DUMMETT and SEARLE) have made the point that practical knowledge can (in some ways, or to some degree) be represented in theoretical terms. However, this is not to say that practice translates into or is reducible to theory. In fact, most of our everyday practical knowledge, according to SEARLE (1992), operates at the level of "background"; we "distort" such practical knowledge when we attempt to express it explicitly in theoretical terms. DUMMETT (1993) regards practical knowledge (in the context of knowing a language) as involving an implicit theoretical component which it might be possible, for some philosophical purposes, to make explicit. But, he maintains, it would be unreasonable to demand this ability to represent practical knowledge in theoretical terms as a necessary condition of the possession of the practical knowledge in question. We may apply these kinds of consideration to our discussion of technical knowledge or practical inference in relation to physical education. From this perspective, we can see that inability to give an explicit formulation of the relevant propositions cannot be taken as evidence of incomplete or defective practical knowledge. It would be at least as serious a mistake to regard the ability to give explicit expression to such theoretical knowledge as constituting a *sufficient* condition of knowledge as such in physical education. This is precisely the error made by those who wish to square physical education with the academic standpoint, in the mistaken belief that since knowledge is essentially propositional, then the knowledge component of physical activities must be so also. The criterion of practical knowledge is practical performance, and the mastery of the rational techniques or methods which constitute the inferential link between purpose and achievement is shown in their consistent and flexible use. Assessment of performance, then, is assessment of practical knowledge, and if some test of theoretical or propositional knowledge is required in addition, it can only be because we consider such knowledge to be worth having, either for its own sake or for its interest and relevance in illuminating the background to, or context of, the physical activities which are our main concern.

The Science and Technology of Human Movement

In considering propositional knowledge in its "technical" role or capacity in practical inference, it is reasonable to inquire into the general character of the propositions or beliefs which come into play when we try to identify strategies which will enable us to achieve our purposes. The answer which suggests itself intuitively is that the cognitive premisses, technical prescriptions or hypothetical imperatives employed by sportsmen and sportswomen, games players, athletes, dancers, gymnasts and so on will reflect or draw on what might loosely be called the lore, expertise, pragmatic wisdom, accumulated craft knowledge, collective experience and traditions of the activity in question. Technical knowledge, in other words, is an expression of what has been learned about the activity and the conditions of successful or effective practice, and is capable of being communicated among practitioners, for example in the contexts of teaching, coaching, advice, demonstration, and the like.

Now it may be supposed that we can distinguish, with reference to practical activities, between a "craft" or pre-scientific approach or stage, which draws on technical knowledge of the kind described here, that is, knowledge based on accumulated experience and expressed in everyday language; and a "technological" approach or stage, which purports to be based on rigorous, systematic, scientific knowledge and research (see HABERMAS, 1987). On the basis of such a distinction, it might be argued that the propositional knowledge which is relevant in physical education will, ideally, be of this latter kind: that is, scientific knowledge, for example of the biomechanical or physiological principles which underlie and explain human motor activity. This view has some degree of surface plausibility. Knowledge advances, becomes more systematic and precise, more scientific. Rough working generalisations become subject to strict experimental testing. The loose, anecdotal, subjective, value-laden, impressionistic language of personal experience is replaced by a terminology which aspires to mathematical standards of exactitude and objectivity. It is a characteristic of modern society that human activity in many spheres exhibits just this form of progress from craft to technology, that is, to the planned application of scientific knowledge; it seems reasonable, therefore, to hold that the scientific study of human movement provides the knowledge basis on which technical progress, including the improvement of skill and performance in physical activities, should be founded.

Whatever truth there may be in this view, it should be recalled that if physical activities are to be understood as expressions of practical knowledge and rationality, then their propositional or theoretical component (in the "minor premiss" or "cognitive premiss" sense under consideration here) must be expressible in the form of technical prescriptions, that is, it must specify some action to be taken in order to secure a given purpose. The argument that the propositional content of knowledge in physical education courses or lessons is essentially scientific knowledge, then, must be considered in the light of this requirement. It is not necessary to dispute the claim that physiology and biochemistry and biomechanics can furnish information about the physical causes and effects of motor activity. What has to be examined, however, is the claim that such propositional knowledge can be *applied* in the context of practical reasoning. It is not the function of physiology and biochemistry, as forms of scientific enquiry aimed at increasing our theoretical knowledge and understanding, to produce guidance for the benefit of practitioners of physical activities. The propositions generated by scientific enquiry, in short, do not take the form of hypothetical imperatives. Whether they can be adapted to such constructions must be an open question.

It is generally acknowledged that the familiar, everyday, common-sense language of human action is not reducible or translatable into a "scientific" language of bodily movement rather than intentional or purposive activity (MELDEN, 1968; KENNY, 1973; SEARLE, 1984; TAYLOR, 1964). The question of the role of scientific knowledge and explanation in physical education is, in fact, a particular instance or application of a more general philosophical issue, that is, the question of how mental or psychological activity is related to material, physical or bodily events. The consensus, shared by philosophers of radically divergent views, is that the language of mind and action is conceptually autonomous. At the root of this autonomy is the logical characteristic known to philosophers as "intentionality"; that is, briefly, the inability of everyday talk about belief, purposes and the like to conform to the requirements of the truth-functional logic pre-supposed by scientific discourse. For some, admittedly, this conclusion provides all the more reason for regarding our everyday language (or "folk psychology") as simply confused, outdated, and in need of replacement; this is the standpoint, for example, of the theory known as "eliminative materialism", which is associated with philosophers such as CHURCHLAND (1988, 1994, 1995).

Whatever side we may take in this debate, however, we are left with the conclusion that practical inference, which plays a necessary part in the practical knowledge comprising the content of the physical education curriculum, presupposes the use of intentionalist concepts derived from the everyday discourse of human action, which cannot be adequately expressed in the non-intentionalist language of the physical sciences. Even where the possibility of translation may look fairly straightforward, such as (for example) in a description of the act of throwing the javelin, the physical or mechanical account of the motor activity involved cannot, as a matter of logic, encompass its intentionality, as expressed in the social or contextual factors which give the activity its human *meaning* and which thus render it intelligible as an act of javelin throwing rather than something physically similar, but having a quite different significance (an act of spear-throwing in battle, for example). So far as physical education is concerned, therefore, the test of the value of this kind of propositional knowledge appears to be its technical use or applicability. If it fails this test, then it is hard to see how it can be considered relevant to the educational purposes of physical education. By this criterion, it is difficult to see how scientific knowledge of processes lying outside the range of voluntary or conscious control, for example of the neuro-physiological causes of muscular contractions, can be of practical use to physical educators and their pupils. This is not to say that such knowledge is not of great theoretical interest in its own right, or indeed of great practical interest to, for instance, practitioners in the field of medicine.

The assumption which must be guarded against, is that the propositional knowledge generated by the sciences of human movement is *necessarily* relevant to the purposes of physical education. There are clearly cases where it would not be difficult to demonstrate such relevance. Where the physical education teacher is concerned with the promotion of knowledge in relation to health and fitness, for instance, it is evident that our understanding of what needs to be done to achieve the goals which are appropriate in this area depends to a considerable degree on the findings of, for example, research in physiology and biochemistry. But the idea that the sciences of human movement are necessary, and not just potentially useful, for our practical knowledge and understanding of curricular physical activity in general is simply mistaken when it is based on a confusion between human action and its associated physical processes, conditions or mechanisms. It represents the dogmatic closure of what I referred to earlier as the open question of the applicability of scientific knowledge in physical education. This move could perhaps be seen as a symptom of *scientism* (the doctrine that science represents the only genuine kind of knowledge), rather than as deriving from a judicious consideration of the proper scope and contribution of science in relation to physical education.

Theory and Practice in Physical Activities (II): Rules and Meaningful Conduct

We have been focusing so far on theoretical or propositional knowledge in relation to its role in the minor, technical or cognitive premiss in practical reasoning, that is, in terms of *applicability*; and there might be a temptation to suppose that this represents the only, or perhaps the most significant, way in which "theory" relates to "practice". We might call this the "technicist" view of the theory-practice relation; or even the technicist *fallacy*. But propositional knowledge, and the intentionality which we have seen to be a crucial factor in our everyday understanding of human action, have a profoundly important part to play elsewhere in the process of practical inference. As we noted earlier, practical reasoning can be said to start with a "major" or "motivational" premiss (AUDI, 1989) in which a *want*, *purpose*, or *intention* is expressed. Now such intentions can only be formulated, insofar as they are intelligible or meaningful, against a background, or from within a context, of recognisable human goals, values, rules, norms, concepts, and the like. The desire to reduce one's handicap, for example, depends for its intelligibility on a fair amount of prior, taken-for-granted understanding about the norms and principles which govern the game of golf. It is with reference to such norms and principles, moreover, that we assess the propriety (and not merely the effectiveness) of the techniques and strategies considered at the "minor premiss" stage of practical inference. The measures we take to achieve our aim of handicap-reduction, that is to say, have to be *legitimate* in terms of the norms and conventions of golf. I have argued that there is room for doubt about the possibility of translating scientific descriptions of the causal mechanisms of motor activity into technical imperatives, that is, about the ways in which propositional knowledge is to be characterised in its technical capacity; but we cannot really have any doubts about the nature of the propositional knowledge which comes into play at the level of the constitutive norms and principles of games and similar activities. For knowledge of this kind can only be understood as a logical *presupposition* of genuine participation in the physical activities which comprise the physical education curriculum, and not merely as useful for their more effective practice. In the case of games, as in our golf example, the adoption of plans, purposes, goals, tactics, moves, responses and so on must take place within an (at least implicit) awareness of the rules and codes governing the game, insofar as such purposes and actions can be regarded as valid or meaningful. Propositional knowledge, in short, does not function here as "theory" which is "applied" to practice. Understanding what it is to play football or tennis is a question rather of mastering the concepts, principles, constitutive rules and norms which define and govern such curricular physical activities, which identify and distinguish them, and which express their nature, meaning and purpose (see RAZ, 1975; SEARLE, 1969; WINCH, 1952; PETERS, 1960). It is a matter, indeed, of grasping certain features of a socially or culturally determined form of life. Such normative principles are not *applied* to (pre-existing) practice, but are logically *prior* to it; they determine what *counts* as football, tennis, and so on. Logical priority, however, does not imply pedagogical priority; it is generally in the context of practical experience and social interactions with others, rather than from a preliminary scrutiny of the rule book, that we gradually develop and sharpen this conceptual knowledge and understanding of what it is to play tennis or football. As is the case with the technical component of practical knowledge, insofar as its proper operation is in the context of practice, the criteria by which this knowledge of constitutive norms and principles is assessed are essentially performative. We need to bear in mind SEARLE's (1992) and DUMMETT's (1993) strictures, noted earlier, upon the demand for an explicit formulation of background pre-suppositions. If we set out to assess knowledge in terms of written examinations and the like, then we are assessing not practical knowledge but theoretical knowledge. No doubt, as with the scientific theory of physical activities, a case could be made out for the educational value of this kind of study in its own right; but the idea that it is necessary to attempt to make out a case for it in relation to physical education is based on the mistake of supposing that the performance of physical activities does not in itself constitute an expression of knowledge.

Conclusion

The new orthodoxy which seeks to redefine physical education in terms of the opportunities which it provides for theoretical study is based on a series of errors. The first and most fundamental of these is its uncritical adoption of the academic standpoint, which identifies the knowledge condition of education as a requirement for the pursuit of propositional knowledge. The second error consists in the distinction which is drawn between the practical performance of physical activities and the knowledge which is related to them. On such a distinction, knowledge in physical education must inevitably be characterised in propositional or theoretical terms, and the scene is set to shift in physical education from the games hall or playing field to the classroom. The third error is to assume that the major theoretical component of physical education activities is supplied by the scientific investigation of human movement, and that this knowledge can be applied unproblematically to the improvement of practice. Where this view is not held as a matter of dogma, the possibility of science making a useful contribution to practice in physical education may be regarded as a question which is open to empirical investigation. But the scope of this contribution must be defined by the principle that practice pre-supposes the concept of rational, voluntary, purposive human action. The fourth error is to construe the theory-practice relationship exclusively or primarily in terms of the improvement of technical knowledge or skill, and thus to overlook the fundamental role of constitutive norms and principles in our understanding of curricular physical activities. The final error is the failure to grasp that since practical human activities such as those which comprise the familiar physical education curriculum are essentially norm-governed, meaningful social constructions, the critical test of genuine knowledge and understanding on the part of those who engage in them is the satisfactoriness and appropriateness, and not merely the technical effectiveness, of the conduct they exhibit. The probable effect of these errors, assuming that they remain uncorrected, will be a radical change in the ways in which physical education is conceived and taught, in comparison with the traditional approach with which this discussion began; but it is not to be expected that change which is rooted in the patterns of confusion outlined above will be change for the better.

References

ANSCOMBE, G.E.M. (1957) *Intention*. Oxford, Blackwell.

AUDI, R. (1989) *Practical reasoning*. London, Routledge.

CARR, D. (1978) Practical reasoning and knowing how. *Journal of Human Movement Studies*, 4, 15-17.

CARR, D. (1978) Practical pursuits and the curriculum. *Journal of Philosophy of Education*, 12, 69-80.

CARR, D. (1979) Aims of physical education. *Physical Education Review*, 2, 2, 91-100.

CARR, D. (1980) The language of action, ability and skill (Part II). *Journal of Human Movement Studies*, 14, 116-118.

CARR, D. (1981) Knowledge in practice. *American Philosophical Quarterly*, 18, 1, 53-54.

CARR, D. (1981) On mastering a skill. *Journal of Philosophy of Education*, 15, 1, 87-96.

CHURCHLAND, P. (1988) *Matter and consciousness*. MIT Press. Revised edition.

CHURCHLAND, P. (1995) Eliminative materialism and the propositional attitudes. In W. LYONS (Ed) *Modern philosophy of mind*. London, Everyman/Dent, pp.214-239.

CHURCHLAND P. and CHURCHLAND, P.S. (1994) Intertheoretic reduction: a neuroscientist's field guide. In R. WARNER and T. SZUBKA (Eds) *The mind-*

body problem: a guide to the current debate. Oxford, Blackwell, pp.41-54.

DAVIDSON, D. *Essays on actions and events*. Oxford, Blackwell

DUMMETT, M. (1993) *The seas of language*. Blackwell, Oxford.

EVERITT, N. and FISHER, A. (1995) *Modern epistemology*. New York, McGraw-Hill.

HABERMAS, J. (1987) *Toward a Rational Society*. Oxford, Polity Press.

HAMM, C. (1989) *Philosophical issues in education*. London, Falmer Press.

HIRST, P. (1974) *Knowledge and the curriculum*. London, Routledge.

KENNY, A. (1973) Freedom, spontaneity and indifference. In T. HONDERICH (Ed) *Essays on freedom of action*. London, Routledge, pp.93-95.

KENNY, A. (1975) *Will, freedom and power*. Oxford, Blackwell.

KENNY, A. (1989) *The metaphysics of mind*. Oxford, Blackwell.

LEHRER, K. (1990) *Theory of knowledge*. London, Routledge.

MELDEN, A.I. (1968) Willing. In A.WHITE (Ed) The philosophy of action. Oxford, Blackwell, pp.70-79.

PETERS, R.S. (1960) *The concept of motivation*. London, Routledge. 2nd edition.

PETERS, R.S. (1966) *Ethics and education*. London, Allen and Unwin.

RAZ, J. (1975) *Practical reason and norms*. London, Hutchinson.

REID, A. (1996) The concept of physical education in current curriculum and assessment policy in Scotland. *European Physical Education Review*, 2, 1, 7-18.

RORTY, R. (1980) *Philosophy and the mirror of nature*. Oxford, Blackwell.

RYLE, G. (1949) *The concept of mind*. London. Hutchinson.

SEARLE, J. (1969) *Speech acts*. Cambridge, Cambridge University Press.

SEARLE, J. (1984) *Minds, brains and science*. London, BBC.

SEARLE, J. (1992) *The Rediscovery of mind.* Cambridge, Mass., MIT Press.

TAYLOR, C. (1955) *Overcoming epistemology. Philosophical Arguments.* Harvard, Harvard University Press.

TAYLOR, C. (1964) *The explanation of behaviour.* London, Routledge.

VON WRIGHT, G.H. (1983) *Practical reason.* Oxford, Blackwell.

WINCH, P. (1958) *The idea of a social science and its relation to philosophy.* London, Routledge.

WITTGENSTEIN, L. (1968) *Philosophical investigations.* Trans. G.E.M. Anscombe. 3rd edition. Oxford, Blackwell.

Chapter 2

The Justification of Physical Education

Jim Parry

Preamble

Twenty years ago, after Prime Minister James Callaghan had initiated the 'Great Debate on Education' that produced the new National Curriculum proposals, Physical Education (PE) was not one of the twelve subjects chosen by Her Majesty's Inspectorate (HMI) for discussion in the 'Red Book' of 1977. Despite a 'Supplementary Working Paper on PE' (HMI, 1979) of scarcely three pages in length, the long-awaited and long-promised 'position paper' (that would outline the position of PE on the new curriculum) had still not appeared when I was writing this article in 1988. Naturally, this was a matter of the greatest concern. Partly (but only partly) because of the above, there had been no organised response or initiative by the PE profession itself, either to chronic problems of self-definition and curriculum development or to the apparent unwillingness or inability of HMI or Department for Education and Science (DES) to show leadership. Everyone was waiting for a lead that took a very long time to come. As PROCTOR (1984) warned in this regard: "Arguably, no other subject at a national level has defaulted to such an extent in this vitally important area" (p.9).

Ten years ago some of us were almost at panic stations. Although many in the PE profession and elsewhere had long thought that PE and Religious Education (RE) were the only two subjects which had a statutory place on the school curriculum, the DES (1984) had set the record straight by announcing that only RE enjoyed that status. It also floated the idea that PE and Games should become a 'free option' in years 4 and 5 (see MEEK, 1986, p.76). Also, there had been severe cutbacks in initial training places for PE students, followed by a readily predictable shortage of PE teachers. At one stage, PE was even quoted in the press in the top three shortage subjects with mathematics and physics. These cutbacks had coincided with an expansion in the provision of places for the training of leisure and recreation professionals and in the privatisation of fitness, health and leisure facilities whilst school playing-fields remained at risk. The following chapter should be read in that context. I was trying, in 1988, both to alert the reader to the seriousness of the situation; and also to suggest a route to a more secure long-term justification of PE as a school subject.

Physical Education, Justification and the National Curriculum

In a chapter of a recently published collection examining the responses of a number of subjects to HMI/DES proposals for the 5-16 National Curriculum (PARRY, 1988a) I remarked upon the "possible threat to the continued existence of (parts of) PE on the school curriculum" (PARRY, 1987). I tried to identify a number of worrying omissions within and alarming implications of, the current debate, arguing that there had been a "virtual absence of PE from serious, detailed informed and open discussion at national level". In examining HMI/DES publications, I tried to show the dangers for PE of the 'areas of experience' approach favoured by HMI, especially as exemplified by the treatment of PE in the documents themselves. An important interim conclusion was that the fashionable position which defines PE in terms of the area of experience called 'the physical' is theoretically weak but also practically suicidal, since it conflicts with the firmly-held and oft-stated view of HMI that no subject bears sole and total responsibility for any one area of experience. Indeed, in one document HMI go out of their way to announce a whole range of 'physical' activities which seem to have nothing to do with PE (such as keyboard skills, writing, craft skills, etc.) whilst omitting to mention PE activities (such as games, gymnastics, dance, etc.).

Whilst rejecting the 'area of experience' or 'process' account of PE, I argued for a 'reactionary' conception of PE which saw it as a *subject* defined by its *activities*. The important task remaining was to make a case for this subject as a justifiable part of the school curriculum, and it is to this task that I now turn.

This is a large and difficult task, as well as an urgent and important one. I would like to begin by illustrating this assertion firstly through an examination of a recent document which looks at one part of the subject, sport, and secondly through a consideration of some traditional claims. We should then, at least, be in a position to see just what kind of situation we are in, and what we might need to do to get out of it.

The Murdoch Desk Study

The Murdoch Desk Study (a comprehensive collection of source materials) was asked to consider "the place of sport in the PE curriculum". Naturally, this brief admits of a variety of interpretations, and could be addressed from the point of view of the historian, sociologist, political theorist, administrator, teacher and a host of others. To my mind, though, to consider the place of sport on the PE curriculum means not only to ask descriptive questions about what is currently the case, or how things have changed, or what is likely to result from certain influences, but also to ask for reasons why sport *ought* to have a place in the PE curriculum. This sort of questioning is conspicuous by its absence from many PE and sport documents, and I believe it to be a very serious weakness which has contributed significantly to present-day difficulties.

The Murdoch study would undoubtedly serve a useful purpose in informing the work of a committee which, indeed, was the reason for its being commissioned. However, for our present purposes, it can afford us only the background information on which our judgements will be based – it does not advance the justificatory arguments a shred.

This is not just my view. The document itself makes quite clear its role as the under-labourer for the reasonings of others. Let me illustrate this by outlining three requirements of a well-grounded judgement. In order to present an argument or a case for X, I would need at least three things:

[i]   I would need to be able to identify the status of different kinds of evidence from different sources and assess the relative merits of particular findings. However, the study says:

> The evidence has been freely used and there has been no attempt to discriminate by appraisal of the quality or value ... The available evidence could therefore be described as (a) substantiated (b) unsubstantiated (c) impressionistic (d) distorted.

That is to say, no attempt has been made to identify the status and assess the merits of the work presented.

[ii]   I would need to present some account of my use of terms above and beyond a simple stipulation. This is because a simple stipulation suffers from the following difficulties:

•   it is difficult to get everyone to agree to your stipulation, in which case (for those who dispute your favoured version) the argument has not even begun;

•   a simple stipulation will constrain further discussion by failing to be sufficiently flexible to respond to the complexity of practice which is precisely the object of enquiry;

•   a simple stipulation gives us no guidance as to how the favoured definition is to be applied and interpreted in practice (this is the difficulty faced, for example, by all codes of practice: how are the crucial terms of the propositions to be construed and applied to particular circumstances?).

So I would need some statement, some general account over and above a bald 'take it or leave it' authoritative edict, which would give me some idea of the overall evaluative positions of the proposer, which would in turn permit me to understand what the definition might mean when I am to apply it in actual practice.

The study recognises the need for something like this (pp.11-12), but merely indicates the problem, rather than offering suggestions and advice as to how to proceed.

[iii]   Most importantly, I would then need to consider a range of justificatory arguments for their adequacy. This is one way of showing that there is actually a genuine question here. Far too often the case for the defence is regarded as having been proven from the outset. The

people writing the documents are themselves already committed to a particular position, and have already decided on the eventual outcome of the argument. No wonder that the justificatory argument is often either very cursory or else is not addressed at all.

This might be well and good whilst we are all sitting round a table looking familiar faces in the eye and stroking each other's prejudices. But in the real world there are actually people who would casually disembowel the PE profession if they could. Even if some people may never be persuaded by our arguments we should seek to address the widest constituency so as to persuade more people than just ourselves of our worth. And this means that arguments concerning the justifiability of including sport in curricular or extra-curricular school time must be fairly and squarely addressed. I would go further than this to claim that such discussions should now be seen by the profession as being of the first importance, rather than being relegated to a few general sentences at the beginning and end of documents.

Again, the study sees the need for something like this, but merely points out:

> ... a felt need for clarification of intent, roles and purposes of both PE and sport in young people's lives ... a reappraisal of the unique role of PE in the total experience of young people. (pp. 52-3)

Now, I think that it has been important to spell out just what the Murdoch study has not set out to do, for it makes clear the enormity of the task still to hand. Often, when we feel our ignorance, it is held that what is needed is 'more research', where 'research' means the collection and analysis of more data. But it must now be clear that a continued consideration of descriptive factors will not advance the task significantly, especially if this is undertaken (as it usually is) with no explicit consideration of the only important question: are there any good reasons for the inclusion of PE and sport in school provision? The task in hand requires critical thinking of a philosophical kind.

On Justifying Justification

Sometimes the view is expressed that there is something wrong in spending too much time on this kind of question. The suggestion is that too much philosophical bone-worrying or navel-contemplation is itself a symptom of decline, and that subjects which are secure and confident of their place don't *have* to justify themselves – they just get on with the job. The complaint is that it is unfair that PE should have to bother with this difficult and irksome chore when other subjects do not. Such a view is mistaken. We must do this kind of work because, firstly, we *need* to, especially at the present time. This is a simple matter of necessity – our survival is at stake. If this does not apply, at the moment, to other subjects, then perhaps this is because they have been successful in this task in the past, or because there is a consensus as to their educational value. If this were true of PE (if we were not under threat) then perhaps I would not be writing this. But it is not, we are, and I am.

However, self-defence or self-promotion are not the only reasons for a justification. Even if a subject did have a secure place in the curriculum, it would still be desirable for teachers of it to be able to produce a reasoned account of that state of affairs – for, secondly, the *reasons* they would give (if followed through into practice) would determine the qualities and values of the subject as taught. The justification is simply a summary of all those practical principles held dear by the teacher – a conscious attempt at articulating what we think we should be doing. Sometimes this may begin with a critical review of our present practice, which may demand an analysis of the premises of our policies and actions. These may be deeply concealed, maybe even from ourselves, but unless they are uncovered and recognised they may continue to determine our practice without the willing consent of our deliberate reason. Every practical proposal will be made from within a philosophical position, whether this is explicitly articulated or implicitly presupposed. Any new proposal will not be clear to its proposers, never mind to outsiders, unless its philosophical commitments are made explicit. This is the internal point of a rationale.

So we need a justification:
* to defend and promote our subject; if we are not doing that, our justification is not good enough;

* to tell ourselves what we think we are (or should be) about. If we are not clear about our values and our direction, we need to think again about our justification.

It seems clear to me that there is general agreement within the profession that we are not doing a good enough job in either of these areas, and so we cannot escape the task, which is of an unavoidably philosophical nature. Let me now try to open up the question in a way which I hope may be helpful in contributing to a conception of PE and sport which will neither presuppose its worth nor make it subservient to other values.

Some Traditional Justifications

Let us begin by examining some traditional claims about the goods promoted by PE and sport to see whether they will advance our search for a justification for PE in the curriculum.

1. Health

It is often argued that PE and sport make a contribution to the health of individuals because it keeps them fit and well-exercised, thus delaying the onset of 'diseases of affluence' and enhancing the quality of life. Well, we cannot deny that sportspeople often look like paragons of health. But it is not at all obvious that it is the physical activity that makes them healthy. Indeed, when I was a PE teacher, I needed to know that the children were *healthy* before they could take part. When I was a footballer, I trained so as to be fit to participate. True, the games also contributed to my fitness – but I trained to be fit to play, rather than playing in order to become fit. The fitness was instrumental to the game, rather than the other way around.

These observations are reinforced by others: for example, it does not appear to be the case that people who have stopped playing games are in better health than those who never played. Possibly, even, games playing induces a certain life-style which becomes destructive if maintained after retiring from activity. Also, the playing of games itself constitutes a health hazard, which in some cases is very severe indeed. I am not saying that a health hazard is necessarily a bad thing. There are many of us whose functions are permanently impaired through sporting injury, but who would not have missed out for the world, and would gladly opt for it again in full knowledge of the risks. Sport may assist a healthy life-style, but it may not. This is not a secure foundation on which to build a justification: maybe, and maybe not.

2. Character

Another suggestion, dating from the days of public-school athleticism (if not before), is that there is some connection between the playing of sport and the development of desirable traits of character. A more modern way of expressing this kind of thought is to suggest that PE and sport makes a contribution to moral education.

Again, the answer is maybe and maybe not. Under certain circumstances, and given good educational leadership, sport may have the potential to affect children for the better. But who would claim the McEnroes and Bests to be amongst the moral giants of our time, regardless of their undoubted sporting prowess? The case here is at best not proven. Sportspeople do not seem to have a monopoly on virtue, and abstainers do not seem to be particularly pernicious or vicious, even on average. The crucial factor here seems to be pedagogical methodology rather than the particular subject-matter – but insofar as the justification relies upon methodology it *weakens* the subject's justification.

3. Socialisation

A less ambitious claim (since it makes no reference to the specific values of education) is that sport can contribute to the socialisation of children. Two examples of this refer to competition and rule-following. It is argued that, since society is competitive (or since we are all innately competitive), sport acts as a microcosm of society, wherein children may learn and practise those qualities which will make them socially successful. Or it is argued that strict enforcement of clear and agreed rules by an impartial authority on pain of a sanction provides children with an unambiguous model of correct social conduct, and encourages their willing obedience to legitimate order.

The problem with this kind of argument is that it fails to address the ultimate questions. It presupposes that the above outcomes, if they occur, *are* desirable. But it is open to us to ask further questions, such as: is competition a social virtue?; do we want our children to be 'successful' in those terms?; if we did, could *everyone* be successful, or would we have to deal with the 'failures' produced as well?; is there a clear right and wrong (even in games)?; do we want our children just to follow the rules obediently?; is sport anyway an agent of conservatism and anti-intellectualism? These are some of the questions which an educational argument would have to address. They cannot be swept under the carpet by presenting them as claims about socialisation.

4. Art

There are those who, supposing art to be deemed respectable without argument, have either claimed that sport is a form of art, or that sport can contribute to an aesthetic education. However, for one thing, it seems clear to me that sport is not art, despite the fact that they may share certain similarities or functions (PARRY, 1986a), and that there may be some tricky borderline cases (such as ice-dance). Secondly, although we may well appraise sport in aesthetic terms, this will not help our case, since it is open to us to appraise *anything at all* aesthetically. Why should it then be thought to be a particularly powerful feature of sport? In either form this claim seems to me to be quite empty.

On Extrinsic or Instrumental Justification

In addition to the specific objections which I have raised against the above claims, it is important to notice that they all advance *extrinsic* or *instrumental* arguments. They point to something outside of sport itself and make the claim that sport can be used as an instrument to promote the values of that other thing, be it health, morality, socialisation, aesthetic awareness, or anything else. There are at least three objections in principle to an instrumental argument:

[i]   It is a weak form of argument, because it is both hypothetical and contingent. Being hypothetical, it asserts:

•   *if (and only if) you value X will you value Y*

This is tantamount to saying, for example, that sport is of value only if it contributes to health (etc.), and it then becomes a matter of contingent fact whether or not sport actually does contribute to health. It seems to follow that :

•   *if it can be shown that sport does not contribute to health,*

> *and insofar as it does not, then sport is not justified;*

- *sport has no value of its own apart from its value as a promoter of health.*

The point is that contingent connections can be easily broken by changing circumstances, and offer only a temporary and uncertain justification. We must never rely on them for our *raison d'être*, since they are so easily challenged and overturned.

[ii]   Apart from it being a weak form of argument, the second objection has already been introduced: it is that an instrumental argument turns a moral argument into a factual matter. We began by inquiring into the value of PE activities, but we now find ourselves asking the quite different question of whether or not (and to what extent) a particular activity *as a matter of fact* serves some other value. We are side-tracked. This is a neat way of marginalising an activity: ask not what value there is in X – ask how X can serve Y. And it is also a neat way of avoiding the moral question by presupposing that one thing (Y) is of value, and that the other thing (X) is to be seen as of value only in instrumental terms.

[iii]   The third objection is that an instrumental argument turns an argument about sport into an argument about something else (health, etc.). This is precisely the way in which projects which are supposed to be looking at the PE curriculum can get hijacked by health agencies into not looking at PE at all, but at the general problem of health maintenance.

The Health-Related Fitness movement accepts the value of a certain definition of fitness and health, and judges all PE activities against this fitness/health value. No wonder that PE activities become marginalised. The fitness/health value could perhaps best be served by encouraging parents not to take children to school by car, or by starting up pre-school aerobics classes.

The Health-Based PE variant accepts the value of the development of decision-making skills as contributing to a healthy life-style. No wonder that it concludes that students should spend the PE lesson sitting in discussion groups. In accepting some other value at the outset we soon forget where we started from and the PE activity is not considered for its own value.

I must emphasise that I am not suggesting that there is no point at all in investigating the instrumental benefits of participation in PE and sport. To the contrary, I believe that such enquiry is very important indeed, for two reasons. Firstly, without investigation we have no way of assessing the validity of empirical claims, and these are often made evidential support, as if they were obviously true. Secondly, the present political climate constrains us and we must act opportunistically within it to the extent that our principled commitments will allow. (This is perhaps not the place to embark upon an extended discussion of what happens when people allow themselves to be diverted *from* their principled commitments by meekly accepting political direction or by chasing funding regardless of its nature and effects). There exists at the moment a strong pressure to be politically compliant and to seek to demonstrate the instrumental worth of the subject. I have no grievance against being politically astute, nor against the presentation of the values of the subject to suit a particular purpose or audience. We should seize the moment and the opportunity to demonstrate instrumental value and contingent benefits if this will suit our purposes. But the tail should not wag the dog. We should be interested first and foremost in our own principled view of PE and should seek to incorporate instrumental values to suit our purposes, not someone else's. To do otherwise would be to accept overt or latent political direction. Instrumental justifications, though sometimes useful if sensibly deployed, must be seen as at best ancillary benefits to a subject which stands or falls by the strength of its primary rationale, which will be intrinsic and educational.

On Intrinsic Justification

So, what is required is some attempt to provide an intrinsic justification – an account of PE activities themselves apart from (even if in addition to) an account of their contribution to other goods.

A number of routes towards an intrinsic justification of PE activities have been tried:

1.   On a 'subjective value' account;
2.   On R.S. PETERS' account;

3. Reconceptualising 'knowledge';
4. Reconceptualising 'rationality';
5. Reconceptualising 'education'.

Let us consider each of these in turn.

1. Subjective value

BAIN (1978) tries to justify PE by comparing 'education' with 'play' (which she defines as "intrinsically valuable human experience"). She begins with PETERS' (1965) 'non-instrumental' view of education, which "defined education as initiation into worthwhile activities and modes of conduct". She perceives this view as emphasising "the student's exposure to immediately satisfying, intrinsically worthwhile activities" (p.75). The introduction of the criterion of "immediate satisfaction", and the imputation of it to PETERS' account, should alert us to the subjective, psychological, hedonistic, experiential basis of BAIN's conception of intrinsic value.

Her own definition is as follows:

> An experience which has intrinsic value has inherent qualities which make it an immediately enriching, prized human activity, regardless of its future or long-range effects ... For example, most people listen to music for the pleasure or satisfaction it brings, not because it will improve their character, their health or their employability.
>
> (BAIN, 1978, p.75)

This means that people listen to music because they like it. When considering the PE curriculum, she likewise says:

> Athletic programmes do seem to be an effective means of initiation into the worthwhile human experience valued by physical educators.
>
> (1978, p.78)

This means that PE does what PE people value.

Now, if the only justification for PE is that some people like or otherwise value it, then the obvious retort is that some people do not. Unless there is room on the curriculum for everything that gives someone some satisfaction, we shall need a more substantial argument than this.

BAIN has simply failed to understand R.S. PETERS who, in arguing in favour of intrinsic justification, meant something altogether different from the subjective value of an activity. As we shall see in the next section, PETERS' account offers a quite different basis for the identification of intrinsic value from that offered by BAIN. Instead of her subjectivity, he offers a transcendental argument (which, if true, renders irrelevant our psychological reactions) and instead of her short-term experiential hedonism, he offers an account of life-long education based on the development of knowledge and understanding.

THOMPSON (1977) takes a similar line to BAIN. He asserts that "for those for whom an activity is of worth it simply is of worth" (p.7); but this only means that people like what they like. Unfortunately, some killers just like killing and some burglars burgling, just as much as some like footballing. In a later paper (1983) he reaffirms his view:

> All that is required to establish the place in the curriculum of a range of intrinsically worthwhile activities is the empirical fact that they have been judged so by many people who have found their lives enriched by them. (p.21)

But this simply says that people who like sport like sport, and we already have reason to know that. What we do not yet have, and what a justification must provide, is a reason why people who like sport may be permitted to inflict it upon others as part of a school curriculum. The simple assertion of intrinsic value does not advance the case a jot. Even if it is true that many people enjoy bingo, nothing follows as to its educational worthwhileness. We cannot accept everything that anyone thinks worthwhile. The whole point of justificatory arguments is to sort out which valued things should find a place on the curriculum.

THOMPSON (1983) sees himself as providing an antidote to the kind of thinking which requires us to justify PE in terms of something else (especially the cognitive), but the only alternative he can see is to assert its subjective value and challenge anyone else to gainsay him. He says:

> ... we can justify those things which we do not value for themselves and no others ... I hold that the search for clinching criteria justifying intrinsic worthwhileness is a total waste of time ... I can only assert it. (p.20)

One corollary of this is that we can never justify anything. All extrinsic justifications are part of a chain of reasoning which must end somewhere in an intrinsic justification. Things which we 'justify' extrinsically in terms of some second thing stand or fall according to the justification of the second thing. Since THOMPSON says that there can be no such thing as intrinsic justification (but only the assertion of intrinsic value) it follows that there can be no such thing as justification at all. For if I cannot gainsay THOMPSON's preferences, neither have I any reason whatsoever to take a scrap of notice of them.

Whilst it can be agreed that we should be looking in the first instance for intrinsic rather than extrinsic values, it is a mistake to suppose that these values can only be asserted. THOMPSON has been led astray by his subjective account of the intrinsic. It is time now to turn to other, perhaps more fruitful, formulations which are prepared to consider the possibility that there may be room for discussion and argument, rather than assertion and counter-assertion.

2. PETERS on intrinsic value

PETERS' (1965, 1966) account of 'education' relies on the idea of intrinsic value. He defines education as initiation into intrinsically worthwhile activities in a morally acceptable manner. One of the major tasks in the development of his account is the provision of a defensible definition of an 'intrinsically worthwhile activity'.

PETERS' view is that education has to do with the development of rational mind, and that this is to be achieved by initiation into certain forms of knowledge. These forms of knowledge are justified as the content of education because, regardless of whatever extrinsic justifications for them or personal satisfactions in them there might be (and these might be considerable), they are constitutive of rational mind. Since education has to do with the development of rational mind, these forms of knowledge are intrinsic to the educational task. Teaching maths, or a science, or an art, just are ways of teaching people just those forms of rationality.

Because of this, there is what PETERS sees as a secure route to justification, since we cannot answer the question, "which activities are justified on the curriculum?", without employing rationality. Anyone who seriously asks our question, then, is committed in advance to give the answer that PETERS does: "those activities that develop rationality". This is an example of the transcendental form of argument, which identifies the presuppositions of a question in order to answer it. Thus, even the most sceptical of questioners is committed by his question to the answer which is contained in its presuppositions.

Education, then, is initiation into worthwhile activities, where this means something altogether more convincing than the subjectivist accounts of BAIN (1977) and THOMPSON (1977, 1983). It is not surprising, then, that many people in the PE world, impressed with the power of this analysis and persuaded of the force of its arguments, responded by seeking to demonstrate a way in which PE could comply with its requirements and so enable itself to develop a secure route to justification.

BAIN was one of these, but we have already seen how she misunderstood PETERS' account of intrinsic value. WESTTHORP (1974) did not misunderstand PETERS in this way. She outlined his three criteria of intrinsic educational value, and then tried to show how PE activities could fulfil them. The main difficulty for such an argument, though, is that PETERS developed his own theory of intrinsic value specifically in contrast to PE activities (see 1966, pp. 144-165). Any attempt to force PE activities into the framework, then, inevitably involves either unsustainable claims about the nature of the activities or distortion of the framework to accommodate them.

On PETERS' account, the strongest arguments in favour of 'theoretical' activities "derive from how they differ from games" (p.158). This difference is spelled out in terms of "seriousness" and "cognitive perspective" well before the transcendental argument makes its triumphal (and, for PETERS, decisive) appearance (pp.164-5). It seems clear that any attempt to slot PE activities into such an account is doomed to failure from the outset, since the account is designed precisely to show in what ways they are deficient when compared with theoretical activities.

The critical literature on PETERS' concept of education and his theory of justification is much too voluminous to comment on here, although we should note that, in some form or another, it has been very resilient. We shall, in any case, shortly return to a consideration of fundamental criteria. For the moment, let us summarise the position so far: PETERS' (1966) account of education defines it in terms of the development of rationality by initiation into forms of knowledge, which effectively excludes PE activities. If, despite criticisms of PETERS' (1966) arguments, the structure of this account is to be retained, only two kinds of modification seem to be available to the PE apologist: s/he must produce a reconceptualisation either of knowledge or of rationality. Both paths have been trodden, and we shall follow them in the next two sections.

3. Reconceptualising knowledge

MEAKIN (1983) presents DEGENHARDT's account (1982) of intrinsic value as :

[i]   a way of escaping the intrinsic/extrinsic dichotomy;

[ii]   a way of demonstrating that the 'practical' knowledge with which PE is especially concerned may be seen as educationally valuable.

The argument is as follows: the dichotomy exists only if we define extrinsic value as 'valuable as a means to an end' and intrinsic value as 'valuable as an end in itself'. However, there is a third kind of value which transcends this dichotomy: "valuable as an aid to us in determining our ends", i.e. that knowledge which "... gives us that picture or understanding of things in terms of which we can decide what to do with our lives, what aims to set ourselves, what ends to live for" (DEGENHARDT, 1982, p.85).

This third formulation seems to me simply a restatement of PETERS' view of intrinsically valuable activities, i.e. activities which contribute to the development of rationality but also constitute it, thus enabling our forming of a world-view. But if we accept this formulation as presenting us with the kind of knowledge of which justifications are made, how does PE fare according to it?

MEAKIN (1983) has two observations. Firstly: "the criticism that I would make here is that it finds no place for PE" (p.16). Surely this is to prejudge the issue. We are supposed to be enquiring into the nature of justifiable activities so that we can judge whether or not PE makes muster, whereas here the third formulation is being judged on whether or not it includes PE. MEAKIN's (1983) second observation, however, seems straightforwardly to concede the case against PE: "I take the point that engagement in PE activities offers little help in forming a world-view" (p.16).

Once conceded, it follows that PE does not have value according to the third formulation, i.e. according to what PETERS calls intrinsic value. All that remains is for MEAKIN to claim that it is the place that these activities have within a world-view that is the important question. We shall return to this matter, for it is indeed important, but the present argument has shown only that a reconceptualisation of knowledge according to the DEGENHARDT/PETERS formulation would serve to exclude PE. Any subsequent claim that PE should have some place within a world-view is a separate issue, requiring a separate argument.

MEAKIN (1983) asserts at this stage that it is necessary to engage in PE activities in order to be in a position to decide their place within one's world-view (although this is contrary to the view expressed by WHITE, 1973). He says: "... it is only by seriously engaging in PE activities that such experiences will be had" (p.17). If this means that one must do it to experience it, this is trivially true but would apply to anything else, too. What would not be justifiable on this argument? It could be argued of anything that one must do it in order to experience it. Whether or not this is necessary in order to decide about its value on the curriculum is another matter.

Underlying MEAKIN's (1983) argument is an account of 'practical' knowledge, which is claimed to be worthwhile. CARR (1983a) has also developed a defence of PE activities along these lines. He says: "In order to be regarded as educational ... an activity should involve the promotion of knowledge and understanding or the rational mastery of some skill" (p.10). He warns us against making wild claims that PE activities lead to the promotion of theoretical or academic knowledge, but reassures us that they do, nevertheless, involve 'knowledge' of a sort. This 'practical knowledge' is justifiable since the curriculum is a selection from culture, and sports, games and the like are an important part of culture.

There is some mileage here, but it is independent of the knowledge-claim. Of course there will be some kind of knowledge in anything that is transmissible as an element of culture. So to provide an argument demonstrating this admissible fact is otiose. What the argument must rather do, since it chooses knowledge as the important criterion for the demonstration of the value of these activities, is to show that this knowledge is especially valuable, not that the activities themselves are allegedly valuable on some other ground, such as their cultural value.

The same objection applies to accounts which suggest that some form of 'acquaintance knowledge' or some kind of 'understanding' approach will satisfy the cognitive demands of a conception of education such as that of PETERS. Even if they succeed in showing that PE contributes to the development of such knowledge and understanding, all such accounts face the 'status problem' – is this the kind of knowledge and understanding with which 'education' ought to concern itself? Thus, the attempt to work within PETERS' framework continually forces us to confront and attempt to overcome the bias against PE activities which is implicit within it.

A reconceptualisation of 'knowledge' succeeds in pushing the problem back one step, only for it to reappear later in another guise. On the PETERSian account it could on the one hand be denied that PE deals in 'knowledge' at all. At one remove, it could be claimed that PE deals in 'knowledge' (in its reworked sense) but then it could be denied that this is the appropriate kind of knowledge to contribute to someone's 'education'. PETERS' (1966) account develops a conception of knowledge within a justificatory argument. The justification therefore works only for knowledge as so defined, not necessarily for any other definition of knowledge. It follows that nothing is gained by reconceptualising knowledge unless it is accompanied by a successful reworking of the justificatory part of the argument.

One final observation: MEAKIN (1983) says, "... practical knowledge is a rich source of satisfaction and it patently involves the use of reason" (p.15). We can agree with both parts of this assertion, although neither will advance the justificatory claims of PE. The first (that PE activities bring satisfaction) may be true, but this refers only to 'intrinsic value' of a subjective kind, and we have already noticed the problem with that. The second (that PE activities involve the use of reason) may be true, but it is irrelevant to their justification.

Just why this is so will be made clear in the next section.

4. Reconceptualising rationality

The second path which has been trodden has been toward the reconceptualisation of rationality. The argument has been developed in a series of interesting articles (refer to *Momentum*, 1983) which have made an excellent contribution to our understanding in this area, and it is the notion of 'rational agency' which has emerged as an important feature. The idea is that, as well as theoretical rationality which is the basis of cognitivist accounts of education, there is such a thing as rational agency, the exercise of which is related to practical knowledge.

MEAKIN (1983) says: "... it follows that agency as well as theoretical thought can be rational" (p.13). CARR (1983a) says: "But clearly not all forms of knowledge and skill pursued by rational agents are educational" (p.10). However, the only disqualifying criterion he mentions is a moral one. He does not consider whether the status of the knowledge involved might affect the educational status of the activity, but assumes that knowledge and rational agency are involved here in a full sense. However, as at the end of the last section, we are left with the suggestion that PE activities are somehow justified because they are pursued by rational agents, or that their pursuit involves the use of reason.

In order to present a serious justificatory case through the notion of rational agency, the claim must surely be that engaging in PE activities actually contributes to the development of rational agency. However, all that these arguments would show, if successful, is that:

[a]   PE activities are engaged in by rational agents, or that

[b]   PE activities require the exercise of rational agency for successful participation.

In both of these cases, the only requirement would be that participants would be rational agents who could, as it were, bring their rationality with them to the activity. To show that an activity might be undertaken by a rational agent, or requires the exercise of rational agency, is not sufficient to show that it can contribute in some relevantly significant manner to the production or development of rational agency.

At the risk of repetition, let me spell out the two problems here:

The first problem is internal to the argument which, I suggest, succeeds only in demonstrating that PE activities are undertaken by rational agents, or require the exercise of rational agency, whereas the argument must seek to demonstrate that they produce or develop rational agency.

The second problem is external to that argument. For even if the case had been made, it would show nothing special about PE activities. It may well be the case that we exhibit, practise and develop rational agency in a thousand ways, some of them not 'physical' at all, some of them very 'physical' indeed, without ever engaging in a 'PE activity'. It would still remain to be shown that those activities bear a special relationship to the development of rational agency, over and above that of other activities, if the above is to count as an argument in favour of the inclusion of PE on the curriculum. Without this step in the argument, we shall be in the same position as we were in at the end of the last paragraph: that of presenting PE activities as simply a range of activities undertaken by rational agents, but not in some relevantly significant sense producing them.

BRUNER (1962) thought that PE activities might be justified on the curriculum:

> in accordance with a rational appraisal of the place and value of physical activities in human life ... that the activities themselves are viewed as part of the life of a developing rational being . . . and that they therefore form part of the life of a rational person. (p.102)

He thought that, even if we subscribed to the values of rationality, or rational agency, it would not follow that the only activities justifiable on the curriculum are those that develop rationality, but rather those that rational agents would have a good reason to choose. He thought that rational agents would have good reason to choose other than develop their rationality all day! On this account, PE activities might be justifiable not because they themselves contribute to the development of rationality, but because such a contribution is not necessary to an educational justification.

Similar thoughts are to be found in PETERS (1966): "... 'physical education' suggests the cultivation of physical fitness as a necessary foundation for a balanced way of life" (p.34); and in KLEINIG (1982): "... physical education, as distinct from physical training, implies an approach to and understanding of physical development which sets it into a larger framework of knowledge" (p.15).

On the face of it this does seem a sensible view to take. If we can assume that a major task of education (which is itself a major function of schooling) is the development of rationality, surely we can accept that, to the extent that this task is achieved, rational agents will make good decisions about their physical condition and their physical activity. This is a view that I would share, but we are still left with our original problem unresolved: how are PE activities to be legitimised? It seems to me not just that it is difficult to provide a link between PE activities and the development of rationality, but that the search is misguided. PE activities are undertaken by rational agents, but so is just about everything else that human beings do, so this could not be the ground of their justification.

The foregoing discussion has been vitiated from the outset. The agenda was set by PETERS, and the debate (even when critical of his views) has been conducted in the terms he laid down. However, the most radical critique is precisely to challenge those terms. We must turn to an analysis of the concept of education on which the whole debate has been founded.

5. Reconceptualising education

So far we have considered mainly those views which have responded to PETERS by accepting a starting point compatible with at least the structure offered by his definition of education. Some of the responses we have so far examined have turned on simple misunderstandings of PETERS. Others have sought to amend one or another feature of his account, and I have tried to show that the result has been that the central PETERSian tenets are left standing and no significant gain is made for PE.

However, there is a more radical response available, and that is to question the basis of the whole account. It is not clear why we should accept the starting-point, especially when it is noticed that the account of 'education' is set up by contrast with PE activities. Twenty years of effort by writers on PE have proven what we knew at the outset: the circle cannot be squared. The radical response is to consider alternative conceptions of education, or alternative accounts of curriculum justification. BARROW (1982) agrees that educational goods are cognitive goods, but includes other goods on the school curriculum by explaining that schools are there for the purposes of *schooling*, which include (but are not exhausted by) educational goods.

As I have explained elsewhere (1986), the problem with this is that it confers second-class citizenship on the PE teacher, who would then be seen as dealing with the 'schooling' side of the business, not the 'education' side. Assurances that these are equally important tasks would not cut much ice, I am sure. In any case, BARROW's (1981) account *incorporates* rather than challenges the cognitivist view.

Another kind of radical response provides a genuine challenge by seeking to reorganise our commitments and priorities – to locate our ideas about physical activities firmly and securely within conceptions of education, PE, the person and culture which will give a full and coherent picture of their social, political and educational value. I can only offer a brief sketch of such a theory here.

Underlying every conception of education there is a philosophical anthropology – an idealised conception of the person or citizen, which inevitably has an ideological basis (see HOBERMAN, 1984, pp.1-3).

Thus any educational practice could be challenged at many levels:

[i]   at the level of actual practices as legitimate expressions of the

educational theory, or as efficient means to its goals;

[ii]   at the level of educational theory as a legitimate expression of the ideology;

[iii]   at the level of ideology.

A radical response might seek to develop a conception of education based on the concept of a person and the development of human capacities and excellences. This seems to provide a broader base than do cognitive models, which limit the range of excellences deemed to be the subject of educational development. An intrinsic justification would then refer to whatever activities could be shown to be a necessary part of the development of a human being making progress towards this ideal.

At the same time, it might seek to develop an account of culture and human experience which gives due weight to those forms of athletic, outdoor, sporting, aesthetic activities which focus on bodily performance, and which are generally grouped under the heading of physical education. Such an account, combining claims about human capacities and excellences with claims about the importance of a range of cultural forms, would seek to develop arguments which could justify the place of PE on the curriculum from the point of view both of the individual learner and of the culture into which s/he is to be initiated. PE activities are located within a cultural context which unevenly affirms their value. Since education involves the initiation of children into a selection from culture, we need to identify whatever cultural value adheres to sport, and to relate that to other important facets of educational decision-making, such as conceptions of personhood, and the role of PE in the various stages of its development.

The next step would be, not simply to accept the list of activities which are currently accepted as constituting PE, but to subject each activity (and each group of activities) to rigorous examination against the above rationale. But we should not put the cart before the horse. Until a rationale has been developed, it remains an open question as to just which activities are justifiable according to it.

My own view is that, if we provide no good account of the intrinsic and cultural value of PE activities, or if we can suggest no role beyond the contingent and the hypothetical for them in the educational development of persons, then we will have no good reason for its inclusion on the national curriculum. The present task is to produce a radical reappraisal of the dominant ideology of education so that a reappraisal of the role of other than cognitive excellences might become a genuine practical possibility.

Retrospective: Since 1988

To my knowledge, very little has been written on the educational justification of PE activities since this paper. Since PE now does have a place on the National Curriculum, albeit a minor one, the justification issue does seem to have been put on the back burner by the profession. However, it seems to me, there is still a great deal to achieve before PE activities are restored to their previous position in schools, perhaps only as a prelude to enhancing their role.

What is required, in my view, is a redefinition of the contribution of PE activities to personal development in an educational context. Sport has become more and more important as a global cultural practice, but at the same time it has become less important within the British educational system. The last government was responsible for encouraging the selling-off of playing fields, discouraging staff from voluntary commitment to extra-curricular activity, promoting one-year teacher training through the PGCE route (and thereby making it almost impossible for teachers to be properly prepared in PE), and so on. This is a set of policies which, by design or accident, amounts to the attempted privatisation and deprofessionalisation of PE activity.

Over the past ten years or so, I have repeatedly argued for the re-valuation of PE activities under a systematic educational rationale (see PARRY, 1988b, 1989, 1994, 1997) appealing to the philosophical anthropology of Olympism. However, there are other considerations to attend to before picking up this theme.

Reid on Knowledge and PE

In a recent addition to the literature, REID (1996) outlines two 'conventional assumptions' made by what he calls the 'new orthodoxy' in PE:

[i]   the 'early Hirstian' account[1], which sees knowledge as propositional, and education as academic;

When applied to PE, this suggests:

[ii]   the distinction between practical performance and the 'theory' related to it – i.e. the propositional knowledge of Human Movement Science (HMS).

The paper is a critique of these two assumptions, and a defence of the claim that PE "can indeed satisfy the knowledge requirements of education; but ... without making claims to academic significance" (REID, 1996, p.95). REID asserts that "The criterion of practical knowledge is practical performance", and that "... practical inference ... presupposes the use of intentionalist concepts ... (which describe) ... factors which give the activity its *meaning* ..." (pp.99-100). These insights are used as sticks with which to beat those who might argue that "the propositional knowledge generated by the sciences of human movement are (sic) *necessarily* relevant to the purposes of PE" (p.101). It is only relevant insofar as it is useful or applicable to the work of the physical educator (and HMS is not always and necessarily so). However, there *is* a kind of propositional knowledge that is *logically* required for successful understanding of, participation in, and appreciation of PE activities: that which expresses the "concepts, principles, constitutive rules and norms which define and govern" them (p.102). But this kind of knowledge, whose proper exercise is practical, must also be assessed in practice (i.e. performatively). This explodes our two 'conventional assumptions', since:

[i]   although such knowledge is propositional, it is not academic;

[ii]   there is no sharp distinction here between practical performance and the propositional knowledge related to it, which is *not* just the propositional knowledge of HMS.

REID's (1996) diagnosis is that the source of these assumptions is the mistake of supposing that the performance of physical activities does not in itself constitute an expression of knowledge. The main outcomes for our purposes are two claims:

[i]   that there is no justification for the view that HMS is necessarily relevant to PE activities;

[ii]   that, however, the autonomous language of human action, which alone can express the *meaning* of PE activities, is necessarily relevant.

These are important conclusions, which neatly encapsulate REID's entirely successful attack on naive 'scientism'; but they do not advance his further claim:

[iii]   that PE can indeed satisfy the knowledge requirements of education ... without making claims to academic significance on the basis of propositional ... knowledge (p.95).

I have two comments on REID's (1996) position here:

Firstly, when he accuses the 'new orthodoxy' of making "the mistake of supposing that the performance of physical activities does not in itself constitute an expression of knowledge" (p.102), I think he exceeds the evidence. Many in his target group would be quite willing to accept that there is knowledge of a *kind* in practical performance. Their point would be that it is not knowledge of the *right* kind to bestow educational significance on the practice.

Secondly, my main criticism of REID would be that he includes in his account no claim at all to educational significance. There is no *ground* given for the inclusion of PE practices within a curriculum. There is no justification – no argument for the epistemological significance of the kind of knowledge he champions, i.e. the knowledge expressed in practical performance. In the absence of such an account, we must suspect the existence of subjectivist or relativist assumptions. It is no use arguing the case that the performance of PE activities requires a kind of practical knowledge, for so do "bingo, bridge and billiards"(PETERS, 1996, p.144) – which brings us back to PETERS' problematic: how to account for the supposed value of curriculum activities. In other words, REID has provided no argument to show that the practical knowledge that he champions can clear the status hurdle. As I say above "nothing is gained by reconceptualising knowledge unless it is accompanied by a successful reworking of the justificatory part of the argument".

This is where we can turn to another paper by REID (1997), in which he presents an account of the concept of PE and an embryonic justification. This paper is a systematic attack on the "strategy of assimilation" (p.9), i.e. the attempt to assimilate physical (and 'non-serious') activities to mental (and serious) activities. However, he simply asserts a range of "givens", the axiological basis of which is "pleasure", or "the hedonic good" (p.14). Later, he acknowledges that there is a problem of identifying what counts as "valuable rather than worthless knowledge" (p.15), but he offers no further account of the value of the knowledge that he promotes. Later still (p.16), he acknowledges the "modest but essential" nature of such knowledge, but still offers no educational justification of it. We are left with mere pleasure.

Those who reason thus are, I think, victims of the 'Hedonic Fallacy': the satisfactions we achieve from the successful pursuit of whatever it is that we value should undoubtedly give rise to pleasure; however, it is not necessarily the *pleasure* that we seek, but rather the values of what we pursue. The hedonist puts the cart before the horse. Unless there is already something that we value (apart from mere pleasure) then there is little possibility of gaining pleasure from it. In addition, there is the tricky empirical – and therefore contingent – question (from the point of view of even a hedonist educational justification) of just who *does* derive pleasure out of PE activities[2].

My own position is that, whilst PE activities are naturally a source of pleasure for those who value engagement in them, pleasure is a concomitant rather than the central value of them, if they are to be seen as of educational value. For education has to do not only with the pursuit of pleasure, or the pursuit of knowledge (of a certain valued kind) but also with the development of human excellences (of a certain valued kind).

REID's (1997) view on 'the axiological dimension' seems to be that, if PE activities are infused with some dimension that raises them above bingo, bridge and billiards, then they are being used as means to the intellectualist project. But this does not follow at all. We need *some* way of showing PE activities to be above the level of ludo, or else there will be no way of showing them to be of educational value (unless ludo is, too). But this way does not have to be intellectualist.

Hirst on Practices

As I have already intimated, arch-intellectualist Paul HIRST (1965) radically revised his earlier position in the early and mid-1980s.[3] In the reformed HIRST we find two interesting features. Firstly, there seems to have been a shift from the PETERSian transcendental deduction in favour of an appeal to a kind of relativism.

He says:

"It is those practices that can constitute a flourishing life that I now consider fundamental to education." (p.6)

and he goes on to suggest that a curriculum should be organised in terms of "significant practices". However, just which practices can constitute a flourishing life, or just which practices are to be deemed significant, remains opaque. Without the theoretical support of the transcendental deduction, and in the absence of a stated alternative, we can only assume that the test is a relativist one: those practices are significant which are deemed so by some social group.

Secondly, we nevertheless find a modified intellectualism, clothed in the language of 'practices'. What is clear from HIRST's account, though, is that he is certainly *not* talking about 'practices' in the sense of 'practical PE activities'. His point seems to be that the forms of knowledge should be reconceptualised for educational purposes as ongoing social and intellectual practices into which students must be initiated, rather than as sets of propositions to be taught.[4]

He says:

"What is required ... is the development by individuals of the overall rational practice of specific rational practices." (p.5)

Whilst I would in general agree with this characterisation, this leaves us no further on than we were at the end of my section on 'reconceptualising rationality'. Is a rational practice one which contributes to the development of rationality; or simply a practice that can be engaged in rationally? If the former, then the case remains to be made for PE activities; and, if the latter, then it is not clear what is excluded, so that no educational justification is forthcoming.

HIRST's (1965) further insistence that those practices are to be specified in terms of "the good life for that individual" (p.5) is hopelessly vague and empty, admitting of an indefinite number of interpretations.

Towards a Philosophical Anthropology

For me, the justification of PE activities lies in their capacity to facilitate the development of certain human excellences of a valued kind. Of course, the problem now lies in specifying those 'human excellences of a valued kind', and (for anyone) this task leads us into the area of philosophical anthropology. I want to suggest that the way forward for PE lies in the philosophical anthropology (and the ethical ideals) of Olympism, which provide a specification of a variety of human excellences which:

- have been attractive to human groups over an impressive span of time and space;

- have contributed massively to our historically developed conceptions of ourselves;

- have helped to develop a range of artistic and cultural conceptions that have defined Western culture;

- have produced a range of physical activities that have been found universally satisfying and challenging.

That is to say, these values stand a chance of gaining wide assent, since they transcend the simply hedonic or relative good. They are widely considered to be pleasurable – but only because they are widely valued as sources of opportunities for the development and expression of valued human excellences. They are widely considered to be such opportunities for the expression of valued human excellences because, even when as local instantiations, their object is to strive to challenge our common human propensities and abilities.

In brief, the Olympic Idea is translatable into a few simple phrases which capture the essence of what, on this account, an ideal human being ought to be and to aspire to. The philosophical anthropology of

Olympism promotes the ideals of:

- individual all round harmonious human development;

- towards excellence and achievement;

- through effort in competitive sporting activity;

- under conditions of mutual respect, fairness, justice and equality;

- with a view to creating lasting personal human relationships of friendship;

- international relationships of peace, toleration and understanding;

- and cultural alliances with the arts.

There is a much longer tale to tell about the classical roots of ancient Olympism, the liberal humanist basis of modern Olympism, and the application of those ideas to education (see PARRY, 1988b). However, the above short phrases give some flavour of the ideals that it promotes. These are not merely inert 'ideals', but living ideas which have the power to remake our notions of sport in education, seeing sport not as mere physical activity but as the cultural and developmental activity of an aspiring, achieving, well-balanced, educated and ethical individual.

Notes

1   I call this the 'early Hirstian' account. Since HIRST later rejected it as "part of the 'rationalist' myth" (1992, p.5). He says (loc. cit.) "we are mistaken if we conceive (the) purpose (of education) as primarily the acquisition of knowledge": and (p.6) "Of course I now consider practical knowledge to be more fundamental to theoretical knowledge ...". I think that REID should have taken account of this, and also of the arguments in HIRST's 1979 paper on Human Movement, Knowledge and Education, to which he does not refer.

2   BETJEMAN, J. in his poem *'Summoned by Bells'*. Presents the case for

the opposition:
The dread of beatings! Dread of being late;
And, the greatest dread of all, the dread of games

3   As evidenced in his mature exposition (HIRST, 1992).

4   See ROSS, G.M. et al (1993) for a full statement of such an account in
         relation to philosophy. If taken seriously, it demands a 'Copernican
         Revolution' in pedagogy (p.6). Requiring an initiation of students into the
         skills and practices of philosophising.

References

ALDERSON, J. and CRUTCHLEY, D. (1990) Physical Education and the
National Curriculum. In ARMSTRONG, N. (Ed), *New Directions in Physical
Education.* vol.1, London, Human Kinetics.

ARCHAMBAULT, R.D. (Ed) (1965) *Philosophical Analysis and Education.*
London, Routledge & Kegan Paul.

BAIN, L.L. (1977) Play and Intrinsic Values in Education. *Quest* XXVIII,
Summer, pp.75-80.

BARROW, R. (1981) *The Philosophy of Schooling.* London, Wheatsheaf Books.

BRUNER, J. (1962) *Essays for the Left Hand.* Boston, Harvard Univ. Press.

CARR, D. (1983a) The Place of Physical Education on the School Curriculum.
Momentum, 8, 1, 9-12.

CARR, D. (1983b) On Physical Education and Educational Significance.
Momentum, 8, 3, 2-9.

DEGENHARDT, M. (1982) *Education and the Value of Knowledge.* London,
Allen and Unwin.

DES (1984) *The Organisation and Content of the 5-16 Curriculum.* London,
HMSO.

HIRST, P.H. (1965) Liberal Education and the Nature of Knowledge. In
ARCHAMBAULT, R.D. (Ed), *Philosophical Analysis and Education*, 113-138,
London, Routledge & Kegan Paul.

HIRST, P.H. (1979) Human Movement, Knowledge and Education. *Journal of Philosophy of Education.* 13, 101-108.

HIRST, P.H. (1992) *Education, Knowledge and Practices.* Papers of the Philosophy of Education Society of Great Britain, April, 26-28.

HMI (1977) *Curriculum 11-16.* The Red Book. London, HMSO.

HMI (1979) *Curriculum 11-16 Supp.* Working Papers. PE, London, DES.

HOBERMAN, J. (1984) *Sport and Political Ideology.* Heinemann.

KLEINIG, J. (1982) *Philosophical Issues in Education.* London, Croom Helm.

MEAKIN, D.C. (1983) On the Justification of Physical Education. *Momentum,* 8, 3, 10-19.

MEEK, C. (1986) PE in the 'New' Curriculum. *British Journal Physical Education,* 17, 3, May/June, 105-108.

MURDOCH, E. (1987) *Sport in Schools - a Desk Study for DES/DoE.* London, Sports Council.

PARRY, J. (1986a) Sport, Art and the Aesthetic. Proceedings of the International Olympic Academy, 26th Session July 1986, 152-9. Reprinted in *Sport Science Review,* 12, 1989, 15-20.

PARRY, J. (1986b) Values in Physical Education. In TOMLINSON P. and QUINTON, M. (Eds), *Values Across the Curriculum.* Brighton, Falmer Press.

PARRY, J. (1987) PE Under Threat. *British Journal of Physical Education,* 18, 6, 243-4.

PARRY, J. (1988a) The PE Curriculum From 5-16. In WIEGAND P. and RAYNER, M. (Eds) *Curriculum Progress.* Brighton, Falmer Press.

PARRY, J. (1988b) Olympism at the Beginning and End of the Twentieth Century. Proceedings of the Main International Session. 81-94, International Olympic Academy, Ancient Olympia, Greece.

PARRY, J. (1989) An Ideal for Living. *Sport and Leisure.* 30, 5, 36-37.

PARRY, J. (1994) The Moral and Cultural Dimensions of Olympism and Their Educational Application. Proceedings of the Main International Session. 181-

195, International Olympic Academy, Ancient Olympia, Greece.

PARRY, J. (1997) Ethical Aspects of the Olympic Idea. Proceedings of the 3rd International Session for Educationists. International Olympic Academy, Ancient Olympia, Greece.

PETERS, R.S. (1965) Education as Initiation. In ARCHAMBAULT, R.D. (Ed), *Philosophical Analysis and Education.* London, Routledge & Kegan Paul.

PETERS, R.S. (1966) *Ethics and Education.* London, Allen and Unwin.

PROCTOR, N. (1984) Problems Facing PE After the Great Education Debate. *Physical Education Review,* 7, 1, 4-11.

REID, A. (1996) Knowledge, Practice and Theory in PE. *European Physical Education Review,* 2, 2, 94-104.

REID, A. (1997) Value Pluralism and Physical Education. *European Physical Education Review,* 3, 1, 6-20.

ROSS, G.M., PARRY, J. and COHEN, M. (1993) *Philosophy and Enterprise.* Leeds, University of Leeds.

THOMPSON, K. (1977) The Intrinsic Value of Physical Activity. *Bulletin of Physical Education.* XIII, 4, 5-8.

THOMPSON, K. (1983) The Justification of Physical Education. *Momentum* 8, 2, 19-23.

WESTTHORP, G. (1974) PE as a Worthwhile Activity. *British Journal of Physical Education,* 5, 1, 4f.

WHITE, J.P. (1973) *Towards a Compulsory Curriculum.* London, Routledge and Kegan Paul.

WIEGAND P and RAYNER, M. (Eds) (1988) *Curriculum Progress.* Brighton, Falmer Press.

PART 2

THE NATIONAL CURRICULUM FOR PHYSICAL EDUCATION

Chapter 3

Policy, Process and Power

John Evans and Dawn Penney

Introduction

The 1988 Education Reform Act (ERA) acted as a catalyst for renewed study of educational policy in the UK. A significant number of researchers, including ourselves, set about the task of monitoring the various requirements of the ERA and evaluating their 'effects'; particularly on the content of school curricula and work of teachers in schools. The research generated in this process has drawn attention to both important theoretical and methodological issues. Here our attention is on the former, and specifically, how policy is conceptualised. This issue has been central to our own and others' research and is a focus of ongoing debate within the sociology of education (see LINGARD, 1993; EVANS, DAVIES and PENNEY, 1994). This attention stems from a belief that the exploration of the complexities of policy 'making' and 'implementation' is fundamental to understanding why both 'policy' and 'practice' take particular forms in the context of education. Our ongoing research[1] addressing the introduction and 'impact' of the ERA, and specifically within this, the development of the National Curriculum for Physical Education (NCPE) in England and Wales, has enabled us to develop and refine our theoretical ideas. As 'implementation' progresses and new initiatives arise (see chapter 4), they remain a focus for our own critical reflection.

Our research has, therefore, centred on the development of the NCPE and, as it interacts with other ERA legislation, its impact upon the provision of physical education (PE) and sport in schools. This interaction has certainly been critical and specifically has centred on the dynamic and tensions between the introduction of the National Curriculum (NC) and an associated system of testing, and the parallel establishment of Local Management of Schools (LMS) and Open Enrolment (OE). These latter policies signalled the application of market principles to education and saw the devolution of financial responsibilities from local education authorities to schools. The Conservative government's assumption was that as a whole the ERA would raise standards in state education. As we illustrate below, however, the development and 'implementation' of the NCPE brought to the surface the tensions between the stated educational commitments of the NC and the economic intentions and constraints inherent in LMS and OE. Meanwhile the emergence of these tensions has helped inform our progressive conceptualisation of the complexities of policy.

The National Curriculum for Physical Education (NCPE)

What is to count as PE within the curricula of state schools has been the subject of some of the most public, emotional and vitriolic educational debates in recent years. Media figures and politicians alike have variously charged 'progressive' physical educationalists with prompting the nations' moral, physical and economic decline while bringing PE and sport into disrepute (see EVANS, 1990). The development of the NCPE brought this contestation to the fore once again. Furthermore, it has demonstrated that the 'making' of state education policy is a far from neutral activity, but rather, a complex social and political process in which vested interests and values are always and inevitably expressed. It has revealed both the range and the limits of the central state's power to determine the thinking of educationists and control the constitution of school curricula. Below we pursue the complexities of this process, firstly by the discussion of key concepts in our analysis, and secondly by the presentation of data that is illustrative of the concepts and the complexities that they attempt to address.

Policy 'Making' and 'Implementation'

A key feature of our efforts to conceptualise the processes that we have researched has been to stress that policy 'making' and 'implementation' are very difficult to divide. In pursuing how policy developments have acted to produce, reproduce or challenge inequalities and inequities between and within schools, we like others (see BALL, 1990; BOWE and BALL with GOLD, 1992) have been inclined to dissolve, or certainly underplay, the boundaries between these two notions. We have supported HILL's (1980) observation that

> It is hard to identify a dividing line at which making can be said to be completed and implementation to start. There is also a considerable amount of feedback from implementation which influences further policy making and many policies are so skeletal that their real impact depends upon the way they are interpreted at the implementation stage.
>
> (p.44)

In this view policy is not an event nor an action undertaken only by powerful 'others' who operate 'somewhere' outside of schools or in the upper echelons of institutions and who hand policies on – and down – to others to 'implement'. Policies are always and inevitably interpreted in a number of educational sites and in this process may be adapted, adopted, contested and resisted. Thus, conflicts and contestation over the form and content of the curriculum do not end with the issuing of central government legislation, but rather continue throughout their 'implementation'. 'Putting policy into practice' thus involves the recursive making and remaking of this legislation in a vast variety of circumstances of resourcing and educational work. Post the ERA, this variety remains and thus there is no guarantee that a "broad and balanced curriculum" (see DEPARTMENT OF EDUCATION AND SCIENCE (DES), 1989) is what all schools can deliver, nor what all children will, therefore, receive as a National Curriculum.

There are certainly good reasons for taking an approach that acknowledges potential creativity throughout policy development. As BOWE and his colleagues (1992) have emphasised, the 'state control' model of policy distorts the policy process with its conception of distinct 'makers' and 'implementors', and in so doing reinforces a linear conception of policy in which theory and practice are separate and the former privileged. The major assertion that we and others have thus made, is that policy has to be considered a process that is both protracted and ongoing; a complex series of political interactions involving those inside as well as outside government (O'BUACHALLA, 1988; PENNEY and EVANS, 1994). This view acknowledges human agency and draws our attention to the way in which it is expressed in action which contests, resists, or in some other way mediates what sometimes seem to be immense and 'determining' powers of the state and the interests of capitalism.

In many respects our empirical work has provided considerable evidence to support this less deterministic view of policy. However, at the same time, we have been led to question the emphasis on process and human agency and draw attention to the way in which this occludes analysis of the way in which power operates, resides and moves within the social system (EVANS, DAVIES and PENNEY, 1994). While emphasising the continual nature of policy 'making' and the ongoing struggles and contestation inherent in this, we have also observed the constraints operating in this process; the fact that policies are not always made in conditions of agents' own making (BALL, 1993) and that the policy process like all other forms of human endeavour has to be viewed as a "relational activity" (EVANS and PENNEY, 1992); a process in which the actions of individuals not only act upon and help shape, create and/or recreate the social and organisational contexts in which they are located, but are also shaped by those contexts and the political, social and cultural constraints inherent in them.

From a pluralist viewpoint (see DAHL, 1970; KOGAN, 1975) in democracies power is widely distributed among different interest groups that then play an important part in the policy process. Such groups, with interests in particular issues, form 'issues communities' and in many cases, policy is then formed within these communities, thus segmenting the process (O'BUACHALLA, 1988). While this view may offer a reasonably accurate description of an important feature of policy development, it does not adequately address some of the other matters with which we are concerned, and particularly how the capacities and capabilities of actors to influence policy are differently distributed within and between individuals and interest groups. A FOUCAULTian contribution offers some insight into these matters. For FOUCAULT, power cannot be located either in agency or structures; instead it is everywhere, expressed discursively through "a multiple and mobile field of force relations where far reaching but never complete stable effects of domination are produced" (FOUCAULT, 1980, p.102). Modern power is

> ... relational power that is exercised from innumerable points ... highly indeterminate in character, and is never something acquired, seized or shared. There is no source of power or centre of power to contest, nor are there any subjects holding it; power is purely a structural activity for which subjects are anonymous conduits or by products.
>
> (BEST and KELLNER, 1991, p.52)

As BEST and KELLNER (1991) point out, this is a "pluralised analysis of power and rationality as they are inscribed in various discourses and institutionalised sites" (p.52). Power literally is everywhere and as such it is purportedly indissoluble either from 'structures' or 'agency', from contestation and struggle:

> I am saying: as soon as there is power relation, there is possibility of resistances. We can never be ensnared by power: we always modify its grip in determinate conditions and according to precise strategy.
>
> (FOUCAULT in BEST and KELLNER, 1991, p.123)

The intellectual shimmy here is glorious, deftly side-stepping all the difficult questions about the precise nature of the relationships between human agency and structure (see EVANS, DAVIES and PENNEY, 1994). Nevertheless it does, as BEST and KELLNER (1991) stress, "sensitise us to how power is woven through discourses into all aspects of social and personal life", including the policy process. Furthermore, a FOUCAULTian view also brackets "the questions of who controls and uses power for which interests in order to focus on the means by which power operates" (p.70).

Like pluralist theory, it, therefore occludes the extent to which power is still controlled and administered by specific and identifiable agents in positions of economic and political power, thereby underplaying the analysis of so called 'macro-powers', such as the state and globalised

corporate capitalism. While pluralist and structuralist theories force us
to both complexify our view of power and consider it not just as a state
of affairs but as a 'property', a potential which resides in all human
endeavour, the other dimensions of power, "the capability of actors to
secure outcomes where the realisation of these outcomes depends upon
the agency of others" (GIDDENS, 1979, p.93) is largely overlooked.
Both aspects must be addressed. The latter in particular challenges us
to look at the "resources" which are "the media through which power
is exercised and how structures of domination are reproduced" (ibid,
1979, p.91). Below we report some of our research of the development
of the National Curriculum for Physical Education to illustrate and
endorse these views of policy and power in relation to education.

Power in the Development of the National Curriculum for Physical Education (NCPE)

In our exploration of the policy process, we as others (BALL, 1990;
BOWE et al, 1992) have conceptualised policy texts as constituted by
discourses, which emerge from, and continually interact, with a variety
of interrelated contexts. Our claim (further illustrated in chapter 4) has
been that the power of the texts (i.e. policy documents) is never
complete. From this viewpoint, the ERA legislation is regarded as but
one aspect of a continual process in which "the loci of power are
constantly shifting as various resources implicit and explicit in a text
are contextualised and employed in the struggle to maintain or change
views of schooling" (BOWE et al, 1992, p.13). As BOWE et al, have
emphasised, although there are elements of intended state control
embedded in the ERA, inevitably, there is a re-contextualisation of
policy from central government to agencies of sub-government and
thence on to arenas of practice in schools. For BOWE et al the efforts
of the NC subject working groups, appointed to advise the government
on curriculum content, nicely illustrated and underlined the view that
policy as knowledge and practices, as a discourse, is always subject to
"slippage". Progressively, however, our own investigations have
indicated the limitations to this slippage; the unevenness of the power
relations inherent in the policy process; and the differences in the
capabilities of actors to influence a policy text. In the development of
the NCPE, we have seen both the explicit and very subtle ways in
which power is exercised in the policy process.

The planning of the NCPE, like that for all of the NC subjects, was conducted in distinct phases. Firstly, an overall structure was established by the government and its aids. This identified "Programmes of Study" and "Attainment Targets" for each of the four "key stages" of education identified as the central organising concepts for the development of each subject. The key stages comprised the periods of schooling from the beginning of school until age 7 (key stage 1), age 7-11 (key stage 2), age 11-14 (key stage 3) and age 14 to the end of compulsory education (key stage 4). Programmes of Study addressed the "matters, skills and processes which must be taught to pupils during each key stage in order for them to meet the objectives set out in the attainment targets" (DES/WELSH OFFICE (WO), 1991a, p.3). Attainment Targets are groupings of objectives for each subject, "setting out the knowledge, skills and understanding that pupils of different abilities and maturities are expected to develop within that subject area" (DES/WO, 1991a, p.2).

Secondly, professionals from education and industry were brought in to form a working group that would construct a curriculum and detail its form and content. Thirdly, the group's findings (in the form of an interim and final report) were referred back to the government via, and with modification by, the agency established to oversee this process, the National Curriculum Council (NCC). Following consultation on, and modification to, the final report, the statutory order for the NCPE was issued in 1992. This order then underwent a review and revision in 1994-5. The modified order for the NCPE, along with revised orders for all other subjects, was issued in 1995.

Throughout this development, a struggle over the meaning given to the teaching of PE has been in evidence. Equally apparent, however, have been inequities in the exercise of power within this contest. Notably, physical educationalists had no control over the structure of the NC, the selection of working group members, nor the terms of reference for this group. It was the Secretary of State who selected the actors and determined quite firmly the parameters for their action. In the construction of the NCPE we have seen clear incidents of matters being "non-negotiable". For example, the working group was consistently reminded of the resource implications of their recommendations, and requested to modify these recommendations in the light of the fact that the NCPE was to be implemented within existing (and very different) levels of resourcing in schools. In his

response to the working group's interim report (DES/WO, 1991a) the Secretary of State specifically underlined the need for the group to reconsider the economic 'feasibility' of the proposals and to ensure that the recommendations in their final report were "... realistically related to the general level of school funding which can reasonably be expected to be available" (DES/WO, 1991a). Effectively, the group were being 'asked' to construct a curriculum with respect to its economic viability, rather than its educational desirability. Thus, although there is certainly evidence of resistance and opposition in the actions of the working group, it would be folly to ignore the way in which their actions were strongly framed by more powerful others. Ultimately in relation to several critical matters, the group did not have the resource (the authorisation; GIDDENS, 1979) to contest the authority and power of the state.

In this respect, the development of the NCPE vividly illustrated not only the tension between the stated educational intention of the ERA, that a "broad and balanced" curriculum should be the entitlement of all children, and the harsh economic realities of its development (i.e. the limits of funding), but also that policy making is a political process in which not all parties have similar capabilities to influence 'outcomes'. The development demonstrated that the form of control inherent in the policy process can simultaneously be very obvious and very subtle. In response to the acute dilemma the government faced – of how to establish, or at least be seen to establish, a major initiative in education without investment implications – the concept of "flexibility" emerged as a critical feature of the government's discourse. The importance of this concept as a rhetorical device cannot be overstated. It has been used systematically not only to reduce the level of prescription in the NCPE throughout the various stages of its development, but also to obscure the limited commitments of the state to PE, and shift the onus of responsibility for the development and delivery of this curriculum from central government to individual schools.

For example, the NCPE recommendations for the curriculum at key stage 3 (age 11-14 years) and key stage 4 (age 14 -16) have undergone significant changes in the course of the phases of development outlined above. In their interim report, the working group recommended that in the interests of breadth and balance of experiences, pupils in key stage 3 should experience physical activities from each of six areas of activity: games activities, dance forms, gymnastic activities, athletic activities, swimming and water based activities, and outdoor education and adventure activities; and at key stage 4, activities from at least three areas, including games and either gymnastics or dance (DES/WO, 1991a). Their final report, both expressing and anticipating pressure from central government to reduce the resource implications of recommendations made significant amendments to these requirements. The number of areas of activity for key stages 3 and 4 was reduced to five, with "swimming and other water based activities" now to be pursued within the context of another area (for example, competitive swimming within athletic activities; canoeing within outdoor and adventurous activities). It was then recommended that pupils in key stage 3 should experience all areas, but in any one year at least four, including games and gymnastics or dance; and pupils in key stage 4, two activities from the same or different areas (DES/WO, 1991b). In introducing flexibility, these changes also reduced the guarantee of the delivery of a broad and balanced physical education curriculum. Furthermore, the introduction of differences between the various areas of activity in terms of coverage and frequency of coverage on the one hand created an explicit hierarchy of areas, and on the other, further reduced the notion of balance between them.

The working group's recommendations for key stage 4 were endorsed by the National Curriculum Council (NCC). However, the Secretary of State deemed those for key stage 3 to be "too prescriptive" and in the interests of "greater flexibility" the NCC therefore recommended that activities from four areas be experienced during the key stage, with games a compulsory activity in each year of the key stage (NCC, 1991). Explicit at this point of the development were not only the demands for flexibility and the privileging of a pragmatic discourse, but also increasing pressures for a parallel privileging of a particular view of physical education; centring on performance in traditional team games. This dual direction was even more evident in the revision of the NCPE in 1995. Once again there was the establishment of a critical element of greater flexibility, but with the proviso of increased prescription in relation to the experience of games. The revised order for the NCPE strengthened the distinction between games and other areas of activity, by defining all areas apart from games in terms of "full" and "half units" at key stage 3. It then stipulated that pupils should be taught games in each year of the key stage, plus at least one other full unit of activity and two further half-units during the key stage, with at least one half unit having to be either gymnastics or dance. The requirements for key stage 4 were amended to stipulate that at least one of the two activities pursued be a game (DFE/WO, 1995).

End Comment: Framing the Game

Essentially, in line with its broader cultural restorationist agenda (see EVANS and PENNEY, 1995), the Conservative central government sought to reinforce and/or re-establish via the NCPE, a physical education curriculum modelled on the long-standing traditions of physical education in the English public schools, in which it is performance in sport and in particular the traditional 'male' team games, that is the focus of attention (see also KIRK, 1992). This pressure and direction became increasingly explicit in the development of the NCPE and with it, the critical difference between the discourses of physical education and sport. As we explain and illustrate in chapter 4, the difference in these discourses remains a tension in the continued implementation of the NCPE.

On the surface, ascribing 'flexibility' to a subject area may sound appealing, appearing to offer scope for the level of human agency in policy 'making' which we and others (see for example BOWE et al, 1992) have portrayed in our conceptualisations of the policy process. However, in a highly differentiated school system, and organisational contexts of competition for limited resources, this ascription can be neither equated with freedom from constraint nor unlimited possibilities for either policy making or curriculum development. Although in a liberal discourse, flexibility does signify possibility, in this instance schools and teachers have been issued 'opportunity' without statutory support for their curriculum initiatives. They have responsibility without power. Teachers' capacities to act upon the 'freedom' granted by the texts is inevitably dependent upon existing levels of physical and human resources, and this may vary considerably between schools and across subject departments within them. Significantly, in the eyes of the government, the lower the status of a curriculum subject, the greater the 'flexibility' it can be afforded, and this stance was directly reflected in the development of the NCPE (together with the NC for Art and Music) as compared to other curriculum subjects. Needless to say, within schools, the status imputed to a subject has an important bearing on whether it is privileged or disadvantaged in the acquisition of resources. In a context of scarce resources, 'entitlement' and 'flexibility' may be fundamentally incompatible. Armed with the key rhetorical device of 'flexibility', schools (or rather headteachers and governors) are effectively free from the obligation to deliver the educational ideals of the NC. In our research we have seen that despite the stated commitment in the NC to the provision of a broad and balanced curriculum for all pupils, it is issues of resourcing that invariably continue to dominate discussions of what the provision of PE will be. Looking to the future, the strong obligation that we see emerging for schools and teachers (discussed further in chapter 4) is for an increasing focus within PE on the provision of competitive team games.

Thus, when we look closely at the policy process and interrogate the discourses embedded in policy texts, those marginalised or excluded, and the mechanisms or arrangements for 'creating' policy, we begin to see the need for caution in advocating a view of policy which places too great an emphasis on its dynamic nature or on opportunities for resistance or innovation by individual teachers of schools. Certainly as a social process, policy is always and inevitably made and remade, but not always in conditions of actors' own making (BALL, 1993). Nor in the 're-making' are all elements of a policy open to negotiation and change. The policy process is not always like a game of 'Chinese Whispers' in which the initial story line becomes increasingly and creatively more extravagant and altered. Texts can also be replicated or substantially reduced in the policy process and particular discourses repeatedly privileged and reinforced. In the recursive or cyclical flow of policy, creative activity may occur, but the narrative of the text and the conditions and contexts in which people work may constrain and narrow possibilities for action. Thus, if we understate either the constraints on practice or the different capabilities that actors have to influence the actions and decisions of others, we may be in danger not only of misrepresenting the policy process, but also of obfuscating the ways in which both democracy and the professionalism of teachers are being eroded.

Notes

1.   Our research on the curriculum and pedagogy of PE is ongoing. EVANS'
     research is now focussed centrally upon pupils' interpretations of Physical

Education and the relationships between physical culture, nationalism and identity. PENNEY's research is continuing to pursue the processes of policy and curriculum development via comparative research, and is examining the development and implementation of national curriculum initiatives in Australia.

References

BALL, S.J. (1990) *Politics and Policy Making in Education*. London, Routledge.

BALL, S.J. (1993) Education Policy, Power Relations and Teachers' work. *British Journal of Educational Studies*, XXXXI, 2, 106-121.

BEST, S. and KELLNER, D. (1991) *Postmodern Theory. Critical Interrogations*. London, Macmillan.

BOWE, R. and BALL, S.J. with GOLD, A. (1992) Reforming Education and Changing Schools. *Case Studies in Policy Sociology*. London, Routledge.

DAHL, R. (1970) *Who Governs?* New Haven, Yale University Press.

DEPARTMENT OF EDUCATION AND SCIENCE (1989) *National Curriculum – From Policy to Practice*. London, DES.

DEPARTMENT OF EDUCATION AND SCIENCE/WELSH OFFICE (1991a) *National Curriculum Physical Education Working Group Interim Report*. London, DES.

DEPARTMENT OF EDUCATION AND SCIENCE/WELSH OFFICE (1991b) *Physical Education for ages 5-16*. Proposals of the Secretary of State for Education and the Secretary of State for Wales. London, DES.

EVANS, J. (1990) Defining a Subject: The rise and rise of the new PE? *British Journal of Sociology of Education,* 11, 2, 155-169.

EVANS, J., DAVIES, B and PENNEY, D. (1994) Whatever happened to the Subject and the State in Policy Research in Education. *Discourse*, 14, 2, 57-64.

EVANS, J. and PENNEY, D. (1995b) Physical Education, Restoration and the Politics of Sport. *Curriculum Studies*, 3, 2, 183-196.

FOUCAULT, M. (1980) *Power/Knowledge*. New York, Vintage Books.

GIDDENS, A. (1979) *Central Problems in Social Theory*. London, The Macmillan Press.

HILL, M. (1980) *Understanding Social Policy*. Oxford, Basil Blackwell.

KIRK, D. (1992) *Defining Physical Education*. London, The Falmer Press.
KOGAN, M. (1975) *Educational Policy-Making*. London, Allen & Unwin.

LINGARD, R. (1993) The Changing State of Policy Production in Education: Some Australlian Reflections on the State of Policy Sociology. *International Studies in Sociology of Education*, 3 1, 25- 47.

NATIONAL CURRICULUM COUNCIL (1991) *Physical Education in The National Curriculum*. A Report to the Secretary of State for Education and Science on the statutory consultation for the attainment target and programmes of study in physical education. York, NCC.

O'BUACHALLA, S. (1988) *Education Policy in Twentieth Century Ireland*. Dublin, Wolfhound Press.

PENNEY, D. and EVANS, J. (1994) From 'Policy' to 'Practice': The Development and Implementation of the National Curriculum for Physical Education. In D. SCOTT (Ed) *Accountability and Control in Educational Settings*. Cassell Publications.

Chapter 4

Dictating the Play:
Government Direction in Physical Education and
Sport Policy
Development in England and Wales

Dawn Penney and John Evans

Introduction

The ongoing implementation of a National Curriculum for Physical Education (NCPE) in England and Wales has continued to highlight the *range* of values and vested interests at play within and upon the subject matter of Physical Education (PE) (TALBOT, 1993; EVANS and PENNEY, 1995a,b). Elsewhere we have documented the struggles inherent in the 'making' of this policy, over *what* was to constitute the NCPE for state schools in England and Wales. We have drawn attention to the way in which the Conservative central government in the UK has succeeded in progressively privileging *particular* discourses in its texts. Specifically the development between 1990 and 1992 saw a shift in emphasis, with 'restorationist' ('back to basics') and pragmatic discourses increasingly prominent, and in parallel, educational discourses marginalised, subordinated and/or excluded (see chapter 3 and EVANS, DAVIES and PENNEY, 1994; EVANS and PENNEY, 1995a, 1995b; PENNEY, 1994).

Two policy texts issued by central government in 1995 were critical to the reinforcement of this emphasis: the *revised* National Curriculum for Physical Education issued by the DEPARTMENT FOR EDUCATION (DFE) and the WELSH OFFICE (WO) (DFE and WO, 1995) and a policy statement entitled *Sport – Raising the Game* issued by the Department of National Heritage (DNH, 1995). In the first part of this paper we examine the nature of the discourses that are privileged within and by these texts. In the second part, we focus on the relationships between the two policy documents and the contexts of education and schooling in which they are being 'read' and implemented. We consider the way in which these contexts may nurture and frame particular interpretations of the texts and presage readings that further reinforce and legitimate the discourses privileged within and by them. We highlight the limits that in our view now exist in relation to the ability of PE teachers in schools in England and Wales to define and shape their subject, and question the scope that remains in the system for innovation, interpretation and 'resistance' in their implementation of the NCPE; for the kind of 'slippage' between centrally determined policy and practice in schools that some analyses of policy (and the National Curriculum specifically; see for example BOWE and BALL with GOLD, 1992) have emphasised. Finally, we note that the making of the NCPE has illustrated vividly not only the contested nature of the curriculum but also the inequalities and inequities inherent in education, which recent policies seem set to sustain. Thus, although our analysis centres on PE, it points to processes that have relevance across subject boundaries and to all concerned with the future of democracy and the professional autonomy of teachers in state schools.

Our analysis and discussion is set within the conceptual framework introduced in chapter 3 and developed further in other work (see EVANS, DAVIES and PENNEY, 1994; EVANS, PENNEY and BRYANT, 1993a; PENNEY, 1994; PENNEY and EVANS, 1994a), in which policy is viewed as a *complex process* involving the production of *multiple texts*, which may be written, spoken or mental conceptualisations of policy and inherent in which are a *variety of discourses* each expressing particular interests and ideologies. Like others (APPLE, 1986; BALL, 1993a) we draw attention not only to the inclusions and exclusions in and from texts, but also to the influence of discourses *surrounding* the texts, and to their location within power relations which influence their production and 'implementation'. As our discussion in chapter 3 indicated, discourses are not only about what is said and thought, "... but about who can speak where, when and with what authority" (BALL,1993b, p.14). The discussion that follows illustrates these matters vividly and highlights not only that discourses are created under particular conditions and rules, but also that the control of those conditions and rules is a critical factor in the struggle to establish and sustain particular definitions of PE and concomitantly particular forms of consciousness within and through education (BERNSTEIN, 1990).

Defining Physical Education and Sport in England and Wales

The National Curriculum for Physical Education (NCPE), 1995

In 1993, acknowledging the many shortcomings arising in the development and implementation of the National Curriculum (NC) and most notably the "curriculum overload" in schools generated by this initiative, the Secretary of State for Education called for a review of the NC and "the framework for assessment of pupils" progress (DEARING, 1994). The revision proposed a *reduction within the existing structure and framework* of the NC. It prohibited the questioning of either the underlying rationale for, or merits of, the established subject based, strongly classified (BERNSTEIN, 1971, 1990) structure of the NC. Notably, this structure endorses the distinctiveness of knowledge domains, the separation and division between subject areas and between "areas of activity" in the case of the NCPE. The NCPE defined physical education as a set of distinct activities, identifying games, gymnastic activities, athletic activities, dance, swimming and outdoor and adventurous activities as the basis for developing "Programmes of Study" (POS)[1] for the subject. The extent of the dominance of the belief that physical education does and/or should centre on *performance* in *sport*, and that specific sport activites should be the starting point for curriculum planning and design, is such that many readers may find it hard to conceptualise any alternative. The development in Australia of curriculum texts that centre on "Key Learning Areas" (KLAs), one of which is "Health and Physical Education" and within this KLA, the organisation of curriculum content around the three strands of "Human functioning and physical activity", "Community structures and practices" and "Communication, investigation and application" (see AUSTRALIAN EDUCATION COUNCIL, 1994a), illustrates the potential for a very different framework for teaching and learning 'physical education'. Furthermore, it highlights how in the development of the NCPE in England and Wales themes such as health education, personal and social education and equal opportunities have been marginalised, along with the educational emphasis that physical education is first and foremost about the development of the child, over and above the specific activity in which they may be engaged (see also EVANS and PENNEY 1995a; PENNEY, 1994; PENNEY and KIRK, forthcoming).

In the review of the NC and NCPE specifically, the established curriculum structures were not questioned but rather, underpinned and shaped the revision process. Attention centred on which subjects and what aspects within subjects should be retained within a 'slimmed down' curriculum (DEARING, 1994). Consequently, the possibilities for the development of alternative curricula and the expression of integrated codes (BERNSTEIN, 1971, 1990) were again subordinated. The impression that a subject based (and within physical education, activity based) curriculum, is the 'natural' and only possible model for school curricula was reinforced. In addition, the bias emerging within this structure, towards the privileging of *games*, was openly extended.

In chapter 3, we explained how a hierarchy of areas of activity was embedded in the NCPE texts, with '*games*' accorded the highest status in the curriculum (see also EVANS and PENNEY, 1995a; PENNEY, 1994). Despite innovations in physical education in the UK such as the development of educational gymnastics and the promotion of outdoor education, it is games, with its origins in male traditions of physical education, that have retained dominance in school curricula (see KIRK, 1992), and a residual feature of the development and dominance of games has been the gendered nature of provision, with girls and boys being offered different and stereotypically 'appropriate' activities. As explained in chapter 3, in the 1992 statutory order for the NCPE games was defined as the sole compulsory component of the curriculum in *each year* of key stage 3[2] (incorporating school years 7, 8 and 9) with the requirements specifying that three other areas of activity were to be addressed at *some point during* the key stage. In key stage 4 (years 10 and 11) pupils had to experience two activities, from the same or different areas of activity (DES/WO, 1992). The revised order for the NCPE further endorsed this position of games as the dominant and defining feature of PE, especially in the requirements relating to the secondary years of schooling (key stages 3 and 4). Notably it strengthened the distinction between games and other areas of activity, by defining all areas *apart from games* in terms of "full" and "half units" at key stage 3. It was stipulated that pupils should be taught games in *each year* of the key stage, plus at least one other full unit of activity and two further half-units *during the key stage*. At least one half unit has to be either gymnastics or dance. In addition the requirements for key stage 4 were amended to stipulate that at least one of the two activities pursued be a game (DFE/WO, 1995).

This privileging of games subordinated other areas of activity and concomitantly the commitment to providing breadth and balance within the curriculum of PE. Games was established as the *only* area of activity compulsory throughout the 5-16 curriculum. Given that research has consistently pointed out that competitive games have limited appeal to many children, particularly young women, and indicated the importance of variety between and within areas of activity if the varying needs and interests of children are to be met (OFSTED, 1995; OHMCI, 1995; PENNEY and EVANS, 1995a; PENNEY and EVANS, 1994b; PENNEY and EVANS with HENNINK, 1994) any further narrowing of the curriculum may be very regrettable. Furthermore as well as being in danger of restricting experiences in these terms, the revised NCPE also offers teachers the 'flexibility' within the statutory requirements to provide a sex differentiated curriculum. Again, therefore, the text effectively endorsed long-standing practices and biases in PE in the UK. Recent inspection reports have drawn attention to the effects of these continuing practices; the limiting of both girls' and boys' experiences of, and learning in, PE (see OFSTED, 1995; OHMCI, 1995). Certainly with the statutory requirements as they stand, in years ahead it may be particularly difficult for the stated aim of the NC, to ensure the provision of a broad and balanced education for *all* children (DES, 1989), to be achieved in the context of PE.

Sport – Raising the Game

The revised NCPE clearly reflected central government's 'restorationist' belief that games has "... the advantage of perpetuating the best of English traditions and cultural heritage" (NCC, 1991, p.14). This ideological leaning was even more apparent in the policy statement entitled *Sport – Raising the Game* subsequently issued by the DEPARTMENT OF NATIONAL HERITAGE (in July 1995). This initiative was described by the UK Prime Minister, John MAJOR, as "... the most important set of proposals ever published for the encouragement and promotion of sport" (John MAJOR in DNH,

1995). Certainly the strength of direction and potential 'control' inherent in this 'encouragement' seemed unprecedented. The proposals appeared set to reach out to *regulate* not only the provision of sport in schools, in higher education and by clubs and governing bodies of sport, but also teacher training in PE. Key elements of the policy text reflected very clearly the government's privileging of elitism, nationalism and cultural restorationism within the arenas of PE and sport policy. This policy highlighted that definitions of PE and sport are never neutral, but rather, promote and legitimate *particular* values and interests and in parallel, exclude and/or subordinate others.

Naming the Game ...

In his letter of introduction to the policy statement, the Prime Minister stated "We want to sustain the place of minor sports that bring much enjoyment. *But I am determined to see that our great traditional sports – cricket, hockey, swimming, athletics, football, netball, rugby, tennis and the like – are put firmly at the centre of the stage."* (John MAJOR in DNH, 1995; our emphasis). Absent from this list, just as they were progressively subordinated and silenced in the NCPE, are sports with an aesthetic emphasis, or an emphasis on, for example, personal fitness rather than team performance. The privileging of games and more specifically 'competitive', 'traditional' team games ran strongly throughout the proposals. For example, in relation to school provision, one of the requirements outlined in the policy statement was for schools to publish for parents and governors details of their aims for and provision of sport and how these have been met during the school year. The 'suggestions' were that these might include details of "... what sports and, *in particular, what traditional team* sports are played at the school" and "the *results of school teams* ..." (DNH, 1995, p.11; our emphases). Similarly it was stated that future inspections of schools would specifically address "... the range, time spent and quality of *games*, including *competitive team games*, offered as part of the formal PE curriculum" and the "... sporting provision that schools offer to pupils outside formal lessons ... *paying particular attention to traditional team games*" (DNH, 1995, p.12; our emphasis).

The ideological leanings of these measures were mirrored in the proposals concerning teacher training. It was stated that "the new criteria for teacher training will mean that all teachers of PE will be equipped to teach at least one mainstream game played in the summer and one mainstream game played in the winter" and that it was the government's belief that "every training teacher, not just those with PE as their first qualification, should have the opportunity to acquire coaching qualifications, and be strongly encouraged to do them" (DNH, 1995, p.15). It was then explained that funding would be tied to evidence of institutions having complied with the government's desired aims: "... inspectors will be asked to monitor training to teach the *main traditional and competitive team sports*, and to see that all trainee teachers are made aware of the increased opportunity to gain *coaching* qualifications". In the light of the evidence gathered "quality indicators" would be developed to ensure that future funding supports "the most effective training" (DNH, 1995, p.17; our emphasis).

The narrow, anglocentric, male, view of PE and sport inherent in this document conveniently overlooked the more dubious and negative 'qualities' of citizenship that any sport may promote, as well as the multicultural environment of sport and PE in the UK. As WINDER (1995) pointed out, the emphasis on team sports, "discipline" and "commitment" "... all harks back to some ludicrous Victorian ideal of manly camaraderie, leadership, competition, cold showers and so on ..." (ibid, THE INDEPENDENT, 15/7/95, p.17). Others observed that "... non-team games, such as rockclimbing or judo, can be just as challenging and character building" (THE GUARDIAN LEADER, 15/7/95, p.24). We would stress that neither this nor any other outcome is guaranteed simply by participation in a particular activity; the needs and interests of children are not likely to be met through their relationship with an activity alone. Development, whether in sport or PE, has to be mediated and nurtured by good teaching and the actions of individuals well trained, imbued with sophisticated pedagogical skills. Regrettably these are qualities that the recommendations for teacher training in *Raising the Game*, together with the increasingly short time training teachers have in higher education institutions (see EVANS, PENNEY and DAVIES, 1996) appear likely to do little to either foster or sustain.

As well as this emphasis on particular sports, the proposals in *Raising the Game* presaged more *elitism* in PE. Although "health", "fun" and "enjoyment" were mentioned in the Prime Minister's opening letter, it was clear that they are not the government's priorities in its "support" for sport and physical education. *Raising the Game* laid the foundations for the establishment of a British Academy of Sport specifically for the development of excellence, and it was prospective stars who were clearly privileged throughout many of the proposals. For example, it was stated that "Alongside teachers, clubs have an important role to play by expanding the range of sports on offer and providing coaching *to the most talented*" (DNH, 1995, p.9; our emphasis). Meanwhile, with respect to provision of sport in further and higher education, it was explained that a working party would be established to investigate the existing provision of university sport scholarships directed towards supporting individuals training and competing *"at the highest level"* during their studies and how such schemes could be developed.

Much of this would be well and good if accompanied by the equivalent resourcing and celebration of PE and sport for *all*. In the absence of such investment, with WINDER (1995) we pose the question "... is it better to promote a small elite of winners whom the rest of us can watch on telly, or a nation of participants?" (p.17). In his view it is "Far better to spread facilities, coaching, equipment and encouragement as widely as possible, rather than buying new bats for the first eleven" (p.17). Notably the parallel policy statement issued by the Welsh Office highlighted that encouraging the elite and catering for the needs and interests of others less talented are not necessarily mutually exclusive aims. Launching the Welsh initiative, the Secretary of State for Wales, William HAGUE, explained that "Participating in sport goes much further than achievement at national or international level ... Although Wales has a wealth of sporting talent – which I hope this blueprint will further encourage – we should not forget that sport is fun and we can enjoy it at whatever level of achievement we reach." (WELSH OFFICE, 1995) .

From 'Policy' to 'Practice' ...

Following the revision of the NCPE and the issuing of *Raising the Game*, our concerns centred on how these texts would be read by PE teachers. Were the texts likely to be interpreted in ways that were responsive to the needs of all children, to the circumstances of the school and the communities they serve? Would teachers have the autonomy and the 'freedom' to decide what their responses would be? In addressing the likely answers to these questions we draw attention to the significance of the dynamic between the two policies, and the importance also of their inter-action with the broader educational contexts in which responses to them are being made.

As with the previous NCPE text (DES/WO, 1992), the revised NCPE nurtured the illusion that individual schools and teachers have considerable choice in matters of curriculum design and delivery relating to sport and PE. With the exception of the prescriptive requirements concerning games, the areas of activity to be included in the curriculum and the attention to be devoted to them are matters for individual schools and teachers to determine. Furthermore, neither the allocation of time between areas within the subject nor the 'teaching methods' to be used are matters that the statutory requirements explicitly address. Much, it seemed, was to be left in the hands of a teacher's innovatory ideals. However, once we register on the one hand the powerful discourses inherent in these documents, and on the other those dominant in the contexts of their implementation, we begin to see the limits to the 'flexibility', 'choice' and opportunities for "slippage" (BOWE et al, 1992) between the intentions of government and the implementation of the NCPE in schools.

As mentioned above, the 'official' NCPE text endorses a definition of, and structure for, the curriculum of PE which has long featured in PE. Although the text does not exclude the possibility of adopting alternative curriculum structures, founded for example on the theme of health education and 'integrated' rather than 'collection' codes, (BERNSTEIN, 1971) neither does it encourage such developments. Discussion of, or guidance on, 'alternative structures' has been noticeably absent from the texts of the NCPE (see EVANS and PENNEY, 1995a; PENNEY, 1994) and is a much needed debate in the subject. As indicated, the National Statement and Profile for Health and Physical Education developed in Australia (Australian Education Council, 1994a, 1994b) may be a useful first point of reference in our endeavours to make explicit what such alternatives might 'look like'. At present, however, such enlightenment is certainly lacking. Furthermore, the contexts in which teachers are working may serve to further obstruct the development of innovative approaches and ideals, and instead reinforce the biases inherent in both the NCPE text and much current practice.

Returning to our focus on the position of games within PE, on the surface the text of the NCPE provides as much scope to challenge the dominance of games within PE as it does to endorse its privileged position. The requirements of the NCPE are identified as only the *minimum* required provision for PE, leaving the scope for schools to achieve 'breadth and balance' by supplementing the NCPE with additional provision. Theoretically, therefore, considerable attention could be given to those areas of activity accorded a lower status in the government's texts, with schools perhaps ensuring that other areas of activity are experienced with the same frequency and in a similar depth as games. However, in the absence of any explicit encouragement for such an approach to curriculum design and within conditions that (as we explain further below) may be far from supportive of such developments, neither the willingness nor ability on the part of schools and teachers to 'even out' this imbalance in PE can be assumed. Not all schools have the staff expertise, facilities, equipment and funding to support diversity in the curriculum. Others lack the support of head teachers and/or senior staff in timetabling and staffing arrangements to facilitate curriculum development, or face conflict with them over the direction that development should take (see EVANS, PENNEY and BRYANT, 1993b; PENNEY, 1994). In addition, in a climate in which pupil intakes are the very basis of school survival and/or prosperity[3], headteachers and school governors with heightened consciousness of the importance of 'marketing their school' may see merits in a games centred PE, seeing this as the basis for achievement in the publicly visible and valued arena of extra-curricular *sport*. Furthermore, the prospects of newly qualified teachers emerging from training with an ability or a desire to innovate or reflect critically upon present practice may also be diminished once the recommendations of *Raising the Game* outlined above come into play.

The above pressures within schools *in part* help to explain the tendencies towards consolidation and assimilation rather than innovation and development that we have observed in the implementation of the NCPE. Our research has drawn attention to the failure of the introduction of the NCPE to sponsor widespread or comprehensive critical review and development of PE curricula, its requirements instead being in many instances *accommodated within* largely unchanged practices (see EVANS and PENNEY, 1995a; PENNEY, 1994). However, our investigations have also directed us to some of the other factors contributing to this response. Certainly, feelings of having little 'ownership' of the changes required, and a lack of time and support to reflect on and review them, have also played their part in sustaining the 'status quo'. Teachers were not positioned centrally as active 'agents of change' in the making of the official NCPE texts and they have been similarly marginalised in the production of *Raising the Game*. Once again they are being asked to implement policies over which they have had little say or control. In relation to time for planning a response and subsequent directions in development, the publication of the statutory orders in 1992 allowed teachers only a matter of weeks to plan their implementation for the forthcoming academic year. Although the revision of the NC allowed more time for preparation, the timescale for its introduction was nevertheless acknowledged as "demanding" (DEARING, 1994, p.26). Time and space for reflection and development, thus, remain absent from the contexts of teaching and to make matters worse, teachers have been increasingly burdened by heavy administrative demands that in many instances have taken precedence over, and detracted from development of the 'practice' of teaching PE (see PENNEY, 1994; GRAHAM with TYTLER, 1993). Clearly these are not conditions likely to sponsor a positive approach to curriculum development.

Also significant is the fact that the implementation and revision of the NCPE has come at a time of diminishing support, guidance and professional development opportunities for teachers in England and Wales. Requirements for assessment and 'accountability', rather than, for example, the development of critical pedagogies, have emerged as the priorities for the limited support available (see EVANS and PENNEY, 1994). The issuing of *Raising the Game* may further direct and narrow the range of in-service provision and demands. Its text not only *threatens* inspections focused on schools' provision of games in school, but also provides accompanying *incentives* for schools to direct PE provision more towards competitive sport. The document advocates formal recognition of "effective policies for promoting sport" via the introduction of "SportsMark" and "GoldStar" awards for schools, and identifies the awards as beneficial acquisitions in schools' bids to attract parents and hence prospective pupils. At the time of writing the criteria for the awards are yet to be confirmed, but will clearly be critical in shaping future provision. The suggestions voiced in *Raising the Game* are that schools be required to devote at least 50% of in- and extra-curricular PE time to games, develop links with local sports clubs, and that teachers improve their coaching skills. Our fear is that the increasing emphasis on "coaching" and links with clubs may together further presage an emphasis on sport performance and the needs of the able few. In considering likely responses from schools, we need again to look to the wider context in which texts will be read. As explained earlier, post the ERA, schools in England and Wales have to attract sufficient pupils to finance their existing staffing levels and their curricula. In these conditions, the pressures to adopt rather than adapt or resist the dominant discourses of games and sport are considerable. If they are to survive, or indeed prosper in the 'education market', many schools may feel that they have little choice but to "play the government's game" (PENNEY, 1994), particularly when one considers the views and interests likely to be prevalent amongst the parents that schools are seeking to attract. Given the messages repeatedly peddled in the public domain by central Government and the media (see EVANS, 1990), it is perhaps not surprising that parents, (paradoxically it often seems in the light of their own unfavourable experiences of being taught games in schools) continue to endorse the importance of *sport* in PE. Attempting to inform or change these perceptions is no easy task and in present conditions, a 'risk' few schools may feel able or encouraged to take.

Conclusion: Autonomy and Control in Policy Implementation

Given the 'authority' of the discourses inherent in the texts of the NCPE and *Raising the Game* and acknowledging the economic and socio-cultural conditions in which these texts will be interpreted and read, in the years ahead we should not be surprised to find schools and institutes of further and higher education increasingly adopting, and thereby appearing to endorse, a C/conservative view of PE as sport. Indeed, with further policy initiatives and even more significantly, both human and financial resources following the direction set by *Raising the Game*, any deviation seems increasingly unlikely. Specifically, the Youth Sport Trust (YST) has emerged as a key player in (and provider to) future curriculum developments, particularly in primary schools. Its "Top Play" and "BT Top Sport" programmes provide a clear focus and resources for primary teachers, that under present conditions neither initial teacher training nor further professional development can adequately deliver. While welcoming the support, we have concerns about the limitations of these initiatives. Although the YST itself emphasises that its materials "... are not a substitute for the National Curriculum but an additional resource for teachers that can complement the planning for the school physical education programme" (CAMPBELL, 1996, p.22), we highlight that these may be the only resources and support received by some teachers.

However, whilst acknowledging what we regard as very real constraints now placed upon the flexibility and freedom of teachers and schools, and the noted absence of support for alternative developments, we also guard against an overly deterministic and pessimistic view of the impact and influence of government policy on schools. Teachers and teacher educators are not automatons or mere puppets in the policy process. Although they face ever increasing pressures to respond in set ways, they remain key and influential elements in the interpretation and expression of policies as practice in schools. Here is the paradox in a top down view of policy implementation, and the check on the extent of central state control. Policy cannot implement itself (sic). Central government has to rely on the good will and cooperation-operation of teachers (who it has often sought to deride) if its policies are to materialise in schools. As others have noted, the actions of teachers are fundamental to the success of particular initiatives and hence the dominance of particular discourses and values in physical education. Certainly, we need note with BALL (1993b) that "... there is agency and there is constraint in relation to policy – this is not a sum-zero game" (p.13). Thus as THE DAILY TELEGRAPH observed following the launch of *Raising the Game*, "Crucial to this grand design is the goodwill and practical support of the teaching profession" (THE DAILY TELEGRAPH, 15/7/95, p.14). However, whilst acknowledging this 'agency', we have highlighted how governments may nonetheless still subtly frame the opportunities of and for individuals to think and act otherwise, outside the frame set by 'negotiated' policy measures. Regrettably in the UK we have witnessed increasing constraint on the policy process. Texts are not being 'read' in circumstances of the respondent's own making (BALL, 1993a). The conservative 'Right' have established an unprecedented degree of control over education, perhaps particularly in the arenas of PE and sport. We have witnessed what CLEGG (1989) has described as a central feature of power, the "fixing of the terrain for its own expression" (p.183). As one of the members of the NCPE working group, Elizabeth MURDOCH (1992) observed, whilst there may still be talk of flexibility for teachers, "It might be questioned just how free we are to make judgments on our practice. The pressures are subtle but nonetheless significant" (p.18) and together with the more obvious directives of legislative measures they directly contradict a view of policy as a process best established and realised by "communities of people within and across schools who talk about the provisions, enquire into them, and reformulate them, bearing in mind the circumstances and the children they know best" (HARGREAVES, 1995, p.5).

Many of the agencies concerned with sport in the UK, such as the British Association of Advisers and Lecturers in Physical Education (BAALPE), the Physical Education Association United Kingdom (PEAUK) and The Central Council for Physical Education, have welcomed *Raising the Game* "with great enthusiasm" and regarded the "carefully crafted" initiative as representing "outstanding good news for sport throughout the United Kingdom" (LAWSON, 1995). We have been more guarded in our acclaim. Whilst not wishing to dismiss or temper any interest in sport in schools, we would encourage all to ask exactly what the government is providing support for, towards whom is this support directed towards, why the particular direction is being taken, and what the consequences of these initiatives will be for the identities and opportunities of children in schools? Certainly our analysis suggests that statements that "The joint impact of National Curriculum PE with this significant initiative [i.e. *Raising the Game*] for school sport *makes it more possible for the Physical Education profession to meet the needs of all young people in schools*" and that "Teachers of physical education *will continue to offer the balance of experience expected within the National Curriculum*" (BAALPE/ PEAUK, 1995; our emphasis) may turn out to be at best optimistic, at worst somewhat naive.

Notes

1   Programmes of Study specified the essential teaching within each subject area in the National Curriculum (DES, 1989).

2   In the National Curriculum schooling years are defined in relation to age of pupils as follows: Age 5 or under: Reception (R); Ages 5-7: Years 1 and 2; Ages 7-11: Years 3-6; Ages 11-14: Years 7-9; Ages 14-16: Years 10 and 11; and the curriculum is structured around four "key stages": Key stage 1 includes pupils in years R,1 and 2; key stage 2 those in years 3 - 6; key stage 3 years 7-9 and key stage 4 years 10 and 11 (DES, 1989).

3   Local Management of Schools (LMS), introduced by the Education

Reform Act (ERA) (1988), introduced the allocation of funds to schools on a formula basis, related to the number and age of pupils. Another policy within the ERA, Open Enrolment, removed previous restrictions on and LEA control of school intakes. Together these policies created conditions of competition between schools for pupils (see MACLURE, 1989).

References

APPLE, M.W. (1986) *Teachers and Texts. A Political Economy of Class and Gender Relations in Education.* London, Routledge and Kegan Paul.

APPLE, M.W. (1993) *Official Knowledge. Democratic Education in a Conservative Age.* London and New York, Routledge.

AUSTRALIAN EDUCATION COUNCIL (1994a) *A statement on health and physical education for Australian schools.* Carlton, Curriculum Corporation.

AUSTRALIAN EDUCATION COUNCIL (1994b) *Health and physical education – a curriculum profile for Australian schools.* Carlton, Curriculum Corporation.

BALL, S.J. (1993a) Education Policy, Power Relations and Teachers' work. *British Journal of Educational Studies,* XXXXI, 2, 106-121.

BALL, S.J. (1993b) What is Policy? Texts, Trajectories and Toolboxes. *Discourse,* 13, 2, 10-17.

BAALPE/PEAUK (1995) Press Release: Joint Statement from the British Association of Advisers and Lecturers in Physical Education (BAALPE) and the Physical education Association United Kingdom (PEAUK) on "Sport – Raising the Game." 14 July 1995.

BERNSTEIN, B. (1971) On the Classification and Framing of Educational Knowledge. In YOUNG, M.F.D. (Ed) *Knowledge and Control. New Directions for the Sociology of Education.* London, Collier Macmillan.

BERNSTEIN, B. (1990) *The Structuring of Pedagogic Discourse. Volume IV Class, Codes and Control.* London, Routledge.

BOWE, R. and BALL, S.J. with GOLD, A. (1992) Reforming Education and Changing Schools. *Case Studies in Policy Sociology.* London, Routledge.

CAMPBELL, S. (1996) Raising the Game. *British Journal of Physical Education*, 27, 3, 21-24.

CLEGG, S.R. (1989) *Frameworks of Power*. London, Sage Publications.

DEARING, R. (1994) *The National Curriculum and its Assessment: Final Report*. London, School Curriculum and Assessment Authority.

DEPARTMENT FOR EDUCATION/WELSH OFFICE (1995) *Physical Education in the National Curriculum*. London, DFE.

DEPARTMENT OF EDUCATION AND SCIENCE (1989) *National Curriculum – From Policy to Practice*. London, DES.

DES/WO (1992) *Physical Education in the National Curriculum*. London, DES.

DEPARTMENT OF NATIONAL HERITAGE (1995) *Sport – Raising the Game*. London, DNH.

EVANS, J. (1990) Defining a Subject: The rise and rise of the new PE? *British Journal of Sociology of Education*, 11, 2, 155-169.

EVANS, J., DAVIES, B. and PENNEY, D. (1994) Whatever happened to the Subject and the State in Policy Research in Education? *Discourse*, 14, 2, 57-64.

EVANS, J. and PENNEY, D. (1994) Whatever Happened to Good Advice? Service and Inspection after the Education Reform Act. *British Educational Research Journal*, 20, 5, 519-533.

EVANS, J. and PENNEY, D. (1995a) The politics of pedagogy: making a National Curriculum Physical Education. *Journal of Education Policy*, 10, 1, 27-44.

EVANS, J. and PENNEY, D. (1995b) Physical Education, Restoration and the Politics of Sport. *Curriculum Studies*, 3, 2, 183-196.

EVANS, J., PENNEY, D. and BRYANT, A. (1993a) Theorising Implementation: A Preliminary Comment on Power and Process in Policy Research. *Physical Education Review*, 16, 1, 5-22.

EVANS, J., PENNEY, D. and BRYANT, A. (1993b) Improving the Quality of Physical Education? The Education Reform Act, 1988 and Physical Education in England and Wales. *Quest*, 45, 321-338.

EVANS, J., PENNEY, D. and DAVIES, B. (1996) Back to the Future? Education Policy and PE. In N. ARMSTRONG (Ed) *Issues in Physical Education* vol.3. Cassell Publications, pp.1-18.

GRAHAM, D. with TYTLER, D. (1993) A Lesson for Us All. *The Making of the National Curriculum.* London, Routledge.

HARGREAVES, A. (1995) Working with Paradox: Why We Have to Reinvent Educational Change. In CEDAR, *Re-Thinking UK Education: What Next?* Roehampton Institute, London, pp.4-7.

KIRK, D. (1992) *Defining Physical Education.* London, The Falmer Press.

LAWSON, P. (1995) Press Release: Sport Wins the Jackpot. CCPR, 14 July 1995.

MACLURE, S. (1989) *Education Re-formed* (2nd Edition). London, Hodder and Stoughton.

MURDOCH, E.B. (1992) Physical Education Today. *The Bulletin of Physical Education,* 28, 2, 15-24.

NATIONAL CURRICULUM COUNCIL (1991) *Physical Education in The National Curriculum.* A Report to the Secretary of State for Education and Science on the statutory consultation for the attainment target and programmes of study in physical education. York, NCC.

OFFICE OF HER MAJESTY'S CHIEF INSPECTOR OF SCHOOLS (1995) *Physical Education. A review of inspection findings 1993/4.* London, HMSO.

OFFICE OF HER MAJESTY'S CHIEF INSPECTOR OF SCHOOLS IN WALES (1995) *Report by HM Inspectors. Survey of Physical Education in Key Stages 1, 2 and 3.* OHMCI, Cardiff.

PENNEY, D. (1994) "No Change in a New Era?" The Impact of the Education Reform Act (1988) on the Provision of PE and Sport in State Schools. PhD Thesis, University of Southampton.

PENNEY, D. and EVANS, J. (1994a) From 'Policy' to 'Practice': the Development and Implementation of the National Curriculum for Physical Education. In SCOTT, D. (Ed) *Accountability and Control in Educational Settings.* Cassell Publications.

PENNEY, D. and EVANS, J. (1994b) It's Just Not (and not just) Cricket. *British*

Journal of Physical Education, 25, 3, 9-12.

PENNEY, D. and EVANS, J. with HENNINK, M. (1994) (Unpublished report) The implementation of the National Curriculum for Physical Education: report of findings of a questionnaire survey of state secondary schools. Department of Physical Education, Sports Science and Recreation Management, Loughborough University.

PENNEY, D. and KIRK, D. (forthcoming) National Curriculum Developments in Australia and Britain: A Comparative Analysis. *Journal of Comparative Physical Education and Sport.*

TALBOT, M. (1993) Physical Education and the National Curriculum some Political Issues. In McFEE, G. and TOMLINSON, A. (Eds) *Education, Sport and Leisure: Connections and Controversies.* University of Brighton, 34-65.

THE DAILY TELEGRAPH (1995) A Sporting Chance. *The Daily Telegraph,* 15/7/95, p.14.

THE GUARDIAN LEADER (1995) Mr. Major's sporting wish-list. *The Guardian,* 15/7/95, p.24.

WELSH OFFICE (1995) *Press release:* "William Hague Launches Sports Blueprint for Year 2000" 25/9/95. Cardiff, The Welsh Office.

WINDER, R. (1995) Comment. *The Independent,* 15/7/95, p.17.

PART 3

HEALTH, HEALTH-RELATED EXERCISE
AND PHYSICAL EDUCATION

Chapter 5

Aerobic Fitness and Physical Activity Patterns of Young People

Neil Armstrong, Joanne Welsman and Brian Kirby

In adult life the effect of regular physical activity and/or aerobic fitness in reducing high blood pressure, enhancing blood lipid profile, countering obesity, retarding osteoporosis, improving blood glucose control, and increasing psychological well-being is extensively documented (FENTEM, BASSEY and TURNBULL, 1988). It appears that adults' physical activity patterns and aerobic fitness may have their origins in childhood (ACTIVITY AND HEALTH RESEARCH, 1992; KUH and COOPER, 1992) therefore, encouraging children to adopt physically active lifestyles and to maintain adequate levels of aerobic fitness may have significant long-term health benefits. However, until recently little was known about British young people's aerobic fitness and physical activity patterns.

In this chapter we focus on data generated in the PEA Children's Health and Exercise Research Centre over the last decade and address the question, are British young people fit and active?

Young People's Aerobic Fitness

Aerobic fitness depends upon pulmonary, cardiovascular and haematological components of oxygen delivery and the oxidative mechanisms of the exercising muscle. Maximal oxygen uptake (VO_2 max), the highest rate at which an individual can consume oxygen during exercise, limits the capacity to perform maximal aerobic exercise and, therefore, serves as the best single indicator of adults' aerobic fitness (ASTRAND and RODAHL, 1986). The conventional criterion for the attainment of VO_2 max during an exercise test is a levelling-off or plateau in VO_2 despite an increase in exercise intensity. However, it is well-documented that many young people can exercise to exhaustion without demonstrating a true VO_2 max plateau (ARMSTRONG, WELSMAN and WINSLEY, 1996b). The appropriate term to use with young people is therefore peak oxygen uptake (peak VO_2), the highest elicited during an exercise test to exhaustion, rather than VO_2 max which conventionally implies the existence of a VO_2 plateau (ARMSTRONG and WELSMAN, 1994).

An analysis of 420 British 11 to 16-year-olds revealed that peak VO_2 increased with chronological age in both sexes and that boys exhibited significantly higher values than girls at all ages studied (ARMSTRONG, WILLIAMS , BALDING, GENTLE and KIRBY, 1991). The difference between boys' and girls' values was attributed to the boys' greater muscle mass and haemoglobin concentration. When peak VO_2 was expressed in ratio with body mass, in accord with the extant literature, a different picture emerged, with boys' mass-related peak VO_2 being remarkably consistent over the age range studied whereas girls' mass-related peak VO_2 showed a gradual decrease with age. Mass-related peak VO_2 remained unchanged with maturation in both sexes.

We have, however, subsequently demonstrated that there is sufficient evidence to seriously question the use of ratio standards (ie expressing peak VO_2 in ratio with body mass) to partition out body size differences in the interpretation of peak VO_2 (ARMSTRONG and WELSMAN, 1997; WELSMAN and ARMSTRONG, 1996). In our view, the uncritical acceptance of ratio standards may have clouded our understanding of growth and maturational changes in aerobic fitness (ARMSTRONG and WELSMAN, 1994; WILLIAMS, ARMSTRONG, WINTER and CRICHTON, 1992).

A recent study of 156 10 to 22-year-olds used appropriate statistical methods to model and interpret functional changes in peak VO_2 during growth and, after partitioning out body size, demonstrated that peak VO_2 increases progressively in males from prepuberty through to adulthood and from prepuberty to circumpuberty in females (WELSMAN, ARMSTRONG, KIRBY, NEVILL and WINTER,

1996). Subsequently, a study of 212 12-year-olds demonstrated a significant effect of maturation on peak VO_2 independent of body size in both boys and girls (ARMSTRONG, WELSMAN and KIRBY, under review). This effect had probably been masked in previous studies by the inappropriate use of peak VO_2 in ratio with body mass.

Data on the aerobic fitness of prepubescent children are sparse and only one published study has examined British children. The peak VO_2 of 111 boys and 53 girls, classified as TANNER (1962) stage one for both pubic hair and either genitalia rating (boys) or breast rating (girls), were determined on a treadmill (ARMSTRONG, KIRBY, MCMANUS and WELSMAN, 1995). The boys' peak VO_2 was 22% higher than the girls' values and even when the influence of body mass was removed using a log-linear adjustment model the boys' peak VO_2 remained 16% higher than the girls' values. As there was no sex difference in haemoglobin concentration, subcutaneous fat or habitual physical activity likely to influence peak VO_2, it is not readily apparent why prepubescent boys have significantly higher levels of aerobic fitness than prepubescent girls and the data invite further investigation. DAVIES, BARNES and GODFREY (1972) had speculated that the lower peak VO_2 of young girls may be due to their smaller leg volume but more recent work using magnetic resonance imaging has indicated that when data are scaled appropriately peak VO_2 in children is not related to either thigh volume or thigh muscle volume (WELSMAN et al, in press).

The peak VO_2 values of British youngsters compare favourably with those of similarly aged children from other countries. Although comparative data need to be interpreted cautiously, the literature indicates that the aerobic fitness of children and adolescents has changed very little since the pioneering studies of ROBINSON (1938) and MORSE, SHULTZ and CASSELS (1949) in the United States and P.O. ASTRAND (1952) in Europe. Members of the European Pediatric Work Physiology Group (BELL, MACEK, RUTENFRANZ and SARIS, 1986) have expressed the view that a lower limit of VO_2 in the absence of other health-related problems may represent a health risk during childhood. They have identified "risk" levels for children but less than 2% of the 2,500 young people we have tested over the last 10 years could be classified as "at risk" using these criteria.

In our view, the well-publicised belief that young people's aerobic fitness is low and has deteriorated over time stems from a misunderstanding of the concept of aerobic fitness and its assessment and interpretation. There is no substitute for a direct determination of young people's peak VO_2 and a misinterpretation of data derived from submaximal predictions of peak VO_2, performance tests (e.g. 20 m shuttle run), and motor skill tests has led to erroneous conclusions about children's true level of aerobic fitness.

In summary, boys have higher levels of aerobic fitness than girls even in primary school and the sex difference becomes more pronounced as young people progress through secondary school, reaching about 37% at 16 years of age. There is, however, no scientific evidence to show that young people's aerobic fitness is low or that it has deteriorated over the last 50 years.

Young People's Physical Activity Patterns

The measurement of adults' habitual physical activity is one of the most difficult tasks in epidemiological research and the assessment of the daily physical activity of free-ranging children is even more problematic. A range of methods for estimating the level of adults' physical activity has been developed and several of these methods have been used in the assessment of children's habitual physical activity without due consideration being taken of the differences between children and adults (see ARMSTRONG and WELSMAN, 1997, for a review). With young people the technique used must be socially acceptable, it should not burden the subject with cumbersome equipment, and it should minimally influence the subject's normal physical activity pattern. Ideally the intensity, frequency, and duration of activities should be monitored and if a true picture of habitual physical activity is required some account should be taken of any day to day variation. A minimum monitoring period of 3 days has been recommended (BAR-OR, 1983). Few studies of British children's and adolescents' physical activity patterns have satisfied these criteria.

A series of studies used the Polar Sports Tester to continuously monitor the heart rates of 743 10 to 16-year-olds from 0900 to 2100 hours over three normal schooldays (ARMSTRONG, BALDING, GENTLE and KIRBY, 1990a; ARMSTRONG and BRAY, 1991; McMANUS and ARMSTRONG, 1995; WELSMAN and ARMSTRONG, 1992). In order to interpret the heart rate data, a representative sample of youngsters exercised at various speeds on a horizontal treadmill. It was noted that brisk walking at 6 Km.h^{-1} elicited steady state heart rates averaging 146 bts·min^{-1} so 140 bts·min^{-1} was used as the criterion of moderate exercise. The mean heart rate of the subjects at peak VO$_2$ was 200 bts·min^{-1} therefore moderate exercise was classified as 70% of maximum.

The data have been re-analysed on the basis of primary schoolchildren (165 girls and 167 boys) and secondary schoolchildren (243 girls and 168 boys). The primary schoolboys spent a significantly greater percentage of time with their heart rate above 139 bts·min^{-1} (9.2%) than both primary schoolgirls (7.7%) and secondary schoolchildren (boys, 6.3%; girls 4.7%). Two hundred and fifty two of the secondary schoolchildren (115 boys and 137 girls) and 114 of the primary schoolchildren (56 boys and 58 girls) also had their heart rates monitored from 0900 to 2100 on a Saturday. The secondary schoolgirls spent significantly less time (2.8%) with their heart rates above 139 bts·min^{-1} than secondary schoolboys (5.5%), primary schoolboys (5.5%), and primary schoolgirls (6.0%). Interestingly, no significant differences were detected between the primary schoolgirls and the two samples of boys.

Because of the limitations of simply reporting percentages of time above a threshold value and to provide a clearer picture of the youngsters' physical activity patterns, the number of 10 minute periods with heart rate sustained above 139 bts·min^{-1} was calculated. Forty seven percent of the secondary schoolgirls and 38% of the boys did not even experience the equivalent of a 10 min brisk walk during the whole period of monitoring. The comparable figures with primary schoolchildren were 28% of the girls and 21% of the boys not experiencing the equivalent of a 10 min brisk walk. Ninety two percent of secondary schoolgirls and 71% of the boys did not experience the equivalent of a 10 min brisk walk on a Saturday. Seventy one percent of the primary schoolgirls and 82% of the primary schoolboys were equally torpid on a Saturday. Overall the boys were significantly more active than the girls. The volume of physical activity of both sexes decreased through adolescence but the decline was both more marked and statistically significant in girls.

These studies were carried out throughout the school year, but in order to investigate whether there was any difference between physical activity levels during the Autumn and Summer terms 24 children were monitored for 3 days during each term (ARMSTRONG and BRAY, 1990). No significant differences were detected. Young people's physical activity during the Summer vacation does not appear to have been studied using heart rate monitoring, probably because of the logistics involved.

There are no data on young people's habitual physical activity which can be used to examine whether their physical activity has declined over time. However, although studies of energy intake provide little insight into young people's physical activity patterns an analysis of historical data put together by DURNIN is of interest. DURNIN (1992) pooled data collected from the 1930s to the 1980s and demonstrated a progressive decline in the energy intake of adolescents in the United Kingdom. The body mass of both boys and girls was almost identical within each sex for each group studied and the methodology of data collection was the same on each occasion. The only conceivable explanation for the very marked reduction in energy intake, which must reflect energy expenditure, is that adolescents' physical activity has radically decreased over the last 50 years.

In summary, young people have surprisingly low levels of physical activity and many youngsters seldom experience the frequency, intensity and duration of physical activity recommended for health-related outcomes (SALLIS and PATRICK, 1994). Boys are more active than girls and girls' activity levels deteriorate markedly as they move through secondary school. Energy intake data indicate a radical decrease in young people's physical activity over the last 50 years.

Aerobic Fitness and Habitual Physical Activity

The evidence linking young people's aerobic fitness to their level of physical activity is conflicting and must be interpreted in the light of the problems associated with assessing both physical activity and aerobic fitness (ARMSTRONG and WELSMAN, 1997). Correlations have, at best, been small to moderate and typically about $r = 0.16$ (MORROW and FREEDSON, 1994).

In two studies the heart rates of 85 boys and 111 girls, aged 11 to 16 years (ARMSTRONG, WILLIAMS, BALDING, GENTLE and KIRBY, 1991) and 86 prepubescent boys and 43 prepubescent girls, aged 10 to 11 years (ARMSTRONG, MCMANUS, WELSMAN and KIRBY, 1996) were monitored for at least three 12 hour periods, to estimate habitual physical activity. Peak VO_2 was directly determined and used as the criterion measure of aerobic fitness. No significant relationship between physical activity and aerobic fitness was detected in either study. In a third study (WELSMAN and ARMSTRONG, 1992) the same methodology for estimating daily physical activity was used but the percentage of peak VO_2 at the 2.5 mmol·L^{-1} blood lactate reference level was utilized as a criterion of aerobic fitness. No significant relationships were revealed with a sample of 73 young people, aged 11 to 16 years.

The evidence relating habitual physical activity to peak VO_2 in children and adolescents is equivocal perhaps because most studies have involved small sample sizes, limited periods of monitoring physical activity, or predictions of peak VO_2 from submaximal data. That a relationship between peak VO_2 and habitual physical activity remains to be proven is not unexpected, given the complexity of any relationship that may exist. Peak VO_2 is a physiological variable whereas habitual physical activity is a behaviour, and although it has been suggested that high levels of aerobic fitness may encourage individuals to engage in strenuous leisure-time activities this has yet to be established. The evaluation of any relationship between level of physical activity and peak VO_2 is further confounded by the presence of an as yet unquantified genetic component of peak VO_2. However, the data support the hypothesis that the habitual physical activity levels of British children and adolescents do not stress aerobic metabolism sufficiently to influence peak VO_2.

Aerobic Fitness, Physical Activity and Physical Education

The data which we have reported here have been collected from British children and adolescents over the last 10 years and they emphasize the importance of distinguishing between aerobic fitness and physical activity patterns. There is no scientific evidence to suggest that young people's aerobic fitness is either low or deteriorating over time. Yet, the majority of British schools still include compulsory fitness testing within their curriculum (HARRIS, 1994).

Fitness tests that are suitable for use in the school environment and that provide valid and objective measures of fitness are simply not available. Fitness tests determine the obvious, at best only distinguishing the mature and/or motivated youngster from the immature and/or unmotivated youngster. The use of norm tables promotes ego orientation and confounds the issue of relative fitness because tables constructed on the basis of chronological age cannot be used to legitimately classify children at different levels of maturity (see ARMSTRONG and MCMANUS, 1996, for a review). Furthermore, having different norms for boys and girls results in different expectations. Norms are based on performances rather than capabilities and if teachers accept lower norms for girls as reflecting acceptable performances, girls will tend to meet these lower expectations (THOMAS and THOMAS, 1988). Students view fitness testing unfavourably and as a major contribution to negative attitudes towards physical education (LUKE and SINCLAIR, 1991). Teachers must ask themselves why they persist in using curriculum time to test students' fitness, and if the answer is to classify students, then we suggest that they would be better employed seriously addressing the problem of young people's sedentary lifestyles.

Our data demonstrate that it is young people's current level of physical activity which gives cause for concern and, in our view the physical education profession should foster active lifestyles from an early age and place less emphasis on activities concerned solely with the promotion of aerobic fitness. Girls are less active than boys and girls' level of physical activity decreases as they move through secondary school. Encouraging girls to become more active should be a priority. Physical educators should take a more reflective view of the organization and presentation of their programmes in order to challenge the gender ideologies reflected in many physical education curricula. We have argued at length elsewhere that physical educators are well-placed to promote physical activity (ARMSTRONG and WELSMAN, 1997). They must meet this challenge. The future health and well-being of our children may depend upon it.

Note

This review is based on data generated in the PEA Children's Health and Exercise Research Centre and draws upon previously published material. It has been developed at the Editors' request from ARMSTRONG, N., McMANUS, A.,

WELSMAN, J. and KIRBY, B. (1996). Physical activity patterns and aerobic fitness among prepubescents. *European Physical Education Review* 2, 1, 19-29 and related papers itemized in the list of references.

References

ACTIVITY AND HEALTH RESEARCH (1992) *Allied Dunbar National Fitness Survey.* London, Sports Council and Health Education Authority.

ARMSTRONG, N., BALDING, J., GENTLE, P. and KIRBY, B. (1990) Patterns of physical activity among 11 to 16 year old British children. *British Medical Journal*, 301, 203-205.

ARMSTRONG, N., WILLIAMS, J., BALDING, J., GENTLE, P. and KIRBY, B. (1990b) Peak oxygen uptake and physical activity in 11 to 16 year olds. *Pediatric Exercise Science,* 2, 349-358.

ARMSTRONG, N. and BRAY, S. (1990) Primary schoolchildren's physical activity patterns during Autumn and Summer. *Bulletin of Physical Education,* 26, 23-26.

ARMSTRONG, N. and BRAY, S. (1991) Physical activity patterns defined by continuous heart rate monitoring. *Archives of Disease in Childhood*, 66, 245-247.

ARMSTRONG, N., KIRBY, B.J., MCMANUS, A.M. and WELSMAN, J.R. (1995) Aerobic fitness of pre-pubescent children. *Annals of Human Biology*, 22, 427-441.

ARMSTRONG, N. and MCMANUS, A. (1996a) Growth, maturation and physical education. In N. ARMSTRONG (Ed), *New Directions in Physical Education – Volume 3, Change and Innovation.* London, Cassell, pp.19-32.

ARMSTRONG, N., MCMANUS, A., WELSMAN, J. and KIRBY, B. (1996a) Physical activity patterns and aerobic fitness among pre-pubescents. *European Physical Education Review*, 2, 7-18.

ARMSTRONG, N. and WELSMAN, J.R. (1994) Assessment and interpretation of aerobic fitness in children and adolescents. *Exercise and Sport Sciences Reviews,* 22, 435-476.

ARMSTRONG, N. and WELSMAN, J.R. (1997) *Young People and Physical Activity.* Oxford, Oxford University Press.

ARMSTRONG, N., WELSMAN, J.R. and KIRBY, B.J. (under review) Peak oxygen uptake and maturation in 12-year-olds.

ARMSTRONG, N., WILLIAMS, J., BALDING, J., GENTLE, P. and KIRBY, B. (1991) The peak oxygen uptake of British children with reference to age, sex and sexual maturity. *European Journal of Applied Physiology*, 62, 369-375.

ASTRAND, P.O. (1952) *Experimental Studies of Physical Working Capacity in Relation to Sex and Age*. Copenhagen, Munksgaard.

ASTRAND, P.O. and RODAHL, K. (1986) *Textbook of Work Physiology*. New York, McGraw-Hill.

BAR-OR, O. (1983) *Pediatric Sports Medicine for the Practitioner.* New York, Springer-Verlag.

BELL, R.D., MACEK, M., RUTENFRANZ, J. and SARIS, W.H.M. (1986) Health indicators and risk factors of cardiovascular diseases during childhood and adolescence. In J. RUTENFRANZ, R. MOCELLIN and F. KLIMT (Eds), *Children and Exercise XII*. Champaign, Illinois, Human Kinetics, pp.19-27.

DAVIES, C.T.M., BARNES, C. and GODFREY, S. (1972) Body composition and maximal exercise performance in children. *Human Biology*, 44, 195-214.

DURNIN, J.V.G.A. (1992) Physical activity levels past and present. In N. Norgan (Ed), *Physical Activity and Health*. University Press, Cambridge, pp. 20-27.

FENTEM, P.H., BASSEY, E.J. and TURNBULL, N.B. (1988) *The New Case for Exercise*. London, Sports Council and Health Education Authority.

HARRIS, J. (1994) Health-related exercise in the National Curriculum: results of a pilot study in secondary schools. *British Journal of Physical Education Research Supplement*, 14, 6-11.

KUH, D.J.L. and COOPER, C. (1992) Physical activity at 36 years: patterns and childhood predictors in a longitudinal study. *Journal of Epidemiology and Community Health*, 46, 114-119.

LUKE, M.D. and SINCLAIR, G.D. (1991) Gender differences in adolescents' attitudes toward school physical education. *Journal of Teaching in Physical Education*, 11, 31-46.

McMANUS, A. and ARMSTRONG, N. (1995) Patterns of physical activity among primary schoolchildren. In F.J. RING (Ed), *Children in Sport.* Bath, University Press, pp.17-23.

MORROW, J.R. and FREEDSON, P.S. (1994) Relationship between habitual physical activity and aerobic fitness in adolescents. *Pediatric Exercise Science,* 6, 315-329.

MORSE, M., SCHLUTZ, F.W. and CASSELS, D.E. (1949) Relation of age to physiological responses of the older boy to exercise. *Journal of Applied Physiology,* 1, 683-709.

ROBINSON, S. (1938) Experimental studies of physical fitness in relation to age. *Arbeitsphysiologie,* 10, 251-323.

SALLIS, J.F. and PATRICK, K. (1994) Physical activity guidelines for adolescents: A consensus statement. *Pediatric Exercise Science,* 6, 302-314.

TANNER, J.M. (1962) *Growth at Adolescence (2nd Edition).* Oxford, Blackwell Scientific Publications.

THOMAS, J.R. and THOMAS, K.T. (1988) Development of gender differences in physical activity. *Quest,* 40, 219-229.

WELSMAN, J. and ARMSTRONG, N. (1992). Daily physical activity and blood lactate indices of aerobic fitness. *British Journal of Sports Medicine,* 26, 228-232.

WELSMAN, J.R. and ARMSTRONG, N. (1996) The measurement and interpretation of aerobic fitness in children: current issues. *Journal of the Royal Society of Medicine,* 89, 281-285.

WELSMAN, J.R., ARMSTRONG, N., KIRBY, B.J., NEVILL, A.M. and WINTER, E.M. (1996) Scaling peak VO2 for differences in body size. *Medicine and Science in Sports and Exercise,* 28, 259-265.

WELSMAN, J.R., ARMSTRONG, N., KIRBY, B.J., WINSLEY, R.J., PARSONS, G. and SHARP, P. (in press) Exercise performance and magnetic resonance imaging determined thigh muscle volume in children. *European Journal of Applied Physiology.*

WILLIAMS, J., ARMSTRONG, N., WINTER, E. and CRICHTON, N. (1992) Changes in peak oxygen uptake with age and sexual maturation in boys: physiological fact or statistical anomaly? In J. COUDERT and E. VAN PRAAGH (Eds), *Children and Exercise XVI.* Paris, Masson, pp. 35-37.

Chapter 6

Activity Promotion
in Physical Education

Jo Harris and Lorraine Cale

Introduction

A number of significant developments have occurred in the area of
children's exercise and health over the past few years which have
reinforced the value of regular physical activity to young people.
Research on children's physical activity levels in England has
increased (ARMSTRONG and BRAY, 1991; ARMSTRONG,
BALDING, GENTLE and KIRBY, 1990; CALE and ALMOND,
1993; SLEAP and WARBURTON, 1992; SPORTS COUNCIL, 1995)
and specific recommmendations relating to the amount of exercise that
children and adolescents should be doing to improve their health have
been developed in the U.S.A. (CORBIN, PANGRAZI and WELK,
1994; SALLIS and PATRICK, 1994). There have also been
developments within the fitness industry in Great Britain with an
increased number of training courses on children's exercise, the
emphases of which are the differing responses, needs and desires
between children and adults regarding physical activity.

Given that the learning of health-related knowledge, attitudes and
behaviours is known to begin at an early age and that physical activity
patterns set in childhood persist into adult life (PUHL, GREAVES,
HOYT and BARANOWSKI, 1990), the targeting of young people in
the promotion of physical activity is clearly vital. Research findings
suggest that only about a third to a half of children and adults in

England are doing enough exercise to benefit their health (CALE and ALMOND, 1992; SPORTS COUNCIL and HEALTH EDUCATION AUTHORITY, 1992). It would seem that sedentary lifestyles are commonplace and that, whilst physical activity is considered to be 'a good thing', it is simply not done on a regular basis by most people. However, due to the difficulties of accurately measuring activity levels (especially in children), further research is necessary to confirm the concerns about activity levels and to establish more precisely the minimal and optimal levels of exercise associated with specific health gains (RIDDOCH and BOREHAM, 1995).

In 1992 the *Health of the Nation* white paper (the Government's strategy for the health of the population of England) acknowledged the role of physical activity in promoting good health and identified schools as a key setting for health promotion work. The paper also recognised the value of school physical education (PE) in teaching young people the necessary skills and understanding associated with adopting an active way of life (DEPARTMENT OF HEALTH, 1992). Furthermore, 'health related exercise' (HRE), a term used to encompass the understanding, skills and attitudes associated with the adoption of active lifestyles, is now an established component of the prescribed National Curriculum for Physical Education (NCPE) in England and Wales and is also a component of the cross-curricular theme of health education (DEPARTMENT FOR EDUCATION and THE WELSH OFFICE, 1995; NATIONAL CURRICULUM COUNCIL, 1990). Indeed, FOX (1993) has reported increased commitment from the PE profession in the past decade with respect to the promotion of exercise for health and strongly believes that there has been an upgrade in the quantity and quality of exercise education and promotion in schools.

However, physical education programmes in America have been criticised for failing to foster current and future healthy exercise and other lifestyle habits in youth (DOUTHITT and HARVEY, 1995). Could the same be said of physical education programmes in the United Kingdom and elsewhere? Whilst the authors of this chapter appreciate that there are numerous factors outside the physical education context which determine physical activity levels, it is also recognised that PE may not always maximise its potential in terms of fostering lifelong health habits.

There is no doubt that the PE profession has a key role to play in promoting physical activity, in providing appropriate exercise guidance, and in empowering young people to make informed exercise choices. Indeed, student display of regular physical activity has been identified as a principal component of the definition of a physically educated person (NATIONAL ASSOCIATION FOR SPORT AND PHYSICAL EDUCATION, 1991) and FOX (1992) believes that preparation for lifetime exercise represents the singular greatest contribution that PE can make to the quality of life of people. It is thus fitting that the National Curriculum requirements for PE in England and Wales incorporate teaching young people the necessary knowledge, understanding and skills to be able to exercise independently. The influence that PE teachers potentially have in the promotion of active lifestyles in young people has yet to be capitalised upon.

This chapter will consider the major issues and considerations relating to children's exercise and health, and the promotion of physical activity within the PE curriculum in schools. In addition, it will attempt to clarify the messages and advice that the PE profession may provide young people about exercise.

Evaluating Exercise Prescriptions for Children

In terms of exercise prescription, recent developments have provided age-appropriate guidelines for young people with regard to the volume of exercise generally considered necessary to promote short term benefits and enhance future health and well-being. The Children's Lifetime Physical Activity Model (CORBIN, PANGRAZI and WELK, 1994) recommends both minimal and optimal levels of physical activity for young people and guidelines for adolescents have emanated from the International Consensus Conference on Physical Activity Guidelines for Adolescents (SALLIS and PATRICK, 1994) (Table 1).

These recommendations are welcomed as they represent the most up to date scientific guidelines available for children and adolescents. Previously, the emphasis in exercise prescription has been on the promotion of the adult fitness guideline of 3 x 20 minutes of aerobic activity, the applicability and appropriateness of which has been questionned for most children (CALE and HARRIS, 1993; CORBIN, PANGRAZI and WELK, 1994). Given the knowledge that children do not favour or respond well to high intensity physical activity (CORBIN, PANGRAZI and WELK, 1994; EPSTEIN, SMITH AND VARA, 1991) the new age-appropriate guidelines are particularly encouraging because they highlight the notion that exercise does not have to be incredibly strenuous for benefits to be gained. It is interesting to note that guideline one for adolescents does not stress intensity or duration of activity as it is considered that these are probably less important than the fact that energy is expended and a habit of daily activity is established (SALLIS and PATRICK, 1994).

As Table 1 shows, two quite distinct elements or types of physical activity have emerged from the new recommendations; namely lifestyle physical activity and moderate to vigorous physical activity. The minimum standard in the Children's Lifetime Physical Activity Model highlights lifestyle activities and is one that, according to CORBIN, PANGRAZI and WELK (1994), inactive children can achieve with a modest commitment to childhood games and activities, or lifestyle activities such as walking or riding a bicycle to school or performing physical tasks around the home. Similarly, guideline one of the physical activity guidelines for adolescents, encourages the incorporation of physical activity into daily life such as walking upstairs, walking or riding a bicycle for errands or doing household chores (SALLIS and PATRICK, 1994). The rationale provided for this guideline is that daily weight-bearing activities are critical for enhancing bone development that affects skeletal health throughout life and that substantial daily energy expenditure is expected to reduce risk of obesity and may have other positive health effects (SALLIS and PATRICK, 1994). Guideline two, however, focuses on moderate to vigorous activities which are defined as activities which require at least as much effort as brisk or fast walking. In this respect a diverse range of activities are recommended which use large muscle groups as part of sports, recreation, chores, transportation, work, school physical education or planned exercise. The rationale for guideline two is that continuous moderate to vigorous physical activity during adolescence enhances psychological health, increases HDL cholesterol and increases cardiorespiratory fitness (SALLIS and PATRICK, 1994).

Table 1
Exercise guidelines for children and adolescents

| | ACSM (1988) | Children's Lifetime Physical Activity Model (1994) | | Physical Activity Guidelines for Adolescents (1994) | |
| | | Children | | Adolescents (11-21 years) | |
		Minimum	Optimal	Guideline 1	Guideline 2
Frequency	every day	daily, 3 or more sessions a day	daily, 3 or more sessions a day	daily or nearly every day	3 or more sessions a week
Intensity	vigorous	moderate (to expend at least 3 kcal/kg/day)	moderate to vigorous (to expend at least 6-8 kcal/kg/day)	intensity not as important as fact that energy is expended	moderate to vigorous
Time	20 - 30 minutes	30 minutes or more	60 minutes	time not as important as fact that energy is expended	20 minutes or longer
Type		childhood games and lifestyle activites (e.g. walking to school)	childhood games, lifestyle activities and a variety of enjoyable activities which use large muscle groups and include some weight bearing	variety of activities which are enjoyable, involve a range of muscle groups and include some weight bearing activities	range of activities using large muscle groups

Increasing Children's Activity Levels

Just as there are concerns over children's low levels of physical activity generally, there are similarly concerns over the low level of moderate to vigorous physical activity that children experience during PE lessons (CURTNER-SMITH, CHEN and KERR, 1995). Some studies have successfully shown that PE lessons can be made more active for pupils (MACCONNIE, GILLIAM, GREENEN and PELS, 1982; MCKENZIE et al, 1993a, 1993b; SIMONS-MORTON, PARCEL and O'HARA, 1988; TAGGART, 1992) and this is highly desirable in terms of health benefits and pupil involvement and enjoyment. However, the issue of increasing activity levels within PE prompts a range of potential responses, some of which may be considered less than desirable. For example, some PE teachers may respond to reports of low activity levels of children by adopting a hard-line approach and increasingly forcing pupils into 'hard' exercise, such as arduous cross-country running or fitness testing, at the expense of acquiring knowledge and understanding about exercise and developing physical and behavioural skills and positive attitudes towards physical activity. Such attempts serve only to simplify the complex nature of physical activity promotion and overlook the multi-faceted nature of exercise education. Indeed, KIRK (1991) has expressed concern over the neglect of learning in daily PE programmes in Australia whilst HARRIS and ALMOND (1994) argue that activity without learning is not appropriate nor desirable within the PE curriculum.

A major issue in promoting physical activity relates to the type and volume of physical activity children should be encouraged to do. Physical education teachers may well accept the role they have to play in promoting physical activity, but may be unaware of the recent exercise recommendations highlighted earlier (CORBIN, PANGRAZI, and WELK, 1994; SALLIS and PATRICK, 1994) and may not fully appreciate their implications for physical activity promotion. In terms of types of activity, the acknowledgement of children's low activity levels both in leisure time and PE time may result in vigorous physical activity being promoted at the expense of less strenuous forms of exercise. However, as the recent recommendations highlight, vigorous activity is only one form of physical activity and features in only one of the guidelines. The traditional view that sustained bouts of vigorous activity are necessary to achieve health benefits has now been challenged and strong evidence exists to support the promotion of lower intensity exercise (AMERICAN COLLEGE OF SPORTS MEDICINE AND THE CENTERS FOR DISEASE CONTROL AND PREVENTION, 1993; RIDDOCH and BOREHAM, 1995), in other words the lifestyle type of activity proposed in the Children's Lifetime Physical Activity Model and guideline one for adolescents (CORBIN, PANGRAZI and WELK, 1994; SALLIS and PATRICK, 1994). Similarly, the national physical activity campaign in England, a three year initiative aimed at encouraging the sedentary population of England to take more physical activity, focuses primarily on the benefits of moderate rather than vigorous activity (DEPARTMENT OF HEALTH, 1995).

Whilst vigorous activity may be more effective in enhancing cardiovascular fitness than moderate activity, an important message in terms of public health is that vigorous activity is not necessary for cardiovascular health benefits nor for effective weight management. Different types and amounts of physical activity contribute differently to health and it is important to recognise that there are health benefits to be gained from all activity types including cardiovascular activity, exercises to enhance flexibility, muscular strength and muscular endurance, and relaxation. Furthermore, moderate activity is associated with improved adherence in children (EPSTEIN et al, 1991) and a lower risk of injury (HEALTH EDUCATION AUTHORITY, 1995; PATE and MACERA, 1994).

That is not to say, of course, that the promotion of vigorous activity in young people is no longer desirable or applicable. Indeed, the rationale provided to support the physical activity guideline two for adolescents clearly highlights the importance of moderate to vigorous physical activity for young people. However, it has been suggested that this guideline will not be immediately attainable by a number of children and will need to be progressed towards gradually (CALE and HARRIS, 1996). Any reluctance by teachers to recognise the value of more moderate as well as vigorous forms of activity to health may be detrimental to the promotion of physical activity.

This raises other issues with regards to the new guidelines. Whilst these guidelines are undoubtedly very useful, it remains prudent to apply them with common sense and sensitivity and to regard them as recommendations rather than strict or rigid prescriptions (CALE and HARRIS, 1993, 1996). Thus, any exercise formula is more appropriately viewed, not as a starting point, but as a goal for young people to progress towards at their own pace. Children have different activity histories, fitness levels, functional capacities, personal circumstances and varying preferences and dislikes for particular activities which need to be taken into account when applying recommendations (CALE and HARRIS, 1993). Each child should be treated as an individual and encouraged to engage in the types and amount of physical activity which are appropriate for them. It is, therefore, desirable that exercise recommendations are flexible and that initial advice and guidance stresses to young people that all forms and amounts of exercise, performed safely, are beneficial and that any level of physical activity is better than none. An appropriate message would simply be to 'gradually do more'. Indeed, in terms of activity promotion in children, the short-term social and psychological benefits such as fun and enjoyment alongside friends are likely to be more appealing than an over-emphasis on longer term physiological benefits. Research consistently shows fun and enjoyment to be the major motive for participation in physical activity and sport in youth (GOUDAS and BIDDLE, 1993; WEISS, 1993) and findings from the recent SPORTS COUNCIL survey on young people and sport in the UK (SPORTS COUNCIL, 1995) reveal a clear relationship between enjoyment of activities in physical education lessons and frequency of participation out of lessons.

Finally, to achieve these guidelines, children need to be helped to recognise the broad nature of physical activity, to recognise exercise opportunities at school, at home, and within the community, and to develop ways of incorporating such activities into their daily lives. In this respect teachers are encouraged to draw children's attention to the new national physical activity campaign and to take advantage of the information the campaign provides, discuss its key messages and evaluate its effectiveness.

Exercise Education and Activity Promotion

Another major issue relates to the approach adopted to educating children about exercise within the PE curriculum. Although the search for the most effective method of promoting physical activity still remains a challenge for PE, and there are some who question whether HRE is likely to encourage lifelong participation any more than 'traditional' PE (GREEN, 1994), clearly the processes of implementation need to be effective with physical activity promotion as a distinct objective within a structured PE programme.

In England and Wales, the absence of an activity area for HRE in the NCPE has been interpreted by some physical educators as indicating that HRE is to be delivered solely through the activity areas (i.e. athletics, dance, games, gymnastics, outdoor and adventurous activities and swimming), rather than in discrete blocks or units of work (OXLEY, 1994). HARRIS and ALMOND (1994) however, contest this view reminding us that "the National Curriculum specifies content, not delivery" (p.65) and they advise teachers to determine the most effective method of delivery for themselves. The permeation model of approach, however, has been criticised on the grounds that it tends to be rather 'hit and miss' and past evidence would suggest that it has not been very effective in producing exercise literate, active young people (HARRIS and ELBOURN, 1992a, 1992b). Furthermore, such an approach may deny children the opportunity to engage in a variety of popular health promoting lifetime exercise activities. A recent survey of HRE in secondary schools has revealed that the most common approach to delivering HRE (adopted by a third of schools) is through focused units of work in PE, through some or all of the PE activity areas, as well as in other areas of the National Curriculum (HARRIS, 1994a, 1995). This combined approach has the advantage of focusing on HRE through a range of activities, maintaining valuable links with the PE activity areas and other subjects, and minimising the possibility of HRE being taught in isolation from other practical experiences in PE (HARRIS, 1995). HARRIS (1995) reminds us though, that the critical issue is the effectiveness of the learning rather than the particular approach adopted.

In order to encourage children to develop a pattern of regular activity, it is vital that physical activity is perceived as an achievable and positive experience. Regardless of the approach adopted for delivering HRE, it is desirable that it involves enjoyable exercise experiences, a practical knowledge base and caring teaching strategies. Such strategies have been identified by HARRIS and ALMOND (1991) as central to effective HRE. Exercise and physical activity need to be promoted in a positive way with emphasis on the beneficial short and long term effects, improved functional capacity, weight management, and psychological well-being associated with exercise participation.

Highlighting the risks of inactivity (hypokinetic diseases) and threats of death and illness will do little to promote physical activity with young people. As FOX (1993) notes, teenagers believe that they are either immortal or immune from such problems. Rather, the aim is to empower young people to make considered and informed choices over their lifestyles, whilst at the same time acknowledging and, where possible, challenging the obstacles and constraints to participation. Constraints may be environmental and may require long term strategies such as a revised transportation policy as proposed by HILLMAN (1993), or they may simply result from prejudiced and stereotyped views of who physical activity is for and what form it takes. Such views have yet to be fully confronted and resolved within the physical education profession.

There is also concern over the inconsistent and limited approach to HRE in some schools. A recent survey of 1000 secondary schools in England (HARRIS, 1995) revealed that delivery of HRE varies tremendously between schools. Only a third of PE heads of departments described the overall teaching of HRE in their schools as structured and many teachers were unaware or unsure about the 'knowledge base' associated with HRE. The knowledge which was imparted tended to be primarily physiologically based with limited attention to psychological and social issues. SMITH and BIDDLE (1995) consider that the mistaken belief that HRE is simply a matter of getting children to be more active takes no account of the socio-cultural and behavioural factors influencing children's participation in activity and claim that such factors are usually ignored or only implicitly recognised in schools. Similarly, in the USA, DOUTHITT and HARVEY (1995) are of the opinion that the PE profession has "been trying to force youth into a PE curriculum mold which does not include sensitivity to individual psycho-emotional needs and preferences" (p. 34). They confirm the accepted view in health promotion that knowledge alone is insufficient to bring about behaviour change.

It is known that fitness testing has become common practice in many schools with about 60% of secondary schools in England including compulsory fitness testing in the PE curriculum (HARRIS, 1994a, 1995). A major issue with fitness testing in PE lessons is the amount of time spent on it without necessarily positively influencing either pupils' activity levels or their attitudes towards physical activity.

Indeed, ROWLAND (1995) goes so far as to say that programmes of field testing children are antithetical to the goal of promoting physical activity in children, that they are demeaning, embarrassing and uncomfortable to those children about which there is most concern, and that they only reinforce the belief that exercise is competitive and unpleasant. Whilst not adopting ROWLAND's anti-fitness testing stance, the authors are certainly in agreement with SMITH and BIDDLE (1995) that fitness tests are not automatically beneficial for the promotion of exercise and physical activity, and that, given the tendency towards reduced PE time in schools (HARRIS, 1994b), it is crucial that time is used wisely.

Finally, the trend towards PE being focused more explicitly on competitive team games with an emphasis on performance (DEPARTMENT FOR EDUCATION and THE WELSH OFFICE, 1995) and the SPORTS COUNCIL's enforced abandonment of the 'sport for all' ethos in favour of a 'commitment to excellence' may counteract messages about physical activity being for all abilities. Similarly, the Government's proposals within *Raising the Game* (DEPARTMENT OF NATIONAL HERITAGE, 1995) for the Sportsmark scheme with specific criteria biased towards competition and the requirement on all schools to record their sporting achievements in their governors' annual report have a tendency to emphasise performance over participation and to imply an activity hierarchy rather than a wide and open choice of physical activity. Certainly, to be effective physical activity promotional strategies need to ensure provision of more opportunities, incentives and rewards for all young people.

Conclusion

The past decade has witnessed major developments with respect to children's exercise and health including acceptance by the British government that physical activity is a desirable health behaviour to be promoted from a young age. Statements made by the DEPARTMENT OF HEALTH (1992, 1995), the SPORTS COUNCIL and THE HEALTH EDUCATION AUTHORITY (1992) suggest that much faith and responsibility are being placed on school PE to educate children about exercise and to promote lifetime physical activity. The role and responsibility PE has in the promotion of physical activity needs to be highlighted and guidance given from within the profession on the issues addressed within this chapter. Appropriate resources and training would assist teachers in providing consistent, co-ordinated messages to young people about physical activity. In the UK, much can be achieved through the HRE components of the National Curriculum although the wide ranging interpretations of the HRE requirements within the NCPE and the inconsistent guidance from within the PE profession to date suggest that there is still much to be done in terms of clarifying the purpose, content and effectiveness of HRE in schools. Furthermore, the SPORTS COUNCIL and the PE profession both seem to have been reluctantly drawn towards a greater focus on 'competitive team games' which may counter activity promotion messages and impinge upon opportunities to increase mass participation in health-promoting physical activity.

Activity promotion is an important aspect of physical education and, arguably, one that is attracting more attention given the media hype regarding young people's sedentary lifestyles leading to an impending health crisis for future generations. Whilst the authors would not go along with the dramatic notion of an impending 'crisis', there are certainly some concerns relating to the tendency towards reduced physical activity levels (especially in girls) and the superficial and piecemeal approaches evident in some schools to the promotion of physical activity for all pupils. Hopefully and thankfully, school PE is losing the 'aversion therapy' image of the past and is no longer driving pupils away from activity. Indeed, there is evidence to suggest that progress has been made in exercise education and promotion in the past decade. Nevertheless, there is little doubt that school PE could be yet more effective in contributing to increased levels of physical activity and enhancing public health.

References

AMERICAN COLLEGE OF SPORTS MEDICINE AND THE CENTERS FOR DISEASE CONTROL AND PREVENTION (1993) *Summary Statement: Workshop on Physical Activity and Public Health.* 'Experts Release New Recommendation to Fight America's Epidemic of Physical Inactivity'. News Release: 29/7/93. Authors.

ARMSTRONG, N., BALDING, J., GENTLE, P. and KIRBY, B. (1990) Patterns of physical activity among 11 to 16 year old British children. *British Medical*

Journal, 301, 203-205.

ARMSTRONG, N. and BRAY, S. (1991) Physical activity patterns defined by continuous heart rate monitoring. *Archives of Disease in Childhood,* 66, 245-247.

CALE, L. and ALMOND, L. (1992) Children's activity: A review of studies conducted on British children. *Physical Education Review,* 15, 2, 111-118.

CALE, L. and ALMOND, L. (1993) Physical activity levels in children: The implications for physical education. *Proceedings of the FIEP World Congress,* Israel.

CALE, L. and HARRIS, J. (1993) Exercise recommendations for children and young people. *Physical Education Review,* 16, 2, 89-98.

CALE, L. and HARRIS, J. (1996) Understanding and evaluating the value of exercise guidelines for children. *Proceedings (Part 1) of the AISEP Conference,* Israel, June 1995 (pp. 161-166).

CORBIN, C.B., PANGRAZI, R.P. and WELK, G.J. (1994) Toward an understanding of appropriate physical activity levels for youth. *Physical Activity and Fitness Research Digest Series 1,* 8, 1-8. President's Council on Physical Fitness and Sports.

CURTNER-SMITH, M.D., CHEN, W. and KERR, I.G. (1995) Health-related fitness in secondary school physical education: a descriptive-analytic study. *Educational Studies,* 21, 1, 55-66.

DEPARTMENT FOR EDUCATION and THE WELSH OFFICE (1995) *Physical education in the national curriculum.* London, HMSO.

DEPARTMENT OF HEALTH (1992) *The health of the nation. A strategy for health in England.* London, HMSO.

DEPARTMENT OF HEALTH (1995) *The health of the nation. More people more active more often. Physical activity in England. A consultation paper.* Physical activity task force. London, Author.

DEPARTMENT OF NATIONAL HERITAGE (1995) *Sport: Raising the game.* London, HMSO.

DOUTHITT, V.L. and HARVEY, M.L. (1995) Exercise counselling – how physical educators can help. *Journal of Physical Education, Recreation and Dance,* 66, 5, 31-35.

EPSTEIN, L.H., SMITH, J.A., VARA, L.S. et al, (1991) Behavioural economic analysis of activity choice in obese children. *Health Psychology,* 10, 5, 311-316.

FOX, K. (1992) Education for exercise and the National Curriculum proposals: a step forwards or backwards? *British Journal of Physical Education,* 23, 1, 8-11.

FOX, K. (1993) Exercise and the promotion of public health: More messages for the mission. *British Journal of Physical Education,* 24, 3, 36-37.

GOUDAS, M. and BIDDLE, S. (1993) Pupil perceptions of enjoyment in physical education. *Physical Education Review,* 16, 2, 145-150.

GREEN, K. (1994) Meeting the challenge: health-related exercise and the encouragement of lifelong participation. *The Bulletin of Physical Education,* 30, 3, 27-34.

HARRIS, J. (1994a) Health related exercise in the national curriculum: results of a pilot study in secondary schools. *British Journal of Physical Education Research Supplement,* 14, 6-11.

HARRIS, J. (1994b) Physical education in the National Curriculum: is there enough time to be effective? *British Journal of Physical Education,* 25, 4, 34-38.

HARRIS, J. (1995) Physical education: a picture of health? *British Journal of Physical Education,* 26, 4, 25-32.

HARRIS, J. and ALMOND, L. (1991) Learning to care. *Bulletin of Physical Education,* 27, 1, 5-11.

HARRIS, J. and ALMOND, L. (1994) Letter of response. *Bulletin of Physical Education,* 30, 3, 65-68.

HARRIS, J. and ELBOURN, J. (1992a) Highlighting health related exercise within the National Curriculum – Part 1. *British Journal of Physical Education,* 23, 1, 18-22.

HARRIS, J. and ELBOURN, J. (1992b) Highlighting health related exercise within the National Curriculum – Part 2. *British Journal of Physical Education,* 23, 2, 5-9.

HEALTH EDUCATION AUTHORITY (1995) *Health Update 5.* Physical Activity. London, Author.

HILLMAN, M. (1993) *Children, Transport and the Quality of Life.* Policy Studies Institute.

KIRK, D. (1991) Daily physical education research: A review and critique. In D. KIRK and R. TINNING (Eds) *Daily Physical Education. Collected papers on health based physical education in Australia.* Victoria, Australia, Deakin University Press, pp.64-76.

MACCONNIE, S.E., GILLIAM, D.L., GEENEN, D.L. and PELS A.E. III. (1982) Daily physical activity patterns of prepubertal children involved in a vigorous exercise program. *International Journal of Sports Medicine,* 3, 202-207.

MCKENZIE, T.L., SALLIS, J.F., FAUCETTE, N., ROBY, J.J. and KOLODY, B. (1993a) Effects of a curriculum and inservice program on the quantity and quality of elementary physical education classes. *Research Quarterly for Exercise and Sport,* 64, 2, 178-187.

MCKENZIE, T., SALLIS, J., ROBY, J., KOLODY, B. and FAUCETTE, N. (1993b) Effects of project SPARK on the physical education classes and physical fitness of fourth-grade children. *Research Quarterly for Exercise and Sport,* March Supplement, A-44.

NATIONAL ASSOCIATION FOR SPORT AND PHYSICAL EDUCATION (1991) *Physical education outcomes.* Reston, VA, Author.

NATIONAL CURRICULUM COUNCIL (1990) *Curriculum guidance 5. Health education.* York, National Curriculum Council.

OXLEY, J. (1994) HRE and the National Curriculum – an OFSTED inspector's view. *Bulletin of Physical Education,* 30, 2, 39.

PATE, R.R. and MACERA, C. (1994) Risks of exercising: Musculoskeletal Injuries. In C. BOUCHARD et al, (Eds) *Physical activity, fitness and health: International proceedings and consensus statement.* Champaign, IL: Human Kinetics, pp. 91-92.

PUHL, J., GREAVES, K., HOYT, M. and BARANOWSKI, T. (1990) Children's Activity Rating Scale: Description and calibration. *Research Quarterly For Exercise and Sport,* 61, 1, 26-36.

RIDDOCH, C.J. and BOREHAM, C.A.G. (1995) The health-related physical activity of children. *Sports Medicine,* 19, 2, 86-102.

ROWLAND, T.W. (1995) The horse is dead; Let's dismount. *Pediatric Exercise Science*, 7, 117-120.

SALLIS, J.F. and PATRICK, K. (1994) Physical activity guidelines for adolescents: consensus statement. *British Journal of Physical Education Research Supplement*, 15, 2-7.

SIMONS-MORTON, B.G., PARCEL, G.S. and O'HARA, N.M. (1988) Implementing organizational changes to promote healthful diet and physical activity at school. *Health Education Quarterly*, 15, 1, 115-130.

SLEAP, M. and WARBURTON, P. (1992) Physical activity levels of 5-11 year old children in England as determined by continuous observation. *Research Quarterly for Exercise and Sport*, 63 (3), 238-245.

SMITH, R.A. and BIDDLE, S.J.H. (1995) Psychological factors in the promotion of physical activity. In S.J.H. BIDDLE (Ed) *European Perspectives on Exercise and Sport Psychology*. Champaign, IL, Human Kinetics, pp. 85-108.

SPORTS COUNCIL (1995) *Young people and sport. National survey selected findings*. London, Author.

SPORTS COUNCIL and HEALTH EDUCATION AUTHORITY (1992) *Allied Dunbar national fitness survey. Main findings*. London, Authors.

TAGGART, A. (1992) The systematic development of fitness skills for primary school children: A planned intervention. In T. WILLIAMS, L. ALMOND and A. SPARKES (Eds) *Sport and physical activity*. London, E. & F. N. Spon, pp. 401-410.

WEISS, M.R. (1993) Children's participation in physical activity: are we having fun yet? *Pediatric Exercise Science*, 5, 205-209.

PART 4

PHYSICAL EDUCATION
AND SPORTS PARTICIPATION

Chapter 7

Youth Cultures and Sport: The Success of School and Community Sport Provisions in Britain

Kenneth Roberts

The Success Story

The findings from three major national surveys, all sponsored by government departments, into sport, schools and young people in England and Wales, were published during 1995 (DEPARTMENT FOR EDUCATION, 1995; HUNTER, 1995; MASON, 1995). These enquiries investigated school sport facilities, the participation of children aged 6-16 in sport in and out of school, and overall uses of leisure by 11-25 year olds. Together the investigations offer a comprehensive, nationally representative picture of the position of sport in schools and young people's lives in England and Wales in the mid-1990s. The evidence, which is reviewed in detail elsewhere (see ROBERTS, 1996), shows that in the years up to 1994 Britain's schools were improving their sports facilities, that young people were playing more sports in and out of school than in the past, that the drop-out rate on completion of statutory schooling had fallen dramatically, that social class and gender differences had narrowed, and that by the mid 1990s sports had higher youth participation and retention rates then any other structured forms of leisure.

The picture is not recognisable in the government policy statement, *Sport: Raising the Game,* which was also issued in 1995 (DEPARTMENT OF NATIONAL HERITAGE, 1995). This statement suggested that there had been a decline in school sport and that a rescue job was needed to promote physically active recreation among Britain's youth and restore a flow of talented athletes. It constructed an image of the 'good old days' when competitive team sports were supposed to have been entrenched at the heart of school cultures and timetables, and in young people's lives. It is impossible to square the analysis in *Sport: Raising the Game* with the government departments' own research evidence. The policy statement prescribes a cure for a fictitious illness. School sport in Britain has been a recent success story, not a disaster zone, if success can be measured in terms of the numbers of pupils playing and continuing to play after leaving school.

It is always difficult to attribute causality confidently, and impossible to prove it, but the following passages identify features of schools' sports curricula and community sports provisions that are likely to have been responsible for the success, and explain why they will have been effective. Since the 1960s there have been major changes in young people's day-to-day and week-to-week leisure styles, and corresponding changes in the ways in which they participate in sport. These developments are deeply rooted in youth's new social condition. Young people do not need sport any more than formerly, but sport can now appeal to young people on an unprecedented scale if presented appropriately. School and community provision for sport have in fact reflected and responded to trends in young people's leisure styles because schools and local authorities have been sensitive to 'what works' and have applied research findings that have filtered through the professions though not, it would appear, into some ministerial thinking. The real trends in school sport and in young people's levels and patterns of involvement supply no arguments for a return to traditional ways which, in fact, had only modest success in the 1950s and 60s. At that time football was the only competitive sport that was played regularly by a substantial proportion (more than 10 per cent) of young people. They were nearly all males, and the majority had lapsed by age 20. Subsequent trends in young people's leisure styles suggest that if traditional games regimes are re-adopted in the 1990s they will be even less successful than earlier in the twentieth century.

From Life Cycle to Life Course

In their study of *Leisure and the Family Life Cycle* (1975) Rhona and Robert RAPOPORT argued that during their lifetimes most individuals were experiencing three main careers – work careers, family careers and leisure careers. The RAPOPORTs illustrated how these careers typically interacted to create successive life stages, each with its own pre-occupations, usually arising from the actors' work and family situations, which gave rise to particular interests which, in turn, led to characteristic uses of leisure. They argued that adolescents were typically preoccupied with identity problems. 'Who am I?' was said to be the preoccupation characteristic of the age group, and in order to discover themselves young people were said to seek a variety of leisure experiences. Hence their high but fickle participation rates in out-of-home recreation. Young adults, in contrast, were said to be preoccupied with starting work and family formation, so their leisure became more focused around particular partners and, subsequently, more home-centred. Afterwards individuals were said to become preoccupied with establishing themselves in their careers and families, and their leisure became even more home and family centred, usually in ways that strengthened family bonds. The RAPOPORTs argued that life cycle transitions associated with starting employment, getting married and becoming a parent, for example, were important moments for leisure because it was at these points in life that patterns of day-to-day living were likely to unfreeze and become available for reconstruction. One feature of the reconstruction that occurred in adolescence was a flight from sports as soon as individuals left full-time education.

Needless to say, the RAPOPORTs recognised that each life cycle stage had a rather different significance for males and females, and that there were important social class differences throughout. However, their evidence suggested that most people joined particular social class and gender groups early in life, then followed the life cycles characteristic of their groups. It was as if the members of each group were herded into public transport vehicles when young, after which each group would travel through successive life stages together (see BERGER, STEINMULLER and SOPP, 1993). The members of any age group could look ahead, see what had happened to the cohorts who had been in their own situations some years previously, and thereby glimpse how their own lives were most likely to unfold in employment, the family and leisure. In 1975 the RAPOPORTs' use of the life cycle concept was uncontroversial. Its introduction to leisure research was generally applauded. At that time family relationships usually lasted for life, and there were clear and firm links between age and most other social positions.

Since then life seems to have stopped going round and round in cycles. The social sciences are now littered with references to the life course being destandardised. This is one example of a recent loosening of older structures. Labour markets have become more flexible, occupational careers have become less secure, risks of unemployment have risen, and work schedules have become more varied. Alongside these economic trends neighbourhoods have become less close-knit than they once were, families have become less stable, and researchers now recognise a variety of masculinities and femininities. Major life events are no longer as closely linked to given ages as in the past. People today often retire from their main occupations when, in other respects, they are at the peak of adulthood. People in mid-life have been restarting careers, sometimes by returning to full-time education or training. More people in their 30s and 40s are experiencing the dissolution of their domestic partnerships and rejoining the singles scenes. An upshot is greater variety within all age groups. It has become more hazardous than in the past to try to generalise about the circumstances and behaviour of people at given life stages.

The full effects of the recent destandardisation of the life course will become evident only during the lifetimes of current and future generations of young adults. They have been exposed immediately and directly to the full force of the trends, and it is they who will experience marriage dissolution risks of 40 per cent or more if current rates continue. Up to now no cohort has gone through life and experienced this degree of family flexibility whereas youth has already become a different kind of life stage than in the recent past for the majority of young people. Teachers of physical education and other subjects need to be aware of these trends because their own roles are inevitably affected.

Youth's New Condition

'New' here means post-1970s. There are several stark contrasts with young people's earlier situations. First, the life stage has been prolonged. Perhaps it is more accurate to say that its length is now more varied. There are still some young people entering employment at age 16. Some teenagers still marry and become parents. But the typical ages at which young adults cross all these thresholds have risen. This is partly because jobs have become more difficult to obtain amidst the higher levels of unemployment that have followed the so-called 30 glorious post-war years. Simultaneously, young people have become keener to remain in education so as to become as well qualified as possible. A desire for qualifications was once considered middle-class whereas nowadays parents and young people from all social classes recognise the advantages, especially in tight labour markets, of entering as well-qualified as possible. Family transitions have slowed down partly as a result of transitions into employment being delayed. However, young women's control of their own fertility, their improved labour market opportunities, some parents' enhanced ability to support their children through prolonged transitions, and young people's own worries that their partnership may dissolve have all contributed to this slow-down (HOBCRAFT and KIERNAN, 1995; IRWIN, 1995). There has been no upward movement in the characteristic ages at which youth commences. Sixteen has remained the statutory school-leaving age since 1972. By then the majority of young people have adopted some adult leisure practices. For example, the majority are drinking alcohol regularly, usually with at least the tacit consent of their parents (SHARPE, GREER and LOWE, 1988). Nor has there been an all round upward movement in the ages at which young people first leave their parents' homes to live independently. The mean age has actually fallen as more young people have progressed into higher education (JONES, 1995). Most young people now experience an intermediate stage between leaving their parents' homes and marrying. Until the 1960s, for most young people, these transitions occurred simultaneously (see LEONARD, 1980), whereas nowadays most marrying couples are already living at the same address.

Second, young people's biographies have been individualised (see ROBERTS, CLARK and WALLACE, 1995). This is partly due to the variety of courses in post-compulsory education, training schemes, part-time and temporary jobs, and periods of unemployment, that young people experience nowadays. It is also due to the contraction of the major firms and industries that once dominated many local labour markets. There was never a village where absolutely every boy went down the pit or every girl into the cotton mill, but in many parts of the country there used to be main types of employment into which most males or females, with specific educational backgrounds, would progress. Individualisation is also a product of the break-up of neighbourhoods that were once knit together by their residents' lifelong acquaintance. These trends have made it more difficult to conduct youth ethnography in the traditional ways. It was once possible for fieldworkers to make contact with (usually male) peer groups in given localities and emerge with portraits of their typical backgrounds, attitudes, lifestyles and futures. These groups are no longer present in most districts. Individualisation does not mean that young people's family origins and achievements in secondary education have become unrelated to their future life chances. These old predictors remain in excellent working order (see ROBERTS and PARSELL, 1992). The old predictors are proving resilient but nowadays operate in a variety of configurations which means that young people themselves are less likely to be aware of all that they share in common with other members of any social category. They are more likely to feel personally responsible for their current circumstances and for building their own futures.

Third, young people's futures have become uncertain. It is more difficult than formerly for young people to know the types of adults that they will become. This is partly a straight forward consequence of individualisation. When large numbers from a cohort travelled into adulthood together, following a predictable life cycle, it was relatively easy for them to look ahead, at what had happened to earlier cohorts of young people like themselves, and become aware of their own most likely futures. Uncertainty is also a consequence of the substantial numbers of young people who enter recently introduced educational courses and training schemes with no track records. Equally, it arises from the larger numbers on longer established routes, in higher education for example. Nowadays there are so many university students that their qualifications cannot unlock as attractive career prospects for them all as rewarded earlier generations of graduates. Perhaps most basically, uncertainty is a consequence of the sheer pace of economic and social change which means that the adult roles that many of today's children will play are still unknown. This is a different situation than confronted young people in the 1960s and before when life ran in more predictable cycles. By age 19 the few who remained in full-time education were an academic elite who could be confident of entering commensurate employment. Others were completing apprenticeships and could expect to be skilled for life. Others knew that they were unlikely to obtain anything better than ordinary jobs. For young people today basing their self-concepts on what they hope to become is hazardous. Rebelling and dropping-out from predictable futures have not become unfashionable so much as impossible.

Fourth, a corollary of their uncertain futures is that all the steps that young people can take have become risky. They cannot avoid risk taking. Higher education may lead to an excellent career but a university entrant today would be unwise to rely on this. Employer based training may lead to a skilled job. If so, the occupation may last for a long time. But there is simply no way of being sure. Personal relationships have become equally risky. Marriage may lead to lifetime domestic security or despair. Young people have lost much of their former security. Their new situation can appear threatening but it is helpful to recall that some members of earlier generations felt stifled by their predictable futures. An indeterminate future can be more attractive than knowing the limitations of one's prospects.

Fifth, young people's dependence on their families has been prolonged. Needless to say, families differ in their ability and willingness to discharge their prolonged responsibilities. The parents in a Dutch study of 120 young people were nearly all extremely supportive. They did not try to exercise authority but advised and negotiated with their grown-up children and tried to prepare them for "choice biographies" (DU BOIS-RAYMOND, DIEKSTRA, HURRIEMAN and PETERS, 1995). Young people without families on whom they are able and wish to depend are at a heavy disadvantage. Family support is often crucial in enabling young people to complete their full-time studies and to make the transition into independent households (COLES, 1995; JONES, 1995). Remaining in an intact family is a huge advantage (see SPRUIJT and DE GOEDE, 1995). The young people who are still making quick transitions – leaving education and seeking employment as soon as they are legally able to do so, and becoming teenage parents – are mostly from heavily disadvantaged family and educational backgrounds (KIERNAN, 1995).

The Constant Functions of Young People's Leisure

It would be amazing if the above changes in young people's situations had not affected their leisure, and we shall see that there have indeed been changes but these have occurred alongside strong continuities.

Leisure performs some functions for all age groups: it allows individuals to express themselves (to let off steam, if they feel the need), and to acquire skills that may subsequently prove useful in other domains, and bonds participants into groups. Young people's leisure has always kept them apart, and continues to set them apart from adults, because, being young and, therefore, having no deeply ingrained tastes, they are receptive to the latest fashions. There are additional functions that young people's leisure has performed in all modern (in some pre-modern) societies. It enables them to assert their independence from adults, typically with the blessing of their elders, and acts as a milieu in which they can learn to play sexualised roles and acquire the associated feelings and self-identities (see HENDRY, SHUCKSMITH, LOVE and GLENDINNING, 1993).

Its special functions give young people's leisure a different significance even when they take part in the same leisure activities as adults such as going out for a drink, or staying in to watch television or listen to music and converse. The crucial differences – the independence that young people find it necessary to assert and their sexual expressiveness – often alarm adult observers. Young people have always been regarded as a threat, liable to overturn normal patterns of family life and commit offences. Adults tend to regard themselves as potential victims but from the standpoint of the young they are the vulnerable, harassed, victimised age group. Sheila BROWN's (1995) questionnaire study among over 1,000 11-16 year olds and interviews with 200 found that 30 per cent of this age group could recall being followed by an adult on foot and 18 per cent had been followed by an adult in a car. Over a fifth had been physically assaulted by other young people. The young people's main defence strategy was to stay with their own groups. Another such strategy in recent years has been to carry a weapon of some description. Most young people are telling the truth when they explain this behaviour, which most adults find offensive, as a defensive precaution.

The continuities in young people's leisure can easily beguile all age groups into believing that nothing of significance has changed. Parents who are shocked by the rave culture and body piercing can recall that they themselves provoked outrage with their football hooliganism or punk styles in the 1970s and 80s, or as mods or hippies earlier on. While expressing horror at today's youth, adults can comfort themselves in the belief that they understand present-day young people's behaviour and problems. Adults have always been able to respond to the latest youth scenes with such ambivalence. However, in the past, alongside the continuities, there have been major transformations in the significance of youth cultures. One such transformation occurred after the Second World War and in the late twentieth century we are witnessing a comparable shift.

Post-War Youth Cultures

Youth cultures pre-date 1945. Throughout the nineteenth and early twentieth centuries, young people in urban industrial Britain found space for themselves, usually on the streets, where they established their independence and built sexual reputations. But these youth cultures were local phenomena which only occasionally acquired national reputations, usually for their exceptional toughness or criminality (see DAVIES, 1992). There was little commercial leisure targeted specifically at young people. Between the wars the dance halls catered for the young but the cinema, spectator sports and pubs had mainly adult customers. Young people were dependent on their families. Teenagers were paid boy and girl wages which, until they were 21 or became engaged, were usually handed over to their mothers in exchange for pocket money. Young people on the streets were generally considered 'at risk'. The boys were said to be at risk of becoming criminals while the girls risked pregnancy or, almost as disastrous, blighted reputations. Middle-class families protected their children by keeping them at home, in schools and universities. Youth movements and clubs were intended for working class youth. The sports that were offered to young people at that time – in teams that represented schools and clubs – were developed in an age when teenagers had few alternatives in out-of-home leisure, and when 'the problem' was to keep them under control and out of temptation. Those not 'in contact', the 'unclubbables', were regarded as the high risk group. They tended to be from the most disadvantaged, often 'rough' rather than 'respectable', working class households.

After the second world war a new kind of youth culture appeared. There were Teddy Boys and, later on, Mods and Rockers. These youth cultures were unexpected and unprecedented. At the time they were regarded as a threat to civilisation. The new youth cultures were associated, in media discourse, with the risking rates of juvenile delinquency and teenage pregnancy. With hindsight, in practice from the 1960s onwards, it has been easy to see that these new youth cultures were products of full employment, narrowing differentials between young people's and adults' earnings, teenagers going 'on board' from the beginning of their working lives, and the affluent teenager becoming a market segment that was targeted by the suppliers of a range of leisure goods and services, especially music and fashion clothing (ABRAMS, 1961). When commercial options became available young people began to vacate the traditional youth clubs and movements. Young people's new ways of life, or at least their styles, gained unprecedented visibility. By virtue of how they dressed and their musical tastes young people could identify, and be identified with, flamboyant national youth scenes. In the 1950s it was mostly working class young people, who left school at age 15 and earned 'good money' quickly, who became involved in these youth cultures. In some respects these young people were simply an avant garde group in the consumer culture and lifestyles that have subsequently spread to all sections of the population.

By the 1960s it was possible to see that the young people who became involved in these new cultural scenes were not threatening civilisation as formerly known. Sociological studies began to re-interpret the post-war youth cultures as processes of continuous socialisation. The young people were not really dropping-out. Actually they were making accelerated transitions to adulthood. Progression into adult employment accelerated and the mean age of marriages fell. Young people's new situation and their new youth cultures were enabling them to establish adult identities and play adult sexual roles at younger ages than their pre-war counterparts. The 'teenage rebels' of the 1950s and 60s grew into the next generation of respectable parents, often retaining their teenage idols – Elvis, Cliff and Cilla for example.

Another feature that became apparent as soon as researchers were able to 'stand back' and identify the main patterns in post-war youth scenes was that they incorporated conventional gender and social class divisions. A generation war was not replacing earlier class struggles. The central actors in most of the new youth cultures were male. Girls had peripheral roles. Their "lives of their own" were likely to remain based around "bedroom cultures" (see GRIFFIN, 1985; SHARPE, 1977). Participation in youth cultures was also class related. The new youth cultures of the 1950s and 60s were mostly working class phenomena. Young people on working class trajectories made the most rapid transitions to adulthood and earned adult wages at the youngest ages. It was not just that the most active and youngest participants tended to be working class. It also became apparent that their youth styles often incorporated specifically working class values – about masculinity, the importance of solidarity between mates, being able to enjoy a good time and display disrespect towards authority (see HALL and JEFFERSON, 1975; HEBDIGE, 1979; MUNGHAM and PEARSON, 1976; WILLIS, 1977). Far from challenging, the new youth cultures were reflecting and helping to reproduce established gender and social class divisions. Through the styles that they developed or adopted, young people were expressing values, and sometimes addressing problems and contradictions, arising from their gender and class situations. Some of the studies which emphasised these features of the post-war youth cultures could be accused of ignoring the extent to which the participants were also addressing problems rooted in the process of growing up and overlooking the fact that the committed participants were not statistically representative of their social classes (see SMITH, 1981). The crucial point remained that rather than a revolutionary threat the post-war youth cultures were socially conservative.

These trends affected sport in a variety of ways. On the one hand, young people had more alternatives to 'traditional' provisions such as sport teams and youth clubs. Some were growing up and out of such juvenile pastimes more rapidly than in the past. On the other hand, sports (usually football) teams, based on schools, youth clubs, firms, pubs or neighbourhoods, became a focal point for some male peer groups. Watching sport (once again, usually football) became a peer group activity for some males who could afford to follow their sides home and away. Before long the presence of these supporters became associated with a growing problem of football hooliganism. Overall the 1950s and 60s were years when sport was affected by, rather than responsive to broader social trends. The (Advisory) Sports Council[1] was created only in 1965 and did not gather momentum for several years. Local authorities operated playing fields rather than sports policies. Attendance at spectator sports was declining. The mass media were neither creating new markets nor generating new money for sport. The 1950s and 60s were certainly not a golden era for sport. In contrast, during subsequent changes in young people's situations, sport has been developing all-round rather than stagnating or retrenching, and has been much more responsive to wider trends.

The Latest Transformation

It is always important not to lose sight of the continuities but there have been a number of trends which indicate that youth cultures in the 1990s are not basically just the same as in the 1950s and 60s. First, a wider age group is involved in today's youth scenes. This is a result of transitions to adulthood becoming prolonged or, at any rate, more variable in length. Today's 30-somethings are often still mingling with the young singles while some of their age peers are parents of teenage children. When he interviewed a sample of young adults who were visiting the night scene in Newcastle city centre, HOLLANDS found that his respondents were aged up to 31. There has been speculation about whether youth cultures are disappearing (see WALLACE and KOVATCHEVA, 1996). If so, youth unemployment will not be the reason. Young people without jobs face similar leisure problems to the unemployed in other age groups. They have sub-normal rates of participation in virtuallly all types of recreation that cost money. However, most students and youth trainees, and many of the young unemployed, manage to participate in a wide range of leisure activities with the cash that they raise from parents, grants, loans and part-time jobs (see ROBERTS and PARSELL, 1991). There are huge inequalities in young people's incomes and spending levels, but their spending patterns prove that it is possible to participate in most youth scenes at different levels of expense. Nights out, holidays and new outfits can cost a lot or can be managed much more cheaply. If youth cultures disappear this will not be a consequence of young people's poverty. It is more likely to be a consequence of pre-teen children being introduced to youth fashions in dress and becoming an important market for pop music, individuals staying young into their 30s, and the spread of popular consumer cultures into adult age groups. Unlike in the 1950s, it is no longer only, or even mainly, young people who now purchase leisure wear and recorded music.

A second post-1970s trend has been that gender and social class divisions within youth cultures have become less clear cut. This is not to say that either type of difference has disappeared. Despite unisex fashions and the gay villages in some cities, most young (and older) people still succeed in looking unmistakably male or female, and heterosexual masculinity and femininity are expected if not demanded in most informal social settings. One change is simply that most youth cultures are not as male dominated as formerly. Young women have broken out from the bedroom culture. The recent changes in their leisure behaviour will be related to young women making more headway in education (out-performing males at all levels) and in the labour market, and gaining effective control over their own fertility. Nowadays young women are as likely as young men to use indoor sports facilities (DEPARTMENT FOR EDUCATION, 1995). They have been claiming space in other public places also – city centres, wine bars and throughout the club scenes. Young women no longer need male escorts in order to go out.

There has been a similar blurring of social class divisions. Since the 1960s, popular culture has been adopted by young people on middle class trajectories in secondary schools' academic streams and in higher education. This has not driven out high culture; it is more a case of young (and older) people now feeling able to enjoy both classics and pop. There is more intermingling of the social classes in comprehensive secondary schools and in post-compulsory education. This, along with the less certain futures of all young people, has made them harder to 'classify' by researchers, and by one another. An outcome is that there are no longer clear social class differences in the kinds of music that young people listen to, the fashions that they wear, or the places they go to. Those from middle class home backgrounds, who are educationally successful, still tend to do more leisure activities, but the 'more' is of the same kinds of things in which working class youth are also involved (see ROBERTS and PARSELL, 1994).

A third trend has been the splintering of youth cultures. Needless to say, there are still many things that most young people do. The majority go on nights out and consume alcohol, listen to popular music, watch television and, nowadays, play sport (see ROBERTS, 1996). However, there are no longer any particular musical genres or fashions that can claim to be the dominant style. There is a rapid turnover in hit parade numbers and artists. None seem able to exert the appeal of the Beatles, Elvis and Cliff. New technology is part of the explanation. The music production and distribution industries have more players. There are more radio stations, all trying to appeal to specific taste publics. But technology is not the reason why it is now equally fashionable to have short-cropped or long hair, or why no 'uniform' is worn as widely as blue denim in the 1960s and 70s. Young people's tastes do not map neatly onto either social class, gender or geographical divisions (see ROBERTS and PARSELL, 1994). There is simply more variety within all social groups which will be related to the broader processes of individualisation. Young people use leisure to develop and express their individuality but can only do this via their specific sub-cultural affiliations.

A fourth trend has been towards young people's sub-cultures acting as bases for proto-communities (WILLIS, 1990) or "new tribes" (MAFFESOLI, 1994) rather than expressing membership of pre-existent groups. The groups of young people (and adults) who become fans of specific sports teams, and who attend raves and similar scenes where their preferred types of music are played, can experience intense camraderie. Much of the appeal of these occasions is that they are incredibly social. Everyone is friendly. Individuals find that they are accepted and 'absorbed' into the scenes. Needless to say, none of this is completely new. The change over time has been that the young people who play together nowadays are less likely than in the past to have grown up together in the same districts and attended the same local schools. Their participation in the "new tribes" is usually temporary. Participants are always drifting off to other scenes. Sometimes the sub-cultures simply disappear. Yet being part of these scenes is extremely important to young people (see HOLLANDS, 1995).

Through their sub-cultural affiliations today's young people do not so much express as build (albeit temporary) social identities and self-concepts. Education, occupations and gender no longer confer the clear unambiguous identities that they offered in the past. Today's young people cannot be sure about the kinds of adults they will become; what their occupational and social class destinations will be. Hence their need to become part of specific sub-cultures in order to define who they are.

Young People's Uses of Sport

School sport in Britain has evolved alongside young people's changing leisure styles. Neither the changes in school sport nor in young people's general uses of leisure will have been a simple cause or effect of the other. School sport has been changing throughout the twentieth century. The broadening of curricula has been occurring for several decades. However, in recent years this trend cannot have avoided interacting in a mutually reinforcing way with broader trends in young people's leisure styles. This will be one of the processes whereby sports participation has become part of present-day youth cultures. It was different in the 1950s and 60s when 'on scene' young people left sport to the 'good pupils' (see HENDRY, 1978; SUGARMAN, 1967.) School sport will have adapted, among other reasons, because teachers have been responsive and innovative, have known 'what works' with their pupils, and have ranked 'sport for all' ahead of producing winning teams (MASON, 1995). The curriculum has adapted by complementing the older team games, and upgrading facilities for a variety of additional sports such as badminton, squash, swimming, and even golf and skiing that can be practised individually and played by small groups of young people (and adults) at times and places of their choosing without any ongoing commitment to teams or clubs. Over the past 20 years, Britain's schools have increasingly been using lesson time to introduce pupils from primary age upwards to a wide variety of sports and have made it possible for pupils to play their favoured games out of lessons also. Simultaneously, local authorities have opened multi-sport indoor centres which can be used throughout the year, and which individuals can attend to play their preferred sports, with their own friends, at times of their choice. Sports offered by the commercial sector invariably operate on this basis. In European countries, where community sports provisions are overwhelmingly club based, there has been a decline in participation by young and older people (see DECKERS and GRATTON, 1995). In Britain, in contrast, levels of participation have risen, especially steeply among the young, and this will have been because the mode of delivery has coincided with the age group's preferred leisure styles.

In and out of school, young people in Britain are now able to play their preferred sports in places and in groups that express their individuality. Sport has adapted to the splintering of young people's tastes. The new school sports menus contain items that appeal to males and females in all age bands. Both sexes can use sports to assert their independence (playing what they want, when they want, with whom they want), and display their preferred forms of masculinity and femininity. Sport has been made available to, and proves capable of performing these functions for young people in all social class locations, and the varied provisions allow today's young people to continue playing while 'acting their ages' as they move from childhood to adulthood. The sports skills that young people are currently acquiring become personal leisure capital and other things need only remain equal for a high proportion to continue using these skills throughout their adult lives. Sports participation can be expected to rise in all adult age groups in Britain as the current cohorts of young people carry their higher propensity to participate into later life stages (see ROBERTS and BRODIE, 1992).

Returning to the traditional games regime in schools, and making clubs more prominent in community provisions (if such policies are implemented) will almost certainly lead to a flight from sport by Britain's young people. This is the only plausible interpretation that can be placed on the evidence, much of it from government sponsored research, on recent trends in sports promotion and delivery on the one hand, and young people's participation rates on the other, in Britain and other European countries. There is absolutely no evidence that trends in sports education in Britain have failed if an aim has been to broaden and deepen participation. In fact all the evidence points to the opposite conclusion. Traditional games regimes have been far less effective wherever and whenever they have been tried. In the past the traditional regime roughly corresponded with the leisure styles of young males who tended to spend their time in groups from their home areas, who also attended the same local schools. However, these forms of sport participation never appealed to the majority of young women, and males' participation rarely survived the break-up of their same-sexed crowds. The broader trends in young people's situations and leisure patterns in the intervening years can mean only that the recipe will be even less effective if it is tried again in the late twentieth century.

Note

1.   The Advisory Sports Council was established as an advisory body in 1965 and with receipt of its Royal Charter in 1972 became a statutory body with executive powers to oversee the administration of Sport in Britain.

References

ABRAMS, A. (1961) *The Teenage Consumer.* London Press Exchange, London.

BERGER, P.A., STEINMULLER, P. and SOPP, P. (1993) Differentiation of life courses? Changing patterns of labour market sequences in West Germany. *European Sociological Review*, 9, 43-61.

DU BOIS-RAYMOND, M., DIEKSTRA, R., HURREIMANN, K. and PETERS, E. (Eds) (1995) *Childhood and Youth in Germany and The Netherlands.* de Gruyter, Berlin.

BROWN, S. (1995) Youth 2000: a youth based research project. Paper presented at Youth 2000 conference, Middlesborough.

COLES, B. (1995) *Youth and Social Policy.* UCL Press, London.

DAVIES, A. (1992) *Leisure, Gender and Poverty.* Open University Press, Buckingham.

DECKERS, P. and GRATTON, C. (1995) Participation in sport and membership of traditional sports clubs: a case study of gymnastics in The Netherlands. *Leisure Studies,* 14, 2, 117-131.

DEPARTMENT FOR EDUCATION (1995) *Young People's Participation in the Youth Service.* Statistical Bulletin 1/95, London.

DEPARTMENT OF THE ENVIRONMENT (1977) *Leisure and the Quality of Life, Vols 1 and 2.* HMSO, London.

DEPARTMENT OF NATIONAL HERITAGE (1995) *Sport: Raising the Game.* London.

GRIFFIN, C. (1985) *Typical Girls?* Routledge, London.

HALL, S. and JEFFERSON, T. (Eds) (1976) *Resistance Through Rituals.* Hutchinson, London.

HEBDIGE, D. (1979) *Sub-Culture: the Meaning of Style.* Methuen, London.

HENDRY, L.B. (1978) *School, Sport and Leisure.* Lepus, London.

HENDRY, L.B., SHUCKSMITH, J., LOVE, J.G. and GLENDINNING, A. (1993) *Young People's Leisure and Lifestyles.* Routledge, London.

HOBCROFT, J. and KIERNAN, K. (1995) *Becoming a Parent in Europe.* Welfare State Programme 116, London School of Economics.

HOLLANDS, R.G. (1995) *Friday Night, Saturday Night.* Department of Social Policy, University of Newcastle.

HUNTER, P. (1995) *Community Use of School Sports Facilities.* Office of Population, Censuses and Surveys, London.

IRWIN, S. (1995) *Rights of Passage.* UCL Press, London.

JONES, G. (1995) *Leaving Home.* Open University Press, Buckingham.

KIERNAN, K.E. (1995) *Transition to Parenthood: Young Mothers, Young Fathers – Associated Factors and Later Life Experiences.* Welfare State Programme 113, London School of Economics.

LEONARD, D. (1980) *Sex and Generation.* Tavistock, London.

MAFFESOLI, M. (1994) *The Time of the Tribes.* Sage, London.

MASON, V. (1995) *Young People and Sport – a National Survey.* 1994, Sports Council, London.

MUNGHAM, G. and PEARSON, G. (Eds) (1976) *Working Class Youth Culture.* Routledge, London.

RAPOPORT, R. and R.A. (1975) *Leisure and the Family Life-Cycle.* Routledge, London.

ROBERTS, K. (1996) Young people, schools, sport and government policies. *Sport, Education and Society,* 1, 1, 47-48.

ROBERTS, K., CLARK, S.C. and WALLACE, C. (1995) Flexibility and individualisation: a comparison of transitions into employment in England and Germany. *Sociology,* 28, 31-54.

ROBERTS, K. and PARSELL, G. (1991) Young people's sources and levels of income, and patterns of consumption in Britain in the late-1980s. *Youth and Policy,* 35, December, 20-25.

ROBERTS, K. and PARSELL, G. (1992) Entering the labour market in Britain: the survival of traditional opportunity structures. *Sociological Review,* 30, 727-753.

ROBERTS, K. and PARSELL, G. (1994) Youth cultures in Britain: in the middle class take-over. *Leisure Studies,* 13, 33-48.

SHARPE, D.J., GREER, J.M. and LOWE, G. (1988) The normalisation of under-age drinking. Paper presented to British Psychological Society, Leeds.

SHARPE, S. (1977) *Just Like a Girl.* Penguin, Harmondsworth.

SMITH, D.M. (1981) New movements in the sociology of youth: a critique. *British Journal of Sociology,* 32, 239-251.

SPRUIJT, E. and DE GOEDE, M. (1995) Changing family structures and adolescent well-being. Paper presented to Second European Sociological Association Conference, Budapest.

SUGARMAN, B. (1967) Involvement in youth culture, academic achievement and conformity in school. *British Journal of Sociology*, 18, 151-164.

WALLACE, C. and KOVATCHEVA, S. (1996) *Youth in Society: Changing Lives and Changing Times in East and West Europe.* Macmillan, London.

WILLIS, P. (1977) *Learning to Labour.* Saxon House, Farnborough.

WILLIS, P. (1990) *Common Culture.* Open University Press, Milton Keynes.

Chapter 8

Sport and Exercise Motivation:
A Brief Review of Antecedent Factors and
Psychological Outcomes of Participation

Stuart Biddle

The study of motivation has been prominent within psychology more or less throughout the entire history of the discipline, albeit in different forms and interpretations. The range of perspectives is broad, from drive reduction and biochemical indicators through to cognition and affect. However, despite the sheer volume of output and the motivated behaviours of motivational psychologists, I share WEINER's (1990) mixed emotions about the state of contemporary motivation theory and knowledge.

Weiner was reviewing the history of motivation in educational research, yet much of what he says also applies to sport and exercise psychology. On the one hand, we have learned a great deal about motivated human behaviour and have shifted theoretical perspectives to a more realistic view of how humans think and act – i.e. we have moved from mechanistic to more complex cognitive interpretations of motivated behaviour. However, are we better able to answer the practical questions asked by sports coaches or exercise leaders? I fear that at times the volume of motivational research in sport and exercise psychology has not provided the practitioner with sufficiently useful answers as it should have done. Whether this is attributable to the researcher, educator, practitioner, or participant is not possible to say. However, a greater understanding of translating theory into practice is still required and is a challenge for all those working in this area.

This chapter provides a summary of key motivational antecedents and consequences of participation in sport and exercise from a lifespan developmental perspective. To use the research analogy, I will tackle the issue of motivation in a 2 x 2 x 2 design: antecedent/consequent factors x sport/exercise distinction x child/adult distinction. This itself is over-simplified through the use of dichotomous variables. However, I hope to broaden the scope of discussion on motivation and physical activity by using such a plan.

The history of sport psychology has been dominated by the competitive sport experience and by the psychology of skill acquisition. REJESKI and BRAWLEY (1988) attempted to define the boundaries of sport psychology. 'Sport psychology' was defined as:

> the educational, scientific and professional contributions of psychology to the promotion, maintenance, and enhancement of sport-related behaviour, whereby sport is defined by LOY (1969) as an institutionalised competitive game occurrence characterised by physical prowess, strategy and chance in combination.
> (REJESKI and BRAWLEY, 1988, p.239).

Sport psychology research in motivation has been concerned primarily with three broad areas: [i] the identification of the reasons why people participate or cease participation in sport; [ii] cognitive factors associated with the sport experience, but which have motivational applications (e.g. attributions and self-efficacy); and [iii] strategies that promote goal-directed behaviour in sports performers (e.g. goal-setting). The research has been dominated by investigations on children, youth and young active adults; less is known about factors associated with older adults. This chapter addresses the issues associated with why people do or do not participate.

'Exercise psychology' is defined as:
> the application of educational, scientific and professional contributions of psychology to the promotion, explanation, maintenance, and enhancement of behaviours related to physical work capacity. These behaviours ... have the express purpose of stimulating and/or maintaining range of

motion, muscular strength and endurance, and
cardiorespiratory endurance.
(REJESKI and BRAWLEY, 1988, p.239).

Research in exercise psychology has tended to be dominated by factors
affecting adherence to exercise, and the mental health outcomes of
participation in exercise (BIDDLE and MUTRIE, 1991; DISHMAN,
1988). A distinction between participation in sport and exercise is
made. The former refers to competitive contexts whereas exercise is
used to refer to non-competitive moderate to vigorous physical
activities that are associated with the promotion and maintenance of
health-related fitness or participation in health-related exercise.

Finally, in order to redress the balance of prior research, a lifespan
developmental perspective is provided by discussing factors under the
separate headings of children and adults. Where research findings
permit, these broad categories are further sub-divided.

Why Do People Participate?

Sport: Children

The literature on children in sport contains a number of summary
papers on the underlying reasons why children participate in, or
withdraw from, sport (BIDDLE and FOX, 1988; GOULD and
PETLICHKOFF, 1988). The sport experience appears to be attractive
to children for one or more of the following reasons: fun and
enjoyment, learning and improving skills, being with friends, success
and winning, and physical fitness and health. The strength of these
motives is likely to differ as a function of sport, level of participation,
and developmental stage, although they do appear regularly across
diverse settings and groups.

WANKEL and KRIESEL (1985) studied four age groups between 7-14
years and across three sports. They found that the motives were
consistent across the age groups and that two categories could be
identified. These were intrinsic factors, including winning prizes and
pleasing parents and coaches, and social factors, which included being
part of a team or being with friends. Intrinsic factors were rated the
most important and extrinsic factors the least.

Sport: Adults

Surprisingly, less is known about why adults may take up sport. Most adult surveys adopt a broad approach and ask about participation in physical activity rather than just sport. However, the HEARTBEAT WALES (1987) survey did ask about incentives that were thought to be necessary to take up sport. The three main factors that would encourage those 16 years of age and above were fitness/weight loss, having more free time, and maintaining health. Free time became less important with age, as did fitness/weight loss. Those over 60 years of age were much more likely to say that nothing would be an incentive to take up sport, or to give no answer at all.

Another British study investigated a more restricted type of sport participation, that of marathon running. CLOUGH, SHEPHERD and MAUGHAN (1988) investigated the reasons, given by 500 runners, for taking part in a marathon in Scotland. A factor analysis of over 70 reasons revealed the following six factors: well-being, social, challenge, status, addiction, and health/fitness. The researchers highlighted the similarity of these findings to those associated with participation in other leisure pursuits, and in particular the motives of well-being, social factors, status, and challenge. BARRELL, HIGH, HOLT and MACKEAN, (1988) also found that challenge, well-being, social factors and fitness featured as reasons for participation in marathons and half-marathons in their study of English runners.

Other data suggest that adults do change their reasons for participation with age (ASHFORD, BIDDLE and GOUDAS, 1993). Community sports centres in one English city were surveyed and it was found that participants over 25 years of age were much more likely to report motives associated with health and relaxation than younger subjects, whereas the younger participants over 25 years of age were much more likely to report motives associated with challenge and skills. Similarly, MIHALIK, O'LEARY, MCGUIRE and DOTTAVIO (1989), using data from the 'Nationwide Recreation Survey' in the United States (n = 6720), found that sport participation contracted and expanded at different times in the adult life cycle. In particular, there was a decline in participation amongst 29-36 year olds, presumably as a result of pressures of job changes and family circumstances, such as children. More is needed to be known about such changes across the adult lifespan.

Exercise: Children

As outlined already, the data on children tend to refer to sport settings. This is natural given the greater likelihood of children, particularly younger children, to play sport if they are involved in physical activity at all. However, some data exist that point to why children and youth might also want to participate in health-related exercise beyond the competitive sport environment.

The CANADA FITNESS SURVEY (1983a) provides insight into the motivations of Canadian youth to participate in physical activity. However, no distinction was made between sport, exercise or other forms of physical activity. The results showed that from a sample of over 4,500 10-19 year olds, the major "reasons for being active" were fun, feeling better, weight control, flexibility, and challenge. In Finland, TELAMA and SILVENNOINEN (1979) investigated the motives of over 3,000 11-19 year olds. They found that the main area of change in motivation with age occurred in respect of competition and achievement. Boys and younger subjects were more interested in achieving success in competition. By late adolescence, very few showed much interest in competitive success, whereas this trend was reversed for motives of relaxation and recreation – motives that might be more associated with exercise than sport.

A more recent study showed that for a sample of 15-17 year old American youth, competition was not a particularly important factor in exercise participation. TAPPE, DUDA and MENGES-EHRNWALD (1990) found that the main incentives for exercise in boys were strength, mastery, appearance, flexibility and competition, whereas for girls the main factors were appearance, mastery, flexibility, strength, and weight management. However, we need to know more about how children and youth view exercise and sport and the extent to which they are motivated to exercise outside of the sport context.

Exercise: Adults

Rather more is known about adult involvement in exercise and their stated reasons for participation. The CANADA FITNESS SURVEY (1983b) showed that feeling better, fun, weight control, flexibility and stress reduction were all important reasons for being active. Gender differences were not great although women were more likely to state weight control as a reason than men. However, the same survey also showed that physical activity was rated as less important to health than adequate sleep, good diet, medical/dental care, non-smoking, maintaining weight, and control of stress.

DUDA and TAPPE (1989) studied "exercise incentives" in older American adults engaged in an exercise programme. They found that adults over 40 years of age tended to exercise more for health reasons than younger participants. They also reported that older adults were interested in exercising for social reasons as well as stress reduction. Women were more motivated by stress reduction and personal fitness than men.

British research has also shown that what appears to be just one type of exercise setting – exercise classes – can reflect multiple motivations among participants. SCHLACKMANS (1986) studied nearly 2,000 active and inactive women in ten towns in England. Several types of exercise classes were studied, including 'traditional' keep-fit, jazz-dance, and aerobic exercise-to-music. Six different clusters of participants were identified which reflected reasons for participation. These were "sporty socialisers", "weight conscious", "keen exercisers", "modern mothers", "social contact", and "get out of the house". Explanations of these groupings are given in Table 1.

Why Do People Not Participate?

Sport: Children

Many researchers and authors have commented on the high attrition rate from youth sports (GOULD and PETLICHKOFF, 1988). However, one of the problems in surveying the literature on sport withdrawal is that some individuals identified as having dropped out of one sport may or may not transfer their participation into another. GOULD and PETLICHKOFF (1988) have made the distinction between sport-specific dropout (ceasing participation in one sport) and domain-general dropout (ceasing sport participation altogether). Certainly research studies must try and take this distinction into account.

The results of research to date suggest that children cease participation, either in a sport-specific or domain-general form, for reasons of competitive stress, parental pressure, lack of fun, lack of playing time, limited opportunity for improvement, and dislike of the coach (BIDDLE and FOX, 1988; GOULD and PETLICHKOFF, 1988). The nature and extent of competing demands in sport have yet to be explored systematically.

WHITE and COAKLEY (1986), in their qualitative analysis of the English Sports Council's 'Ever Thought of Sport?' campaign, found that school leavers did not take part in community sport and recreation for a variety of reasons and that "decisions about sport participation reflect a wide range of personal preferences going beyond organised, competitive sport" (p.39). Specifically, they found that the following factors were important influences on participation and non-participation: [a] desire to display competence; [b] external constraints, such as money and opposite sex friends; [c] support from significant others; and [d] past experiences, including those in school physical education and sport. Also, negative memories of physical education, and in particular boredom, lack of choice, feelings of incompetence, and negative evaluation from peers, were associated with non-participation.

Sport: Adults

Little research is available on why adults cease participation in competitive sport. BOOTHBY, TUNGATT and TOWNSEND (1981) conducted in-depth interviews with over 250 adults in the north-east of England and used content analysis to cluster 815 reasons for ceasing participation into 43 main factors. The most frequently cited reasons were loss of interest, lack of facilities, physical problems (e.g. poor fitness, disability), moving away from the area, and not having enough spare time.

The HEARTBEAT WALES (1987) survey also showed that lack of time was the most frequently cited reason for having stopped playing sport, and this was followed by loss of interest. As expected, as age increased, so the reasons of old age, disability, and lack of fitness became more prominent.

Table 1

Clusters of participant groups for women's exercise classes (SCHLACKMANS, 1986)

Group (% of exercise market) and Description

Sporty socialisers (25%):

[a]	interested in social aspects of participation
[b]	physically quite fit
[c]	good at other sports
[d]	interested in their own exercise progress

Weight conscious (18%):

[a]	exercise as a means to weight loss
[b]	self-perception of being overweight
[c]	less likely to take part in other sports

Keen exercisers (17%):

[a]	interested in physical fitness benefits
[b]	not so interested in social aspects
[c]	concerned for quality instruction
[d]	good at sport and perceive themselves to be quite fit

Modern mothers (16%):

[a]	keen on sport
[b]	perceive themselves to be quite fit
[c]	interested in their exercise progress
[d]	older than 'get out of the house' group

Social contact (15%):

[a]	older than modern mothers group
[b]	women who live alone or had children who had left home
[c]	exercise was seen primarily for reasons of social contact

Get out of the house (8%):

[a]	youngest group
[b]	little interest in social or physical benefits
[c]	class used a means of getting away from the house

Exercise: Children

Little is known about why children give up exercise outside of the sport context. However, indirect evidence is available through the CANADA FITNESS SURVEY (1983a) and HEARTBEAT WALES (1987). The CANADA FITNESS SURVEY (1983a) reports that lack of time, competing time demands, and lack of facilities are seen to be important obstacles to physical activity. Similarly, HEARTBEAT WALES (1987) found that for 12-17 year olds, the main reasons stated for non-participation were lack of time, money and personal transport, as well as lack of facilities and interest.

Exercise: Adults

Dropping out of exercise may not be an 'all or none' phenomenon (SONSTROEM, 1988), but an on-going process that changes through the adult life cycle. However, with the exception of the study of MIHALIK et al (1989) cited earlier, little is known about such changes. Current research shows that the main reasons stated by adults ceasing participation in exercise are associated with lack of time and inconvenience. In a study of why people quit an aerobic exercise programme in Australia, LEE and OWEN (1985) found over 200 reasons were reported for dropping out. The main factors were lack of time, medical problems, lack of motivation, and situational and practical constraints, such as travel or expense. Some studies have found that those who quit an exercise programme might be biologically disadvantaged at the outset. For example, DISHMAN and GETTMAN (1980) reported that high body fat levels at the start of a supervised exercise programme were predictive of later dropout.

From Motives to Integrating Theories

GOULD and PETLICHKOFF (1988) have provided an integrated model of motivation and attrition as it relates to youth sports. They make a distinction between "surface levels" motives and more fundamental underlying theoretical perspectives. From the viewpoint of research and further understanding of motivation in sport and exercise, integrating theoretical perspectives are important, although they will be seen to be less valuable by those attempting to deliver practical strategies. It is not intended to review such theoretical perspectives. However, major themes and theories in psychology, such as perceptions of control, self-efficacy, attributions, competence perceptions and achievement orientations have been studied in sport and exercise psychology and may provide future research directions for a more fully integrated view of motivation for the future (BIDDLE and MUTRIE, 1991). However, recognition of a lifespan developmental perspective is also required here (DISHMAN, 1990).

One of the emerging themes in contemporary research is that of competence perceptions. This has been studied mainly with children, both in sport (DUDA, 1987) and other contexts such as classroom education (HARTER, 1978). The extent to which competence perceptions underpin motivational factors associated with children in physical activity remains to be seen. Indeed, they form just one part of HARTER's model, alongside motivational orientations and perceptions of control. Similarly, perceptions of competence are difficult to untangle from related constructs such as attributions and self-efficacy.

For the study of adults, individual differences may also play an important role in the understanding of motivation. However, the study of traditional cross-situational traits is currently less 'fashionable' in sport and exercise psychology. This may be a premature move that researchers will regret. From a motivational standpoint in sport and exercise, more needs to be known about how adults of different ages view the constructs of sport and exercise and how they define 'success' within each. Goal orientation research is built on this notion (DUDA, 1989; MAEHR and NICHOLLS, 1980).

Motives and Dropout: Summary and Implications

The data currently available from North America, Europe and Australia tend to cover children in sport and adults in exercise. More is needed on children in exercise and adults in sport, particularly why people cease participation. The information currently available shows that individuals have multiple motives for participation and that these change with age and vary between genders. Most groups appear to be motivated by reasons associated with health and well-being, and this is more pronounced for older adults. Reasons of challenge, skill and competition are associated with the younger age groups, and competition appears to decline rapidly as a major motive during adolescence.

Application of this information in the field can be made in several ways. First, the way physical activity is advertised and marketed will need to be modified to be appropriate for different ages and genders. This will also apply to the distinction between competitive sport and recreational exercise. Radical thinking is needed since the norm is often to equate exercise with sport. This will lose many potential exercisers who are not motivated by the image of sport. For example, the *Health of the Nation* document produced by the DEPARTMENT OF HEALTH (1991) in the UK states that the medium through which children will be taught an active lifestyle is sport. No mention is made of health-related exercise in physical education.

Research in Scotland by EADIE and LEATHAR (1988) showed that adults view sport and exercise quite differently with sport being seen as competitive and aggressive, whereas exercise was said to be primarily about the development of physical qualities such as strength and endurance. Their recommendations for marketing fitness and exercise in the community included making activities less formal and structured, to highlight the social and mental benefits of participation, and to emphasise "universal representation". This is where exercise becomes a socially accepted activity by all and not just the young, active and fit. This is only likely to happen by making a wider choice of activities available to all ages. These recommendations have implications for school curricula too. Current content of physical education programmes tend to reflect traditional sports and codes of conduct that are generally inappropriate for the promotion of "universal representation" and a broad-base of involvement in adulthood.

Psychological Outcomes of Participation as Motivators

This section discusses briefly the issue of psychological outcomes. What psychological outcomes result from participation and to what extent do these act as motivators for participation? Although a great deal has been written on the potential psychological benefits of participation, little has been written about the potential motivational effects of such outcomes. The literature reporting psychological outcomes of participation in physical activity cannot easily be divided into sport and exercise. Consequently, these will be combined, but separate reference will be made where appropriate.

Children

Self-esteem

One of the most commonly believed outcomes of participation in sport and exercise for children is that of personality and 'character' development. However, the extent to which this is a motivational issue, at least in the short term, is debatable. Nevertheless, a related issue – that of self-esteem development – has featured prominently in recent research on motivation and mental health (see BIDDLE and MUTRIE, 1991; SONSTROEM, 1988).

In a meta-analytic review of physical activity and self-esteem development in children, GRUBER (1986) supported the link between activity and self-esteem. Specifically, he found that the average "effect size" (strength of effect for self-esteem expressed in standard deviation units) was 0.47, showing that children in studies experiencing a physical activity intervention displayed self-esteem scores nearly one-half of a standard deviation higher than children in control groups. Subsequent analysis showed that the effect was larger for children with disabilities compared with 'normal' children, and for fitness activities over creative, sports or skill-based activities, although all types of activities had a positive link with self-esteem development.

FOX and CORBIN (1989) report on the development of a multi-dimension scale for the measurement of physical self-perceptions. They suggest that a more informative way to look at self-esteem is to investigate the relationships between global self-esteem and more discrete aspects of the self, such as physical self-worth. Their research shows that American college students tend to view physical self-worth as comprising sport competence, body attractiveness, physical strength, and physical condition. Preliminary evidence of a similar structure in American children was reported by WHITEHEAD and CORBIN (1988). However, the structure of physical self-worth and physical self-perceptions in British children has not been clear

(BIDDLE et al, 1993). Nevertheless, other research has shown that physical self-perceptions are related to performance on an endurance run task, and to involvement in moderate to vigorous physical activity in 12 year old children (BIDDLE and ARMSTRONG, 1991; BIDDLE et al, 1993).

The direction of the link between self-esteem and physical activity in children has yet to be clarified. Do children high in self-esteem choose physical activity? Or do children in physical activity develop high self-esteem? SONSTROEM's work with adolescents suggested that it was perceptions of physical ability that were related to self-esteem, rather than actual physical ability. Whatever the direction, those charged with promoting involvement in sport and exercise in children should seek the development of self-esteem and positive physical self-perceptions. The likelihood that these will stimulate and maintain participation is strong.

Enjoyment

The outcome of 'enjoyment' must be a critical variable to sport and exercise motivation in children. To date, the literature on children and physical activity has focused on sport enjoyment only. WANKEL and KRIESEL (1985) found that for Canadian children factors leading to sports enjoyment were associated with intrinsic and 'process' factors – those of skills, testing abilities, personal accomplishment, and excitement. The least important were extrinsic or 'product' factors, such as winning. WANKEL and SEFTON (1989), after a study of 7-15 year olds, concluded that 'fun' was best explained as a positive mood state associated with personal accomplishment and the ability to meet a challenge. This is close to CSIKSZENTMIHALYI's (1975) work on enjoyment, flow and intrinsic motivation.

SCANLAN and LEWTHWAITE (1986), in a study of 9-14 year old male wrestlers, found that the best predictors of sport enjoyment were satisfaction expressed by parents, lack of negative maternal interactions, high perceived ability, and positive adult involvement. Enjoyment was shown to be higher among younger participants. A model of sport enjoyment, based on the dimensions of achievement/ non-achievement and intrinsic/extrinsic, proposed by SCANLAN and LEWTHWAITE (1986), awaits further testing.

Despite the apparently high ecological validity of a construct such as enjoyment, little is known about the nature and extent of enjoyment experienced by children in sport and exercise. Similarly, the relationship between enjoyment and motivation is understood merely at the anecdotal level. This appears to be a strange state of affairs.

Adults

Mental Health Outcomes

Perhaps the most widely reported aspect of physical activity and psychological outcomes for adults has been in the area of 'mental health'. This is usually seen as changes in negative affect, such as anxiety and depression, and positive affect, such as self-esteem. Consensus statements suggest that such mental health benefits from exercise are likely, although the underlying reasons or mechanisms are not well understood (BIDDLE and MUTRIE, 1991; MORGAN and GOLDSTON, 1987). Nevertheless, recent meta-analytic reviews provide further information and directions. Such reviews are now available on the effects of exercise on anxiety (PETRUZZELLO, LANDERS, HATFIELD, KUBITZ and SALAZAR, 1991), depression (NORTH, MCCULLAGH and TRANS, 1990), and stress reactivity (CREWS and LANDERS, 1987). One aspect of the mental health benefits of exercise that has been ignored is that of the motivational consequences of changed affective states. Evidence does exist to show that high levels of physical effort are related to dropout in exercise (ANDREW et al, 1981), and recent British research by STEPTOE and his colleagues has shown that positive changes in mood after exercise are associated more with moderate, rather than high, levels of exercise intensity (MOSES, STEPTOE, MATTHEWS and EDWARDS, 1989; STEPTOE and BOLTON, 1988; STEPTOE and COX, 1988).

Similarly, the motivational effects of prescribed exercise levels requires investigation. For example, research has shown that effort perceptions may differ as a function of personality (WILLIAMS and ESTON, 1989), and that individuals may differ in their preference for different levels of exertion. Rigid prescriptions based on physiological principles alone, therefore, may be inappropriate and have a negative effect on exercise motivation in adults.

STEPHENS (1988), in his analysis of four large surveys in North America, found that the mental health benefits of physical activity were more likely to be detected in women and in older adults. Again, studies taking account of life cycle influences and stages are required to understand the motivational consequences of mental health outcomes.

Enjoyment

CSIKSZENTMIHALYI (1975) studied a range of activities that adults participated in for apparently intrinsic reasons, including sport. Such activities he labelled "autotelic", meaning self-directing or "self-purpose". He found that states of high-level enjoyment or "flow" were only likely to occur when there was a match between the challenge offered and the available skills of the individual. Mismatches produced anxiety or boredom. WANKEL (1985) reported results from a study of 111 participants and dropouts from an employee fitness programme. Enjoyment of the programme was a strong predictor of whether the participant stayed with the programme or dropped out.

Psychological Outcomes: Summary and Implications

A great deal of time and effort has been spent in the psychology of sport and exercise trying to identify antecedent factors of motivation. However, little has been done to understand the role that psychological outcomes of participation may play in the reinforcement or encouragement of participation. The large and growing literature on the effects of exercise on mental health appears to be a logical starting point to redress this imbalance. Given that we know that of those who start an exercise programme only about half will still be participating several months later (DISHMAN, 1988), more resources need to go into understanding what it is that people find motivating or demotivating about the sport and exercise experience.

Process Models of Motivation

SALLIS and HOVELL (1990) propose a process model for the study of the determinants of exercise participation in adults (see Figure 1).

The extent to which this is applicable for children remains to be seen. Discrete stages of adoption, maintenance, dropout, and resumption may not be applied easily to children, particularly outside of the more structured sport environment. Spontaneous play of children may be influenced by transient factors such as fashions and seasons. Children's cognitive development will also play a role in the extent to which conscious decisions are made about participation in physical activity. The best we can apply at this stage for children are models developed to explain behaviour outside of physical activity, such as HARTER's (1978) competence motivation theory. In short, a process model of children's motivation in sport and exercise, based on developmental principles, is now needed (GOULD and PETLICHKOFF, 1988). SALLIS and HOVELL's (1990) model provides a useful framework from which to view adult involvement in exercise and sport. It is also consistent with the popular "stages of change approach" in exercise motivation.

Figure 1

**A process model of exercise behaviour,
proposed by SALLIS and HOVELL (1990)**

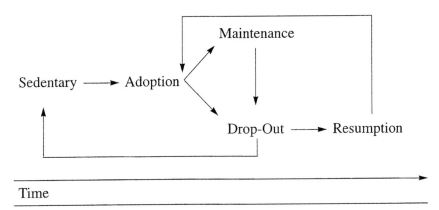

Stages of Change and Exercise

Research into the nature of behaviour change in smokers and those presenting themselves for psychotherapy has suggested that recovery from problem behaviours, or successful behaviour change, involves movement through a series of stages (PROCHASKA and DICLEMENTE, 1984; PROCHASKA, DICLEMENTE and NORCROSS, 1992). This notion has now been successfully applied to exercise behaviours (see reviews by PROCHASKA and MARCUS, 1994; MARCUS and SIMKIN, 1994; see Table 2 for a summary of stages of change and exercise studies). Even those attempting self-change, as well as those in therapy, seem to move through "stages of change" (SOC). The SOC approach is currently popular in psychotherapy and now other areas of health and exercise. The term "transtheoretical model", often used for this area, refers to PROCHASKA's early work in which he identified common change stages and processes across diverse theoretical systems of psychotherapy (see PROCHASKA, 1979).

The following stages have been identified, although not all have necessarily been used in all exercise studies:

- **precontemplation:** includes people who are not currently exercising and have no intention of doing so in the near future. Prevalance information from a large sample (n=1063) of worksite employees in the USA (MARCUS, ROSSI, SELBY, NIAURA and ABRAMS, 1992b) showed that only 8% were at this stage. If the definition is changed to those who are not at criterion level of physical activity (e.g. 5 periods per week of 30 minutes of moderate activity) and have no intention of reaching criterion within a specified time period (say six months), then the prevalance is likely to rise steeply;

- **contemplation:** this stage includes current non-exercisers but who have an intention to start exercising in the near future. MARCUS, SELBY, NIAURA and ROSSI (1992c) identified 21.1% of their sample in this category;

- **preparation:** these are individuals who are "currently exercising some, but not regularly" (MARCUS and OWEN, 1992, p.6), or, as PROCHASKA and MARCUS (1994) suggest, these people are intending to take action in the next month or so. This stage has not always been used in exercise research and could be quite unstable as sporadic involvement occurs;

- **action:** this stage represents people who are currently exercising, but have only recently started. As such, PROCHASKA and MARCUS (1994) suggest that it is an unstable stage during which individuals are at high risk of relapse. MARCUS et al (1992c) identified 36.9% of their sample at this stage;

- **maintenance:** this stage includes those who are currently exercising and have been doing so for some time – at least 6 months – and included 34% of the sample studied by MARCUS et al (1992c);

- **termination:** this has not been used in exercise research but does feature in other SOC research, such as on smoking and alcohol abuse in which about 15-17% of those in maintenance group were classified. PROCHASKA and MARCUS (1994) define this stage as the point at which people have "no temptation to engage in the old behaviour and 100% self-efficacy in all previously tempting situations" (p.163);

- **relapse:** this has not been tested much in exercise but is consistent with SALLIS and HOVELL's (1990) model. While data are available from smoking and alcohol research on the risk of relapse from the maintenance phase, little data are available in exercise, although MARCUS and SIMKIN (1994) suggest that maybe 15% fall into the category of being "relapsers" (i.e. regressive movement back to either contemplation or precontemplation).

The stages outlined suggest a steady linear progression from one stage to the next. However, certainly in addictive behaviours, where most of the SOC approach has been investigated (PROCHASKA et al, 1992), a linear pattern has given way to the belief that change is cyclical. In the context of exercise, MARCUS and SIMKIN (1994) suggest that several attempts at change are likely before maintenance is reached. Indeed, PROCHASKA et al (1992) say that for many the process of cycling may help strengthen behaviour change in the long run as people learn from their mistakes and relapses.

The research on SOC and exercise is still in its infancy with still only a few published studies, as shown in Table 2. Nevertheless, there is sufficient consistency in the evidence to suggest that SOC is an important construct. MARCUS and her colleagues, who have undoubtedly led the way in applying SOC to exercise, have provided evidence showing that increasing self-efficacy is associated with greater exercise readiness, and that perceived benefits increase and costs decrease through the stages in a predictable way (MARCUS and OWEN, 1992). The 'pros' and 'cons' of exercise and decision balance is also consistent with SOC (MARCUS et al, 1992a). In addition, progress has been made on the measurement of stages and processes of change (MARCUS et al, 1992c, 1992d; WYSE, MERCER, ASHFORD, BUXTON and GLEESON, 1995), and it has been shown that interventions can move people between stages (CARDINAL and SACHS, 1995; MARCUS et al, 1992b).

The stages of change refer to the temporal patterning of behaviour change. By also identifying processes of change we are able to understand why and how this temporal shift takes place. Processes of change, therefore, are important for interventions – for moving people between stages. MARCUS et al (1992d) define processes of change as "the cognitive, affective, and behavioural strategies and techniques people use as they progress through the different stages of change over time" (p.425).

There is no doubt that a dynamic approach to understanding exercise and physical activity that includes different stages of 'readiness' is an appropriate way forward. The success of the SOC model in other health settings also lends confidence to its application to physical activity. Similarly, MARCUS and co-workers, as well as other researchers, have shown the utility of SOC in exercise across three countries and in adults of differing ages, and processes of change have been proposed, thus increasing the likelihood of SOC being applied successfully in intervention trials.

Peer-reviewed published SOC research in physical activity, however, is still relatively small, although growing. It is often descriptive and has merely identified different, and at times predictable, cognitions associated with each stage. Limited information is available on processes of change or on how best to move people from one stage to another. The following limitations have been identified (see MARCUS and SIMKIN, 1994):

•   studies have mainly relied on self-report of physical activity;

- studying SOC across both structured exercise and habitual physical activity settings is required;

- studies are largely cross-sectional; longitudinal research is required to study behaviour change more effectively;

- more intervention studies are required for testing the effectiveness of matching processes and stages;

- greater use of representative and diverse samples is desired.

A somewhat speculative summary of an integration between SALLIS and HOVELL's model and SOC is shown in Table 3. The principle appears to be correct that different stages in the process model will require different motivational interventions, but the state of our knowledge is such that we are still unsure as to which factors are most important and at which stage.

Motivation Research Challenges

It is important for those working in Europe that any findings that emanate from elsewhere are replicated in the European culture. For example, the youth sport context in North America, on which the participation motives research is largely built, may not be appropriate when applying findings here. Similarly, research on adult motivation in sport within certain political structures may not generalise beyond that system. In short, cross-cultural research is required (DUDA and ALLISON, 1990). For example, the proposed factorial structure of the Physical Self-Perception Profile, a scale developed by FOX and CORBIN (1989) with American college students, has now been shown to be replicated with British students, but less clearly for children (BIDDLE et al, 1993; PAGE et al, 1993).

Much of the research into adult involvement in exercise has been reported in North America. The evidence is biased towards supervised exercise settings. More is needed on the motivational influences of Europeans involved in unsupervised community programmes or simply habitual physical activity in 'free-living' contexts. Use of motivational inventories or other measurement tools need to be

Table 2

A summary of stages of change and published exercise research

Study	Sample[1]	Purpose(s)	Results
Barke & Nicholas (1990)	Adults (N=59) aged 59-80 years from a). exercise programme, b).'elderhostel', c). retirees.	i). to test for differences in stages of change (SOC) in physical activity (PA) for groups differing in PA ii). to test the stereotype that older adults are 'set in their ways'.	i). contemplation (CONT), action (ACT) and maintenance (MAIN) scores higher than precontemplation (PRE), stereotype refuted. ii). exercise and elderhostel groups higher than retirees on ACT and MAIN, and lower on PRE.
Marcus et al (1992a)	Employees (N=778) from 4 worksites. Mean age = 41.5 years.	i). To develop decision balance (DB) questionnaire ii). study the relation between DB and SOC	Measures of exercise 'pros' and 'cons' and DB (pros - cons) showed expected differences between majority of stages.
Marcus et al (1992b)	Employees (N=1172) from 2 worksites	i). to develop 'Processes of Change' (POC) questionnaire; ii). to investigate processes used at different stages	i). POC questionnaire shown to have hierarchical structure; 2 higher and 10 lower order factors; ii). POC highly related to SOC
Marcus et al (1992c)	Worksite employees. Study I:N=1063 Study II:N=429 Study III: N=20	i). to develop SOC scale ii). to obtain prevalence information of stages iii). to test the ability of self-efficacy to differentiate people at different stages	Prevalence from Studies I & II: PRE I=8%, II=7.3% CONT I=21.2%; II=23.1% PREP II=30.4% ACT I=36.9%; II=16.6% MAIN 1=34%; II=2.6% Efficacy scores increased through the stages in both studies. Study III. Test-retest correlations for SOC and efficacy measures confirmed.
Marcus et al (1992d)	Volunteers (N=610) in community exercise intervention. Ages ranged 18-82 years.	To motivate and support movement through stages for exercise adoption for those in CONT and PREP stages. Intervention = 6 weeks.	31.4% CONT at baseline moved to PREP after 6 weeks, a further 30.2% moved to ACT. 61.3% at PREP at baseline moved to ACT.
Marcus & Owen (1992)	1093 American and 801 Australian employees	To examine relationship between SOC, self-efficacy, and perceived costs and benefits of exercise	Increasing efficacy and benefit and decreasing 'cost' scores shown across stages rom PRE to MAIN in both samples.
Marcus & Simkin (1993)	Worksite employees (N = 235)	To ascertain the degree of relationship between stage and 7 day recall of PA	Prevalence: PRE=22.4% CONT=28.3% PREP=17.8% ACT=8.7% MAIN= 22.8% ACT+MAIN was higher on vigorous PA than other stages, For moderate PA, both ACT+MAIN and PREP were higher than PRE+CONT.

Study	Sample[1]	Purpose(s)	Results
Lee (1993)	50-64 year old Australian women (N=286)	Telephone survey asking about psychological variables that might differentiate women at the different exercise stages.	PRE were older and had poorer exercise knowledge than others. PRE differed from ACT by perceiving fewer benefits. ACT perceived fewer practical barriers to exercise
Armstrong et al. (1993)	Adults (N= 1719)	To examine relationships between stages, self-efficacy and adoption of vigorous PA over 2 years, prospective design	Stage was significant predictor of PA at 6 months after controlling for age, gender and efficacy. More CONT moved to ACT and MAIN than PRE.
Marcus et al. (1994)	Employees (N=698) from 4 worksites	To examine the relationship between stage and self-efficacy1 , costs and benefits of exercise, as well as PA. A subsample (N= 433) were also assessed 6 months later.	Structural equation models for both cross-sectional and longitudinal PA prediction showed that pros, cons and efficacy predicted PA indirectly through stage of exercise. Variance accounted for in PA by the model was 34.4% (cross-sectional) and 48.2% (longitudinal).
Prochaska et al. (1994)	Worksite employees (N=717) from Marcus et al. (1992a) study2	To examine the generalizability of the transtheoretical model across 12 health behaviours, specifically looking at the relationship between stage and decision balance.	See Marcus et al. (1992a)
Prochaska (1994)	As for Prochaska et al. (1994)2	To test whether progression from PRE to ACT involves a greater increase in pros than a decrease in cons.	Pros increased more (Max T score increase=15.9) than cons decreased (max T=5.1).
Cardinal (1995a)	Adult women (N= 178)	To study the relationship between exercise stage and level of exercise, level of PA and VO2peak.	Consistent differences across stages for for all three dependent variables.
Cardinal (1995b)	Undergraduate females (N=31) and males (N=43).	To ascertain relationship between PREP, ACT & MAIN stages and leisure-time exercise, frequency of sweating, body fat%, PA rating, difficulty with relance snfl VO2peak	Consistent differences across stages for all variables except body fat%.
Cardinal & Sachs (1995)	Female university employees (N= 81)	To study stage of exercise and three different mail delivered self-instructional exercise materials	Positive shift in exercise stage across time, with only 14.8% regressing in stage. No difference between type of exercise material used.
Wyse et al. (1995)	British tertiary college students aged 16-21 years (N=244)	To examine concurrent validity of 'Stages of Exercise Behaviour Change' (SEBC) scale and to see if a range of bio-behavioural and psychological variables would	distinguish people by stage. SEBC scale validity was supported withdifferences across stage for self-reported levels of exercise, exercise efficacy, physical self-perceptions and self-esteem.

Notes:

1. All samples are American unless otherwise stated.

2. 11 other health behaviours were also examined with separate samples. These are not reported here.

Table 3

Possible determinants of exercise across different stages and phases of exercise and physical activity

Stages¹	Pre / Con	Prep Action Maintenance		
Phases²	Adoption	Maintenance	Relapse / Dropout	Resumption
Factors/Determinants [adapted from Biddle, (1992)]				
attitudes	**	*	*	**
social norms	**	**	*	**
self-efficacy / control / competence	***	***	***	***
personality / self-motivation	*	**	**	*
environmental	**	**	*	**
biological	*	**	***	*
mental health outcomes	*	***	***	**
self-regulatory skills	**	***	***	***
attributions	*	*	**	***
Determinants categories [from Sallis & Hovell (1990)]				
environmental	**	**	*	**
social	**	**	*	**
cognitive	**	**	***	**
physiological	*	**	***	*

* some influence possible   ** expected influence   *** likely strong influence

Notes:

1. Stages: according to the Transtheoretical 'Stages of Change' model; pre = precontemplation; con = contemplation; prep = preparation.
2. Phases: according to Sallis & Hovell's (1990) 'Natural History' model.

compared across countries. This will serve two functions. First, the validity of instruments can be tested across different countries, and second, comparisons of results can be made more easily if instrumentation is better standardised.

Finally, this chapter review has attempted to highlight a number of issues associated with motivation. The area is vast and so I have been selective. However, one of my aims has been to highlight that future approaches to the study of motivation must account for the context, such as whether it is competitive sport or health-related or recreational exercise, and account for the developmental status of the individuals. This should take a life span approach if we are to understand how people of all ages are predisposed to be physically active.

References

ANDREW, G.M., OLDRIDGE, N. et al (1981) Reasons for dropout from exercise programmes in post-coronary patients. *Medicine and Science in Sports and Exercise,* 13, 164-168.

ARMSTRONG, C.A., SALLIS, J.F., HOVELL, M.F. and HOFSTETTER, C.R. (1993) Stages of change, self-efficacy, and the adoption of vigorous exercise: A prospective analysis. *Journal of Sport and Exercise Psychology,* 15, 390-402.

ASHFORD, B., BIDDLE, S.J.H. and GOUDAS, M. (1993) Participation in community sports centres: Motives and predictors of enjoyment. *Journal of Sports Sciences,* 11, 249-256.

BARKE, C.R. and NICHOLAS, D.R. (1990) Physical activity in older adults: The stages of change. *The Journal of Applied Gerontology,* 9, 216-223.

BARRELL, G., HIGH, S., HOLT, D. and MACKEAN, J. (1988) Motives for starting running and for competing in full and half marathon events. In *Sport, Health, Psychology and Exercise symposium proceedings.* London, Sports Council/Health Education Authority.

BIDDLE, S.J.H. (1992) Adherence to physical activity and exercise. In NORGAN, N. (Ed) *Physical activity and health.* Cambridge, Cambridge University Press, pp. 170-189.

BIDDLE, S.J.H. and ARMSTRONG, N. (1992) Children's physical activity: An exploratory study of psychological correlates. *Social Science and Medicine,* 24,

325-331.

BIDDLE, S.J.H. and FOX, K.R. (1988) The child's perspective in physical education: II. Children's participation motives. *British Journal of Physical Education,* 19, 2, 79-82.

BIDDLE, S.J.H. and MUTRIE, N. (1991) *Psychology of physical activity and exercise: A health-related perspective.* London, Springer-Verlag.

BIDDLE, S.J.H. and SMITH, R.A. (1991) Motivating adults for physical activity: Towards a healthier present. *Journal of Physical Education, Recreation and Dance,* 62, 7, 39-43.

BIDDLE, S.J.H., PAGE, A., ASHFORD, B., JENNINGS, D., BROOKE, R. and FOX, K.R. (1993) Assessment of children's physical self-perceptions. *International Journal of Adolescence and Youth,* 4, 93-109.

BOOTHBY, J., TUNGATT, M.F. and TOWNSEND, A.R. (1981) Ceasing participation in sports activity: Reported reasons and their implications. *Journal of Leisure Research,* 13, 1-14.

CANADA FITNESS SURVEY (1983a) *Canadian youth and physical activity.* Ottawa, Canada Fitness Survey.

CANADA FITNESS SURVEY (1983b) *Fitness and lifestyle in Canada.* Ottawa, Canada Fitness Survey.

CARDINAL, B.J. (1995a) The stages of exercise scale and stages of exercise behavior in female adults. *Journal of Sports Medicine and Physical Fitness,* 35, 87-92.

CARDINAL, B.J. (1995b) Behavioural and biometric comparisons of the preparation, action and maintenance stages of exercise. *Wellness Perspectives,* 11, 3, 36-43.

CARDINAL, B.J. and SACHS, M.L. (1995) Prospective analysis of stage of exercise movement following mail delivered, self-instructional exercise packets. *American Journal of Health Promotion,* 9, 430-432.

CLOUGH, P., SHEPHERD, J. and MAUGHAN, R. (1988) Motivations for running. In *Sport, Health, Psychology and Exercise symposium proceedings.* London, Sports Council/Health Education Authority.

CREWS, D. and LANDERS, D.M. (1987) A meta-analytic review of aerobic fitness and reactivity to psychosocial stressors. *Medicine and Science in Sports and Exercise,* 19, 5, (Supplement), S114-S120.

CSIKSZENTMIHALYI, M. (1975) *Beyond boredom and anxiety.* San Francisco, Jossey-Bass.

DEPARTMENT OF HEALTH (1991) *The health of the nation.* London, HMSO.

DISHMAN, R.K. (Ed) (1988) *Exercise adherence: its impact on public health.* Champaign, IL, Human Kinetics.

DISHMAN, R.K. (1990) Determinants of participation in physical activity. In BOUCHARD, C., SHEPHARD, R.J., STEPHENS, T., SUTTON, J.R. and MCPHERSON, B.D. (Eds) *Exercise, fitness and health: A consensus of current knowledge.* Champaign, IL, Human Kinetics, pp. 75-101.

DISHMAN, R.K. and GETTMAN, L. (1980) Psychobiologic influences on exercise adherence. *Journal of Sport Psychology,* 2, 295-310.

DUDA, J.L. (1987) Toward of a developmental theory of children's motivation in sport. *Journal of Sport Psychology,* 9, 130-145.

DUDA, J.L. (1989) Goal perspectives and behaviour in sport and exercise settings. In AMES, C. and MAEHR, M. (Eds) *Advances in motivation and achievement: VI. Motivation enhancing environments.* Greenwich, CT, JAI Press, pp. 81-115.

DUDA, J.L. and TAPPE, M.K. (1989) Personal investment in exercise among adults: The examination of age and gender-related differences in motivational orientation. In OSTROW, A. (Ed) *Ageing and motor behaviour.* Indianapolis, Benchmark Press, pp. 239-256.

DUDA, J.L. and ALLISON, M.T. (1990) Cross-cultural analysis in exercise and sport psychology: A void in the field. *Journal of Sport and Exercise Psychology,* 12, 114-131.

EADIE, D.R. and LEATHAR, D.S. (1988) *Concepts of fitness and health: An exploratory study.* Edinburgh, Scottish Sports Council.

FOX, K.R. and CORBIN, C.B. (1989) The Physical Self-Perception Profile: Development and preliminary validation. *Journal of Sport and Exercise Psychology,* 11, 408-430.

GOULD, D. and PETLICHKOFF, L. (1988) Participation motivation and attrition in young athletes. In SMOLL, F.L., MAGILL R.A. and ASH, M.J. (Eds) *Children in Sport.* Champaign, IL, Human Kinetics (3rd edition), pp. 161-178.

GRUBER, J.J. (1986) Physical activity and self-esteem development in children: A meta-analysis. In STULL, G. and ECKERT, H. (Eds) *Effects of physical activity on children.* Champaign, IL, Human Kinetics, pp. 30-48.

HARTER, S. (1978) Effectance motivation reconsidered: Towards a developmental model. *Human Development,* 21, 34-64.

HEARTBEAT WALES (1987) *Exercise for health: Health-related fitness in Wales.* Heartbeat Report 23. Cardiff, Heartbeat Wales.

LEE, C. (1993) Attitudes, knowledge and stages of change: A survey of exercise patterns in older Australian women. *Health Psychology,* 12, 476-480.

LEE, C. and OWEN, N. (1985) Reasons for discontinuing regular physical activity subsequent to a fitness course. *The ACHPER National Journal,* March, pp.7-9.

LOY, J. (1969) The nature of sport: A definitional effort. In LOY, J. and KENYON, G. (Eds) *Sport, culture and society.* London, McMillan, pp. 56-71.

MAEHR, M. and NICHOLLS, J.G. (1980) Culture and achievement motivation: A second look. In WARREN, N. (Ed) *Studies in cross-cultural psychology,* vol.2. New York, Academic Press, pp. 221-267.

MARCUS, B.H. and OWEN, N. (1992) Motivational readiness, self-efficacy and decision-making for exercise. *Journal of Applied Social Psychology,* 22, 3-16.

MARCUS, B.H., RAKOWSKI, W. and ROSSI, J.S. (1992a). Assessing motivational readiness and decision making for exercise. *Health Psychology,* 11, 257-261.

MARCUS, B.H., ROSSI, J.S., SELBY, V.C., NIAURA, R.S. and ABRAMS, D.B. (1992b). The stages and processes of exercise adoption and maintenance in a worksite sample. *Health Psychology,* 11, 386-395.

MARCUS, B.H., SELBY, V.C., NIAURA, R.S. and ROSSI, J.S. (1992c) Self-efficacy and the stages of exercise behaviour change. *Research Quarterly for Exercise and Sport,* 63, 60-66.

MARCUS, B.H., BANSPACH, S.W., LEFEBVRE, R.C., ROSSI, J.C., CARLETON, R.A. and ABRAMS, D.B. (1992d) Using the stages of change model to increase the adoption of physical activity among community participants. *American Journal of Health Promotion,* 6, 6, 424-429.

MARCUS, B.H., EATON, C.A., ROSSI, J.S. and HARLOW, L.L. (1994) Self-efficacy, decision making, and stages of change: An integrative model of physical exercise. *Journal of Applied Social Psychology,* 24, 489-508.

MARCUS, B.H. and SIMKIN, L.R. (1993) The stages of exercise behaviour. *The Journal of Sports Medicine and Physical Fitness,* 33, 83-88.

MIHALIK, B., O'LEARY, J., MCGUIRE, F. and DOTTAVIO, F. (1989) Sports involvement across the lifespan: Expansion and contraction of sports activities. *Research Quarterly for Exercise and Sport,* 60, 396-398.

MORGAN, W.P. and GOLDSTON, S.E. (Eds) (1987) *Exercise and mental health.* Washington, Hemisphere.

MOSES, J., STEPTOE, A., MATHEWS, A. and EDWARDS, S. (1989) The effects of exercise training on mental well-being in the normal population: A controlled trial. *Journal of Psychosomatic Research,* 33, 47-61.

NORTH, T.C., MCCULLAGH, P. and TRAN, Z.V. (1990) Effect of exercise on depression. *Exercise and Sport Sciences Reviews,* 18, 379-415.

PAGE, A., ASHFORD, B., BIDDLE, S.J.H. and FOX, K.R. (1993) Evidence of cross-cultural validity for the Physical Self-Perception Profile. *Personality and Individual Differences,* 14, 585-590.

PETRUZZELLO, S.J., LANDERS, D.M., HATFIELD, B.D., KUBITZ, K.A. and SALAZAR, W. (1991) A meta-analysis on the anxiety-reducing effects of acute and chronic exercise: Outcomes and mechanisms. *Sports Medicine,* 11, 143-182.

PROCHASKA, J.O. (1994) Strong and weak principles for progressing from precontemplation to action on the basis of twelve problem behaviours. *Health Psychology,* 13, 47-51.

PROCHASKA, J.O. (1979) *Systems of psychotherapy: A transtheoretical analysis.* Homewood, IL, Dorsey Press.

PROCHASKA, J.O. and DICLEMENTE, C.C. (1984) *The transtheoretical approach: Crossing traditional boundaries of therapy.* Homewood, IL, Dow Jones-Irwin.

PROCHASKA, J.O., DICLEMENTE, C.C. and NORCROSS, J.C. (1992) In search of how people change: Applications to addictive behaviours. *American Psychologist,* 47, 1102-1114.

PROCHASKA, J.O. and MARCUS, B.H. (1994) The transtheoretical model: Applications to exercise. In DISHMAN, R.K. (Ed) *Advances in exercise adherence.* Champaign, IL, Human Kinetics, pp. 161-180.

PROCHASKA, J.O., VELICER, W., ROSSI, J., GOLDSTEIN, M., MARCUS, B., RAKOWSKI, W., FIORE, C., HARLOW, L., REDDING, C., ROSENBLOOM, D. and ROSSIE, S. (1994) Stages of change and decisional balance for 12 problem behaviours. *Health Psychology,* 13, 39-46.

REJESKI, W.J. and BRAWLEY, L.R. (1988) Defining the boundaries of sport psychology. *The Sport Psychologist,* 2, 231-242.

SALLIS, J.F. and HOVELL, M.F. (1990) Determinants of exercise behaviour. *Exercise and Sport Sciences Reviews,* 18, 307-330.

SCANLAN, T.K. and LEWTHWAITE, R. (1986) Social psychological aspects of competition for male youth sport participants: IV. Predictors of enjoyment. *Journal of Sport Psychology,* 8, 25-35.

SCHLACKMANS (1986) *Women's fitness and exercise classes: 1. Summary and conclusions.* London, Schlackmans.

SONSTROEM, R.J. (1988) Psychological models. In R.K. DISHMAN (Ed) *Exercise adherence: its impact on public health.* Champaign, IL, Human Kinetics, pp. 125-153.

STEPHENS, T. (1988) Physical activity and mental health in the United States and Canada: Evidence from four population surveys. *Preventive Medicine,* 17, 35-47.

STEPTOE, A. and BOLTON, J. (1988) The short-term influence of high and low intensity physical exercise on mood. *Psychology and Health,* 2, 91-106.

STEPTOE, A. and COX, S. (1988) Acute effects of aerobic exercise on mood. *Health Psychology,* 7, 329-340.

TAPPE, M.K., DUDA, J.L. and MENGES-EHRNWALD, P. (1990) Personal investment predictors of adolescent motivational orientation toward exercise. *Canadian Journal of Sport Sciences,* 15, 185-192.

TELAMA, R. and SILVENNOINEN, M. (1979) Structure and development of 11 to 19 year olds' motivation for physical activity. *Scandinavian Journal of Sports Sciences,* 1, 23-31.

WANKEL, L. (1985) Personal and situational factors affecting exercise involvement: The importance of enjoyment. *Research Quarterly for Exercise and Sport,* 56, 275-282.

WANKEL, L. and KRIESEL, P. (1985) Factors underlying enjoyment of youth sports: Sport and age-group comparisons. *Journal of Sport Psychology,* 7, 51-64.

WANKEL, L. and SEFTON, J. (1989) A season-long investigation of fun in youth sports. *Journal of Sport and Exercise Psychology,* 11, 355-366.

WEINER, B. (1990) History of motivational research in education. *Journal of Educational Psychology,* 82, 616-622.

WHITE, A. and COAKLEY, J. (1986) *Making decisions: The response of young people in the Medway towns to the 'ever thought of sport?' campaign.* London, Greater London and South East Sports Council.

WHITEHEAD, J. and CORBIN, C.B. (1988) Physical competency/ adequacy subdomains and their relationship to global physical self-worth and global general self-worth. Paper presented at AAASP Conference, Nashua, NH, October.

WILLIAMS, J. and ESTON, R. (1989) Determination of the intensity dimension in vigorous exercise programmes with particular reference to the use of the rating of perceived exertion. *Sports Medicine,* 8, 177-189.

WYSE, J., MERCER, T., ASHFORD, B., BUXTON, K. and GLEESON, N. (1995) Evidence for the validity and utility of the Stages of Exercise Behaviour Change scale in young adults. *Health Education Research,* 10, 365-377.

PART 5

TEACHING PHYSICAL EDUCATION

Chapter 9

Systematic Observation of Physical Education Teachers' Behaviours: A Perspective

Colin A. Hardy

Over the last thirty years many studies have been conducted in physical education settings using systematic observation systems to collect data. However, with the more frequent use of other approaches (e.g. ethnographic, anthropological) to unravel the complexities of teaching, the value of observational data to our understanding of teaching needs to be assessed.

It is suggested "that observation involves the sensitive reaction of human or machine to the defined dimensions of behavioural events" (JOHNSTON and PENNYPACKER, 1980, p.157). Therefore, the human observer must be stimulated by the target behaviour in a way that brings this reaction under the necessary control for accurate observation. Furthermore, the selection and training of an observer and the conditions for the observation are crucial for a successful outcome. For example, the researcher must decide whether the life history of the selected observer will facilitate or impair accurate observation, whether the amount of training is adequate to develop the requisite observation skills and whether the presence of extraneous behavioural contingencies will reduce the chances of detecting the target behaviour. However, the replacement of such traditional teaching observation techniques as intuitive judgement, eyeballing, anecdotal recording, behaviour checklists and rating scales (METZLER, 1990) with systematic observation techniques has ensured that human observation has become less problematic. In fact, "the first large-scale entry by researchers into classrooms was made by observers briefly trained in the fluent use of schedules and category systems" (EDWARDS and WESTGATE, 1987, p.79).

The emphasis with systematic observation techniques was to enable teachers to record what actually happened in their lessons, compare that data with their intentions, and to identify and monitor any changes they wished to make. Furthermore, it was only natural for researchers to uphold methods of observation that were easy to learn, reliable and capable of providing quantitative data that could be used for testing hypotheses about classroom events. However, critics of systematic observation techniques note that the procedures are ideologically based in the sense that they focus on some things to the neglect of others and that such systems are totally dependent on the descriptive and explanatory power of the concepts inherent in the system used (MCINTYRE and MACLEOD, 1986). As such, it is suggested that one "risks furnishing only a partial description" of a classroom event (DELAMONT and HAMILTON, 1976, p.9). In addition, it is noted that the data do not take into account the meanings participants give to their interactions and that the links and chains of behaviour are lost (HARGREAVES, 1972). In general, it could be argued that to understand a classroom event it is also necessary to be aware of its history, to be alert to its possible outcomes and, above all, to be sensitive to the thoughts and intentions that guide its participants (HAMILTON, 1977). However, as there is evidence "to show that what teachers do in classrooms cannot be ascertained through extrapolations from teachers' accounts of their intentions or from accounts of what they do" (MCINTYRE and MACLEOD, 1986, p. 21), data from systematic observation techniques can only complement findings obtained from other approaches (e.g. ethnographic).

In the early years the process-product approach to research on teaching was central to many research programmes. In this approach, based on the DUNKIN and BIDDLE model (1974), 'process' variables referred to the visible and audible behaviours of teachers and students systematically recorded during classroom teaching and 'product' variables referred to the objectively measurable results of teaching, and the most effective teacher was the one who achieved the highest results following an instructional period. Furthermore, with the developments of technology (e.g. video tape, computer coding of data) and more powerful statistical techniques, studies became more complex and results more precise. BROPHY and GOOD (1986) in their examination of the findings of process-product research on teacher behaviour and student achievement noted that:

> Students achieve more in classes where they spend most of their time being taught or supervised by their teachers rather than working on their own (or not working at all). These classes included frequent lessons ... in which the teacher presents information and develops concepts through lecture and demonstration, elaborates this information in the feedback given following responses to recitation or discussion questions, prepares the students for follow up seatwork activities by giving instructions and going through practice examples, monitors progress on assignments after releasing the students to work independently, and follows up with the appropriate feedback and reteaching when necessary. The teacher carries the content to the students personally rather than depending on the curriculum materials to do so, but conveys information mostly in brief presentations followed by recitation or application opportunities. There is a great deal of teacher talk, but most of it is academic rather than procedural or managerial, and much of it involves asking questions and giving feedback rather than extended lecturing. (p.361)

As CLARK (1995) comments, "the global image of the good teacher supported by this research is of a business-like person who is clearly in control of the flow of work in an orderly efficient classroom" (p.11). Although the search for the good teacher now includes research on teacher thinking and teacher knowledge, and draws on such sources as the voices of teachers themselves and what children say about good teaching (CLARK, 1995), these early investigators did provide an image of the effective teacher from a behavioural standpoint.

In physical education many systems have been used to view teacher and pupil behaviours in the school context. In general they have been designed to record the number of times a behaviour happens (i.e. event recording), to measure the length of time a behaviour occurs within a teaching episode (i.e. duration recording), to note behaviours at predetermined intervals (i.e. time sampling) and to focus on different kinds of behaviour using a combination of techniques (METZLER, 1990). The problem with much of the data collected from physical education lessons is that many types of instruments have been used in a variety of physical education settings with different age and gender groups in many cultures. Therefore, the data collected must be viewed with caution but, on the other hand, must be regarded as data that contributes to an understanding of the 'effective' teacher.

Table 1

Characteristics of effective or experienced teachers of motor skills

- Plan for class management and student learning

- Anticipate situations and make contingency plans

- Are aware of student skill differences and use the information in planning and monitoring

- Require much information to plan

- Have a repertoire of teaching styles and know when to use them

- Provide accurate and focused explanations and demonstrations

- Provide adequate time for student practice

- Maximize appropriate student practice or engagement

- Minimize inappropriate student practice or engagement

- Minimize student waiting

(SILVERMAN, 1991)

Teacher Behaviours

SILVERMAN (1991), in his review of "'research on teaching in physical education'", suggested that "teacher effectiveness", with its emphasis on observation systems, was a major research stream in physical education, and that it included:

• descriptions on behaviours and actions that occur during physical education classes;

• process-product investigations involving teacher behaviour, teaching methods, class organisation and student engagement;

• comparison among teachers, students, curricula and settings.

Although SILVERMAN "tossing caution to the wind" (p.358) is accused of being too simplistic in compiling a list of the characteristics of effective physical education teachers (DODDS and PLACEK, 1991) based on his interpretation of the research findings, MAWER (1995) does feel that such lists do offer pointers for identifying the skills of effective physical education teachers (Table 1). However, as the compilation of such a list does depend very much on being able to draw conclusions from many investigations, the problematic nature of summarising observation data needs to be examined.

Based on the Data Bank Research project at Teacher's College, Columbia University, ANDERSON and BARRETTE (1978) reported teachers spending 36.9% of the lesson on active instruction (including preparatory instruction and feedback to pupils), 21.2% silently observing pupils, 20.4% on managing pupils and the environment and 16.9% on instruction-related activities such as officiating. A direct comparison cannot be made with SPACKMAN's English study (1986) because the two systems contained different sets of categories of teacher behaviours. However, both investigations revealed that "talk" was the most significant mode of interaction and communication. In a study by HARDY (1993a), using the SPACKMAN system, the average teaching behaviours for four teachers showed differences from those reported by SPACKMAN (1986) in that there were more teaching than management behaviours, more class teaching but less audible teaching and over 20% more audible-physical communication (Table 2).

Table 2

Teaching behaviours of the physical education teachers in the studies by HARDY (n = 4) and by SPACKMAN (n = 11)

Categories	Author	
	SPACKMAN (1986)*	HARDY (1993)
Management	26.7%	21.6%
Teaching	67.2%	78.4%
Direction One Group Class	24.2% 32.8% 39.8%	21.6% 35.3% 43.1%
Mode Audible Silent Physical Audible-Physical	67.8% 18.7% 0.6% 10.9%	42.2% 25.4% 0.9% 31.5%

Percentages do not add up to 100% because the categories of 'other interaction', 'non-interaction' and 'inadequate record' were included in the totals.

The reason for there being more audible-physical communication and less management behaviours in the latter study may be due to the environment and the nature of the activity. Whereas SPACKMAN's observations did not include swimming lessons, the study by HARDY was conducted in the swimming pool. Therefore, it is possible that the noise in a swimming pool encourages teachers to talk and demonstrate simultaneously and the act of swimming does not give pupils many opportunities to become distracted by other things.

Nevertheless, SPACKMAN reported that the nineteen lessons taught by the eleven teachers (male and female) did show a remarkable level of consistency in their selection of behaviours regardless of the activity, environment, pupils' age or their own personal attributes including their training. Similarly, UNDERWOOD (1988), in his comparison of teachers in five schools, reported no significant difference at the context or learner involvement level for the male and female teachers studied, although VARSTALA (1989) concluded that Finnish female physical education teachers were carrying out their teaching more thoroughly than male teachers. However, GUSTHART (1985) noted that research had relied heavily on observing teaching behaviours for relatively short periods of time, and questioned whether the data collected were representative of the teacher's "typical" behaviour. In a study to investigate the variation of teaching behaviour of three male teachers over a ten lesson volleyball unit, GUSTHART reported as much variability in teaching behaviours for each teacher during the ten lessons as between the three teachers. For example, the most prominent behaviour for one teacher was informing (40%) but there was a range of 28% for that behaviour over the ten lessons, and, although informing and organising were the most frequent behaviours for the three teachers, the less frequent behaviours concerned with refining, observing, extending, applying and with conduct varied according to the teacher. RINK (1983), in her study of teaching behaviours over a 15-lesson volleyball unit, reported "unstable" behaviours that could not be attributed to any specific event; for instance, a teacher who is normally active, giving specific feedback to students during skill practice becomes inactive. Furthermore, HARDY (1993a) noted how the behaviour patterns of four physical education teachers varied during lessons, perhaps indicating the importance of understanding how behaviours are put together as part of the total unit.

TOBEY (1974), using FISHMAN's category system for describing augmented feedback, reported that augmented feedback comprised a substantial portion of teacher behaviours. He found that words were used almost exclusively to convey feedback about movements being performed and that feedback was directed primarily to a single student. He found that a larger proportion of feedback was non-specific (44%) although MAWER and BROWN (1983), in a study of twenty teachers from four primary and six middle schools, found that three-quarters of teacher's interactions seemed to be general comments rather than specific guidance information concerning how to improve movement attempts or indicating why movement attempts were good. TOBEY (1974) found that the instances of positive feedback (42%) were outnumbered by instances of negative feedback (56%), but PIÉRON (1982a) reported a ratio approximately three to one in favour of positive interventions in studies at the University of Liège. This evaluation type of feedback varied between 25% and 50% of all feedback (PIÉRON, 1983). Corrective feedback, which is intended to provide instructions for the future performance of a skill, came to approximately 40% (ARENA, 1979). However, PIÉRON (1983) reported that feedback occurrence was extremely variable and ranged from less than 10% to more than 25% of the behaviours recorded and from less than one feedback to approximately four per minute. SPACKMAN (1986) recorded an 8% feedback occurrence with English teachers.

The importance of feedback to student progress in physical education was questioned by studies that concluded that high amounts of teacher verbal feedback were not found to be significantly correlated with student achievement (GRAHAM, SOARES and HARRINGTON, 1983; YERG, 1977). Also there were even suggestions that feedback impeded student achievement because it decreased the time for actual skill practice. However, a study by YERG and TWARDY (1982) concluded that practice without feedback might even be detrimental to student achievement, and PAESE (1987) reported that specific verbal feedback, when given along with high rates of student opportunity to practise a skill, did make a difference in the overall student learning of a motor skill.

GRAHAM (1983) reported that the influence of teacher feedback has yet to be documented through process-product research in physical education; based on five physical education "Experimental Teaching Unit" (ETU)[1] studies, he suggested that teacher feedback that severely inhibits opportunities to practise would restrict rather than enhance student learning, regardless of the type of quality of the feedback. In a recent ETU study, BEHETS (1989) concluded that the direct influence of teacher feedback on pupil performance seemed to be limited and needed further research in laboratory situations.

With reference to opportunities to practise there has been a great deal of literature on the amount of non-movement or movement of pupils in physical education teachers' lessons.[2] In a review of literature, PIÉRON (1983) reported that the time devoted to movement activity varied from below 20% (BRUNELLE et al, 1980; METZLER, 1979;

SHUTE, DODDS, PLACEK, RIFE and SILVERMAN, 1982), between 20% and 30% (COSTELLO and LAUBACH, 1978; MCLEISH, HOWE and JACKSON, 1981; PIÉRON and DOHOGNE, 1980; PIÉRON and HAAN, 1980) to over 45% (TELAMA, PAUKKU, VARSTALA and PAANANEN, 1982; VARSTALA, TELAMA and AKKANEN, 1981). UNDERWOOD (1988), in his study of five English schools, corroborated PIÉRON's conclusion that physical education lessons were characterised by a great deal of non-movement. On average, UNDERWOOD found that pupils spent 16% of the lesson either waiting to take part or waiting for instructions, and another 27% was spent in cognitive tasks such as listening or watching an aspect of skill acquisition.

Apart from the study by TELAMA et al (1982), boys appear to be marginally more engaged in motor activities than girls in physical education lessons (PIÉRON and HAAN, 1980; SHUTE et al, 1982). Although SHUTE et al (1982) found small differences in engaged motor responses between learners of different skill levels, PIÉRON (1982b) found that high achievers were significantly more engaged in motor responses than low achievers in volleyball and gymnastics lessons. The kind of activity seems to have a bearing on the amount of motor engaged time, with games (MCLEISH, HOWE and JACKSON, 1981; PIÉRON and DOHOGNE, 1980; RATE, 1980) and swimming (MCLEISH et al, 1981) involving a high level of student activity and gymnastics a low level of student activity (COSTELLO and LAUBACH, 1978). However, TELAMA, VARSTALA, HEIKINARO-JOHANNSON and UTRIAINEN (1987) suggested that, although teachers may try to treat pupils with different skill levels equally, a certain inequality may make itself apparent on the level of the pupil's behaviour and experiences; in non-differentiated teaching, low-skill pupils have inadequate opportunities for participation on their own terms whereas high-skill pupils benefit most and are most motivated by teaching. When the practice of a movement task was differentiated the rate of responding by high- and low-ability pupils during lessons was comparable although the high skilled pupils tended to have more successful responses (GRAHAM, 1988).

PARÉ, LIRETTE, CARON and BLACK (1987) were more pessimistic about the way teachers deal with their students. In a study of seventeen experienced teachers' lessons, it was found that there were small differences in their class time distribution, their student engagement time distribution and their student motor engagement time distribution even though the subjects being taught and the ages of the students differed. PARÉ et al (1987) felt that the total absence of any significant differences questions the amount of consideration teachers really give to their students and that we may have to look more closely at the type and quality of their professional preparation.

Intervention studies to modify teachers' behaviours in a way that will influence the amount of pupil activity provided in their classes have met with varying degrees of success (BIRDWELL, 1980; BEAMER, 1983; MANCINI, WUEST, VANTINE and CLARK, 1984; WHALEY, 1980) although a more recent study (HARDY, 1993) reported that pupils increased the amount of distance covered during swimming lessons when the teachers intentionally used brief instructional cues. Some physical education investigators have attended to the sequential patterning of instructional events (NYGAARD, 1975; PIÉRON and DRION, 1977; CHEFFERS and MANCINI, 1978) arguing that good teaching involves more than a command of a few isolated behaviours. OLSON (1983), using the Adaptation of the Observational System for Instructional Analysis for use in physical education (OSIA-PE), analysed twenty-four videotapes of elementary, junior high, and senior high (eight at each level) physical education classes, and reported that "the total number of three- or four-event chains after collapsing was forty six" (p.291). The greatest number of different chains (or catenas) was found to begin in the categories labelled initiating, responding, soliciting clarification and soliciting. OLSON recommended that attempts should be made to find extensions of the already located chains, and that investigations should continue to identify chains across different classes with different activities taught by the same teacher, and in classes of the same activity taught by the different teachers. GUSTHART and SPRIGINGS (1989) also noted that "no single element of instructional behaviour should exclusively be considered apart from all of the other behaviours or from the total situation in which it is found" (p.310), and that the interaction of the instructional variables is an important consideration.

Conclusion

Data have been collected on teacher behaviours for nearly four decades using systematic observation instruments. Such issues as the stability of teaching and managing behaviours, the individuality of teachers, the importance of physical education settings and the relationship between time and pupil achievement have been central to the examination of such data. However, because of the complexity of the teaching process, researchers using such an approach cannot claim a privileged insight into the minds of teachers as the data is only representative of the technique being used and, furthermore, may not be typical of that kind of data. Nevertheless, "all researchers have to make simplifying assumptions about that part of the social world which they seek to investigate if they are to gather data at all" (EDWARDS and WESTGATE, 1987, p.93) and, in this sense, researchers using systematic observation systems are no different from those using alternative techniques. Systematic observation is one way of viewing teaching events and, as such, has a contribution to make in disentangling the complex world of teaching.

Notes

1   An Experimental Teaching Unit (ETU) is a brief series of lessons on a topic of general interest to the year level of pupils to be taught by the teachers in the experiment. Ten lessons is a typical ETU length (GRAHAM, 1983).

2   Many physical education researchers have used Academic Learning Time - Physical Education (i.e. "the portion of engaged time in which the pupil is performing motor tasks at a low error rate" (PIÉRON, 1983, p.21) as a proxy measure of pupil achievement, but as the direct relationship of ALT-PE with pupil achievement has not been established (SILVERMAN, 1985), a high level of engaged time cannot be regarded as a sufficient condition for learning.

References

ANDERSON, W.G. and BARRETTE, G.T. (1978) Teacher behaviour. In W.G. ANDERSON and G.T. BARRETTE (Eds) What's going on in gym? *Motor skills: Theory into Practice. Monograph 1.* Newtown, CT, A.L. Rothstein, pp.11-24.

ARENA, L. (1979) Descriptive and experimental studies of augmented feedback in sport settings. Doctoral Dissertation, Ohio State University. In R. TELAMA, V. VARSTALA, J. TIAINEN, L. LAAKSO and T. HAAJANEN (Eds) 1983.

Research in School Physical Education. Report of Physical Culture and Health, No. 38. Jyväsklä: The Foundation for Promotion of Physical Culture and Health, 17.

BEAMER, D.W. (1983) The effects of an inservice education program on the academic learning time of selected students in physical education. *Dissertation Abstracts International* 43, 2593A. (University Microfilms No. DA 8300208.)

BEHETS, D. (1989) Feedback behaviour and skill level of pupils. In *Movement and Sport – A Challenge for Life-Long Learning* (Abstracts), World Convention, July 1989, 11, AIESEP, Jyväsklä.

BIRDWELL, D. (1980) The effects of modification of teacher behaviour on the academic learning time of selected students in physical education. *Dissertation Abstracts International* 41, 1472A, (University Microfilms No. DEM80-22239).

BROPHY, J.E. and GOOD, T.L. (1986) Teacher behaviour and student achievement. In M.C. WITTROCK (Ed) *Handbook of Research on Teaching,* 3rd Ed. New York, MacMillan, pp.328-375.

BRUNELLE, J., GODBOUT, P., DROUIN, D., DESHARNAIS, R., LORD, M and TOUSIGNANT, M. (1980) Rapport de recherche sur la qualité de l'intervention en education physique. Cited in R. TELAMA, V, VARSTALA, J. TIAINEN, L. LAASKO and T. HAAJANEN, 1983. *Research in School Physical Education.* Reports of Physical Culture and Health, No. 38. Jyväsklä, The Foundation for the Promotion of Physical Culture and Health, 22.

CHEFFERS, J.T.F. and MANCINI, V.H. (1978) Teacher-student interaction. In W.G. ANDERSON and G.T. BARRETTE (Eds) What's going on in gym? *Motor skills: Theory into Practice.* Monograph 1. Newtown, CT, A.L. Rothstein, pp.39-50.

CLARK, C.M. (1985) *Thoughtful Teaching.* London, Cassell.

COSTELLO, J. and LAUBACH, S. (1978) Student behaviour. In W.G. ANDERSON and G.T. BARRETTE (Eds) What's going on in gym? *Motor Skills: Theory into Practice.* Monography 1. Newtown, CT, pp.11-24.

DELAMONT, S. and HAMILTON, D. (1976) Classroom research: A critique and a new approach. In M. STUBBS and, S. DELAMONT (Eds) *Explorations in Classroom Observation.* London, Wiley.

DODDS, P. and PLACEK, J.H. (1991) Silverman's RT-PE review: Too simple a summary of a complex field. *Research Quarterly for Exercise and Sport,* 62, 4,

365-368.

DUNKIN, M.J. and BIDDLE, B.J. (1974) *The Study of Teaching.* New York, Holt, Rinehart and Winston.

EDWARDS, A.D. and WESTGATE, D.P.G. (1987) *Investigating Classroom Talk.* London, Falmer Press.

GRAHAM, G. (1983). Review and implications of physical education experimental teaching unit research. In T.J. TEMPLIN and J.K. OLSON (Eds.) *Teaching in Physical Education.* Champaigne, IL, Human Kinetics, pp.244-253.

GRAHAM, K. (1988) Research note: effects levels in pedagogical research. *Journal of Teaching in Physical Education, 7*, 4, 353-357.

GRAHAM, G., SOARES, P. and HARRINGTON, W. (1983), Experienced teachers' effectiveness and intact classes: An ETU study, *Journal of Teaching in Physical Education, 2*, 2, 3-14.

GUSTHART, J.L. (1985) Variations in direct, indirect and non-contributing teacher behaviour. *Journal of Teaching in Physical Education, 4*, 2, 111-122.

GUSTHART, J.L. and SPRIGINGS, E.J. (1989) Student learning as a measure of teacher effectiveness in physical education. *Journal of Teaching in Physical Education, 8*, 4, 298-311.

HAMILTON, D. (1977) *In Search of Structure.* London, Hodder and Stoughton.

HARDY, C.A. (1993a) Teaching behaviours of physical education specialists. *Physical Education Review, 16*, 1, 19-26.

HARDY, C.A. (1993b) Teacher communication and time on-task. *Research in Education, 49*, 29-38.

HARGREAVES, D.H. (1972) *Interpersonal Relations and Education.* London, Routledge and Kegan Paul.

JOHNSTON, J.M. and PENNYPACKER, H.S. (1980) *Strategies and Tactics of Human Behavioral Research.* Hillsdale, NJ, Lawrence Erlbaum Associates.

MANCINI, V.H., WUEST, D.A., VANTINE, K.W. and CLARK, E.K. (1984) The use of instruction and supervision in interaction analysis on burned-out teachers: Its effect on teaching behaviours, level of burnout, and academic learning time. *Journal of Teaching in Physical Education, 3*, 2, 29-46.

MAWER, M. (1995) *The Effective Teaching of Physical Education.* London, Longman.

MAWER, M. and BROWN, G. (1983) Analysing teaching in physical education. In M. MAWER (Ed.) *Trends in Physical Education.* Aspects of Education, No. 29. University of Hull, Institute of Education, pp.71-95.

MCINTYRE, D. and MACLEOD, G. (1986) The characteristics and uses of systematic observation. In M. HAMMERSLEY (Ed) *Controversies in Classroom Research.* Milton Keynes, Open University Press.

MCLEISH, J., HOWE, B. and JACKSON, J. (1981) *Effective Teaching in Physical Education,* Victoria, B.C., University of Victoria.

METZLER, M. (1979) *The measurement of academic learning time in physical education.* Doctoral dissertation, Ohio State University. Cited in R. TELAMA, V. VARSTALA, J. TIAINEN, L. LAASKO and T. HAAJANEN (Eds) 1983. *Research in School Physical Education.* Reports of Physical Culture and Health, No. 38, Jyväskylä, The Foundation for Promotion of Physical Culture and Health, 22.

METZLER, M.W. (1990) *Instructional Supervision for Physical Education.* Champaign, IL, Human Kinetics.

NYGAARD, G.A. (1975) Interaction analysis of physical education classes. *Research Quarterly,* 46, 351-357.

OLSON, J.K. (1983) Catenas: Exploring meanings. In T.J. Templin, and J.K. Olson, *Teaching in Physical Education,* 1983. Champaign, IL, Human Kinetics, pp.286-297.

PAESE, P.C. (1987) Specific teacher feedback's effect on academic learning time and on a novel motor skill. In G.T. BARRETTE, R.S. FEINGOLD, C.R. REES, and M. PIÉRON (Eds) *Myths, Models and Methods in Sports Pedagogy.* Champaign, IL, Human Kinetics, pp.207-213.

PARÉ, C., LIRETTE, M., CARON, F. and BLACK, P. (1987) The study of active learning time: Profile of behaviour. In G.T. BARRETTE, R.S. FEINGOLD, C.R. REES, and M. PIÉRON (Eds) *Myths, Models and Methods in Sport Pedagogy.* Champaign, IL, Human Kinetics, pp.255-261.

PIÉRON, M. (1982a) Analyse de l'ensignement des activités physiques. In R. TELEMA, V. VARSTALA, J. TIAINEN, L. LAAKSO and T. HAAJANEN, *Research in School Physical Education.* Reports of Physical Culture and Health,

1993, No. 38. Jyväskylä. The Foundation for the Promotion of Physical Culture and Health, 17.

PIÉRON, M. (1982b) Behaviours of low and high achievers in physical education classes. In M. PIÉRON and J. CHEFFERS (Eds) *Studying the Teaching in Physical Education*. Liége, University of Liége, pp.53-60.

PIÉRON, M. (1983) Teacher and pupil behaviour and the interaction process in PE classes. In R. TELAMA, V. VARSTALA, J. TIAINEN, L. LAAKSO and T. HAAJANEN (Eds) *Research in School Physical Education*. Reports of Physical Culture and Health, 1983, No. 38, Jyväskylä, Foundation for the Promotion of Physical Culture and Health.

PIÉRON, M. and DRION, C. (1977) Analyse de l'interaction entre le professeur et ses élèves en education physique, par le system de Hough. *Revue de L'Education Physique*, 17, 27-37.

PIÉRON, M. and HAAN, J.M. (1980) Pupils' activities, time on-task and behaviours in high school physical education teaching. *Bulletin of the Fédération Internationale d'Education Physique*, 50, 3/4, 62-68.

PIÉRON, M. and DOHOGNE, A. (1980) Comportements des élèves dans des classes d'education physique. Conduites par des enseignants en formation. *Revue de L'Education Physique*, 20, 4, 11-18.

RATE, R.A. (1980) *A Descriptive Analysis of Academic Learning Time and Coaching Behaviours in Inter-scholastic Athletic Practices*. Unpublished Ph.D. dissertation, Columbus, Ohio State University.

RINK, J.E. (1983) The stability of teaching behaviour over a unit of instruction. In T.J. TEMPLIN and J.K. OLSON (Eds) *Teaching in Physical Education*. Champaign, IL, Human Kinetics, pp.318-328.

SHUTE, S., DODDS, P., PLACEK, J., RIFE, F. and SILVERMAN, S. (1982) Academic learning time in elementary school movement education: A descriptive analytic study. *Journal of Teaching in Physical Education*, 1, 2, 3-14.

SILVERMAN, S. (1985) Relationship of engagement and practice trials to student achievement. *Journal of Teaching in Physical Education*, 5, 1, 13-21.

SILVERMAN, S. (1991) Research on teaching in physical education. *Research Quarterly for Exercise and Sport*, 62, 4, 352-364.

SPACKMAN, L. (1986) *The Systematic Observation of Teacher Behaviour in*

Physical Education: The Design of an Instrument. Unpublished Doctoral thesis, Loughborough University of Technology.

TELAMA, R., PAUKKU, P., VARSTALA, V. and PAANANEN, M. (1982) Pupils' physical activity and learning behaviour in physical education classes. In M. PIÉRON and J. CHEFFERS (Eds) *Studying the Teaching in Physical Education.* Liège, University of Liége, pp.23-35.

TELAMA, R., VARSTALA, V., HEIKINARO-JOHANSSON, P., and UTRIAINEN, J. (1987) Learning behaviour in P.E. lessons and physical and psychological responses to P.E. in high-skill and low-skill pupils. In G.T. BARRETTE, R.S. FEINGOLD, C.R. REES and M. PIÉRON (Eds), *Myths, Models and Methods in Sport Pedagogy.* Champaign, IL, Human Kinetics, pp.239-248.

TOBEY, C. (1974) A descriptive analysis of the occurrences of augmented feedback in physical education classes. Unpublished Doctoral thesis, Teachers College, Columbia University. In V. MELOGRANO (Ed), *Designing Curriculum and Learning: A Physical Co-education Approach,* 1979. Dubuque, 1A, Kendall/Hunt Publishing Co, p. 344.

UNDERWOOD, G.L. (1988) *Teaching and Learning in Physical Education: A Social psychological perspective.* London, Falmer Press.

VARSTALA, V. (1989) Teacher behaviour in school physical education classes. In *Movement and Sport: A Challenge for Life-long Learning,* AISEP World Convention, July 1989, (p. 133). Jyväskylä, Press of the University of Jyväskylä.

VARSTALA, V., TELAMA, R. and AKKANEN, O. (1981) Teacher and student activities during physical education lessons. In H. HAAG et al (Eds) *Physical Education and Evaluation.* Proceedings of the XXII SUPER World Congress, Kiel, Schorndorf, July 23-27, 1981, pp.368-374.

WHALEY, G. (1980) The effects of daily monitoring and feedback to teachers and students on academic learning time – physical education, *Dissertation Abstracts International* 41, 1477A. (University Microfilms No. DEM 80-22365).)

YERG, B.J. (1977) Relationships between teacher behaviours and pupil achievement in the psychomotor domain. *Dissertation Abstracts International,* 38, 1981a. (University Microfilms No. 77-21229.)

YERG, B.J. and TWARDY, B. (1982) Relationship of specified instructional teacher behaviours to pupil given on a motor task. In M. PIÉRON and J.

CHEFFERS (Eds) *Studying the Teaching in Physical Education.* Liége, University of Liége, pp.61-68.

Chapter 10

The Reflective Physical Education Teacher: Implications for Initial Teacher Education

Anne Williams

In a survey of initial teacher education (BARRETT et al, 1992), reflective practice was identified as the most common philosophy underpinning courses in England. A follow-up project by the same team (WHITING, WHITTY, FURLONG, MILES and BARTON, 1996) found that reflective practice remained the most common model of professionalism in initial teacher education although less dominant than in the previous survey. It seems clear from discussions with colleagues involved in the initial training of physical education teachers, that this philosophy is seen as applicable to physical education as well as to other subject areas. Others have described difficulties associated with fostering reflective practice in work with students and more experienced teachers (CALDERHEAD, 1987; VALLI, 1992; HATTON and SMITH, 1994). Exactly what is meant by reflective practice is far from clear. CALDERHEAD (1987) comments on the variations which exist both in conceptions of reflective activity and in the content on which teachers are expected to reflect. This chapter examines a range of meanings of reflective practice and the implications for the physical education teacher educator of their adoption. It also considers the relationship between different interpretations of reflective practice and distinctive perspectives on research into pedagogy. These considerations are particularly timely given the far reaching changes to initial teacher education which have been imposed by the government in recent years.

A number of factors lead to the conclusion that it seems legitimate to ask two questions about reflective practice. The first is whether it has a future? The second is about the relationship between various aspects of reflective practice and the ways in which beginning teachers learn and develop as professionals? The future of reflective practice may be considered in relation both to overall teacher education policy and to issues specific to physical education. The current context is one of increasing central control and direction in teaching and in teacher education exemplified by the requirements of Circular 9/92 (DFE, 1992) and by the modus operandi of the Teacher Training Agency, set up in 1992 and with oversight of both initial teacher training and teachers' continuing professional development. Specific to physical education is what MACDONALD and TINNING (1995) have described as proletarianisation resulting from the relative increase in the status of sports science sub-disciplines in undergraduate courses and the relative subordination of pedagogy and social science courses. This, they would argue leads students to conceptualise teaching as a matter of acquiring certain technical skills rather than as a value-laden activity subject to critical enquiry.

The answer to the question of whether there is a future for reflective practice depends crucially of course on how the concept is defined. This is not a straightforward task. Many meanings are attached to it and there is not always agreement on what conditions may be required to foster it. HATTON and SMITH (1994) suggest that the term is often used rather loosely to embrace a wide range of concepts and strategies. MCINTYRES's (1993) definition of reflection as "systematic enquiry into one's own practice to improve that practice and to deepen one's understanding of it" (p.43), which he acknowledges as a broad one, exemplifies conceptualisations which are open to several interpretations with markedly different implications for practice. A number of perspectives will be discussed here, which may be seen as constituting a continuum. At one end of the scale is an interpretation which sees reflection as a utilitarian mechanism for improving the execution of teaching skills and, thereby, the learning of pupils. At the other end of the scale, reflective teaching involves consideration of all aspects of the education process as problematic and demands the reconstruction of experience in the light of political, institutional, social and moral constraints. These perspectives are similar to the hierarchies outlined by VAN MANEN (1977) and TOM (1984).

Approaches to Reflection

The first perspective to be examined sees reflection as a tool which involves instrumental mediation of action. That is, it is a process which leads to action determined by conscious thought, usually involving the putting into practice of research findings and theoretical formulations of education. Reflection in this context is instrumental in that the reflective process is used to help teachers replicate classroom practices that empirical research has found to be effective. The knowledge source is usually that of an external authority. An assumption behind this interpretation of reflection is that new information usually comes from authorities who publish in journals rather than from the practice situation itself. This perspective is encapsulated in CRUIKSHANK's (1985) view of the use of reflective teaching, which sees reflection as instrumental in enabling trainee teachers to replicate teaching strategies or behaviours which have been 'proved' effective by empirical research. Research literature provides a source of propositional or prescriptive knowledge which can be used for the application and analysis of practice.

In the context of physical education, this approach can be seen in practice, although there are issues about the lack of research knowledge available particularly in the United Kingdom. Nevertheless, there is some, particularly in the North American literature. SIEDENTOP (1982) has been influential in leading research which aims to identify models of teaching which are seen as effective in producing student learning. For example, factors such as "academic learning time in physical education" (altpe) are identified and studies have been made of lessons in order to establish the extent to which time is used profitably in them. This has been replicated in England by UNDERWOOD (1988).

Because relatively little has been published in England, discussion of the use of such research in the training process has to rely largely on anecdotal evidence. Perhaps the most obvious example of its use and of the development of this particular perspective on reflective teaching is in the various micro-teaching programmes which have been implemented in recent years by a number of training institutions. BUTTERWORTH (1989) describes a micro-teaching programme for physical education students and their reactions to it. This usually involves the identification of a number of specific strategies which are seen to be central to 'good teaching' and discussion subsequent to a lesson which may be taught to small groups, to a whole class for a short time, or to a whole class for a whole lesson, about the student's success or otherwise of putting these strategies into action. In many instances, the lesson is video-taped for later analysis. Where this is not possible, common practice is for other students to act as observers who record the event with a specific brief: for example one student might have the task of commenting on the extent to which the teaching student used his or her voice effectively, while another might be given the task of noting the kind of feedback given by the teaching student and to whom. Feedback from students participating in such programmes has been positive and its seems to be seen as a valuable learning experience.

These examples raise many questions in the context of the alternative interpretations of reflection which are described and discussed below. They also raise questions about the extent to which the context in which the experience takes place encourages one kind of reflection at the expense of others. Having engaged in such a programme with a group of physical education Post-Graduate Certificate of Education (PGCE) students, I was confronted with the issue of whose views of what had gone on were seen as legitimate or valued and whose were seen as less significant. Where students have made judgements about their peers, inevitably made in the light of their own, probably limited experience, it can be tempting to impose one's own judgements and standards upon the group. Is this encouraging or stifling reflective practice? On the other hand, if one does not give one's own judgement, is the development of competent practice being hindered?

Whatever the answers to these questions, the key feature of these approaches is that they take as their main focus the achievement of the learning task with little attention to the context in which that learning is taking place or to the content itself. This is not to belittle the achievements of researchers such as SEIDENTOP or to place such an approach at the bottom of some kind of hierarchical ordering. He, himself (SIEDENTOP, 1980), notes that physical education's history is rooted firmly in cultural transmission rather than social reconstruction, that is, it follows the activity preferences of the culture rather than shaping them. In this context and against a background of little if any empirical evidence about effective teaching behaviour, research which enables us to be better informed about any aspect of teaching is to be welcomed. Moreover, HATTON and SMITH (1994) note that students early in their training place the mastery of the technical skills and content of teaching at the top of their agenda and suggest that if teacher-educators fail to recognise the importance of what they call basic descriptive reflection to the neophyte teacher, they are unlikely to succeed in fostering other kinds of reflection. The issue then, is not that this form of reflection should be criticised as inappropriate but that it should not necessarily be seen as sufficient.

A second perspective sees reflection as a form of deliberation among competing views of teaching, that is, the consideration of educational events in practice. Research knowledge in this context is used not to direct practice as in the previous examples, but to inform it. The context of educational events is an important focus. There is a belief that in reflecting about particular events in context, one deliberates between and among competing views of teaching and examines each in the light of the consequences of the action it entails. Followers of this perspective subscribe to an eclectic view of knowledge, the test of which is whether it benefits student learning.

Extensive work on a range of teaching styles in physical education has been carried out by MOSSTON (MOSSTON and ASHWORTH, 1986), relating specific styles to particular learning outcomes and pupil activities. MOSSTON's work has underpinned much practice in initial teacher education in physical education in recent years. There have, for example, been programmes in which students are asked to teach a particular skill or concept using a specific style from MOSSTON's spectrum either given to them or self-chosen. Early applications of MOSSTON's work assumed that the range of teaching styles presented could be seen as competing alternatives. Subsequent work by MOSSTON and ASHWORTH (1986) however, stresses that the styles are intended to be complimentary. A teacher who is able to use a variety of styles is more likely to be able to select the most effective for a specific learning activity. In the context of reflective teaching, MOSSTON's work offers a framework which goes wider than earlier research, in that he considers the relationship between specific teaching styles and learning outcomes other than the physical. He thus goes beyond what TINNING (1991) describes as performance pedagogy and considers factors such as social and emotional development.

The fact that the active involvement of pupils in decision-making increases as one moves through MOSSTON's spectrum actually raises many questions about relative priorities in the learning process. For example, MOSSTON describes the "reciprocal" teaching style as one where pupils work in pairs with one playing the teacher role. This approach has been suggested as a way of teaching gymnastics which emphasises personal and social skills as well as physical performance (UNDERWOOD and WILLIAMS, 1991). For some teachers, the time spent talking through the requirements for helping a peer effectively (and, for example, looking at visual resources such as worksheets) is seen as time taken away from practising physical skills and as a result they reject this style. For others, the personal and social benefits which accrue far outweigh any time taken from performance.

Both of the above positions are, to an extent, utilitarian in their orientation, that is, they are concerned with doing a competent job. The second goes further than the first in questioning taken-for-granted assumptions and enabling the individual to characterise the problematic. Nevertheless, it remains concerned with what is at root an instrumental approach to the skills of teaching. The third perspective sees reflection as the reconstruction of experience.

Within this third perspective, the source of knowledge is found in both the action setting and in the practical application of personal knowledge. This generates various kinds of new understandings and involves consideration of the situational and institutional context of teaching. Reasons for certain choices of practice need to be articulated and constraints upon them identified. This is the nature of reflective practice as described by SCHON (1988), who stresses valuing the competency already embedded in skilful practice. Although ADLER (1991) views SCHON's approach as being primarily concerned with "doing the job effectively" and as an extension of an instrumental approach to teacher education rather than with calling into question a wide range of curriculum goals and structures, the distinction between this approach as compared with those described earlier seems to lie in his valuing of knowledge arising from practice.

This approach leads to the reconstruction of oneself as a teacher, with an expectation that teachers will become more aware of the cultural milieu in which they operate. Experience embodied in one's personal biography is seen to constitute both the content and consequences of reflective teaching. Reconstructing taken-for-granted assumptions about teaching is equally important. This includes consideration of the worth of competing educational goals and introduces moral and ethical issues. It is a means by which critical theory can be practised with an emancipatory intent, that is, it allows a practitioner to identify and address the social, political and cultural conditions that frustrate and constrain self-understanding. Reflection is, therefore, the reconstruction of experience. Knowledge provides the metaphors that transform one's understanding of the political, institutional, social and moral constraints that impinge on the practice of teaching. This view of reflection seems to fit well with the constructivist view of knowledge which underpins much current thinking in science and mathematics and which is now being applied to the physical education context.

It is this third perspective which is espoused by ZEICHNER who, in questioning a whole range of taken-for-granted assumptions, promotes a more transformational and, some might say, idealistic role for the teacher. LISTON and ZEICHNER (1990) consider that a reflective orientation to teaching should stress the giving of good reasons for educational actions, should take into account the aims, values and purposes of distinct educational traditions, indicate some awareness of alternative social and cultural frameworks, and show an understanding of schools as educational institutions.

While starting from similar beliefs in the value of teacher knowledge or knowledge-in-action to those discussed by SCHON, ZEICHNER's perspective appears to go further than SCHON's in the range of issues which are treated as problematic. It is an approach which seems to mirror the 'critical theory' perspective which has been adopted by a number of researchers in physical education, and which sees all research as value-based and, of necessity, involved with issues of power and social control. BAIN (1992) doubts the impact of critical theory-based research upon practice in physical education partly because impact has to depend upon the extent to which the results of such theory are accessible to teachers as well as to researchers. EVANS (1992) notes that it is easier to define what might be meant by forms of teacher education which develop a critical consciousness than it is to put them into practice. This is particularly true of an education system which has become increasingly prescriptive both in the classroom and with regard to the training of teachers. Nevertheless, some examples can be given which illustrate the kinds of agenda which might be set and the sorts of issues which confront physical education.

One example of an issue which may or may not be viewed as problematic is related to equal opportunities in the context of the development of proposals for National Curriculum Physical Education (DES, 1991a), based upon the recommendations of the Physical Education Working Group, which include some reference to both gender and cultural diversity. It is noted that tensions may arise both between diverse cultural groups and between different generations and that children frequently have to cope with these tensions. It is recommended that schools should embrace the opportunities offered by diversity, which can enable children to value the extension of their own experience which can be developed. Preconceptions based upon stereotypes are highlighted and reference is made to the inappropriateness of notions of "national forms of dance" given that we live in a multicultural society. The Working Group (DES, 1991a) concluded that the development of equitable practice,

> will entail in both initial and in-service training of teachers, the critical review of prevailing practice, rigorous and continuous appraisal and often the willingness to face up to long held beliefs and prejudices.
> (DES, 1991b, p.18)

The fact that curriculum content can clearly be seen as problematic is important. There is a great deal of evidence that physical education is seen positively by some children and negatively by others and that its content and teaching methodology tends to reinforce certain social values which some would wish to question. For example, as TINNING (1991) points out, the message often given is that one can only succeed in a competitive environment if there is a loser, that girls are inferior to boys in matters physical, that the slim mesomorph is the only acceptable body shape and so on. WILLIAMS and WOODHOUSE (1996) highlight differences in the popularity of specific national curriculum physical activity areas between boys and girls. The issues are problematic. Some have addressed them and changed their practice as a result. Some have addressed them and have chosen to retain the status quo. Others have not addressed them at all. It is this latter group to whom our attention should turn and, in the context of teacher education, I would argue that a priority should be to ensure that all newly qualified teachers have seen such issues as problematic, and that, if they choose to support, for example, a competitive orthodoxy, then it should be a conscious decision and not one taken by default.

It might be argued that the present structure of teacher training in physical education, as in other subject areas, militates against the development of the reflective teacher. All programmes in England today involve an extended period spent in a school in a form of apprenticeship. SCHEMP (1987) suggests that these periods inform the student teacher of the tasks of teaching, influence the way in which the student determines the quality of teaching and helps to shape the student's approach towards professional work. He sees the views thus formed as necessarily personal and individualistic, thereby militating against collective and reflective change in current practices of physical education teachers. The logical conclusion from this seems to be that the more the student is immersed into the culture of the school, with its own bureaucracies and traditions, and the less the opportunity to stand back and reflect upon that experience, the less likely is the development of a teacher capable of using a range of reflective strategies. It may be argued that this is precisely what is desired by those behind the most recent changes in secondary teacher training (DFE, 1992).

Thus far, the discussion has focused mainly upon how far there might be a future for reflective practice. In suggesting that there should be, even within some of the limitations outlined, I would wish to argue that the second question raised at the outset will have a crucial influence upon the extent to which attempts to develop different kinds of reflective practice are successful. That is, the nurturing of reflective practice which involves issues of equity and justice as well as technical effectiveness, will require an understanding of how beginning teachers learn, especially in the context of increasingly school-based initial teacher education.

Several writers offer some insights into this process, specifically in the context of the student teacher placed in the school. CALDERHEAD (1987) characterises phases in the process of learning to teach as "fitting in", "passing the test" and "exploring". FURLONG and MAYNARD (1995) also identify developmental stages which they describe as "early idealism", "personal survival", "dealing with difficulties", "hitting a plateau" and "moving on". They go on to make the point that, while stages of student learning can be identified, this does not necessarily lead them to think about different things at different phases of practice. Rather, as GUILLAUME and RUDNEY (1993) have noted, students have a number of concerns which they continue to hold simultaneously and they will think about the same things but think about them in different ways. CALDERHEAD's and FURLONG and MAYNARD's analyses suggest that the early stages of learning to teach are likely to involve a preoccupation with technical effectiveness in that, until the student is beyond the "pass the test" or "survival" stage, they are likely to be preoccupied with professional effectiveness rather than with other aspects of reflection. HATTON and SMITH (1994) echo this when they suggest that the student's early preoccupation with survival in the classroom will limit the scope for reflection and that this should be acknowledged and accommodated in expectations of critical thinking during the early days of the student's development as a teacher. MCINTYRE (1993) puts forward a number of arguments for reflection as a central means of learning for experienced teachers rather than for students. Importantly, he draws attention to the need for student teachers to learn to reflect, rather than to use reflection as a significant means of learning, that is, to acquire the ability to reflect as a tool to be used in their future professional development.

Summary

There is plenty of evidence, albeit not much in empirical form, that the promotion of reflection as a utilitarian activity which takes a behavioural approach to the development of teaching competence has had a place in the initial training of physical education teachers for some time. There is less evidence of reflection as a form of critical pedagogy which works within a social justice paradigm. Much of initial teacher education in physical education remains concerned with initiation into a particular culture in which a performance based pedagogy, underpinned by scientific knowledge and reinforced by personal experience dominates thought and action. While the changes brought about by the introduction of the National Curriculum, as well as developments in initial teacher education, do not seem likely to encourage the extension of reflection beyond its use in supporting rather than challenging the status quo, they do not rule out such developments. What is clear is that assumptions that those who promote reflective practice speak with one voice and work within a common framework with shared understandings, should be challenged.

It is equally clear that the timing of work upon the development of reflective practice in relation to the individual's development as a teacher is crucial. The importance of avoiding seeing the approaches to reflection outlined here as some sort of increasingly desirable hierarchy is noted by HATTON and SMITH (1994) who draw attention to the view espoused by several writers, that technical reflection is an essential aspect of initial student teacher development and is a precursor to other kinds of reflection. This does not exempt physical education teacher education from the need to consider questions of equity and justice or others which fall within the remit of critical reflection. It does suggest that the phases of student teacher development combined with the likely science-based background of physical education make the timing of the introduction of other aspects of reflection critical.

References

ADLER, S. (1991) The reflective practitioner in the curriculum of teacher education. *Journal of Education for Teaching*, 17, 2, 139-150.

BAIN, L. (1992) Research in sport pedagogy: past, present and future. In T. WILLIAMS, L. ALMOND, and A. SPARKES, (Eds) *Sport and Physical Activity: Moving Towards Excellence,* London, E & F.N. Spon.

BARRETT, E., BARTON, L., FURLONG, J., MILES, S. and WHITTY, G. (1992) *Initial teacher education in England and Wales: a topography.* London, Goldsmiths College.

BUTTERWORTH, M. (1989) Student reactions to videotape feedback on teaching performance. *Bulletin of Physical Education*, 25, 3, 37-41.

CALDERHEAD, J. (1987) The Quality of Reflection in Student Teachers' Professional Learning. *European Journal of Teacher Education*, 10, 3, 269-278.

CRUIKCHANK, D.R. (1985) Uses and benefits of reflective teaching. *Phi Delta Kappa,* 66, 10, 704-706.

DES (1991a) *Physical Education in the National Curriculum.* London, DES.

DES (1991b) *National Curriculum Physical Education Working Group: Interim Report.* London, DES.

DFE (1992) *Initial Teacher Training (Secondary Phase)*(Circular 9/92). London, DFE.

EVANS, J. (1992) Reflective Pedagogy and reflective teaching. In T. WILLIAMS, L. ALMOND and A. SPARKES (Eds) *Sport and Physical Activity: Moving Towards Excellence.* London, E. & F.N. Spon.

FURLONG, J. and MAYNARD, T. (1995) *Mentoring Student Teachers.* London, Routledge.

GUILLAUME, A. and RUDNEY, G. (1993) Student Teachers' Growth Towards Independence: an analysis of their changing concerns. *Teaching and Teacher Education,* 9,1, 65-80.

HATTON, N. and SMITH, D. (1994) Reflection in Teacher Education: towards definition and implementation. *Teaching and Teacher Education,* 11, 1, 33-51.

LISTON, D. and ZEICHNER, K. (1990) Reflective teaching and action research in preservice teacher education. *Journal of Education for Teaching,* 16, 3, 235-254.

MACDONALD, D. and TINNING, R. (1995) Physical Education Teacher Education and the Trend to Proletarianisation: a Case Study. *Journal of Teaching in Physical Education,* 15, 98-118.

MCINTYRE, D. (1993) Theory, theorising and reflection in initial teacher education. In J. CALDERHEAD and P. GATES (Eds) *Conceptualising reflection in teacher development.* Brighton, Falmer Press.

MOSSTON, M. and ASHWORTH, S. (1986) *Teaching Physical Education.* Merrill.

SCHEMP, P. (1987) Research on teaching in physical education: beyond the limits of natural science. *Journal of Teaching in Physical Education,* 6, 111-121.

SCHON, D. (1988) Coaching reflective practice. In P. GRIMMITT and G. ERICKSON (Eds) *Reflection in Teacher Education.* New York, Teachers College.

SIEDENTOP, D. (1980) Physical Education Curriculum: an analysis of the past. *Journal of Physical Education and Research,* 48, 7, 40-41.

SIEDENTOP, D. (1982) *Developing teaching skills in physical education* (2nd edition). Palo Alto, Mayfield.

TEMPLIN, T. and SCHEMP, P. (1989) *Socialisation into physical education: learning to teach.* Indianapolis, Benchmark Press.

TINNING, R. (1991) Teacher education pedagogy: Dominant discourses in theprocess of problem-solving. *Journal of Teaching in Physical Education*, 11, 1, 1-20.

TOM, A. (1984) *Teaching as a moral craft.* New York, Longmans.

UNDERWOOD, G. (1988) *Teaching and learning in physical education: a social psychological perspective.* Brighton, Falmer Press.

UNDERWOOD, M. and WILLIAMS, E.A. (1991) Personal and Social Education Through Gymnastics. *British Journal of Physical Education,* 22, 3, 15-19.

VALLI, L. (1992) *Reflective teacher education: cases and critiques.* Albany, State University of New York Press.

VAN MANEN, M. (1977) Linking ways of knowing with ways of being practical. *Curriculum Inquiry*, 6, 205-228.

WHITING, C., WHITTY, G., FURLONG, J., MILES, S. and BARTON, L. (1996) *Partnership in Initial Teacher Education: a topography.* London, Institute of Education.

WILDMAN, T. and NILES, J. (1987) Reflective teachers: tensions between abstractions and realties. *Journal of Teacher Education*, 38, 4, 25-31.

WILLIAMS, E.A. and WOODHOUSE, J. (1996) Delivering the discourse. *Sport Education and Society,* 1, 2, 201-214.

ZEICHNER, K. and LISTON, D. (1987) Teaching student teachers to reflect. *Harvard Education Review,* 57, 1, 23-28.

Chapter 11

Halting Progress?
The Conservative Project
for Teacher Education

John Evans

In recent years Conservative central Government in the UK has attempted to reconstruct both the nature and the meaning of teaching (including the work of physical education (PE) teachers; see PENNEY and EVANS, chapter 4) in state schools in England and Wales. Its education policy legislation on Initial Teacher Education (ITE) has been central to this process. This discussion centres on some of the more influential policy texts, e.g. the *Proposals for The Reform of Teacher Education* (DFE, 1993a) and the more recent *Framework for the Assessment of Quality Standards in Initial Teacher Training* (OFSTED/TTA, 1996) that have both defined and continue to shape practice in ITE and schools. It goes on to consider whether they have also helped nurture, or hinder, progress towards forms of practice in ITE and schools that are innovative and progressive, capable of promoting both quality teaching and forms of practice that enable teachers and pupils to act reflectively, independently and creatively in the lives that they lead.

Conservative Government legislation on ITE has ensured that much of the work of initial teacher education in England and Wales now takes place in schools rather than in Institutes of Higher Education (IHE) (see PIOTROWSKI and CAPEL, 1996). The reasons why central government has shifted responsibilities for training away from IHEs to schools have been discussed in some detail elsewhere (for example, see HUSBANDS, 1996) and will be addressed briefly later in this chapter. The effect on pupils and teachers of placing around 24,000 trainee teachers in schools for the majority of their time throughout the school year have yet to be seriously evaluated. However, with GILROY (1992) we can ask, will it raise standards of teaching, or damage them? Will it enhance or devalue the professionalism of teachers? Will it mean that the best teachers are taken away from their classes to mentor students? Will parents be happy with this situation? Will the best teachers make the best trainers? Critically, will teachers have the time to take a leading role in planning courses? Teachers in England and Wales have had to face the massive task of implementing a large number of education reforms in recent years, and PE teachers are no exception to this rule. This has produced what some have termed "innovation overload" (GILROY, 1992, p.14); teachers struggling to deal effectively with an array of demands, unable to master effectively one set of initiatives before having to deal with the arrival of another. This begs the question, what kind of 'training' will student teachers receive if it is delivered in contexts such as this? Will teachers be in a position to teach student teachers the content of a subject, as well as how it should be taught? What kind of teacher will a school-based or school-centred (see later discussion) ITE produce?

The Changing Workplace of Physical Education

Before the detail of recent Conservative Government legislation on teacher *education* (significantly redefined in Government discourse as initial teacher *training* (ITT); a symbolic shift made concrete in the dissolution of the Council for the Accreditation of Teacher *Education* (CATE) and the creation in 1994/5 of the Teacher *Training* Agency (see PIOTROWSKI and CAPEL, 1996, p.194)) is considered, it may be useful to remind ourselves of the harsher realities currently being experienced by some PE teachers in state schools. This extract is taken from field notes[1] reporting a visit to a smallish secondary school in the South of England:

> Thursday March 1993. I arrive at Updown School at 10.30 to meet the Head of PE at 10.45. It is a pleasant school, small, 600 pupils, coeducational, set in a rural setting, probably built in the 1950s/60s, all glass and concrete, well resourced with its own outdoor swimming pool and playing fields. The foyer is light, colourful,

carefully decorated with children's work, designed to make instant good impressions on prospective 'clients'. I sit waiting for the Head of PE, watching children playing badminton in the gymnasium, Mr D in Charge. 10.30 the school bell rings. I am greeted by Mr D and taken to the staffroom. We sink into armchairs (which have seen better days). I make my introductions and say a little about the research. Mr D seems very agitated, at first, I think, by my presence and the research interests.

I do my best to reassure him. But still he seems edgy and concerned more than anything to tell me of the pressures that he and his department feel. He outlines the paperwork demands that his department has had to meet to revise their programmes of study in respect of the NCPE and he stresses the difficulties of finding the time to do this. With only two full time members of staff he has not been able to share the load of revising (re-writing) the curriculum to meet NC demands. He stresses that in a larger school the load would/could be distributed amongst more PE staff. Clearly he is stressed. My blood pressure is rising with his. I suggest that we drop the interview and go for a stroll, perhaps to see his pupils at work. He leads me through the hall to the Gymnasium, I assume to watch the ongoing PE lesson. But we do not stop in the Gymnasium. Instead we enter the storeroom and there, excitedly, proudly, he shows me his filing cabinets, pulling out the shelves, each overflowing with the product of his and his colleagues efforts. At last he seems contented. 'Here', he seems to be saying, 'here', (not out there in the Gym) 'here in these cabinets is the NCPE. Here is the evidence of what my Department has achieved'.

Although this, perhaps, is an extreme example, it does highlight some of the more worrying characteristics of curriculum provision in PE post the 1988 *Education Reform Act* (ERA) (see PENNEY and EVANS, chapter 4). The extract points to the administrative pressures and bureaucratic tendencies that have emerged in teaching in recent years, presaged by the curriculum and assessment requirements of the National Curriculum PE (NCPE) and the accompanying 'threat' of inspection. Teachers in contexts such as these may hardly be in a position to give student teachers the support that they need, while meeting the demands of managing large groups of children, teaching the NCPE and endeavouring to become effective teacher 'trainers'.

So what kind of teacher education will go on in the turbulent environments created by ERA legislation and National Curriculum and assessment demands? What kind of curriculum will teachers turned 'trainers' be able to provide? What knowledge, skills, aptitudes will children and young people derive from their experience of PE? What kind of citizen will teachers cultivate and produce? Will Government legislation help produce *professionals* able to focus on the quality of their teaching and the responsibilities of the teacher, or individuals able to deal only with norms, benchmarks, average performance and normative data? Will it produce teachers able to concentrate on the uniqueness and diversity of individuals and the complexities of the learning process, or those only concerned with the subject rather than the young person or child? (LAWTON, 1989).

The stance I take in this analysis is that now more than ever we need well trained, highly skilled *professionals*, able to deliver what Denis LAWTON calls a "reconstructionist curriculum": a curriculum that, in the context of PE, lays as much stress upon physical development as it does upon social values, that provides experiences appropriate for developing citizenship and social co-operation (in sport, leisure and health, as in other walks of life); a curriculum in which knowledge for its own sake is not ignored, but is questioned, and in which knowledge is justified in terms of social needs, not in terms of custom, tradition, nor cultural heritage *per se* (LAWTON, 1989). This, as LAWTON emphasises, is not to imply that there is no value in other models but that, "given a democratic society which values certain kinds of freedom, a version of social reconstruction is the most appropriate planning model" (1993, pp.47-48). Unfortunately this is not, I suggest, the kind of curriculum that Conservative Government policy on ITE is pressing us to achieve.

Reconstructing Teacher Education

There is nothing new in a central Government in the UK endeavouring to exercise some measure of control over teacher education. As others have pointed out, from its origins in the mid-nineteenth century teacher education has been subject to state prescription and regulation. These prescriptions and regulations have been 'motivated' in a number of ways,

> Politically: recurring moral crises concerning the behaviour and values of urban youth and the social authority of the state have focused upon the deficiencies of 'the teacher' and the need for 'better' or different forms of preparation. Demographically: the changes in the size of the school population has produced a helter skelter of scaling-ups and scaling-downs of the number of teachers in training. Despite (or perhaps because of) this knee jerk approach to planning there have been very few periods when the numbers of teachers in training have matched the needs of the school system. Shortages or surplus have been more or less the norm. Concomitantly the number of institutions and departments of teacher education has increased and decreased. Economically: as with many other areas of public spending teacher education is subject to the vicissitudes of economic policy and financial crises. Ideologically: during the 1980's the Thatcherite/ Hayekian critique of state professionals as an inefficient, self serving clique, determined to maintain restricted access, restrictive practices and resist innovations was aimed at teachers (as it was at health service workers, civil servants and local government). In policy terms this critique had two major outcomes for teachers. One, the introduction of market forces into education, to 'brake producer capture'. The other, the deregulation of employment and training (which I return to below).
> (MAGUIRE and BALL, 1993, pp.1-2)

Clearly, in this view, *politics* and *ideology* as well as *economic concerns* (essentially the need to cut public spending drastically) are the main nodal points of contemporary teacher education policy. In this respect it is both necessary and productive to view Government reforms of teacher education in the UK not as isolated policy events, but as tied into a broader package of legislative measures on education which together represent an attempt at radical and thorough-going reform of the whole education system in England and Wales. Re-defining the meaning of teacher education is fundamental point of *struggle* in this process, as are moves towards greater centralisation over the curriculum of teacher education (in the mid 1980s the creation of CATE – a Council for the Accreditation of Teacher Education), combined with various attempts to 'open up' and deregulate routes into teaching (in the late 1980s the Licensed and Articled Teachers schemes, and the "Mums Army", (DFE, 1993a)) which are in turn related to the process of de-professionalising teacher education in the early 1990s (see MAGUIRE and BALL, 1993). How are physical educationalists to position *themselves* in this struggle to define teacher education, if they have quality teaching, professional development and democracy uppermost in their minds?

In many respects our personal politics, and our vision of the kind of society that we want to achieve and sustain, are going to determine how we answer that question. This in turn will influence how we think teacher education should be structured and concomitantly how much it would cost to provide. It is worth bearing in mind that even if we are critical of Government policy on ITE we can, and should, neither romanticize past practices in ITE nor idealise the alternatives that we might proffer. Certainly this is not the time to substitute one form of ideologically driven dogmatism with another, or for posturing and empty gesture. That will get us nowhere. We need careful and considered appraisal of the forms of ITE needed to sustain a democracy and quality PE. This must mean that questions about the *structure* of teacher education have to be placed alongside those concerning its *content*. Only once we are clear about *what* our student teachers need to know in order to teach PE effectively in, and for, a modern democracy can we consider the structures that should be put in place to ensure that such a curriculum is achieved. Any discussion of this kind is going to be contentious. All of us, teachers, teacher educators, educational administrators, politicians, "operate with some kind of 'social theory' in the sense of assumptions, values and ideas about a good society" (LAWTON, 1989). This means that just about every statement that we make about education is value laden, connected to ideas about the purpose of education, probably connected with more general values and beliefs, and maybe about the purpose of life. These beliefs may lack coherence and even be contradictory, but that rarely stops us expressing them passionately. Many individuals enter teaching because they believe that schools and teachers can have a positive impact on children and society.

For this reason education is inevitably a contested domain, a site of struggle to define what the individual and society ought to be. Not everyone, however, has the authority or the 'power' to ensure that their particular vision is embedded in the structure of teacher education or the PE curriculum in schools (see PENNEY and EVANS, chapter 4 and EVANS and PENNEY, chapter 3). Indeed the traditional policy process of open debate, consultation, and the hammering out of some degree of consensus has in recent years given way to a different regime (MAGUIRE and BALL, 1993). Central Government has allowed very little space for the voices of those whom it considers not to share its views, even if such individuals do have something valuable to say. Nowhere has this been more evident than in the making of the NCPE (see EVANS and PENNEY, 1995, and chapter 3) As WRAGG (TES, October 22nd, 1993) pointed out,

> the Government has been in power so long, some of its members think they can fly. Patten (in 1993 the Secretary of State for Education) calls parents' representatives 'Neanderthal' for their views, teachers 'Luddites', and Tim Brighouse a 'madman', but he remains fireproof. Nothing he says or does threatens his position, no matter how contemptuous he is of people trying to do their job.
> (p.48)

WRAGG, never one for mincing his polemic, properly points out that this is the chilling political climate in which we live and we do need to consider its consequences for democracy and the profession we serve. The merits of Government legislation on ITE, thus have to be appraised very carefully. In particular we have to explore where, ideologically, politically and culturally, its policies for ITE come from and what purposes and whose interests they serve (APPLE, 1996). We can then relate these interests to more general ideologies, particularly the larger programme of conservative restoration (see EVANS and PENNEY, 1995; PENNEY and EVANS, chapter 4; and APPLE, 1996) and to patterns of domination and exploitation in wider society, in order to make clear what the practical, pedagogical and political choices are before us.

You Are Not Paranoid. Someone Really Is Out To Get You

Let us take a step back for a moment and consider how we arrived at where we are now in terms of policy prescriptions for teacher education in England and Wales. The detail of this story had been provided elsewhere (MAGUIRE and BALL, 1993; PIOTROWSKI and CAPEL, 1996; HUSBANDS, 1996). Certainly GILROY (1992) is on the mark when he states that it is difficult to communicate to those who have not been directly involved in teacher training in England and Wales the quite spectacular changes that have beset those institutions involved with initial teacher education over the last decade.

A series of steps (for example, in 1983 *The Content of Initial Teacher Training*, followed by the White Paper on *Teaching Quality*, then Circular 3/84, the Green Paper 1988 advocating the *Licensed and Articled Teacher Schemes*; see GILROY, 1993) effectively began a process of reconstructing ITE, defining course content and concomitantly the conception of what it is to be a teacher educator. These changes seemed to reach a peak in 1992 when Kenneth CLARKE, then Secretary of State for Education, stated in a speech to the annual North of England Education Conference on the 4th January that he proposed that the vast majority of initial teacher education would, within nine months, begin to be located in schools and away from colleges, polytechnics and universities. These proposals were subsequently developed into a *Consultation Document* issued on 28th January. As GILROY pointed out, the proposals contained in that document represented a dramatic and abrupt reversal of the direction taken by developments in the policy for teacher education over the last 100 years. It had, he reminds us, taken teacher education 150 years to develop from a rejection of a school-based pupil-teacher apprenticeship scheme to one whereby students were inducted into the profession of teaching through structured combination of training and education in both school classrooms and institutions of higher education (GILROY, 1992). A situation has been achieved in which virtually all new entrants to the teaching profession were graduates who had experienced professional training in education. So why then was central Government apparently bent on turning the clock back to a state of affairs which educationalists and politicians from across the political spectrum, for so many years, had fought to remove?

MACLURE (1993) the former editor of the TES reminds us that the thing to remember about Government plans for teacher training is that there is a plot and a sub-plot. The plot, he says, is straightforward. Get more ITE into schools. Give practising teachers a bigger part to play in the professional preparation of their future colleagues. There are many reasons why this could be good news. Certainly, there are many teachers who would testify to the merits and benefits of developing closer relationships, a genuine 'partnership' with teachers in schools as part of the enterprise of developing a quality ITE. However, as MACLURE pointed out, the sub-plot is more sinister. It is to take teacher training out of higher education and ultimately to sever the connections between the study of education in higher education and its practice in school. I share MACLURE's view that this is a deeply damaging idea. PATTEN's *Proposals* (DFE, 1993a) were a further advance on CLARKE's proposals, recommending not just a "school-based" teacher education but a "school-centred training", a form of practice in which relationships between schools and higher education are not just further weakened but potentially dismantled.

However, I am leaping ahead of myself. I will return to the *Proposals* and more recent legislation (OFSTED/TTA, 1996) for teacher training later. Before that, it is important to note that alongside and complementary to the emerging proposal for new routes into teaching of the 1980s and 1990s were the well publicised attacks on teacher education articulated by a number of right-wing 'think tanks', the Centre for Policy Studies and the Hillgate Group in particular (see MAGUIRE and BALL, 1993). These unrepresentative, unelected cabals had a powerful impact on Government policy on education, with views such as these:

> Teachers with Cert. Ed. after their names have studied nonsense for three years. Those with BEd for three or four years. Those with PGCE have had a rest for one year studying nonsense after doing a proper subject and those with MEd or Adv. Dip. Ed. have returned for super nonsense.
>
> (ANDERSEN, 1982, p.11)

To these individuals teacher education is just a waste of time. Teachers are over trained and badly trained. It can seem incredible that such views were neither contested nor refined by those given political authority and responsibility for the welfare of teachers and the education system as a whole. Take this view for example,

> Barmy theory had led teachers into dangerous paths of
> pedagogical untruth. As is well known, teachers do not
> need training, they just need to be able to walk into a
> school and read the instructions delivered from the
> centre. It may help to know a 'subject' but having any
> ideas about how children learn, or develop, or feel,
> should be seen as subversive activity. Teacher educators
> who have peddled their subversions should be hunted
> down and hanged by the entrails of the last educational
> sociologists.
>
> (quoted in STONES, 1992, p.111)

This is no marginal, insignificant, right-wing extremist speaking, this
is Kenneth CLARKE (in 1992) the Secretary of State for Education
delivering this message in a speech to teacher educators with the rubric
Check on Delivery in January, 1992. As GILROY (1992) pointed out,
the rubric said it all. In this view, teaching is delivery of a commodity,
a process which does not need theory or professionals of any standing.
It needs effective managers, educational technicians. In this discourse
of derision, theoretically informed professional teachers and teacher
educators are defined as either mad or bad. Given statements of intent
such as this, teacher educators have every right to be worried for their
professional well being. BRIGHOUSE is right, to be paranoid does not
preclude the possibility that someone is out to get you. Physical
educationalists do need to look over their shoulders given 'leadership'
of this kind.

As GILROY pointed out, virtually all the shibboleths of the cabal who
had CLARKE's ear could be identified in that January speech.
Teachers were to play a much larger part in ITE with schools "being
handed the responsibility to train our PGCE students in their
classroom" (CLARKE, 1992, p.10). He proposed, amongst other
things, "breaking the hold of the dogmas about teaching methods and
classroom organisation" (p.7) which higher education perpetuated.
Unsurprisingly, the speech received major coverage in the press, most
of it favourable to CLARKE in his attack on higher education's
perpetuation of "'trendy' teaching methods" (Sunday Express, 5th
January, 1992). The material of CLARKE's speech was then represented in a *Consultation Document* (DES, 1992a). The whole

process of teacher training was to "be based on a more equal partnership between school teachers and tutors ... with the schools themselves playing a much bigger part" (DES, 1992a, p.7). The 'partnership' was defined as "one in which the schools and its teachers are in the lead in the whole of the training process, from the initial design of a course through to the assessment of the performance of the individual student" (DES, 1992a, p.8). Eighty percent (later reduced to 60%, following widespread criticism from the educational establishment) of the secondary PGCE was to be school based (four days a week). Resources for teacher training were to move from higher education to schools identified by certain criteria (academic results, staying on rates, truancy figures and so on) and would include private schools. These changes were to be implemented with effect from September 1992 with all secondary PGCE courses meeting their requirements by September 1994. The length of the BEd/BA was to be reduced and these courses subjected to the 80% ruling for the school based elements of their work. The profession had until 31st March 1992 to consider the proposals (See GILROY, 1992, p.7).

John PATTEN's *Proposals for the Reform of Initial Teacher Training* (DFE, 1993a) continued the job begun by Kenneth CLARKE in 1992, but the pace of change increased, the pressure intensified and the stakes got even higher (MAGUIRE and BALL, 1993). PATTEN's *Proposals* (including the proposals for changes in the criteria for Primary Teacher Training published in June 1993) marked another stage in the re-definition and reconstruction of the work of teacher educators and the professional standing of teachers. Again we have to look beneath the surface rhetorical justification of these proposals to see what ends they were intended to serve. At a glance the proposals reflected,

• a concern to raise educational standards and levels of skill, and to equip people to cope with change;

• a growing emphasis on the competencies necessary for effective practice;

• the importance of training being closely linked to its practical application;

• the need for continuing training and development through

working life; and,

•   increasing the effectiveness of expenditure on training (DFE,
        1993a).

All the old motives, political, demographic, economic and ideological
are hidden in these claims and few, I guess, would disagree with them
as statements of intent. The claim is that 'higher standards' will be
achieved through reforms which ensure that "teachers have the key
classroom skills to maintain discipline, introduce pupils to the National
Curriculum, and use testing and assessment to improve their own
teaching, as well as keep pupils and their parents informed about
progress" (DFE, 1993, p.1). They again imply a transfer of power from
higher education to schools and a transferred location for much of the
learning involved in ITE. But what model of the student is implicit in
this locational shift? (MCCULLOCH, 1993). What assumptions are
being made about the nature of knowledge and 'competence' and what
is to be learned in the course of becoming a professional teacher of PE?

It is worth noting what support there was 'in the market' for these
changes. In fact there was very little evidence to suggest that either the
'consumers' (parents) or the 'producers' (teachers and teacher
educators) of education wanted these reforms. However, such was the
government's commitment to these policies that it was announced that
in October 1994 a Teacher Training Agency was to be established to
'encourage' the development of school centred ITT (SCITT), with a
statutory responsibility not only for the central funding of all courses
of initial teaching training in England but also for research.

The Secretary of State also announced that "he would take advice from
those best placed to give it, including the new Agency, *as and when he
sees the need to revise course criteria,* rather than maintaining a
standing body (CATE) to advise him on such matters" (DFE, 1993a,
p2; emphasis added). Thus the Teacher Training Agency would run all
teacher education under regulations made by the Secretary of State.
The press referred to this as a quango, but as NEWSAM pointed out
(TES, September 17th, 1993) there was going to be nothing quasi or
autonomous about it. Given its terms of reference the agency was
likely to consist of friends of the Minister: "It is a FOM and should be
known as such". It would, as NEWSAM goes on to argue, be required
to assume in advance, in the face of HMI advice on previous schemes,

that a wholly school-based system of initial teacher education, which had yet to start, would prove successful and that less time could be spent on the initial teacher training of teachers. No educational justification was thought necessary. Neither 'fact' nor reason, it seems, was to stand in the way of central Government's ideologically driven judgements.

The *Proposals* signalled an alarming increase in the control of teacher education, teaching in schools and professions which need protection against political manipulation. As EDWARDS (1993) pointed out, teacher education was to have imposed upon it a specialised funding body not thought necessary for any other profession which has a strong base in higher education. He warned that its remit would, in time, extend to undergraduate degrees in education, thereby placing the academic as well as the vocational under political control. It also covered higher degrees in education, an extension, in EDWARDS' (1993) view, deeply threatening to academic freedom. Further, it embraced educational research in teacher education, thereby threatening to take over functions that would remain the preserve of the Higher Education Funding Council if the education of teachers was an integral part of the higher education system with the defence of freedom of thought and enquiry which it should provide (EDWARDS, 1993).

Again we need to read these *Proposals* (DFE, 1993a) and all subsequent policy texts (OFSTED/TTA, 1996) in context. Like earlier attempts to discipline teacher education (e.g. *Circular 9/92*) the Proposals sought to amplify and extend specific elements of the conservative project. They tightened up "the regimes of control in and around teacher education and furthermore attempted to shut down any gaps or spaces for accommodations or subversions" (MAGUIRE and BALL, 1993, p.11). It is, therefore, not surprising that these *Proposals* met with stern resistance from many quarters. Indeed it is unusual to find consensus amongst educationalists on educational matters, yet this is exactly what the *Proposals* achieved. It was difficult to find a good word for the recommendations in the educational literature.

For example, in a scathing attack on the Blue Paper proposals the TES (not noted for its radical positioning) commented that "even by the standards to which we have unhappily grown accustomed lately, the Government's *Proposals for the Reform of Teacher Training* is a singularly dishonest document". It goes on, "The need, we are told 'to raise the professional skill of new teachers has been pointed up (sic) by recent evidence from the Office of Standards in Education (OFSTED) that around a (sic) third of lessons taken by new entrants were unsatisfactory". The TES pointed out that Her Majesty's Inspectorate (HMI) 'pointed up' no such thing. The opening words of HMI's own summary (*The New Teacher in School*) are: "In 1992, over 90 per cent of headteachers considered their new teachers to have been adequately prepared for their first teaching post and over 70 per cent of lessons taught by new teachers were considered by HMI as satisfactory or better". In the body of their report HMI say that this proportion closely matches that of teachers in general, "For any training system to match the attainments of an established profession is an indication of its competence not the reverse" (TES, September 17th, 1993). The proposals for a new one year course "for mature students, with accreditable experience of working with children, who wish to specialise in teaching nursery and infant pupils up to the end of key stage 1" (ages 5-7) (DFE, 1993a, p.5), termed a "Mums Army" in the outcry that accompanied this proposal, were received with similar levels of derision and dismay.

Indeed, so extreme and potentially deleterious to educational standards in the primary sector were the recommendations of this proposal, some commentators surmised that it may not have been a serious proposal at all, but merely a quasi-policy created to obfuscate the shortcomings of the other initiatives which are to be thrust on teacher education and teachers in schools. Whatever its status the idea seemed a monstrously retrograde proposal. It confused experience with understanding, child rearing with education, teaching technique with pedagogy and worst of all it assumed that the younger the child the cheaper and easier he or she is to teach. The reverse is true. This recommendation if implemented would have thrown away all that was won by the pioneers of early education (MACLURE, 1992). The *Proposals* also offered the prospect of a new style restricted 'QTS' for Nursery and Infants, in MACLURE's view, the thin end of a thick wedge to separate primary from secondary training, and to introduce a three year BEd including a six subject BEd to prepare teachers for work across the primary curriculum. Although in November 1993 the Government stepped back from the widely disliked proposal for a "Mums Army" when Baroness BLACK announced that the proposal would be dropped, she instead announced a new qualification for primary school classroom assistants – specialist teacher assistants (STAs) to strengthen the teaching of reading and arithmetic. All of the other controversial measures in the *Proposals* remained in place, and have since been consolidated in further legislation (DFE, 1993; DFE, 1994) and policy texts (OFSTED/TTA, 1996) and are beginning to find expression in programme of ITE.

What will all this mean for PE and the quality of what is taught? Will student teachers, in the time available, be taught what to teach, but not what they need to know to be able to teach? Will it lead to the preparation of teachers sophisticated in their understanding of children and young people, knowledgeable of the relationships between their physical, social and cultural development, able to innovate as well as manage and sustain order and control? I think not. Certainly the available evidence on current practice in ITE is beginning to give the PE profession serious cause for concern (see PIOTROWSKI and CAPEL, 1996).

The 'Knowledge Base' of Physical Education

Let us look briefly, but carefully, at the conception of knowledge implicit in Government legislation on ITE. Government circulars (DES, 1992b; DFE, 1993b; OFSTED/TTA, 1996) require higher education institutions, schools and students to focus on the competencies of teaching if they are to satisfy the criteria for accreditation (PIOTROWSKI and CAPEL, 1996). For example, the *Proposals* (DFE, 1993a) state that courses will be required to,

> equip students with essential 'competencies', including the subject knowledge and professional and personal skills which new teachers need to manage, maintain order and teach effectively in their classrooms. The development of complete profiles of new teachers' competencies will help ease the transition from initial training to induction.
>
> (p.4)

This is a requirement spelled out in greater detail in the recent *Framework* (OFSTED/TTA, 1996). Arguably, no one in their right mind would contest the view that teachers need to be competent. But again we have to be clear about what this term really means. As MCNAMARA (1992) pointed out, it has been a fundamental and dominant assumption within Government education policy on the curriculum in recent years that the 'outcomes' of teacher education courses can be articulated in and as a set of competencies. From CATE, through *Circular 9/92*, to the *Proposals* and the recent *Framework* (OFSTED/TTA, 1996), we have been encouraged to conceptualise teaching as a shopping list of constituent components which relate to composite skills and knowledge, none of which, I guess, would be objectionable to most teacher educators; but would be regarded as a simple minimum rather than an adequate conceptualisation of what it means to be a teacher (MAGUIRE and BALL, 1993). However, as MCNAMARA points out, these competencies are now assumed to be measurable and amenable to expression as profiles which map out students teachers' abilities at the completion of their initial training. In his *Proposals*, for example, the Secretary of State stated:

> all teachers should start their careers with profiles of competencies, which set out their professional capabilities and give a picture of relative strengths and weaknesses. Such developments will help those recruiting newly qualified teachers to plan induction and development programmes, and can form the basis for a permanent record of the teacher's professional development throughout his or her career.
>
> (DFE, 1993a, p.16)

Again we have to see this proposal not simply as an attempt to state the knowledge base of teaching, but as a means of further deregulating entry to the teaching profession. As MCNAMARA (1992) pointed out, the switch of emphasis from the process of teacher training to a focus upon competencies has a number of advantages for policy makers and politicians, but few, for teachers: "First, it provides a means of (superficially) demonstrating to the lay public that teacher training courses are being made 'relevant' to the needs of children and the schools. Second, by shifting the emphasis from course *process* to course *outcomes* it may be possible to persuade some teacher trainers that they have more autonomy and control over the training process, so long as their students manifest the appropriate competencies at the completion of their course" (p.274). MCNAMARA cautions against this because, embedded in this view, is a more fundamental challenge to teacher education. As he goes on to point out, once the emphasis is placed upon 'outcomes' the training process itself is called into question and is 'up for grabs':

> There is no longer any difficulty in reconciling criteria so that they relate to different routes into teaching be they conventional or non-conventional modes of training. In this way the institutional context and form of teacher training ceases to be important, what matters are the competencies students can demonstrate after the completion of a variety of training experiences. Moreover, any form of training becomes problematic; a prospective teacher who has worked in industry, the services, or other walks of life may be presumed to already possess many of the required competencies and, so it may be argued, training may need to offer little more than provide the requisite extra competencies.
>
> (MCNAMARA, 1992, p.273)

This view is not far fetched. It undergirds the *Proposals for Reform* and the more recent *Framework* (OFSTED/TTA, 1996). Prescribing teacher education in terms of competency outcomes not only determines the structure and content of ITE, it also ensures that teacher trainers are no longer free to decide how to train teachers as they judge professionally appropriate. MCNAMARA (1992) reminds us that the *Consultation Document* (DES, 1992a) statements removed reference to gender and multicultural issues, dimensions of teacher education which many teacher educators consider it essential for their courses to address (p.274). However, achieving competence is not the same as being an effective teacher. As MCNAMARA (1992) pointed out, teacher education,

> involves assisting individual students, whatever their particular repertoires of dispositions and aptitudes, to develop the all-round competence which will enable them to teach effectively in the variety of contexts they will encounter during their careers. This requires more than 'instilling in students units of competence, made up of a number of elements of competence (with associated performance criteria). (Employment Department Group, 1989)' (p.283)

Instead it warrants practices informed by knowledge and understanding and an engagement with suitable amounts of appropriate theory (EVANS and PENNEY, 1996).

So again we must consider what the *Proposals* and more recent competency criteria (OFSTED/TTA, 1996) were designed to achieve? Were the de-theorising of teacher education, the privileging of the practical over the critical, and through this the de-skilling of teachers, designed to raise standards in education? (MAGUIRE and BALL, 1993, p.19). Or were they simply designed to break the connection between higher education and the training of teachers, curb the move towards an all graduate profession, undermine the professionalism of teachers and reduce ITE to a functional and instrumental set of concerns "emphasising only what will be professionally useful to teachers?",

> a form of instrumental knowledge which is typically portrayed as neutral and value free, where education is simply a means to given ends and all that is needed is a check list of competencies which need to be achieved.
> (MAGUIRE and BALL, 1993, p.19)

Sadly, other legislation (the National Curriculum in particular), may have helped facilitate this latter process. On the surface the knowledge base for PE and some other subjects, as listed in National Curriculum documentation looks relatively simple. A cursory glance at the silver ring-leaf folders that accommodate the National Curriculum subjects may suggest that teachers can make do with a brisk year or two (three at most) on-the-job training provided they have had some previous experience of children, or involvement in sport. Is this the quality of teacher, teaching and training that we want to see in PE?

Recent policy texts (OFSTED/TTA, 1996) simply consolidate these trends, further erode the professionalism of teachers and exert yet more control over what teacher educators can think and do. DES (1992) and DFE (1993a) Circulars *9/92* and *14/93*, for example, 'merely' defined the Secretary of State's current criteria for ITT, including the broad competencies which intending primary and secondary teachers should have acquired by the end of their training.

The recent *Framework* (OFSTED/TTA, 1996), however, not only set "out in more detail the basis on which judgements about compliance and quality will be made and provides the basis for inspection and audit" (p.6), it establishes that the allocation of funds and student numbers to institutions, are to be "tied to inspection evidence and other quality assessments provided by the HMI, or to other assessments which the agency or the Secretary of State think appropriate". Evidence that an institution does not meet the Secretary of State's criteria for good practice in ITT will, therefore, result in loss of funding, the potential withdrawal of approval to offer courses of ITT, or a lowly, derisory position in the "performance league table" for ITT that is now being proposed (TTA, 1996).

End Comment

Together, then, a variety of Education Acts (1992, 1994) and many accompanying proposals, circulars and frameworks for action in ITT have ensured that the product of ITE, including the competencies of teaching, is now rigidly specified not by teachers or teacher educators but by the government, the DFE/TTA and the various government appointed agencies who inspect for compliance (PIOTROWSKI and CAPEL, 1996). As a result, very little scope remains in ITE for partner teachers and teacher educators to act professionally, that is to say, to take decisions on curriculum matters, to express imagination, spontaneity and idealism, engage in innovation and construct a curriculum for ITT that can be both sensitive to the needs of 'the nation' and the aspirations of pupils, schools and the communities they serve.

Even if we disagree profoundly with some, or all, of the above analyses, we can and should not ignore the questions being asked. If nothing else, following TAYLOR (1993), we must apply at least three principal criteria to recent legislation and policy texts on ITT in order to assess their merits. First, will the types of training proposed attract good candidates to teaching? Second, will they produce better educated and more competent PE teachers? Third, will those teachers have been given a sound basis for continued career-long professional development? In TAYLOR's view they are likely to fail on all counts. Certainly the current massive shortfall in entry to the teaching profession, the disturbing number of assistants that have to be used in place of teachers in primary schools, and the widespread dissatisfaction in the profession (see TES, 17th January, 1996, p.1 and TES, 31st January, 1996, p.3) is some endorsement of his point of view. Funding ITE separately from higher education, introducing one year training for non-graduate Key Stage 2 (primary school) teachers and shortening BEd courses from four to three years (a trend already evident in ITT PE in England) is unlikely to send clear messages to potential recruits about the status and attractiveness of teaching.

TAYLOR (1993) notes that shorter BEd courses may also fail to take account of the modest educational performance of many candidates for such courses and the need for adequate time in which to equip them with the necessary confidence and skills to work in difficult conditions, and provide support during periods of school based study. It also has to be considered that some universities may no longer wish to engage in ITE under the conditions proposed. Yet, both ITE and the programmes of continuing professional education, mainly higher degree work, provided by universities and colleges are invaluable opportunities for teachers to examine, analyse and criticise both their own actions as well as official policies and actions. Of course this may not always be convenient or pleasant for schools, politicans and administrators, but it is a proper aspect of higher education's responsibilities and a safeguard for democracy (EDWARDS, 1993). In the wake of government legislation on ITT, it is work that is becoming increasingly difficult to sustain.

We do not need to make a blanket defence of teacher education in order to suggest that there is something deeply disturbing about Conservative Government prescriptions for the reform of ITE. With the disestablishment of teacher education in this country, the dismantling of the relationship between schools and higher education, and the over emphasis on competencies as the criteria for adjudging success in ITE, opportunities for reflection on the nature of ITE and teaching could virtually disappear. PIOTROWSKI and CAPEL (1996) remind us that "even a report by HMI (1991) warned that 'a competency-based model' could lead to a technician-style trained teacher". They emphasise that,

> If ITT PE is reduced to preparing teachers to become 'artisan deliverers of authorised curriculum' (DEMAINE, 1988), it will be detrimental to the goal of developing a physically educated population. If this goal is to be

achieved, it is important to educate teachers to understand the needs of individual pupils and to be able to respond to them. It is important that teachers are able to respond to and manage change and this requires adaptability based on an informed point of view. Teachers should be able to challenge, analyse and evaluate rather than merely absorb and imitate. (p.195)

I share this view, and support GILROY's (1992) claim that debate and dialectic are essential both for progress in education and the well being of democracy, and that it is, therefore, crucial to proclaim the essentiality of teacher education in the face of "the breathtaking simplism of those who are currently attempting to destroy it" (STONES, 1992, p.111). Whether Labour Government legislation will help teachers imbue young people with the skills, knowledge and predispositions necessary for their social and physical well being, and for the forms of cultural reconstruction that a modern democracy needs, only time will tell. I have my doubts, but it would be a pleasure to be proved wrong.

Notes

1. This extract is drawn from the *Economic and Social Research Council* project R000233629: *'The Impact of the Education Reform Act on the Provision of PE and Sport in Schools'*.

References

ANDERSON, D. (1982) *Defecting Bad Schools: A Guide for Normal Parents.* London, The Social Affairs Unit.

APPLE, M. (1993) *Official Knowledge. Democratic Education in a Conservative Age.* New York, Routledge.

APPLE, M. (1996) *Cultural Politics and Education.* London, Open University Press.

CLARKE, K. (1992) Check against delivery. Speech to the North of England Conference, January 4, Mimeo.

DEMAINE, J. (1988) Teachers's Work, Curriculum and the New Right. *British*

Journal of Social Education, 3, 8, 247-264.

DES (1992a) *The Reform of Initial Teacher Training (Consultation Document 40/92).* London, DES.

DES (1992b) *Circular 9/92: Initial Teacher Training (Secondary Phase).* London, HMSO.

DFE (1993a) *The Government's Proposal for the Reform of Initial Teacher Training.* Cardiff, Welsh Office.

DFE (1993b) *Circular 14/93: The Initial Training of Primary School Teachers: New Criteria for Courses.* London, HMSO.

DFE (1994) *Education Act 1994: Part 1 Teacher Training.* London, HMSO.

EDWARDS, A. (1993) Change for the Worse. *Times Educational Supplement,* October 29, 1993, p. 15.

EVANS, J. and PENNEY, D. (1995) Physical Education, Restoration and the Politics of Sport. *Curriculum Studies,* 3, 2, 183-195.

EVANS, J. and PENNEY, D. (1995) The Politics of Pedagogy: Making a National Curriculum Physical Education. *Journal of Education Policy,* 10, 1, 27-44.

EVANS, J. and PENNEY, D. (1996) The Role of the Teacher in PE: Towards a Pedagogy of Risk. *British Journal of Physical Education,* 27, 4, 28-37.

GILROY, D.P. (1992) The Political Rape of Initial Teacher Education in England and Wales, a JET rebuttal. *Journal of Education for Teaching,* 18, 1, 5-23.

HUSBANDS, C. (1996) Change Management in Initial Teacher education: national Contexts, Local Circumstances and the Dynamics of Change. In MCBRIDE, R. (Ed) *Teacher Education Policy.* London, The Falmer Press, pp.7-22.

JENKINS, S. (1993) It's Yesterday Once More. *The Times,* October 13, 1993, p.20.

LAWTON, D. (1989) *Culture and the Curriculum.* London, Hodder and Stoughton.

MACLURE, S. (1993) Fight this Tooth and Nail. *Times Educational Supplement,*

June 18, 1993, p.16.

MCNAMARA, D. (1992) The Reform of Teacher Education in England and Wales: Teacher Competence; Panacea or Rhetoric? *Journal of Education for Teaching,* 18, 3, 273-285.

MCCULLOCH, M. (1993) Democratisation of Teacher education : new forms of partnership for school based teacher education. In Gilroy, P and SMITH, M. (Eds.) International Analyses of Teacher Education. *Journal of Education Teaching,* 19, 293-85.

MAGUIRE, M. and BALL, S. (1993) Teacher Education and Education Policy in England. Unpublished Paper. King's College, London.

NEWSAM, P. (1993) Pestered with popinjay. *Times Educational Supplement,* September 17, 1993.

OFSTED/TTA (1996) *Framework for the Assessment of Quality and Standards in Initial Teacher Training* 1996/97. London, Ofsted/TTA.

PIOTROWSKI, S. and CAPEL, S. (1996) Recent influences on the Training of Physical Education Teachers in England and Wales. *Sport, Education and Society,* 1, 2, 185-201.

SAYLE, A. (1993) *The Observer Magazine,* October 10, 1993, p.48.

SHILLING, C. (1993) *The Body and Social Theory.* London, Polity Press.

STONES, E. (1992) Mindless Imperatives and the Moral Order. *Journal of Education for Teaching,* 18, 2, 111-113.

TAYLOR, W. (1993) Why Government should think again on Teacher Reform. *Times Higher Educational Supplement,* October 22, 1993, p.16.

TES (1993) A quango too far. *Times Educational Supplement,* October 9, 1993, p.18.

TEACHER TRAINING AGENCY (1996) Performance Tables for Initial teacher training: Consultation Paper. London, TTA.

WRAGG, T. (1993) Hold the Kwality, give us Some Calibre. *Times Educational Supplement,* October 22, 1993, p.48.

PART 6

EQUAL OPPORTUNITIES IN PHYSICAL EDUCATION

Chapter 12

The Body, Schooling and Social Inequalities: Physical Capital and the Politics of Physical Education

Chris Shilling

Introduction

In this chapter I present an analysis of the relationship between education and human embodiment which highlights some of the sociological issues involved in the schooling of students' bodies. I begin by noting the relative absence of the body in the sociology of education, and then use Marcel MAUSS's concept of "body techniques" to identify what is involved in the processes of education. The paper then concentrates on how schools are implicated in the nexus that exists between social inequalities and the development of specific forms of embodiment by drawing on the work of Pierre BOURDIEU to present a view of the body as a form of physical capital.

The Body in Education

In studying the relationship between schooling and social inequalities, the sociology of education has tended to focus on cognitive development, academic certification and social mobility. As a consequence, little attention has been given to the role of physical education (PE) in the formation of social differences. Indeed, the complete neglect of PE in many sociology of education texts is symptomatic of a much wider underestimate of the importance of the corporeal in schooling (SHILLING, 1993a).

This failure to examine fully the education of bodies compounds the mistaken view that schooling is concerned only with the mind, and with one sort of knowledge; the abstract and intellectual. This proposition is found in the writings of both liberals, who tend to equate education with intellectual development, and most reproduction theorists, who see schools functioning to inculcate dominant ideologies in the minds of pupils. Neither of these perspectives, which otherwise share very little in their analyses of the education system, take adequate note of the embodied nature of schooling or the corporeal implications of educational knowledge.

This neglect of the body is rooted most firmly within a Cartesian philosophical tradition which has identified the mind and consciousness as that which defines our species as specifically human. Nevertheless, it still remains difficult to explain this neglect in educational studies. Schooling is a thoroughly embodied activity and teachers are frequently involved in 'civilising' the bodies of pupils (ELIAS, 1978 [1939]). For example, teachers may encourage young children to dress themselves 'properly', to use tissues instead of picking their noses, to ask to go to the toilet in time for accidents to be avoided, to sit still and be quiet during lessons, and to respect daily rituals such as morning prayers and saluting the national flag. Reflecting on these activities, it should be clear that the moving, managed and disciplined body, and not just the speaking and listening body, is central to the daily business of schooling (SHILLING, 1992, 1993b). Indeed, some commentators have gone further than this to suggest that the usefully schooled body is a docile body (KIRK, 1993). More surprising still is the relative lack of attention given to the body by social studies of PE. Instead, the dominant approach towards PE and social inequalities focuses on questions of access. A major issue here is the effect that middle class values in schools, and mechanisms of academic differentiation, can have in polarising student attitudes to, and involvement in, PE (e.g. WHITEHEAD and HENDRY, 1976; HENDRY, 1978). Useful though this work is, it fails to examine how students' relations to their bodies may induce different attitudes towards sports. The access approach to PE also fails to examine how education systems bestow different values on students' bodies. One example of this phenomenon is the general value accorded to the mesomorphic bodily ideal by PE teachers over the fatter endomorphic, or thinner ectomorphic body (HARGREAVES, 1986). Indeed, the only long term appearance made by the body in a PE tradition comes not in social studies concerned with questions of access, but in the technically oriented work of those concerned with the 'body as machine' – focusing on how to maximise athletic performance and detailing regimented training programmes designed to achieve this end (MACKAY, GORE and KIRK, 1990). It is only very recently that social studies of PE have taken up the issues raised by sociologists of the body (for example, see EVANS, 1993 and the special edition of QUEST, 1991).

Techniques of the Body

Despite the relative absence of the body in social studies of education, the sociology of the body has, since the 1980s, become established as a thriving area of inquiry (e.g. TURNER, 1984, 1992; O'NEILL, 1985; FREUND, 1988; FRANK, 1990; SHILLING, 1993b; SCOTT and MORGAN, 1993). Two assumptions, which form the 'common core' of this sociological work, are particularly relevant to the analysis contained within this paper. First, the body is seen as an increasingly socially constructed phenomenon. This involves the recognition that instead of being simply biological, our bodies are affected in all manner of ways (e.g. in their health, shape, appearance) by social environments, social relationships and technical interventions. Second, as well as being socially constructed in important ways, the body has become a symbol of value in contemporary consumer culture. Bodily representations and meanings have increasingly become extracted from religious meaning systems and placed instead in a market order which sends changing messages to individuals about what constitutes a desirable, achievable and symbolically valued body.

In linking these assumptions to our concern with the education of bodies, Marcel MAUSS's long established work on body techniques still provides important insights (MAUSS, 1979). Body techniques refer to the ways in which people learn how to use their bodies. They involve imagination, practice and accomplishment and serve to mould the body in particular ways. Central to the acquisition of body techniques is what MAUSS terms "the facts of education": "What takes place is a prestigious imitation. The child, the adult, imitates actions which have succeeded ... by people in whom he has confidence and who have authority over him" (MAUSS, 1979, pp.101-102).

Body techniques affect the very fundamentals of social and individual life, involve the ways people learn to walk, talk, look and think, and differ historically and cross-culturally. For example, MAUSS (1979) talks of the importing to France of American ways of walking in the early twentieth century and notes that "The positions of the arms and hands while walking form a *social* idiosyncrasy, they are not simply a product of some purely individual ... arrangements and mechanisms" (MAUSS, 1979, p.100; emphasis added). The notion of body techniques, then, allows us to see in some detail precisely how the body is affected by social forces.

Body techniques are centrally implicated in the ways people relate to, and work on, themselves and the world around them. When people learn how to work, in particular ways, on their social and natural environments, they begin to transform not only their world but their own bodies (HONNETH and JOAS, 1988; MARX and ENGELS, 1970). As such, we may speculate that variations in body techniques across societies are likely to lead not only to differences in character and capabilities, but to differences in social customs and institutions. We might add that although a number of body techniques are common to all members of a society, many others are socially differentiated. Ways of talking and walking, for example, frequently differ depending on the gender and social class of individuals. Indeed, the gender differentiated acquisition of body techniques relates to the control of the environment, the domination of other people, and can be seen as an important part of the bodily basis of gender inequalities (CONNELL, 1987; HOCHSCHILD, 1983).

At an individual level, the acquisition of specific sets of body techniques provides people with the opportunities that arise from having a body, and can also serve to remind them of the limitations which follow from being a body (BERGER, 1969). What I mean by this is that learning certain ways of managing the body often precludes proficiency in other skills. Few champion weight lifters, for example, are also first class pianists. Crucially, it is also the case that the acquisition of body techniques are differently valued by societies: competence in certain skills is more prized than others as is the effect practising these skills can have on one's body.

The use of the term "body techniques" allows us to see the significance of teachers in general, and PE teachers in particular, to the education of children's bodies. This is because techniques of the body have to be taught (implicitly or explicitly), practised, justified, and even enforced. They involve the inculcation of approved ways of doing things (but it is important to remember that they represent an inevitably limited selection from the total number of ways in which bodies could be managed and presented). As such, the transmission of body techniques involves the exercise of power and the creation and deployment of resources. The exercise of power is evident, for example, when we see pupils protesting at dress and behaviour codes, and being victimised by each other when their bodies fail to live up to prevalent standards of femininity or masculinity (MCROBBIE, 1978; WILLIS, 1977).

We can examine further the social significance of body techniques by examining and developing Pierre BOURDIEU's view of the body as a form of physical capital. The body is seen here as fundamental to both schooling and to the social class location of different social groups. I focus on social class in this paper but this is not meant to relegate the significance that other social factors have on people's orientations to their bodies. Elsewhere I have explored in greater detail the importance of gender (SHILLING, 1991b, 1993a), and 'race' (SHILLING, 1993a) in the formation of physical capital. It is also worth saying something here about my use of the concept 'social class'. The sociology of education has most commonly conceptualised social class as membership of an occupational category and this is how the 'access' approach views class. Other traditions within the sociology of education have treated class as a form of consciousness (as in segments of the 'New' sociology of education), or as a position within the relations of production (as in Marxist approaches). What I am attempting to do in this chapter, though, is to develop a notion of class which refers not only to factors external to the individual, such as occupational position, but to the orientations that people possess to their bodies as a result of the acquisition of specific sets of body techniques.

The Body as Physical Capital

At one level, it is not difficult to envisage the body as a form of capital. One only has to think of the rewards received by college athletes in the USA, and professional sports people across the world, to see how specific bodily performances are recognised as valued in certain contexts and can be exchanged for financial rewards. Furthermore, it is not only in sports that particular bodily attributes are recognised and rewarded as valuable. Night clubs and discos employ male bodybuilders as bouncers; fashion and modelling work rewards certain shapes and appearances; labouring jobs with piece work payment reward physical stamina and so, in a different way, does the work of prostitutes. Of course, these 'bodily exchanges' vary in the degree to which their owners profit from and are exploited by such transactions. Common to them all though is the use of the body as a form of capital. Schools are of obvious importance in shaping among pupils particular orientations to their bodies, and viewing the body as a form of physical capital highlights the possibility that formal education is involved in the production of corporeal inequalities. Schools may not only be involved in processes which lead to social inequalities in the acquisition of qualifications, they might also be involved in bestowing on pupils different quantities and qualities of physical capital.

This approach to the body as a form of physical capital inside and outside of schools can be developed further by drawing on the work of Pierre BOURDIEU. BOURDIEU is one of a very few sociologists who place the body at the centre of their theory of social reproduction. BOURDIEU usually analyses embodied or physical capital as a subsection of cultural capital (e.g. BOURDIEU, 1986). However, I want to argue that the corporeal is too important to be seen merely as a subdivision of another form of capital. The development and management of the body is central in its own right to human agency in general, and to the attainment of status and financial capital. Indeed, the management of the body through time and space can be seen as the fundamental constituent of an individual's ability to intervene in social affairs and make a difference to the flow of daily life (SHILLING, 1991a, 1991b). Bearing this in mind, I shall now turn to BOURDIEU's analysis of the production of physical capital, and its conversion into other forms of capital.

The Production of Physical Capital

The production of physical capital refers to the social formation of bodies by individuals through sporting, leisure, waged and unwaged work (and other body-implicating activities) in ways which express a social location (a social position marked by various cultural, economic and social opportunities and constraints) and which are accorded symbolic value. The social production of bodies includes those dimensions of activity involved in the development of body techniques such as how people develop, alter and hold the physical shape of their bodies, and learn how to present and manage their bodies through specific styles of walk, talk and dress. These activities enable people to communicate and interact with others – in short, to be social beings. However, BOURDIEU's work suggests that people acquire different body techniques that give them access to different forms of physical capital. This is because of the influence that people's social location, habitus and taste have on the development of their bodies.

Social locations refer to the degree of "distance from necessity" that people have from financial and material want (BOURDIEU, 1985). The fact that people occupy different social locations means that they have unequal opportunities for developing that physical capital most valued in society. The middle-classes, for example, tend to have more financial and cultural resources than the working-classes. This enables them to keep their children in education for longer, release them from the need to work, and encourage them to engage in activities likely to increase their acquisition of prestigious forms of physical capital. One example of this is those parents who send their children to private schools, or daughters to 'finishing schools', as a way of 'improving' their deportment, manners and speech in ways which express, quite literally, a sense of class. There are, however, numerous other ways in which middle-class parents are more able to buy pre-school or extra-school entry to activities conducive to acquiring certain forms of physical capital (e.g. tennis, ballet).

The social location of individuals from different class backgrounds is also important for BOURDIEU's analysis as they provide the context in which the habitus and taste are developed. The habitus is a set of dispositions, or a "socially constituted set of constituting and motivating structures which provide people with class dependent, predisposed ways of relating to both familiar and novel situations" (BRUBACKER, 1985, p.758). It is constructed through the relationship between children's socialisation and their objective material environment, and is central to the reproduction of social inequalities. The habitus is not only inscribed in the mind, but is embodied, and the way people treat their bodies "reveals the deepest disposition of the habitus" (BOURDIEU, 1984, p.190).

'Taste' is the conscious manifestation of habitus and refers to the processes whereby individuals come to prefer lifestyles which are actually rooted in material constraints. In other words, taste makes a choice out of necessity. BOURDIEU's concept of taste represents an extension of the everyday meaning of this term, and the consumption of food is an obvious example of how taste is shaped by specific material locations. Throughout history, people's taste for food has developed in the context of its availability, and has been affected by the efforts of the dominant in society to appropriate certain foods in order to distinguish themselves from the dominated in terms of what they eat (MENNELL, 1985). These eating patterns have important consequences for bodily development. In contemporary France and England, for example, the working class tend to consume more cheaper, fatty foods which have implications not only for their body shapes, but for their relatively high incidence of coronary disease in relation to the upper classes (BOURDIEU, 1984; TOWNSEND, DAVIDSON and WHITEHEAD, 1988).

A further example of the development of taste concerns the relatively 'passive' orientation to the body possessed by many women compared to the active bodily orientation more frequently developed by men (WILLIS, 1990). This is reinforced by the unequal opportunities women and men have within the household to barter for leisure time (BARRELL et al, 1989). Furthermore, while contemporary consumer culture has promoted the slim, active, 'athletic' body for both women and men (FEATHERSTONE, 1982), it is still considered socially unacceptable for women to develop a heavily muscled body. These attitudes are reflected even in the very organisations that cater for women bodybuilders. The International Federation of Body Builders had the following to say about the criteria which should be used to judge women bodybuilders:

> first and foremost, the judge must bear in mind that he or she is judging a women's body building competition and is looking for the ideal feminine physique. Therefore, the most important aspect is shape, a feminine shape ... muscular development ... must not be carried to excess where it resembles the massive muscularity of the male physique.

(quoted in MACNEILL, 1988, p.206)

As a result of the relationship between social location, habitus and taste, then, social forces play an enormous part in affecting the forms and the contents of body techniques which, in turn, lead to the acquisition of specific forms of physical capital. Because the working class have less time free from material necessities, BOURDIEU argues that they tend to develop an instrumental orientation to the body. The body is a means to an end and this is evident, for example, in relation to illness. 'Getting well' is primarily seen as a means for returning to work, getting ready for a holiday, or enjoying the weekend, and health regimes which seek to prevent indulgence in that time for release free from work tend to be rejected (CRAWFORD, 1987).

Gender divisions mean that most working class women frequently find it difficult to create the time for leisure opportunities apart from those compatible with their waged and unwaged work. Even such 'low-key' activities as watching television tend to be accompanied by such chores as ironing or knitting (DEEM, 1986; GREEN and HEBRON, 1988). Working class women, then, tend to develop an instrumental relation to their bodies marked by the need to earn money and service the needs of a household. This is evident in the widespread evidence which suggests that working class women sacrifice their own bodily needs for rest, recreation and even food, in order to fulfil those of their husbands and children (e.g. CHARLES and KERR, 1988). These sacrifices have real effects on the bodily development of women, as evident by the disproportionately high incidence of physical and mental illness among mothers with children (GRAHAM, 1984; see also MILES, 1991).

In contrast, the dominant classes tend to be further removed from the immediate demands of material necessity and therefore have more freedom to treat the body as an end in itself "with variants according to whether the emphasis is placed on the intrinsic functioning of the body as an organism, which leads to the macrobiotic cult of health, or on the appearance as a perceptible configuration, the 'physique', i.e. the body for others" (BOURDIEU, 1978, p.838; 1984, p.212-213). Orientations to the body become more finely differentiated within the dominant classes. Fitness training for its own sake, for example, is often engaged in by the upwardly mobile middle classes who "find their satisfaction in effort itself and ... accept – such is the meaning of their existence – the deferred satisfactions which will reward their present sacrifice" (BOURDIEU, 1978, p.839). In contrast, professionals in the field of cultural production, such as university teachers, tend towards activities which combine the health-oriented function of maintaining the body with the "symbolic gratifications associated with practising a highly distinctive activity" such as walking in remote places. Such activities can be "performed in solitude, at times and in places beyond the reach of the many" (BOURDIEU, 1984, p.214). Another distinction in physical activity is made for the elite, well established bourgeoisie, who tend to combine the health-giving aspects of sporting activities with the social functions involved in such activities as golf, dance, shooting, polo and equestrianism (BOURDIEU, 1978, p.839-840).

Orientations to the body and the acquisition of specific sets of body techniques, then, are central to the production of particular forms of physical capital. These are shaped through the relationship between social location, the habitus and taste, but it is important to note that participation in body forming activities is irreducible to the influence of these factors in the formative years of an individual's life. A person's financial resources, their access to spare time, and their life situation in general, continue to influence their relation to their body after initial tastes and body techniques have been formed. Flying, for example, usually requires one to have access to considerable resources, and sports organised around elite clubs can require potential entrants to have acquired a certain status before they are able to join (e.g. applicants to prestigious golf or tennis clubs may require social contacts within the club and a certain standing within the local community). Here, if an individual's stock of economic and social capitals has declined, both options may be ruled out and a taste for other activities and a new orientation to one's body may, eventually, be developed.

It also needs to be stressed that BOURDIEU attempts to make his view of taste, sport and relation to the body historically dynamic.[1] For example, the distribution of sporting activities between groups changes over time and between countries and regions, sports such as tennis can become democratised, and some activities will be characterised by genuine cross-class participation. What BOURDIEU supplies us with is a theoretical framework and a method of analysis, not a definitive empirical study. However, the very search by the dominant classes for distinction, a way of marking themselves off from the rest of society, lends a central dynamic in BOURDIEU's work to the question of 'who does what' in the sporting field. If a sport becomes commercialised and popularised, the dominant classes may search out new activities which can serve similar purposes (BOULANGER, 1988).[2]

The significance of bodily orientations is that they shape the formation of bodies for different activities. The lifestyles of people from different social classes become inscribed in their bodies and it becomes more or less natural for them to participate in different forms of physical activity which are themselves invested with unequal social values. This is the production of physical capital.

The Conversion of Physical Capital

The relationship between social location, habitus and taste does not just produce different bodily orientations, it actually shapes the life-chances of people. This is because individuals have unequal opportunities for converting their physical capital into other forms of capital. Physical capital can be converted into economic capital (goods and services), cultural capital (e.g. it can aid entry into private schools), and social capital (social networks which enable reciprocal calls to be made of the goods and services of its members) (BOURDIEU, 1986).

The working classes do not entirely lack opportunities for converting their physical capital into other forms of capital, but these opportunities are limited. For example, the instrumental approach towards sports as a means to an end provides the working class with the potential to convert physical capital into economic capital via entry into sporting careers. Here the power, speed and agility invested in the body become objects of exchange value. However, this form of capital is limiting to the working classes in several respects. First, only a small percentage of its members can hope to earn a living through sport. Second, this form of convertibility is usually transient in that the capacities of the body are limiting even for those who do make it as professional sports people. It only takes one injury to end a soccer player's career and the average length of sporting careers is low, leaving most ex-professionals needing to find work for the rest of their lives. Third, the time working class students spend on sport may detrimentally affect their acquisition of academic qualifications at school (CARRINGTON, 1982). Fourth, this instrumental approach toward the body can also steer working class children away from activities engaged in by the dominant classes and hence reinforce their class distinctiveness. MCROBBIE's (1978) study of working class girls is a useful example of this phenomenon. The girls in MCROBBIE's study had an instrumental relation to their bodies and viewed them as a means to display adult forms of femininity and attract boyfriends. However, in possessing this relation to their bodies, working class girls tended to reject the opportunities available to them in school PE and sport (MCROBBIE, 1978; WOODS, 1979).

If there are limitations in the working class converting physical capital into economic capital, the same is true for cultural and social capital. Working class physical capital is rarely converted into cultural capital in the education system and it has long been argued that working class speech forms and the linguistic codes which underpin them tend to be interpreted negatively by teachers (BERNSTEIN, 1970; KEDDIE, 1971). In the case of social capital, working class physical capital may lead to an admiration among peer groups at school in terms of a prowess at fighting (WILLIS, 1977) or an ability to appear as adult and feminine as possible (MCROBBIE, 1978), but it does little to gain the support of teachers in helping with academic work. In sum, there tend to be high risks and opportunity costs associated with working class efforts to convert their physical capital into other resources.

In contrast, the dominant classes have more valuable opportunities to convert physical capital into other resources. Sport tends not to carry the same means or meanings of upward mobility for the children of the dominant class, and there is a tendency for them to engage predominantly in socially elite sporting activities which stress etiquette and hence facilitate the future acquisition of social and cultural capital. This is reflected in the PE curricula of elite private schools in Britain (SALTER and TAPPER, 1981). Developing a taste for elite sporting and leisure activities is also important as while these activities may not represent a direct route to careers for the dominant classes, they can lead to social situations which indirectly facilitate entry into a profession or allow business contacts to be forged. For dominant groups, elite sporting venues also serve the purpose of finding marriage partners of their own class for their offspring, hence safeguarding the future transmission of their economic capital. Indeed, the prominence of elite sporting venues focused around such activities as eventing and polo in England can be seen as a contributory factor to the high degree of intra-class marriages among the dominant classes in this country.

The physical capital of the dominant class can also be converted into social and cultural capital. Elite social and sporting occasions tend to encompass strict rules of etiquette and allow for the stylised display of the body in formal contexts. This allows members of elite groups to recognise and decode the body as a sign signifying that the bearer shares certain values (e.g. through modes of dress, methods of conversational turn-taking and ways of speaking). Informal contacts can be made on these occasions which can be of great value in acquiring the services of others in such areas as law, finance and politics. Physical capital can also be converted into cultural capital. For example, the interview, in which the management and display of speech and the body is central, is still an integral part of the selection process for many elite private schools and a number of universities in England (including Oxford and Cambridge).

To conclude, the potential exchange value of physical capital is much higher for the dominant classes than for the working class. Furthermore, the development of physical capital for the dominant class does not usually carry the same risks or opportunity costs as working class physical capital.

Schooling and Physical Capital

Having examined BOURDIEU's approach to the body as a form of physical capital, I now want to look at how this analysis might be used to illuminate the relationship between schooling, PE and social class inequalities.

In conceptualising the relationship between schools and physical capital, it is important to state at the outset that there can be no direct 'correspondence theory' between these factors (cf. BOWLES and GINTIS, 1976). The acquisition of body techniques and early development of physical capital takes place in a variety of contexts with the family being of obvious importance. Educational institutions do, however, contribute in important ways to the social formation of bodies. Furthermore, PE is a significant influence on the ways in which children perceive and treat their bodies. Although seldom commented on in the sociology of education, schools in contemporary society are heavily implicated in attempting to internalise in pupils socially acceptable ways of managing and maintaining their bodies (KIRK and COLQUHOUN, 1989). Crucial to this chapter, though, is not simply the point that schools are involved in the formation of bodies, but that they affect differentially the ability of pupils to recognise and develop specific forms of physical capital.

In the next two sections of this chapter I shall briefly sketch some of the ways in which English and Welsh schools have historically influenced the production of physical capital in relation to social class inequalities. The limitations of existing literature make this an inevitably cursory analysis. I shall, however, suggest that there has been a shift in the organisation and control of knowledge about bodies in schools which has affected the ability of different groups in society to produce specific body techniques and forms of physical capital, and to convert physical capital into other resources.

My general argument is that historically there has been a shift in the organisation and control of educational knowledge about bodies. This has moved away from a position existing from the eighteenth century to the middle of the twentieth century, where formal education established rigid boundaries between the bodies of different social classes and schools were implicated in producing 'disciplined bodies'. In the late twentieth century, in contrast, the tendency was for education to treat bodies according to individualist, rather than class-based, criteria. The body was seen more as a shared phenomenon whose biological characteristics and physical potential did not inevitably vary between the social classes. Instead, physical potential varied on the basis of individual characteristics (and, of course, between girls and boys). Here, schools were implicated in producing what I refer to as "regulated bodies".

Schooling the Disciplined Body

From the nineteenth to the mid-twentieth century, formal education established rigid boundaries between the bodies of working and middle-class pupils and the aristocracy, and between the bodies of girls and boys from the dominant classes. It also assisted in sorting out the bodies of the "tidy" from the "untidy" working classes (EVANS, 1988). This was done in order to facilitate the establishment of disciplined bodies; that is, bodies equipped with pre-specified tendencies and capabilities for action.

Separate forms of bodily development were seen as natural for different groups in society, and these were designed to prepare people for particular social positions. Sport was promoted in boys's private schools, for example, as a cultivator of character, moral values and 'manliness' which served to produce the corporeal qualities valued in elite jobs at home and across the Empire. The educational theory implicit in the dominance of sport was that team activity trained individuals – and their bodies – out of individualism and into the corporate membership of a social class which led, and set an example to, the rest of the nation (BEST, 1975). The 'cult of athleticism' prominent in these schools served also to promote a hierarchy of values and status built around a specific orientation to the body which was used to devalue the meritocratic principles of mental (academic) performance promoted by the 'new' bourgeoisie (BOURDIEU, 1978). These orientations to the body were reinforced by statutes which forbade commoners from wearing fabrics and styles reserved for the aristocracy (DAVIS, 1989).

The bodily orientations produced among the English aristocracy by elite private schools were recognised by the higher professions as marks of distinction and prerequisites for entry into elite occupations. Here, the physical capital which private schooling helped produce could be converted into economic capital through the labour market. As the century wore on, and the children of the industrial bourgeoisie started attending in significant numbers prestigious private schools, cultivation of the prestigious 'athletic body' was widened to sections of the middle classes and, ultimately, to the grammar schools.

In stark contrast, team games were not considered suitable for the working class; a people destined to follow rather than lead. Instead, a modified form of drill was introduced into state elementary schools in the late nineteenth century. Indeed, partly as a result of state concerns to maintain a 'fit', 'disciplined' and 'healthy' population that could be mobilised during times of war, drill was incorporated as a recognised subject in the payment-by-results scheme (MCINTOSH, 1952). This emphasis was continued in the early twentieth century and the *Physical Education Syllabus* of 1933 stressed the importance of discipline, alertness, precision, the soundness of body parts, and their harmonious functioning to produce a healthy and efficient whole (HARGREAVES, 1986, p.160).

These class divisions remained even after the establishment of universal secondary education. In the 1950s and 1960s, grammar and private schools continued to provide high-status team games such as cricket and rugby, while the secondary modern school PE curriculum tended to be dominated by games more popular among the working class such as football.

Schools were in the business of producing different body techniques and forms of physical capital which had radically different exchange values. The specific character of the body was not shared by all, but was divided by social class. Furthermore, teachers and pupils did not have much control over this division. The view of the body as divided by social class was so deeply ingrained in English culture that headteachers attempting to change the games orientation of private schools met with overwhelming resistance (MANGAN, 1975).

The education of bodies during this period was not, however, divided simply along class lines. Fundamental biological differences were seen to exist between the bodies of middle class male and female pupils, the implications of which had inescapable social consequences. While the middle class male body was moulded through athleticism, the Victorian image of a middle class woman was of an invalid, ruled by her reproductive organs and limited by the finite amount of energy at her disposal (ATKINSON, 1987). Even when PE did develop in girls' schools, this was within taken-for-granted assumptions about the innate limited capacities of women (SCRATON, 1986; HARGREAVES, 1986) and was underpinned by a concern to counterbalance the strain of mental work for girls. In the early twentieth century, for example, a number of private day and boarding schools stressed the importance of stylish accomplishments for girls, rather than games, and in 1919 the Board of Education's *Syllabus of Physical Training for Schools* recommended certain activities as being more suitable for boys than girls (SCRATON, 1986, p.76-77). The LING system of gymnastics, with its emphasis on remedial and therapeutic work, was recognised and promoted as being particularly relevant for promoting qualities of caring and helping others through physical education. These were qualities associated directly with the ideal of 'perfect motherhood'. Indeed, the notion of woman as mother became part of the general ethos of PE training throughout England.

It was not until the late nineteenth century that there was a genuine shift toward sports, and even here most pioneers accepted the notion of 'limited games' for girls (e.g. hockey was often played on smaller pitches and for shorter periods of time than was usual for boys, MCCRONE, 1988). Male sports were adapted to accommodate women's 'limited abilities' and new sports were introduced, such as netball, which did not carry the stigma of overt masculinity (SCRATON, 1986).

Schools contributed to producing a form of physical capital among middle class girls whose exchange value was directed toward marriage markets. The 'feminine accomplishments' encouraged in these schools prepared girls for future positions in society which were subordinate to men and ill-suited to work pursued out of the limited sphere of the home. Gender inequalities in the education system of the nineteenth and early twentieth centuries, then, were evident not merely in the form of schooling open to the sexes, or in the educational resources on offer to girls and boys, but were, quite literally, embodied.

The education system of the late nineteenth and early twentieth centuries established clear divisions between the bodies belonging to people from different social backgrounds. Natural differences were posited between bodies belonging to different social classes and between those of men and women. However, the education of all these groups was directed toward a common goal; the production of disciplined bodies. This consisted of an approach to the body involving an increasingly better invigilated and rationalised process of adjustment between productive and reproductive activities (FOUCAULT, 1982). Set categories of bodies had definite places in society (e.g. upper class bodies were to lead whereas working class bodies were to follow; middle class men's bodies were primarily implicated in production whereas middle class women's bodies were fitted for and limited by reproduction), and it was the job of schooling to assist in producing strict bodily orientations in line with these roles.

Schooling the Regulated Body

In the early years of the twentieth century, however, the cult of athleticism that previously governed physical education came under attack as academic and occupational pressures rose. Academic concerns came to occupy more of the school curriculum as the occupational system became increasingly bureaucratised and entry into elite jobs became more dependent on qualifications. Furthermore, by the second half of the twentieth century a new ideology of individualism competed with the team oriented cult of the physical. During this time the production of disciplined bodies gradually gave way to the production of regulated bodies, with individual pupils given a role in choosing and monitoring their own physical development. The role of discipline, where necessary, was seen less in terms of external punishment and coercion, and more in terms of the teacher provoking within internalised feelings of guilt and shame. HARGREAVES (1986), following DURKHEIM, has described this shift toward child-centredness as helping to prepare young people for an increasingly complex division of labour in the occupational structure. It is undoubtedly the case that there arose a greater number of acceptable ways of organising and controlling the body in schools. This was partly facilitated by the gradual 'merging' of separate female and male traditions of physical education which stressed gymnastics, dance and movement on the one hand and performance and measurement on the other (FLETCHER, 1984; MCINTOSH, 1952, 1981). Although the latter, male, tradition gained dominance it did not obliterate completely the longer-standing female tradition.

By the late twentieth century there had been a fundamental shift in the educational treatment of bodies. The organisation of bodies in schools no longer treated as fundamentally different pupils from separate class backgrounds. Although differences were not eradicated, especially in the private sector and in the case of gender (where PE remained the most segregated subject in the school curriculum) there was a much greater variety of physical activities open to pupils from all class backgrounds than in the nineteenth century. Curriculum options allowed students a degree of choice, and a growth in the number of health- and fitness-related initiatives available to schools gave teachers more control over how their work related to pupils's bodies.

The increased use of health-related physical education courses in state schools in England and Wales is significant partly because it is parallelled in other countries such as Australia (COLQUHOUN and ROBOTTOM, 1990; TINNING, 1990). In summarising the general orientation of these programmes (programmes such as Health Related Fitness [HRF] and Teaching Games for Understanding [TGFU]), John EVANS (1988) argues that they seek to offer equality of access to activities for each individual irrespective of their level of ability. As he notes, "It is intended that everyone should experience a genuine (but not necessarily the same) level of success, achievement, satisfaction and enjoyment, along with an understanding of the principles which underpin different game forms" (EVANS, 1988, p.179). In order to accomplish this, emphasis is placed on cognitive, rather than (but not at the expense of) technical aspects of games. Mini-games with adapted rules and equipment, for example, are often used on the basis that they are more likely to provide all pupils with opportunities to participate and make decisions irrespective of their physical ability. HRF shares certain characteristics with TGFU such as avoiding labelling pupils as 'winners' or 'losers':

> It is against selection and the creation of ability hierarchies and for 'non-authoritarian', 'non-didactic' approaches to teaching. At the heart of this innovation (at least as officially espoused by the Health Education Council) is concern for the development of each and every individual's 'health career', their positive 'self-esteem' and 'decision-making skills'... The aims are to create the habit of exercise and the belief that this can be fully integrated into one's life style. Within the context of PE ... emphasis is placed upon the development of individual, personalised activity programmes designed to ensure a consistent involvement in physical exercise of an intensity which improves levels of fitness (especially cardiovascular functioning).
>
> (EVANS, 1988, p.180)

Health related physical education courses tend to be child-centred rather than subject-centred (PAYNE, 1985). They appear to encourage individualised orientations to their bodily capacities, and seek to promote an attitude to health and fitness where students monitor their own performance and behaviour and achieve their personal potential. In the terms of these programmes, schools should no longer be implicated in developing disciplined orientations to the body rigidly divided by social class and gender, but prepare students to regulate their own bodies on the basis of individual characteristics. This focus on individual regulation, however, does not necessarily remove completely class based orientations to the body which were so evident in the nineteenth and early twentieth centuries. By focussing on the individual, these initiatives end up failing to confront inequalities in the extra-school opportunities open to people from different social backgrounds (EVANS, 1988). They fail to question how they may be classed or gendered in terms of the unequal ability that pupils may have to attain the aims of these initiatives because of their previous development of body techniques and physical capital. Furthermore, by developing in children flexibility and problem-solving skills, some commentators have argued that they are involved in developing characteristics required for competent occupational performance among the new middle class (HARGREAVES, 1986).

By focussing on the individual in this way, such initiatives run the risk of mystifying, and hence legitimising, socially caused differences in the levels of physical capital open to people from different social backgrounds. Do health related initiatives tend to treat as natural and individualistic, what are in fact socially determined orientations to exercise and to the body? Do such initiatives merely replace a prior notion of 'ability' with other versions which are equally biased in terms of the potential different pupils have for becoming 'skilled'? If so, is this merely replicating the problem of the access approach to PE and games by taking for granted, and treating as technical, concepts of skill which are, in fact, open to contestation? Does this serve to disguise both the body's implication in the production of social inequalities and the social causes and class- and gender-based incidence of mortality and morbidity patterns (as revealed in Britain by *The Black Report* and *The Health Divide* [see also GRAHAM, 1984; MILES, 1991]). These are important questions which have yet to be explored in any depth.

Moving away from health-related initiatives in state schools, the continuation of private schooling means that inequalities in the education of bodies between schools remains untouched. The scope of private schooling has declined since the last century. However, they cater for around 7 per cent of the school population in England (WALFORD, 1991) and can still be seen as aiding the development of physical capital (e.g. through insistence on 'correct' speech and manners) and instilling in pupils a particular confidence and orientation toward the body. Indeed, the importance of managing the body, dress, manner and speech in obtaining elite jobs is reinforced by those studies which suggest that qualifications serve only as an initial screening device, rather than actually determining employment selection decisions (DALE and PIRES, 1984; MOORE, 1989). The informal aspects of employment selection relevant to bodily presentation can, then, play an important part in determining access to economic rewards. These may seem obvious points, but analyses of private schooling and the reproduction of class inequalities have focused on these institutions as providers of cultural rather than physical capital.

The Individualisation of the Body?

This shift in the transmission and control of body techniques in schools, represented by an individualised approach towards physical education, is congruent in a number of respects with broader societal developments in the relationship between the body and self identity.

In the affluent west, the body is no longer simply a mark of social status, but has become an expression of individual personality (SENNETT, 1992). In this context, there is a tendency for the body to be seen as an entity which is in the process of becoming; a project which should be worked at and accomplished as part of an individual's self-identity (SHILLING, 1993b). As a result of the rise of the body in consumer culture on the one hand, and developments in health and fitness programmes, fashion, cosmetics and design, plastic surgery, biological reproduction and genetic engineering on the other, the body is becoming increasingly a phenomenon of options and choices.

Strong norms continue to guide the range of options open to women and men from different social classes, but choices still have to be made from a proliferation of ways in which the body can be developed, and body techniques acquired, relearnt or discarded. This expansion of choices has important implications for the transmission of physical capital between generations.

The Transmission of Physical Capital

There is no guarantee that physical capital will be reproduced in succeeding generations and it is important to note the difficulties that face the dominant classes in maintaining the value of their physical assets. To begin with, physical capital cannot be directly transmitted or inherited. Unlike money, stocks and shares or property rights, it cannot be passed on by mere gift or exchange. Instead, its development is a costly process which can last for years (CONNELL, 1983, pp.30-31). Moreover, physical capital cannot be accumulated beyond the appropriating capacities of an individual agent. Instead, it declines and dies with its bearer (BOURDIEU, 1986, p.245; MELLOR and SHILLING, 1993). Changes in fashion may affect the symbolic value of certain forms of deportment, talk and dress (FEATHERSTONE, 1987). Neither can physical capital be purchased directly as an act of labour is involved in the acquisition of physical capital for each new generation. For example, just as some children fail to acquire academic qualifications despite attending elite private schools, so may some fail to accumulate the physical capital 'appropriate' to their background.

Nonetheless, the natural, biological appearance of physical capital still makes its pursuit attractive to the dominant classes. Physical capital is a hidden form of privilege which is not subject to taxation in the way that can affect economic capital. Indeed, the more the state is able to hinder the official transmission of economic capital, the more the effects of the clandestine circulation of physical capital are likely to affect the reproduction of the social structure (BOURDIEU, 1986, p.254).

The most important factor affecting the relative values of physical capital at any one time, though, is the ability of the dominant class to define their orientations towards the body and lifestyle as superior, worthy of reward, and as, metaphorically and literally, the embodiment of class. This is a process constantly open to challenge and contestation. As writers concerned with the development of consumer culture within high modernity have argued, multinational corporations have become involved in the production of difference through assisting the proliferation of clothing styles and other signs of bodily identity to various social groups (JAMESON, 1984, 1985). Though partly generated through global forms of industrial reorganisation, this degree of proliferation and change poses threats to the ability of the dominant classes continually to impose their physical capital as of greatest social value. As FEATHERSTONE argues (1990), the rapid internationalisation and circulation of consumer and 'lifestyle' goods threatens the readability of those signs used by the dominant to signify their elite physical capital. This would "threaten the logic of differences in which taste in cultural and consumer goods and lifestyle activities are held to be oppositionally structured" (FEATHERSTONE, 1990, p.12).

Conclusion

In contemporary western societies, then, it may be becoming more difficult for any single group to impose as hegemonic a single version of physical capital. One consequence of this is that there is likely to be increased scrutiny of and disagreement over what PE teachers teach and how they teach it (EVANS, 1990). There is also likely to be greater anxiety among class fractions to have their particular orientation to the body recognised as legitimate. No one in the PE profession should be surprised if dominant definitions of what counts as 'ability' or 'skill' in their subject come under even closer scrutiny and even greater debate. The analysis in this paper suggests that PE teachers are faced with enormous challenges in the present period as a result of the body's symbolic significance and its centrality to the formation of self-identities and social inequalities. I have approached these issues by examining Marcel MAUSS's notion of body techniques as central to the education of people, and by looking at the social implications of the differential acquisition of body techniques in terms of Pierre BOURDIEU's work. In an age which has seen the rise of the body as a project, BOURDIEU may overemphasise the degree to which individuals are fated to make particular choices. Nonetheless, his analysis remains a powerful way of looking at the social importance of the body.

Notes

1   For further analysis of BOURDIEU's attempt to construct an approach to the body which is historically dynamic see SHILLING (1993b).

2.   This does not exclude the drive for forms of distinction that occur within working-class cultures. In present circumstances, however, the drive for distinction among the dominant class is a pursuit for an elitism which contains the greatest potential for physical capital being converted into other forms of high value capital.

References

BARRELL, J., CHAMBERLAIN, A., EVANS, J., HOLT, T. and MACKEAN, J. (1989) Ideology and commitment in family life: A case study of runners. *Leisure Studies*, 8, 249-262.

BERGER, P. (1969) *The Sacred Canopy*. New York, Anchor Books.

BERNSTEIN, B. (1970) Education cannot compensate for society. *New Society*, 26, 344-347.

BEST, G. (1975) The Ideal of 'Manliness'. In B. SIMON and I. BRADLEY (Eds) *The Victorian Public School*. Dublin, Gill and MacMillan, pp.129-146.

BOULANGER, R. (1988) Class cultures and sports activities in Quebec, in J. HARVEY and C. CANTELON (Eds) *Not Just a Game: Essays in Canadian Sport Sociology*. Ottawa, University of Ottawa Press.

BOURDIEU, P. (1978) Sport and social class. *Social Science Information*, 17, 6, 819-840.

BOURDIEU, P. (1984) *Distinction. A Social Critique of the Judgment of Taste*. London, Routledge and Kegan Paul.

BOURDIEU, P. (1985) The social space and the genesis of groups. *Theory and Society*, 14, 6, 723-44.

BOURDIEU, P. (1986) The forms of capital. In J. RICHARDSON (Ed) *Handbook of Theory and Research for the Sociology of Education*. New York, Greenwood Press.

BRUBAKER, R. (1985) Rethinking classical theory. *Theory and Society*, 14, 6, 745-775.

BUTLER, N. (1988) An overview of anorexia nervosa. In D. SCOTT (Ed) *Anorexia and Bulimian Nervosa: Practical Approaches*. London, Croom Helm.

CARRINGTON, B. (1982) Sport as a sidetrack. In L. BARTON and S. WALKER (Eds) *Race, Class and Education*. London, Croom Helm.

CHARLES, N. and KERR, M. (1988) *Women, Food and Families*. Manchester, Manchester University Press.

CHERNIN. K. (1983) *Womansize. The Tyranny of Slenderness*. London, The

Women's Press.

COLQUHOUN, D. and ROBOTTOM, I. (1990) Health education and environmental education: Towards a shared agenda and a shared discourse. *Unicorn,* 16, 109-118.

CONNELL, R. (1983) *Which Way Is Up?* Sydney, George Allen and Unwin.

CONNELL, R. (1987) *Gender and Power.* Oxford, Polity Press.

COOPER, T. (1987) Anorexia and bulimia: The political and the personal. In M. LAWRENCE (Ed) *Fed Up and Hungry. Women, Oppression and Food.* London, The Women's Press.

CRAWFORD, R. (1987) Cultural influences on prevention and the emergence of a new health consciousness. In N. WEINSTEIN (Ed) *Taking Care. Understanding and Encouraging Self Protective Behaviour.* Cambridge, Cambridge University Press.

DALE, R. and PIRES, E. (1984) Linking People and Jobs: Indeterminate Place of Educational Credentials. In BROADFOOT, P. (Ed) *Selection, Certification and Control: Issues in Educational Assessment.* Lewis, Falmer Press, pp.51-65.

DEEM, R. (1986) *All Work and No Play?* Milton Keynes, Open University Press.

DORE, R. (1976) *The Diploma Disease.* London, Allen and Unwin.

ELIAS, N. (1978 [1939]) *The Civilising Process Vol. 1: The History of Manners.* Oxford, Basil Blackwell.

EVANS, J. (1988) Body matters: Towards a socialist physical education. In H. LAUDER and P. BROWN (Eds) *Education: In Search of a Future.* London, Falmer Press.

EVANS, J. (1990) Defining a subject: The rise and rise of the new PE? *British Journal of Sociology of Education,* 11, 2, 155-169.

FEATHERSTONE, M. (1982) The body in consumer culture. *Theory, Culture and Society,* 1, 18-33.

FEATHERSTONE, M. (1987) Leisure, symbolic power and the lifecourse. In J. HORNE, D. JARY and A. TOMLINSON (Eds) *Sport, Leisure and Social Relations.* London, RKP.

FEATHERSTONE, M. (1990) Perspectives on consumer culture. *Sociology*, 24, 1, 5-22.

FLETCHER, S. (1984) *Women First: The Female Tradition in English Physical Education 1880-1980*. London, The Athlone Press.

FRANK, A. (1990) Bringing bodies back in: A decade review. *Theory, Culture and Society*, 7, 131-162.

FREUND, P. (1988) Understanding socialised human nature. *Theory, Culture and Society*, 17, 839-64.

GIDDENS, A. (1991) *Modernity and Self-Identity*. Oxford, Polity Press.

GRAHAM, H. (1984) *Women, Health and the Family*. Brighton, Wheatsheaf.

GREEN, E. and HEBRON, S. (1988) Leisure and male partners. In E. WIMBUSH and M. TALBOT (Eds) *Relative Freedoms: Women and Leisure*. Milton Keynes, Open University Press.

HALL, C. (1992) Girls aged nine "are obsessed by weight". *The Independent*, 10th April.

HARGREAVES, J. (1986) *Sport, Power and Culture*. Oxford, Polity Press.

HENDRY, L. (1978) *School, Sport and Leisure*. Lepus Books.

HOCHSCHILD, A. (1983) *The Managed Heart. Commercialisation of Human Feeling*. California, California University Press.

HONNETH, A. and JOAS, H., (1988) *Social Action and Human Nature*. Cambridge, Cambridge University Press.

JAMESON, F. (1984) Postmodernism: Or the cultural logic of late capitalism. *New Left Review*, 146, 53-92.

JAMESON, F. (1985) Postmodernism and consumer society. In H. FOSTER (Ed) *Postmodern Culture*. London, Pluto Press.

KEDDIE, N. (1971) Classroom knowledge. In M. YOUNG (Ed) *Knowledge and Control*. London, Collier-Macmillan.

KIRK, D. (1993) *The Body, Schooling and Culture*. Deakin, Deakin University Press.

KIRK, D. and COLQUHOUN, D. (1989) Healthism and physical education. *British Journal of Sociology of Education,* 10, 4, 417-434.

MCINTOSH, P. (1952) *Physical Education in England Since 1800.* London, G. Bell and Sons.

MCINTOSH, P. (1981) Landmarks in the history of PE since World War Two. In P. MCINTOSH et al (Eds) *Landmarks in the History of Physical Education.* London, RKP.

MACKAY, J., GORE, J. and KIRK, D. (1990) Beyond the limits of technocratic physical education. *Quest,* 42, 52-80.

MACNEILL, M. (1988) Active women, media representations and ideology. In J. HARVEY and H. CANTELON (Eds) *Not Just a game: Essays in Canadian Sport Sociology.* Ottawa, University of Ottawa Press.

MARTIN, E. (1987) *The Woman in the Body.* Milton Keynes, Open University Press.

MARX, K. and ENGELS, F. (1970) *The German Ideology.* London, Lawrence and Wishart.

MAUSS, M. (1979) *Sociology and Psychology. Essays by Marcel Mauss.* London, RKP.

MELLOR, P. and SHILLING, C. (1993) Modernity, self-identity and the sequestration of death. *Sociology,* 27, 3, 411-431.

MENNELL, S. (1985) *All Manners of Food. Eating and Taste in England and France from the Middle Ages to the Present.* Oxford, Basil Blackwell.

MILES, A. (1991) *Women, Health and Medicine.* Milton Keynes, Open University Press.

MORRE, R. (1989) Education, Employment and Recruitments. In COSIN, B., FLUDE, M. and HALES, M. (Eds) *School Work and Equality.* London, Hodder and Stoughton. pp.206-222.

O'NEILL, J. (1985) *Five Bodies: The Human Shape of Modern Society.* Ithaca, NY, Cornell University Press.

ORBACH, S. (1988) *Fat Is A Feminist Issue.* London, Arrow.

PAYNE, S. (1985) Physical education and health in the United Kingdom. *British Journal of Physical Education,* 17, 1, 4-9.

SALTER, B. and TAPPER, T. (1981) *Education, Politics and the State.* London, Grant McIntyre.

SCOTT, S. and MORGAN, D. (1993) *Body Matters. Essays on the Sociology of the Body.* London, Falmer Press.

SENNETT, R. (1992) *The Fall of Public Man.* New York, Norton.

SHILLING, C. (1989) *Schooling for Work in Capitalist Britain.* Lewes, Falmer Press.

SHILLING, C. (1991) Educating the body: Physical capital and the production of social inequalities. *Sociology,* 25, 4, 653-672.

SHILLING, C. (1992) Schooling and the production of physical capital. *Discourse,* 13, 1, 1-19.

SHILLING, C. (1993a) The body, class and social inequalities. In J. EVANS (Ed) *Equality, Education and Physical Education.* London, Falmer Press.

SHILLING, C. (1993b) *The Body and Social Theory.* London, Sage Press.

TINNING, R. (1990) Physical education as health education: Problem-setting as a response to the new health consciousness. *Unicorn,* 16, 81-91.

TOWNSED, P., DAVIDSON, N. and WHITEHEAD, M. (1988) *Inequalities in Health.* London, Penguin.

TURNER, B.S. (1984) *The Body and Society.* Oxford, Basil Blackwell.

TURNER, B.S. (1991) Recent developments in the theory of the body. In M. FEATHERSTONE, M. HEPWORTH and B.S. TURNER (Eds) *The Body. Social Process and Cultural Theory.* London, Sage Press.

TURNER, B.S. (1992) *Regulating the Body.* London, Routledge.

WALFORD, G. (1991) Private Schoolong into the 1990's. In G. WALFORD *Private Schooling.* London, Chapman Publishing, pp.1-13.

WHITEHEAD, N. and HENDRY, L. (Ed) (1976) *Teaching Physical Education in England.* Lepus Books.

WILLIS, P. (1977) *Learning to Labour.* Farborough, Saxon House.

WILLIS, S. (1990) Work(ing) Out. *Cultural Studies,* 4, 1, 1-18.

WOODS, P. (1979) *The Divided School.* London, Routledge and Kegan Paul.

Reprinted with kind permission of the Centre for Research into Sport and Society, University of Leicester.

Chapter 13

Gender, Coeducation and Secondary Physical Education: A Brief Review

Ken Green and Sheila Scraton

Introduction

Physical education (PE) in the United Kingdom has a history of gender segregation: a legacy of single-sex teaching in schools built upon a tradition of single-sex teacher education. Typically, segregation has taken the form of sex-specific teaching groups, separate teachers within separate departments, and differing activities. PE was, and remains, the most gender segregated subject in the school curriculum particularly at secondary level (SCRATON, 1992, 1993; KAY, 1995; FLINTOFF, 1996a; WADDINGTON, MALCOLM and COBB, forthcoming). This fact, and the consequences for young women's PE experiences and post school participation in sport and physical activity are well documented (LEAMAN, 1984; FLINTOFF, 1990, 1994; SCRATON, 1992, 1993; HARGREAVES, 1994; KAY, 1995). This chapter addresses the relationship between physical education and gender and is particularly concerned with the persistence of gender inequalities in secondary PE despite two significant developments – a trend towards coeducational PE and the introduction of the (revised) National Curriculum for Physical Education (NCPE).

Coeducational Physical Education

The guiding principle of equal educational opportunity, which was formally recognised by the 1944 *Education Act*, was applied to opportunities afforded to girls and boys following the 1975 *Sex Discrimination Act*. Coeducation became the norm in most state schools ostensibly to ensure that girls and boys received the same educational opportunities (SCRATON, 1993). The kind of single-sex teaching that had characterised secondary PE inevitably became something of an anomaly in secondary education thereafter, and a clear trend towards coeducation developed even in this bastion of single-sex teaching – secondary PE. This was not, however, a planned nation-wide development towards coeducation in PE. Rather, it was frequently the result of initiatives in the direction of mixed-sex grouping by innovative and enthusiastic PE teachers or, more typically, for administrative convenience – particularly in the upper years of secondary schooling (SCRATON, 1993; FLINTOFF, 1996b).

Coeducational PE at secondary level became increasingly common in Britain through the 1980s (SCRATON, 1993; KAY, 1995; FLINTOFF, 1996b). A rationale for coeducational PE emerged on the premise that mixed-sex grouping was an essential step in the development of equal opportunities and coeducation (SCRATON, 1993). SCRATON points out, however, that whilst the guiding principles and justification for mixed or single-sex teaching were essentially *educational,* in reality pragmatism, rather than principle, provided the driving force behind developments; the reality of mixed-sex grouping had "more to do with economic necessity and a rationalisation of diminishing resources than because of a committed educational philosophy" (1993, p.141).

Whatever the basis for change, mixed-sex grouping, at first glance, appeared a positive step towards equal opportunities for both sexes. The *Education Reform Act* (ERA, 1988) had established the entitlement of all children to a *broad and balanced* curriculum aimed not only at promoting personal development but also preparing young people for adult life (TALBOT, 1996) and the *National Curriculum Physical Education Working Group Interim Report* identified the "rich potential for physical education to transcend categories" such as sex (DES and WO, 1991, p.17). The underlying principle of *entitlement* in the ERA and the NCPE required (and requires) PE teachers to rethink and challenge "attitudes which lead to certain activities being viewed as suitable only for girls, or only for boys" (TALBOT, 1996, p.5).

As the trend towards mixed-sex grouping took hold in the 1980s, it became apparent that equating coeducation with equal opportunities was over-simplistic in principle and by no means straightforward in practice (SCRATON, 1993). The *Interim Report* acknowledged that, as coeducation became increasingly the norm, there had been a failure to consider how teaching the sexes singularly or together "might be more successful or appropriate" (DES and WO, 1991, p.17). The *Report* acknowledged the importance of appreciating that *access* is not necessarily to be *equated* with opportunity:

> In some schools girls and boys ... may be said to have the same access to the physical education curriculum ... But even when this desirable state of affairs exists, do children also have equal opportunities to learn and express themselves through and in physical activity ? The effects of attitudes and expectations of the teachers ... the interactions within mixed-sex ... groups, and the previous experiences ... of the children must also be considered.
> (DES and WO, 1991, p.17)

The *Final Report* of the National Curriculum Working Group on Physical Education, underlined these concerns:

> ... it would be a mistake to equate access with opportunity ... In some schools pupils may be said to have the same access to curriculum physical education regardless of their sex ... But it may not be the case that these children also have equal opportunities to participate ... Children's capacities to take advantage of the activities provided are affected by the attitudes and expectations of teachers ... These effects are particularly important in physical education where teaching methods may have been adopted for traditional rather than educational reasons.
> (cited in TALBOT, 1996, p.6)

Consequently, as FLINTOFF (1996a) observed, the initial expectation of the early 1980s – that mixed-sex PE offered the best way of providing equal opportunities in PE – came increasingly to be questioned. By the mid-1990s inspection reports (OFSTED, 1995; OHMCI, 1995) were drawing attention to the limiting effects on girls' and boys' experiences in PE of the continuing practice of co-educational PE (PENNEY and EVANS, 1997); mixed-sex grouping was not leading inexorably to coeducational PE experiences for girls and boys.

Despite its continuing prevalence, mixed-sex teaching has been a very uneven and varied development: "not all schools have introduced mixed-sex teaching, and some have adopted it for economic or timetabling reasons" (FLINTOFF, 1996b, p.25). HARGREAVES (1994, p.153) observes that: "Although for the first three years of secondary schooling (11-14 years) it has been usual to introduce both sexes to compulsory 'core' activities (including athletics, dance, games, gymnastics and swimming), in many schools boys and girls continue to be taught separately and differently". HARGREAVES adds:

> Even when some aspects of the curriculum are taught to mixed classes, ideologies of sexual difference continue, and traditional divisions along lines of gender are almost always retained in games. The shared experience of mixed PE in primary schools seems to do little to diminish the power of traditional ideas about gender in secondary PE or to change the expectations and experiences of pupils.
>
> (1994, p.153)

Alongside evidence of continuity in terms of single-sex teaching, however, there is also evidence of quite widespread change towards what might broadly be termed coeducational strategies. FLINTOFF's recent study (1996b) reveals that strategies aimed at widening access to areas of the curriculum (especially for girls) through mixed-sex teaching were, and continue to be, commonplace. Indeed, FLINTOFF found that the majority of PE teachers in her research preferred working with mixed-sex groups. Male teachers of PE, however, tended to be far more reluctant towards the 'integration' of girls into traditionally male activities, frequently citing the (alleged) potentially detrimental effects of mixed grouping on the 'levels' of boys' performance. Women teachers tended, on the other hand, to be much more attuned to the possibility of girls losing out in mixed-sex PE: "women teachers, and also younger teachers, are more likely to be committed to equal opportunities than men" (FLINTOFF, 1996b, p.26). In a nutshell, it appears that whilst many PE teachers may be "prepared to agree with the principle of gender equity" (p.25) they tended to be far less committed to action.

The Unforeseen Consequences of Coeducational PE

SCRATON's (1992, 1993) research supported LEAMAN's (1984) conclusion that, despite the trend towards coeducational secondary PE, mixed-sex grouping had not been a marked success. Indeed, SCRATON (1993) argued, the move to mixed-sex teaching made the significance of gender more apparent, frequently intensifying rather than dissipating inequities. SCRATON pointed to educational research demonstrating that in coeducational classroom settings, boys, on the whole, had far more contact with the teacher, received more attention, were allowed to talk more in class and were, generally, far more 'visible'. Subsequent research confirmed that the same could be said for PE. Boys dominated mixed-sex PE lessons, both verbally and physically; they asked more questions; they dominated the 'action'; they were chosen to demonstrate more often; they ordered girls about; and frequently marginalised them to only occasional physical involvement as active-participants (FLINTOFF, 1996a; SCRATON, 1993). KAY (1995) summarises a breadth of similar findings from the 1980s regarding the reality of learning opportunities for girls within mixed-sex grouping:

> (boys) were particularly dominant in certain activities, notably team games, in which they received more contact time with the ball than girls; as boys generally did not pass the ball to girls unless the girls were exceptionally skilful, most female pupils had relatively little involvement in and influence over the flow of the game.
> (p.109)

The obvious consequence of such male-domination of PE lessons has been the reinforcement of gender-stereotypical attitudes (from both boys and girls about their own and those of the opposite sex) and behaviours. Such *attitudes* take the form of stereotypical views about girls and boys physical and sporting capabilities (girls being seen as less skilful and less physically able). Such *behaviour* takes the form of boys dominating girls verbally and physically, and ignoring them by interacting and working in single-sex groupings or being reluctant partners in joint activity. Interaction between pupils within mixed settings "remains single-sex unless there is positive intervention by the teacher" (SCRATON, 1993, pp.143-144). "In these situations", SCRATON (1993) points out, "PE is reinforcing gender power relations with boys reproducing their dominant role and girls learning their subordination" (p.145). She concludes: "In practice mixed-sex organization rarely means coeducational teaching and/or learning" (p.145). The upshot of the reinforcement of gender stereotypical attitudes and behaviour in PE is the reinforcement and reproduction of gender power relations – the dominant role of boys and the subordinate role of girls (SCRATON, 1993).

It is not surprising, then, that "girls' unwillingness to take part in sport may be more a reaction to the terms of participation rather than the activity itself" (KAY, 1995, p.59). In her 1993 research, SCRATON noted that many of the mixed activities that take place in PE are activities that have been traditionally male activities, e.g. soccer, basketball, cricket. In reality, she concludes (citing LEAMAN, 1984), "equal access in PE often means equal access for all pupils to male PE!" (p.143).

Evidently, when coeducational PE in reality means access to traditionally male activities taught in mixed-sex groupings, PE is bound to draw attention to the differential ability of girls and boys and "is more likely to confirm traditional gender stereotypes than challenge them" (KAY, 1995, p.109). Boys and girls do not arrive on the secondary PE starting line together. The prior socialization of boys and girls – the effects of cultural expectations on the experiences of girls and their development of abilities (FLINTOFF, 1996b) – leaves the latter relatively disadvantaged in terms of sporting and physical activity experiences and, thus, skill development. Consequently, offering the same opportunities to both sexes at the outset of secondary PE will not make up for earlier inequities, still less will it be likely to lead to equality of outcome; especially if mixed-sex PE is tantamount to boys PE. According to Talbot (1996), "it is unrealistic to expect that girls and boys of the same age ... but with vastly different experiences of ... sport, should be taught those activities in coeducational groups" (p.6). Indeed, she continues, "many teachers who have attempted this have found that the groupings become parallel rather than coeducational. Just as mixed-ability *grouping* is not the same as mixed-ability *teaching*, so mixed-sex *grouping* is not the same as mixed-sex *teaching*" (p.6; emphases in the original). It is clear, then, that mixed-sex provision will not necessarily lead to equal opportunities in PE, especially for girls (TALBOT, 1996). Indeed, ironically, it may provide inferior learning experiences not only for girls in particular, but for boys as well. For these reasons, ostensibly coeducational PE may do little to halt, let alone reverse, girls' apparent declining enthusiasm for PE in secondary schools. Most girls' interest in sport appears to reach a peak before the end of year 8, i.e. around the age of 12-13 years (KAY, 1995): "The alienation of girls from sport in their middle and later years of secondary schooling is often in contrast to the same pupils' much more enthusiastic involvement in the immediately preceding years" (KAY, 1995, p.58).

Not surprisingly, it seems that many girls do not want mixed-sex PE (SCRATON, 1993); often because of the embarrassment and lack of confidence girls feel during adolescence. This awkwardness is, in a very real sense, 'socially constructed': embarrassment and lack of confidence is frequently directly related to the behaviour of boys in mixed-sex PE settings. This is exacerbated and intensified by what SCRATON (1993) refers to as "the serious problem of sexual harassment (verbal, emotional and physical)" (p.145). SCRATON (1993) describes how, in many physical activity situations, "girls run the gauntlet of persistent comment on their physical appearance and sexuality" (p.145). She adds tellingly:

> The response is either to attempt to disguise their bodies by dressing in loose clothing or to opt out of the activity. During the sensitive years of adolescence when young women are physically and sexually developing, the ideology of woman-as-object becomes dominant in their lives .... Their bodies become the focus of comment, stares, admiration/and or criticism.
>
> (p.145)

KAY (1995) comments that, "Adolescence is a particularly significant time in the development of women's body image" (p.59) and "Concern with body image is closely associated with sexuality and, in particular, the eagerness which most adolescent girls have to establish their heterosexual identity" (p.60). Consequently, PE, like sport, frequently normalizes gender differences (FLINTOFF, 1990; SCRATON, 1992; HARGREAVES, 1994) and coeducational PE thus runs the risk of emphasising rather then diminishing "Conflicts between the cultivation of femininity and the perceived non-feminine characteristics of physical education" (KAY, 1995, p.59).

It should not be remarkable, then, that sport and physical activity become increasingly "less important in the lives of adolescent girls who, encouraged by peer-group pressure, seek other activities linked closely to their preferred perceptions of femininity" (HARGREAVES, 1994, p.155; paraphrasing HENDRY, 1978). SCRATON (1993) highlights the significance of normative expectations regarding physicality and sexuality for boys during adolescence – faced with the expectations of hegemonic masculinity. However, she points out that, "while boys are judged by 'achievement' with regard to masculinity, girls are judged 'against' masculinity. Boys' masculinity is judged against other boys whereas girls are judged by boys in relation to 'desirable femininity'" (p.145).

Girls' apparent alienation from PE, physical activity and sport is more adequately explained in terms of gender and, in particular, the ideology of gender. The lack of priority given to sport has as much, if not more, to do with wider cultural expectations of appropriate feminine behaviour and the concomitant narrowness of appropriate activities, as well as the inappropriate forms of sport offered to girls at secondary school and the unforeseen complexity and disadvantages of coeducational settings. KAY (1995) concludes, "The combination of girls' physical education experience at school, with the external influences which are particularly strong during adolescence, encourage many to dismiss sports activities as 'unfeminine, irrelevant and childish'" (p.59).

It is, then, not merely what is taught under the banner of coeducational PE that is problematic in terms of equal opportunities, it is also the ways in which PE is taught; primarily in terms of the consequences of mixed-sex grouping but also in terms of teachers themselves (SCRATON, 1993; TALBOT, 1993; FLINTOFF, 1996a, 1996b). Teachers' attitudes and behaviours are frequently such that they continue to reproduce and reinforce gender stereotypes (SCRATON, 1993). TALBOT (1993) notes: "While teachers of physical education may claim that they espouse equality of opportunity for all children, their teaching behaviours and practices reveal entrenched sex-stereotyping, based on common-sense notions of what is suitable for girls and boys, both in single-sex and mixed-sex groups and schools" (p.74). FLINTOFF (1996a), in turn, points to the "everyday practices within a P.E. department" which frequently "operate to reinforce and reproduce gender inequalities" (p.21); especially in terms of ideas about femininity and masculinity. FLINTOFF's (1996b) research suggests that, "gender stereotyping of particular physical activities (by teachers) remains a significant feature of secondary school P.E." (p.29). This is evident in attitudes and behaviours. FLINTOFF (1996b) points out that in teachers' minds activities are viewed as the preserve of either sex and, she adds, very few teachers, male or female, use anti-sexist strategies in their teaching. Not only do "male teachers and PE teaching continue to reinforce and reproduce dominant masculinities including ideologies of male sexuality, physicality, homophobia and misogyny" (SCRATON, 1993, p.147), even women PE teachers are prone to stereotypical views about the suitability or otherwise of certain activities for girls (SCRATON, 1992).

The continuance of sex-differentiated views regarding what to teach and how to teach it are illustrated in a recent study by WADDINGTON, MALCOLM and COBB (forthcoming). Their research revealed that traditional forms of gender stereotyping "are most clearly evident in teachers' involvement in, and attitudes, towards the teaching of dance and outdoor activities". WADDINGTON et al's research shows "substantial differences in terms of the ways in which teachers are *involved* in and *perceive* different parts of the NCPE" (forthcoming; emphases added). They observe:

> those activities which teachers taught most and in which they felt most competent were also those which they most enjoyed teaching and which they felt it was most important for pupils to learn; by contrast, those activities which they taught least and in which they felt least competent were also those which they least enjoyed teaching and which they felt it was least important for pupils to learn.

For both male and female teachers of PE, the most popular activities tended to be 'traditional', i.e. sex-stereotyped games. Thus, it becomes apparent that although PE teachers appear to agree with the principle of gender equity, their practices continue to reinforce gender differentiation which in turn potentially reproduces gender inequalities.

For SCRATON (1993), the continued existence of gender-based ideological assumptions among teachers is a crucial issue in coeducational PE. The long-standing male and female sub-cultures within PE mean that "underpinning girls' PE and the training of female PE teachers are dominant gender ideologies concerning expectations of women's physicality, their sexuality and their role as mothers and carers" (p.143). SCRATON's research points out that developments in the direction of mixed-sex grouping driven by putative organizational benefits, risk leaving the gendered presumptions about what to teach and how to teach it untouched, and underlying gender-based ideological assumptions about the 'nature' of boys and girls unidentified.

Recent proposals concerning a 'national curriculum' for teacher training promise little to threaten the tendency towards reinforcement of gender inequities inherent in the narrow, male-oriented model of NCPE. The expectations are that "all teachers of PE will be equipped to teach at least one mainstream game played in the summer and one mainstream game played in the winter" (DNH, 1995, p.15). PENNEY and EVANS (1997) highlight the manner in which the new criteria for teacher training – insisting that funding "is to be tied to evidence of institutions having complied with the government's desired aims" and that "inspectors will be asked to monitor training to teach the main traditional and competitive team sports, and to see that all trainee teachers are made aware of the increased opportunity to gain coaching qualifications" (DNH, 1995, p.17; cited in PENNEY and EVANS, 1997) – serve to reinforce a "privileging" of a narrow male-oriented model of PE.

National Curriculum Physical Education

The arrival of NCPE held forth the promise of a significant contribution to the dissipation of gender segregation in PE (FLINTOFF, 1993; SCRATON, 1993; TALBOT, 1993). However, NCPE seems something of a double-edged sword. On the one hand, the revised NCPE protects and bolsters the traditional female games, such as netball and hockey, that SCRATON (1993) speculated might be in danger of dying with the emergence of coeducational PE in the 1980s. On the other hand, however, the bolstering of 'traditional games' in the revised NCPE (and the reinforcement of this development more recently by the Government's policy statement *Sport: Raising the Game*) threatens to undermine further the quality of girls' PE experience – particularly in mixed-sex groupings – rather than enhance it. By identifying 'activity areas', with games especially prominent, NCPE has, in effect, 'defined' PE "as a set of distinct activities" (PENNEY and EVANS, 1997, p.22) and "(hardened) the hierarchy of areas of activity long established within the subject of PE, in which games is accorded the highest status" (p.23). Consequently, the revised order for NCPE has endorsed and strengthened games "as the dominant and defining feature of PE", especially at key stages 3 and 4 – the secondary years (PENNEY and EVANS, 1997, p.23).

The restoration and "privileging" of team-games in the NCPE has potentially significant consequences not only for coeducational PE but also girls' post-school physical activity and, thus (as we mention below), their likely commitment to health-related exercise – one of the central contemporary justifications for PE. In the first instance, the 'flexibility' available to PE teachers – within the statutory requirements for NCPE – allows for the continued provision of a sex-differentiated curriculum. NCPE, in its revised form, has "effectively endorsed long-standing practices and biases in PE in the UK" (PENNEY and EVANS, 1997, p.24) and appears, whether intended or not, more likely to reinforce the gendered nature of PE provision, "with girls and boys being offered different and stereotypically 'appropriate' activities" (PENNEY and EVANS, 1997, p.23), than to challenge it. The potential for areas of PE that might have provided better opportunities for coeducational experiences, e.g. dance and outdoor and adventurous activities, is undermined by secondary PE teachers' stereotypical attitudes towards teaching them and their alleged differential suitability for boys and girls (WADDINGTON et al, forthcoming).

Added to this, NCPE looks set to reduce time spent on those activities less impacted upon by the earlier sports socialization experiences of girls and boys and which, as such, hold out more hope for coeducational PE. KAY (1995) summarises research which contrasts the differing patterns of behaviour and interaction exhibited by girls and boys in more or less sex-stereotyped activities. She points out that in contrast to those 'male' activities often used for coeducational PE, such as football, in which a strong skill imbalance usually exists in favour of boys, in activities such as gymnastics and dance where the imbalance was neither as obvious nor as relevant, different patterns of interaction between boys and girls were observed. KAY (1995) cites TURVEY and LAWS (1988) example of gymnastics, wherein pupils worked in single-sex groupings initially – observing demonstrations by the other sex – before working together, whereupon "a more productive, equal and shared learning experience seemed to occur ... initial apprehension gave way to uninhibited partnership, and produced the type of constructive co-operation between the sexes which mixed sex grouping is hoped to achieve" (p.109). Clearly, some PE activities are potentially less threatening for girls, more likely to lead to full involvement and learning opportunities for them, as well as being more suited to coeducational teaching. Mixed-sex grouping is most likely to 'work' where skill imbalances are minimal, participation by boys and girls is on equal terms and boys are not able or are prevented from sidelining girls (KAY, 1995). Problems are particularly likely to arise in traditional 'male' games such as football or those that "offer opportunities for gendered personal attributes (e.g. boys' greater self-confidence, aggression and competitiveness)" (KAY, 1995, p.109).

Finally, the "privileging" of games has the potential to be particularly detrimental to girls' likely future participation in sport and physical activity, given the breadth of research pointing out that "competitive games have limited appeal to many children, particularly young women" (PENNEY and EVANS, 1997, p.23) and that "secondary school experiences of physical education are less successful at instilling a long-term interest in sport in girls than in boys" (KAY, 1995, p.58). A mis-match exists, then, between girls' PE and their likely forms of adult participation. The sports that girls have available to them in the PE curriculum do not neatly articulate with those participated in by adult women. "There is", according to KAY (1995), "discontinuity between the types of activities which girls are most likely to have been introduced to through school sport, and the activities which they might expect to take part in as leisure in adulthood" (p.61). She adds:

> For girls, many sport experiences at school are unlikely to be seen as relevant to later life; in the adult world, the activities traditionally offered to schoolgirls do not enjoy either the mass participation or elite status of boys' football, cricket and rugby, and role models are few. P.E. activities can be viewed as 'childish', and the transition to

female adulthood is more likely to involve leaving sport
behind than continuing it.

(KAY, 1995, p.61)

Whilst to some extent the same can be said of boys' PE, because girls
are far more likely to participate in body management activities in their
post-school lives then the revised NCPE is more likely to reinforce the
sporting behaviours of boys than those of girls. KAY (1995) notes,

> The contrast with boys' experiences is marked; the sports
> in which boys participate at school are replicated and
> exalted in later life not just as adult activities, but as
> major, prestigious, national and international institutions.
> For young and adolescent boys, continued involvement in
> the world of sport is part of a rite of passage into a
> communal masculine adulthood. (p.61)

One well-established consequence of the gendered nature of secondary
PE is the apparent disjuncture between girls' PE and their health needs
(ARMSTRONG, MCMANUS, WELSMAN and KIRBY, 1996): "We
have the most sedentary group of children we have ever had. Girls are
less active than boys and are getting less active as they get older"
(ARMSTRONG; cited in MIHILL, 1995). Of particular concern is the
trend for girls' activity levels to show a marked deterioration as they
progress through secondary school (ARMSTRONG et al, 1996). Far
from confronting this issue, NCPE promises to aggravate the situation.
The enhanced status of games at all key stages of NCPE runs counter
to "the overwhelming evidence that the dominance of team games in
the curriculum is doing little to encourage girls' active participation in
physical education" (MCMANUS and ARMSTRONG, 1996, p.35).
This situation has, of course, been exacerbated by the Government's
policy statement *Sport: Raising the Game* (DEPARTMENT OF
NATIONAL HERITAGE, 1995). Insofar as the NCPE and the policy
statement "privilege" games they bolster the discrepancy between
those activities available to girls at school and those they appear to find
enjoyable and might, thus, be likely to take with them into post-school
life, such as aerobics and dance.

In sum, NCPE serves to reinforce wider social pressures operating to
encourage girls away from, rather than towards, active lifestyles. For
all these reasons the combined impact of the revised NCPE and trends

in coeducational secondary PE are cause for major concern regarding girls' continued participation in physical activity and sport in their post-school lives.

Even though sex differences in sport are wider than in any other area of young people's leisure (ROBERTS, 1996), the apparent failure of PE to encourage girls towards lifelong participation in sport is nothing if not a complex and contested issue. Whilst the differences between boys' and girls' participation in sport "remain stark" according to ROBERTS (1996, p.55) nevertheless, "Sex differences ... have probably lessened as young people have taken up more sports, many of which are played by both sexes" (ROBERTS, 1996, pp.54-55). In his studies of recent trends in youth cultures and school sport in relation to government policies ROBERTS (1996) has this to say:

> in 1994 males and females were participating more or less equally in sport during school lessons. Since most of the schools were co-educational the sexes had the same amounts of timetabled sport and PE. Moreover, the mean number of sports played in lessons hardly differed between the males and females in either primary or secondary schools. (p.55)

The significance of this analysis for claims about mixed-group teaching becomes readily apparent: "The girls in coeducational schools were not sitting on the sidelines and watching the boys play. This may have applied in previous years ... but in 1994 the situation was different" (ROBERTS, 1996, p.55). However, whether girls and boys were "participating more or less equally" begs questions about what is meant by 'equally'. Notwithstanding the pertinence of ROBERTS' observations the point we would wish to make here (as discussed earlier) is that the qualitative experiences of mixed-sex groupings may be just as gendered as previous sex-differentiated curricula. Equal participation in relation to time tells us little about experiences or outcomes.

Nevertheless, MILOSEVIC's (1996) research supports much of ROBERTS' analysis. She points out that the majority of pupils in her study favoured mixed-sex PE lessons. She adds, however, that "overall nearly a third of all pupils preferred single sex groups" and, particularly pertinently, "The greatest preference for single sex P.E.

came from 15 and 16 year old girls" (p.20). Both MILOSEVIC and ROBERTS point to extra-curricular PE and out of lessons (both in and out of school) as the point at which the differences in girls' and boys' participation were most marked:

> It was out of lessons where sex differences in sports participation were widest ... Out of lessons, in and out of school, the boys played more sports, were the more likely to participate regularly in seven or more, and less likely to participate regularly in none. The boys played sport on more days during term time, for more hours per day, and also spent more time playing sport during school holidays.
>
> (ROBERTS, 1996, p.55)

Differences, in terms of levels and forms of participation in sport and physical activity within PE, are widest and most evident at the secondary level. As ROBERTS (1996, p.55) observes, "sport illustrates a general leisure tendency: sex differences that are evident in the primary school become wider with age". Nonetheless, whilst differences between the sexes seem wider in sport than any other area of young people's leisure, on the basis of the demonstrable narrowing of the gap in schools, ROBERTS (1996) argues, that,

> the evidence ... does not suggest that the schools bore a major responsibility for the females' lower rates of out-of-school participation. The girls were playing as much sport, and as many sports, as boys in school lessons, and were being offered a wide range, encompassing sports played mainly by girls and others that were played by both sexes. *The main reason for the girls' lower participation outside lessons seemed to be simply that they liked sport less.*
>
> (p.56; emphasis added)

However, this conclusion of ROBERTS fails to adequately recognise the complexities of secondary school, PE which is not simply about numbers and types of sports played, but is implicitly related to pupils' and teachers' gendered attitudes, behaviours and experiences and the likely consequences of these for the place of physical activity and sport in the adult lives of young women.

ROBERTS (1996) goes on to suggest that,

> rather than being created or even strengthened by their school experiences, it seemed rather that the sexes were bringing their different attitudes into school and a result was that the girls were more likely to resent, while the boys were more likely to enjoy, the similar amounts of sport in which they were required to participate. Out of school, of course, the girls had the option of playing less.
>
> (p.56)

Secondary PE may, as ROBERTS (1996) concludes about schooling *per se*, "be unable to countervail against wider socialising influences even if they wish to do so" (p.56). Nevertheless, while accepting that schools cannot accept full responsibility for wider structural inequalities, there seems little doubt that the unintended consequences of coeducational PE and the revised NCPE may indeed be the reinforcement and reproduction of gender stereotypes and inequalities.

Conclusion

On the face of it, coeducational PE has the potential to make teachers and pupils alike address issues of sex discrimination, gender inequalities and equal opportunities. Paradoxically, however, coeducational PE (by failing to appreciate the unintended consequences of mixed-sex grouping and the manner in which oversimplified attempts to bring the sexes together in PE might lead to an exacerbation of girls' disadvantages) is likely to have the opposite effect to that intended. The movement towards coeducational PE has not automatically brought with it the development of equal opportunities for girls or boys. As if to aggravate these difficulties, the revised NCPE, by "privileging" team games and sport, threatens to reinforce a vicious circle of gender-typical attitudes and behaviours among both pupils and present and future PE teachers.

Notwithstanding ROBERTS' (1996) observations about increased participation among girls and young women, a clear difference remains in terms of boys' and girls' experiences of PE. Hence, it is difficult to be particularly optimistic about gender equity in secondary physical education. NCPE has 'privileged' (PENNEY and EVANS, 1997) a 'male' view of suitable PE. PE teachers continue to perpetuate stereotypical teaching behaviours and ideologies at the same time as 'traditional' female sports and physical activities continue to be undervalued. The unintended consequences of some mixed-sex grouping (especially that driven by organizational benefits) is the continuance of stereotypical beliefs about gender-appropriate behaviour among adults and young people alike.

It may be that a combination of single-sex and mixed-sex grouping is the most likely to bring about gender equity in PE (KAY, 1995) if gender differences are to be confronted and eradicated, rather than unthinkingly or unintentionally exacerbated. From the work of ROBERTS (1996) and MILOSEVIC (1996) it seems that it may be possible to identify preferred groupings, interests and activities at the differing stages of secondary PE that may go some way to achieving some of the best of coeducational PE whilst avoiding some of the more obvious pitfalls. MILOSEVIC (1996) takes the view that "There may be a case for offering strongly stereotyped activities in single-sex groups initially". "In this way", she adds, "girls are given a relatively unhindered opportunity to participate in traditionally male activities and boys can do the same for conventionally female activities" (p.20).

The nature of the revised NCPE does nothing to suggest that it will be any different to coeducational PE in failing to deliver the equality of opportunity in secondary PE that it appeared to promise: "Certainly with the statutory requirements as they stand, in years ahead it may be particularly difficult for the stated aim of the NC, to ensure the provision of a broad and balanced education for *all* children (DES, 1989), to be achieved in the context of PE" (PENNEY and EVANS, 1997, p.24; emphasis in the original). Unfortunately, secondary PE shows all the signs of remaining, as TALBOT (1993) succinctly states, "gendered in ideology, content and teaching methods" (p.74).

References

ARMSTRONG, N., MCMANUS, A., WELSMAN, J. and KIRBY, B. (1996) Physical Activity Patterns and Aerobic Fitness Among Pre-Pubescents. *European Physical Education Review*, 2, 1, 19-29.

DEPARTMENT OF EDUCATION AND SCIENCE AND THE WELSH OFFICE (1991) *National Curriculum Physical Education Working Group*

Interim Report. London, DES and WO.

DEPARTMENT FOR NATIONAL HERITAGE (1995) *Sport: Raising the Game*. London, DNH.

FLINTOFF, A. (1990) Physical Education, Equal Opportunities and the National Curriculum: Crisis or Challenge? *Physical Education Review*, 13, 2, 85-100.

FLINTOFF, A. (1993) Gender, Physical Education and Initial Teacher Training. In EVANS, J. (Ed) *Equality, Education and Physical Education*. London, Falmer Press, pp.184-204.

FLINTOFF, A. (1996a) We have no Problems with Equal Opportunities here ... We've got Mixed Changing Rooms! *The British Journal of Physical Education*, 27, 1, 21-23.

FLINTOFF, A. (1996b) Anti-Sexist Practices in Secondary PE. *The British Journal of Physical Education*, 27 (1) 24-31.

HARGREAVES, J. (1994) *Sporting Females: Critical issues in the history and sociology of women's sports*. London, Routledge.

KAY, T. (1995) *Women and Sport: A Review of Research*. London, The Sports Council.

LEAMAN, O. (1984) *Sit on the Sidelines and Watch the Boys Play: Sex Discrimination in Physical Education*. Harlow, Longman.

MCMANUS, A. and ARMSTRONG, N. (1996) The Physical Inactivity of Girls – A school issue? *The British Journal of Physical Education*, 27, 1, 34-35.

MIHILL, C. (1995) Bias against girls' in school sports. *The Guardian*, Friday, September 15th, 1995.

MILOSEVIC, L. (1996) Pupils' Experience of P.E. Questionnaire Results. *The British Journal of Physical Education*, 27, 1, 16-20.

OFFICE OF STANDARDS IN EDUCATION (OFSTED) (1995) *Physical Education: A Review of Inspection Findings*. London, HMSO.

OFFICE OF HER MAJESTY'S CHIEF INSPECTOR OF SCHOOLS IN WALES (OHMCI) (1995) Report by H.M. Inspectors. *Survey of Physical Education in Key Stages 1, 2 and 3*. Cardiff, OHMCI.

PENNEY, D. and EVANS, J. (1997) Naming the Game. Discourse and Domination in Physical Education and Sport in England and Wales. *European Physical Education Review,* 3, 1, 21-32.

ROBERTS, K. (1996) Young People, Schools, Sport and Government Policies. *Sport, Education and Society,* 1, 1, 47-58.

SCRATON, S. (1992) *Shaping Up to Womanhood.* Milton Keynes, Open University Press.

SCRATON, S. (1993) Equality, Coeducation and Physical Education in Secondary Schooling. In EVANS, J. (Ed) *Equality, Education and Physical Education.* London, Falmer Press, pp.139-153.

TALBOT, M. (1993) A Gendered Physical Education: Equality and Sexism. In EVANS, J. (Ed) *Equality, Education and Physical Education.* London, Falmer Press, pp.74-89.

TALBOT, M. (1996) Gender and National Curriculum Physical Education. *The British Journal of Physical Education,* 27, 1, 5-7.

TURVEY, J. and LAWS, C. (1988) Are Girls Losing Out? The Effects of Mixed-Sex Grouping on Girls' Performance in Physical Education. *British Journal of Physical Education,* 19, 6, 253-255.

WADDINGTON, I., MALCOM, D. and COBB, J. (forthcoming) Gender Stereotyping and Physical Education. *European Physical Education Review.*

Chapter 14

Sexism and Homophobia in Physical Education: The Challenge for Teacher Educators

Anne Flintoff

Images of Coeducational Physical Education Initial Teacher Education

A male lecturer is taking a mixed group of first year students for their first canoeing lesson in the swimming pool. Asking one woman to enter a canoe, he leans from the pool side and pushes her knees apart into the correct leg position, saying "that's right, open your legs wide – not like your mother told you!". A major 'put-down' used by male students is to call another a "girlie", or a "nancy". Homophobic comments or gestures by male students are common in practical classes, such as gymnastics or dance, where students are asked to perform movements which include touching or supporting one another. A talented soccer player tells me that she would not consider joining the women's football team because "most of the team are a bit suspect". A group of students and female lecturer are reviewing a tape recording of a gymnastics lesson. At one point, the camera focuses on a young girl performing a straddle roll away from the camera. One of the male students asks loudly for a "close up on that please". The only response was a low snigger from two students.

Each of the above incidents are examples of sexism and homophobia observed during the fieldwork of a research project which explored the relationship between gender power relations and initial teacher education (ITE) in physical education (PE) (see FLINTOFF, 1993a)[1]. They are used here to illustrate the sexist and homophobic nature of the ethos and atmosphere in the two ITE institutions on which the study was based. The research revealed that although the organisation of PE ITE along coeducational lines has clearly raised important issues of physicality and sexuality, as yet, these remain unacknowledged on formal institutional agendas. Evidence drawn from a later piece of research carried out in 1994 suggests that these issues are even less likely to be raised in the new school-based ITE. This chapter argues that attempts to sensitise students to the impact of gender on the teaching and learning process need to be not simply much more systematic and substantial, but must also include attention to sexuality as a fundamental element of sexism. At the same time, it suggests that PE professionals (lecturers and teachers) will have to recognise and to challenge the operation of sexism and homophobia in their own classrooms if real progress in gender equity is to be made.

Gender Equality and Teacher Education

Teacher education has been recognised as having a crucial role to play in the process of challenging gender power relations for some time (e.g. DEEM, 1980), yet it is only recently that feminist critiques have begun to appear (e.g. EQUAL OPPORTUNITIES COMMISSION, (EOC), 1989; LEONARD, 1989; SKELTON and HANSON, 1989). To date, studies have focused largely on the degree to which gender inequality has a legitimacy and presence within the formal curriculum of ITE courses. Few of these studies have specifically considered PE ITE (DEWAR's work, 1987, is a key exception). Whilst not denying that a focus on the structure and content of the formal curriculum is useful, it is necessarily a limited one; as LEONARD (1989, pp.26-28) points out,

> colleges ... have theories about education *and* are practical institutions. To understand the role of ITT [initial teacher training], we must look not only at the theories of education which colleges *teach*, but also at what they *practise* ... the issue is not whether it is counter-productive to raise the topic of sex equity at ITT level, but *what* is taught and learned and *how* it is taught (in the sense of the broadest social relations within which

learning takes place) within universities ... (emphasis in the original).

In an effort to explore how gender relations might be reproduced or challenged through ITE in terms of both the formal curriculum and the nature of everyday interaction, my research centred on the ethnographic study of two institutions, Brickhill and Heydonfield (both pseudonyms) (see FLINTOFF, 1993a, 1993b, 1993c). These were chosen to reflect the separate and distinct historical development of PE, and are typical of the institutions currently involved in the training of intending secondary PE teachers in Britain. The focus of the study was on the training of intending secondary school PE teachers, not because primary PE is any the less important, but because most of my experience has been with the secondary age group. The research used semi-structured interviews with key decision makers (such as course leaders) and document analysis, but a large amount of data was collected through extensive periods of observation and simply 'being around'. Whilst the implications for girls of moves towards coeducational school PE are beginning to be explored (e.g. SCRATON, 1985, 1992, 1993; MILOSEVIC, 1995), the implications for women of moving towards coeducation within PE ITE – a process which is now well established in Britain – has been devoid of feminist analysis or evaluation[2]. My research aimed to contribute to an understanding of this context.

Gender Identities in PE

I have found the work of BRITTAN (1989) on gender identity particularly useful in understanding and unravelling the complex nature of gendered interaction observed during the fieldwork. He argues that rather than seeing gender as a set of role behaviours unproblematically acquired (a position now largely discounted – see CONNELL, 1987), it is better seen as an accomplishment, something which is never static, and which is always subject to renegotiation and redefinition. Masculinity or femininity can never be accepted as a 'finished product' but needs to be accomplished in a permanent process of struggle and confirmation – a process he has called "identity work". BRITTAN's work and others (e.g. CARRIGAN, CONNELL and LEE, 1985; CONNELL, 1987) have also stressed the politics of gender identities, and the differentiation of behaviours and characteristics within gender groupings, as well as between them. As CARRIGAN et al. (1985, p.590) have noted,

> the fissuring of the categories of 'men' and 'women' is one of the central facts about patriarchal power and the way it works. In the case of men, the crucial division is between hegemonic masculinity and various subordinated masculinities.

So although it is important to note that few men actually correspond to "culturally exalted forms of masculinity", very large numbers of men become complicit in sustaining hegemonic models because most benefit from the subordination of women which is central to them.

Attempting to describe some of the characteristics of "identity work" at Heydonfield and Brickhill presents the difficulty of conveying through writing the ways in which gender power relations structure situations without reducing men to one cultural grouping and women to another (see also WOOD, 1984). Here I have space only to note that the institutions were involved in producing a range of masculinities and femininities, but that they were also involved in the processes by which particular ones became hegemonic (see FLINTOFF, 1993a). At Heydonfield, for example, the former men's PE college, there was room for male PE students to negotiate between a variety of masculinities, ranging from the rational, responsible masculinity reflected in, and maintained through, the heavily science-dominated curriculum, to an anti-intellectual, flamboyant, and physical masculinity characteristic of the male 'jock' sporting culture of the institution (see DEWAR, 1990). The definitions of masculinity made available were very much influenced, too, by social class. Many students had come from independent schools, suggesting that middle class values would have been very influential in the kinds of masculinities predominating.

Male Identity Work: Competitive and Heterosexual Display

Observation revealed that for male PE students, 'doing' masculinity involved two main strategies: overt demonstrations of physical prowess and competitiveness, and what I have called heterosexual displays. Both strategies relied heavily on the use of "negative reference groups" (STANWORTH, 1983). In the same way that studies on boys at school level have revealed (e.g. ASKEW and ROSS, 1988), male students brought competition into almost all of the activities they were involved with, and competition seemed to be their primary source of motivation. Practical PE sessions were obviously ideal contexts for the display of physical prowess, and those which demanded an appropriately 'masculine' physicality, such as the contact games, were particularly fierce and competitive. However, even in non-competitive activity sessions, such as gymnastics, some of the male students would set up direct competitive challenges for one another, for example, daring one another to climb to the very top of a rope, and perform higher and higher dive forward rolls over a beam.

A common insult used in these competitive challenges was to trivialise or to put down another man's performance by suggesting that they were performing like a "right nancy" or a "girlie"[3]. Because masculinity is defined in terms of what it is not – not homosexual or feminine (MESSNER, 1987), women and homosexuals were used as negative reference groups in the students' identity work. This frequently resulted in a sexist and homophobic ethos, in which many of the men actively distanced themselves from any behaviour or activity associated with 'femininity'. In dance, for example, a group of men worked hard to demonstrate their lack of commitment by fooling around and being generally disruptive (FLINTOFF, 1991).

A second element of 'doing masculinity' involved heterosexual displays. It was common for male students (as well as male staff too) to deliberately 'sexualise' situations by introducing sexual innuendo. The centrality of the body in the PE Studies work meant that there were numerous opportunities for this, and displays ranged from explicit comments or gestures, to more subtle glances and facial expressions. These were directed at female staff as well as students and served to embarrass them and erode their confidence and status (see also WHITBREAD, 1980; ASKEW and ROSS, 1988).

CONNELL (1987), COVENEY et al (1984) and MAHONY (1985) have all highlighted the important role played by the social construction of male heterosexuality in the maintenance of male power, a major feature of which revolves around the objectification of women. Many of the interactions between men involved boasts and innuendoes centred around "getting" or "having" a woman – of presenting an image (even if it was only an image, rather than reality) as an active heterosexual. These were very much 'public' displays – always performed overtly for an 'audience'. For example, a partner stretch in gymnastics was suggested as a new sexual position; the shortness of a woman teachers' PE skirt 'blamed' for a lack of concentration on a visit to school. On another occasion, a first year student, asked in an introductory ice-breaking session to name something "bizarre" about himself, suggested loudly that he considered the fact that he was still a virgin as "highly bizarre" and something which he would be "working to resolve" that evening in the Student Union bar.

Public displays of 'heterosexuality' came from some of the male staff too – these did not just form part of informal conversations, but were features of their everyday teaching strategies and interactions. One, for example, suggested that women should not be afraid to volunteer to cycle on the stationary bike in the laboratory as he "had had a woman only last week!". Joining in the ensuing laughing from some of the students he added that he had better "rephrase that before anyone gets the wrong idea!". This comment worked, like many others I observed, to restrict women's involvement in learning experiences – it was not surprising to see that there were no women volunteering for this practical exercise.

As these and the examples presented earlier suggest, a predatory heterosexual ethos identified in other educational contexts (e.g. HALSON, 1989; MAHONY, 1989) was also in evidence here. Whilst the incidents I observed might be dismissed as trivial, and may be less extreme than some described in other feminist research, they serve nonetheless to reinforce the 'naturalness' of hetero-sexuality, and a construction of male sexuality based on objectification and conquest[4]. These situations left women with little option but to 'go along with' the 'jokes' or risk having their sexuality – or rather men's definitions of their sexuality – questioned if they complained too strongly. As CLARKE's (1994) recent work shows, for students who are lesbian, the task of managing – or more accurately, in most cases, concealing – their sexual identity is a constant tension in their everyday lives in PE.

Many of the sexualising incidents were specifically homophobic. Any sign of 'weakness' by a man was considered appropriate for others to pick on and use to humiliate: the colour or style of clothing;

involvement in 'feminine' activities or the inability to drink copious quantities of beer (see also CURRY, 1991; SKELTON, 1993)[5]. Although not all men were involved in such incidents, I observed no-one challenging or speaking out against them – such is the power and effect of male bonding, as JACKSON (1990) notes,

> [male bonding] is not just about group dynamics. It's a political process because it viciously exploits men's internal contradictions and uses these to sustain patriarchal power over other people ... to survive [boys and men] learn to consent to the accepted codes and conventions of heterosexual masculinity ... that [make] up the rules of the male club. (p.170)

The rules of the 'male club' within Brickhill and Heydonfield operated to ensure that men responded competitively and aggressively – not just in their involvement in 'male' activities, but also in their interactions and relationships with each other – and worked continually to preserve a heterosexual identity, through homophobic and sexist displays.

Female Identities in PE: A Balancing Act?

For women students, negotiating an identity in PE, involved the adoption of a number of "gender management strategies" (SHEPPARD, 1989). A major part of identity work for women students, and which was especially evident at Brickhill, involved making sure they were recognised as heterosexual and feminine[6]. Particularly in the early years of the undergraduate degree, students took great care to emphasise their femininity and an acceptable (hetero) sexuality, through for example, their dress and appearance, and through the way in which they avoided 'masculine' activities. Many of the women used the label of "girlie" themselves, illustrating the importance of heterosexual attractiveness in the construction of their own identities – they were prepared to collude with the use of the label, despite its other, objectionable characteristics. Being a "girlie" entailed treading a careful line in terms of sexuality. On one hand, women who were not in a visible heterosexual relationship risked the label of a "lezzie" (lesbian); on the other, women who were known to have had more than one sexual partner risked the label of "a bike" (a woman who slept around). As HALSON (1989) and LEES (1987) have noted such terms are used to restrict and control women's and girls' sexuality.

It was clear that some of the women were uncomfortable with being female in specific PE sessions. For example, in practical sessions such as swimming and gymnastics where students' bodies were very much on 'display', conversations with the women confirmed that their choice of wearing long tee shirts over their swimming costumes until the last possible moment, was an attempt to avoid the "really embarrassing" situation of "having to perform in front of the men". The suggestion by SCRATON (1987) that whilst mixed PE might offer a better experience for women and girls, it may also offer more opportunities for male objectification and gaze, seemed to hold true in these particular sessions. It is significant to note that many of the practices and policies of the institutions themselves contributed towards the reproduction of particular images of femininity; for example, women students were often called "girls" by staff, and the compulsory PE "uniform" meant that women had little or no choice about their presentation in practical sessions.

Although identity work by female students at Heydonfield was somewhat different in that here they down-played the fact that they were women, in both institutions, women negotiated identities within the boundaries of what CONNELL (1987) has called an "emphasised femininity", a femininity essentially organised around the interests of men and which is first and foremost heterosexual. However, it is important to note that the reproduction of "emphasised femininity" is not a simplistic, straightforward process, and there was evidence of some women challenging and resisting these definitions. One woman student was noticeable for her feminist stance in discussions; she constantly raised questions about gender, although she confided in me that she had nearly left the course on several occasions because of the way in which she was treated by some of the male students for doing this. I observed male students groaning, or giving a 'time-out' signal whenever she raised her hand.

The account above has described the sexist and homophobic nature of everyday life within PE ITE. However, although gender power relations were very much visible in this sense, as the next section shows, they were largely invisible as part of the formal curriculum, and in the educational discussions in which students were involved.

Sexism and Sexuality as Legitimate Education Issues?

Until its demise in September 1993, all ITE courses in England and Wales were required to fulfil national criteria laid out by the Council for the Accreditation of Teacher Education (CATE). These included making sure that "all students learn to guard against preconceptions based on the race, gender, religion or other attributes of pupils, and understand the need to promote equal opportunities" (DES, 1989, p.10)[7].

However, research suggests that the implementation of the CATE criteria with respect to gender issues is far from adequate (EOC, 1989; LEONARD, 1989; SKELTON and HANSON, 1989). A survey by the Equal Opportunities Commission in 1989 showed how little impact these criteria have had on the inclusion of gender issues in ITE courses. Whilst most institutions recognised the need for 'gender awareness', there was little evidence to suggest that this work was being systematically promoted and good practice owed more to the commitment and energy of individuals than to coherent planning. This scenario held true at both Brickhill and Heydonfield. There was little attention given to gender within the formal curriculum, particularly on the one year Post Graduate Certificate of Education (PGCE) courses[8]. Here staff suggested that "time was limited" and they raised these issues largely through a permeation method – where issues were discussed when or if they emerged within other contexts. However, there was little or no evidence of gender issues being raised sensitively in practice; staff were far more likely to reinforce stereotypical images of boys' and girls' abilities and the attitudes of some male staff were distinctly hostile to the idea that they might permeate such issues through their teaching (see FLINTOFF, 1993b).

On the four year undergraduate programmes, the situation was a little better; here all students were introduced to equality issues in small, compulsory units of work situated in the second year of the Professional Studies aspect of their degree. The location of the compulsory modules within the Professional Studies element of the courses – the area of work which students view as least relevant – together with their on-off nature, and their early placement in the course, are other factors likely to contribute to their overall ineffectiveness (DENSCOMBE, 1982). Although opportunities did exist beyond these short, 'bolt on' courses to help students understand the structural frameworks of inequality, these were within optional rather than compulsory modules situated later in the degree.

Students were no more likely to be involved in discussions of gender power relations within their PE subject study than in their Professional Studies work. Although the structure of the courses was very different at Brickhill and Heydonfield, in both, the PE curriculum was dominated by the behavioural sciences, mirroring trends noted by others (e.g. MCKAY, GORE and KIRK, 1990). After introductory courses in the first year, the remaining socio-cultural knowledge was largely restricted to optional modules in the final (assessed) years of the degree. At Brickhill that year, the course had not attracted sufficient numbers of students to be able to run, suggesting few students see such knowledge as really useful (see also DEWAR and INGRAM, 1987). It is important to stress that there were some staff who worked hard to raise issues of equality with students, particularly those women staff involved in teaching the sociology and curriculum issues courses.

Overall, however, students had limited opportunities to learn about the effects of gender on the teaching and learning process in PE. However, as well as noting the extent to which gender issues were (or were not) raised, the content and focus of such sessions are also significant. LEONARD (1989) has noted the limitation of work within ITE on gender which focuses solely on the pupils' educational experience at the expense of its impact on teachers and their work. But also significant is the silence which surrounds the whole area of sexuality, and sexual harassment in discussions of gender relations with students. Sexuality remains a massively problematic area for girls and women in school and one in which unequal power relations are very much manifest (DEEM, 1991; HALSON, 1991; HOLLY, 1989; KELLY, 1992). It is manifested in particular ways within PE, both at school level (SCRATON, 1987), and as presented here, within ITE. Although very much a dominant aspect of everyday interactions between students, and between staff and students, sexuality remained largely invisible in terms of the explicit agendas of the curricula at Brickhill and Heydonfield.

School Based Training in the 1990s

Since my research was completed, the introduction of school-based training (DFE, 1992a; DFE, 1992b) has significantly altered the nature and shape of PE ITE. There is no space here to explore in detail the nature of the changes (see MAGUIRE and BALL, 1993; FURLONG, 1992), but the emphasis of the new courses is broadly on the development of students' classroom management skills, their knowledge of assessment procedures and familiarisation with the content of the national curriculum. There is now no formal obligation for teacher education courses to make sure that students are aware of how gender and 'race' affect the teaching and learning process.

The following section draws on research conducted with students on the first year of a school-based PGCE course at my own institution, and focuses specifically on their experiences in school, an aspect of ITE which I chose not to include in my earlier research[9]. Like other research which has focused on students' experiences of teaching practice in schools (see MENTER, 1991), I found that gender was a significant aspect of the students' work, although not in any straightforward or consistent way.

Gender as a Professional Issue in School Based Work

Although schools organised students' school based work in different ways, all had a programme which entailed students meeting with their Professional Mentor (a teacher outside PE, such as the deputy head, or senior teacher whose responsibility extended to all students in the school), as well as work in the PE department, supervised by a PE mentor. For most students, this programme included a focus on 'equal opportunities', although gender was much less likely to be addressed than, for example, special educational needs. No student mentioned any sessions on gender specifically, although several had had the opportunity to look at the schools' policy on equal opportunities, and discuss the ways in which the school was working to implement this in practice. This patchy commitment to work on gender equity in school is not surprising, and is supported by the findings of a major piece of research on gender which have recently been reported. ARNOT, DAVID and WEINER's (1996) study focused on the impact of educational reforms on gender equity in schools, and concluded that although there "was a mixed picture of beneficial procedures and policies arising from some of the reforms, pockets of thoughtful and knowledgeable practice from committed individuals and groups ...

overall, [there was] no infrastructure for the delivery of equal opportunities on a wider and more systematic basis".

Whilst equality issues did seem to have had some visibility in students' Professional Studies discussions, this was not the case within their specialist subject area. Only three of the seventeen students had had any discussion about gender issues within PE, and this had been limited to a discussion about the advantages and disadvantages of single-sex versus mixed-sex teaching. It seems that many PE teachers do simplistically equate mixed-sex PE teaching with providing equal opportunities in their subject (FLINTOFF, 1995). Very often, as found elsewhere (e.g. EOC, 1989), it was on the students' own initiative that gender was discussed at all. One student felt that the course had not prepared him to promote gender equity through his teaching at all, suggesting:

> it was a case of if you wanted to raise it, then you raised it I suppose ...The idea that schools should be reinforcing equal opportunity issues is great in theory, but unfortunately, in many cases this has not happened for a variety of reasons, perhaps one of which is that subject mentors in school have had insufficient training and simply do not have the knowledge and expertise to cover these areas.

Equality issues had not been mentioned to any student in the written feedback they had been given from the PE mentors evaluating particular lessons. Interestingly, although all of the students felt that they were able to promote gender equity in their teaching, when I asked them what strategies they used to do this, their responses were mixed and few could give concrete examples. A common response was to suggest that they "had not really thought about it consciously", or that it was essentially "a matter of common sense". Three male students suggested that since they had only taught boys that year, it was not really a relevant question to ask them![10]. It was clear that most of the students had not been involved in any kind of critical reflection on the effects of gender relations on their teaching or their role as a PE teacher. Despite this, gender was a very obvious factor in the process of their training, as the next section describes.

Gender/Sex in the Process of School-Based Training

Gender was a significant factor in the initial placement of students in schools, a key part of my PE tutor role. Schools did not agree to have PE students, but specifically requested male or female students, (or more usually, one of each) reflecting the organisation of school PE around separate girls' and boys' departments. This task was fraught with ethical questions and dilemmas which are rarely openly acknowledged or addressed. On what basis do I decide to place a particular student in a particular school? Do I, for example, place a grammar-school educated, confident and outgoing, games-playing male student to work with a male mentor in a strong games-orientated, single-sex department, where I suspect he would 'do well' – at least in terms of the mentor's assessment of him? Or would it be better for him to work with a female mentor, in a mixed department, where I know he will have more opportunity to develop his weaker areas of dance and gymnastics? These kinds of dilemma are clearly not new to teacher education; the nature of a student's teaching practice school has always been significant to development as teachers. What is new is the extent to which school-based work now forms the central, and most sustained, aspect of that work.

Once allocated to a school, the structure, organisation and philosophy of the specific PE department hugely affected the students' opportunities and experiences – and gender was a salient factor in this. To give some specific examples:

* a number of students only taught children of their own sex;

* women students were more likely to have had the opportunity to teach across the full range of NCPE activities;

* students' opportunities to teach games were heavily limited by stereotypical notions of 'girls' games' and 'boys' games'; men students largely taught rugby and soccer; women students, netball and hockey (although extra curricular opportunities were more relaxed in some schools).

Quality assurance and consistency of provision across schools is clearly a difficult, if not impossible task. Like other institutions, we have barely enough schools wishing to be involved in the scheme, so it is not a question of us being able to pick and choose what kinds of experiences were on offer for our students! The new reforms for teacher education have produced a fragmented and varied training. In terms of PE, the effect appears to be one which may well have strengthened the impact and significance of gender in that process.

The student-mentor relationship was a further aspect of the training which raised specific gendered issues. This relationship is clearly unequally balanced in terms of power in that the student is very firmly in the weakest position. It is the student who is 'inexperienced', usually the younger of the two, who is there 'to learn' and who is being assessed on his or her teaching competence at the end of the course. Many students adopt what TINNING (1988) has called a "pedagogy of necessity" on their teaching practice. They adopt "safe" practices which they perceive will simply "get them through", rather than risk innovatory ones which may fail to win their mentor's approval. However, gender power is rarely acknowledged as playing a part in the student-mentor relationship, and yet as MENTER (1989) suggests, within a patriarchal society there are opportunities for that power imbalance to be amplified, especially where a strong position is occupied by a man, and a weak position is occupied by a woman. In our scheme, there was a notable gender imbalance between PE mentors and students. Eighteen out of twenty-two PE mentors were male, whereas the student cohort was made up of nine women and thirteen men.

This imbalance was significant in a number of ways, not least of which was the amount of help some students received from their mentors. For three of the women students, and one of the men, their placement in departments run on a single-sex basis, and having a PE mentor of the opposite sex, meant, incredibly, they had little or no interaction with them at all! At the end of their first teaching practice, three women students had not been seen teaching by their mentor at all, and had little or no interaction with them, yet their teaching practice report at the end of the three weeks, was written by them. I should note that all of these students did value, and comment upon, what they considered to be the excellent support they had received from the women staff in the school, but clearly, this was not the same as working with a mentor who was knowledgeable about the details of the PGCE scheme.

Several female students mentioned that their relationship with their male mentor was one in which "gender-joking" played a part. CUNNISON (1989) has coined the term "gender-joking" to describe jokes or comments which have a gender content, and are made across gender lines. They are usually initiated by men and take place in front of an audience, thus constituting a public performance. Several students suggested that dealing with such comments was "part and parcel" of their relationship with their male PE mentor, and other male staff; to pass their PGCE year, it was a case of "putting up and shutting up". They told me very matter-of-factly about incidents or comments, suggesting that it was "no big deal", "the usual kind of thing", "they were only having a laugh and it wasn't personal". One woman suggested that in her department "sexism was a standing joke ... they're were always going on, always making a joke, tongue in cheek". It is clear that the 'sexualising' of PE classes at women's expense noted earlier, is not confined to higher education institutions, but is a salient feature of students' school-based work too.

Whilst I have mentioned mostly women's experiences here, it is important to note that one or two of the men told me of situations where they felt gender had been influential to their time in school too. Dealing with girls' 'crushes' on them, for example, was cited as flattering but difficult to deal with, and establishing good working relationships with girls meant, for two male students, having to adopt a "fatherly approach". Two men talked briefly about having to deal with homophobic comments from pupils (but also male PE staff!) when teaching dance. Men as well as women students need help in understanding and problematising the very real ways in which gender affects not just pupils' learning in PE, but their own too.

The second part of this chapter has suggested that despite a very changed context for ITE, gender remains a significant, if largely unacknowledged, feature of school based training. Whilst equity issues are marginal in the formal agendas of school-based work, nevertheless, the process and experience of this work is one in which gender and sexuality form a pervasive feature.

Concluding Remarks

If the findings of my research are endemic elsewhere, it appears that the asexual 'Peter Pan' world of women's PE, described by

FLETCHER (1984), has long since disappeared. In its place is a coeducational environment in which (hetero) sexuality and sexism constrains and limits the opportunities, experiences and identities of women students, and staff, but also of men too. Yet it also shows how feminist knowledge, which could help students understand and challenge gender relations in their teaching, has yet to become a legitimate form of knowledge within ITE. The data presented here (and the research more broadly) make visible some of the ways in which sexism and homophobia are manifest within PE ITE, extending work elsewhere in PE and sport (GRIFFIN, 1989a, 1989b; GRIFFIN, 1992; GRIFFIN and GENASCI, 1990; CLARKE, 1997; WOODS, 1992). The ongoing challenge will be for teacher educators, and school teachers working alongside them, to extend the legitimacy of these issues within professional debate, and to work for action and change, in order to make PE a more rewarding and enriching experience for all.

Notes

1.   Although the focus of the research was gender relations, it is recognised that these are cut across and compounded by relations of class and 'race'. Since there were very few black students or staff at Brickhill or Heydonfield (reflecting the picture nationwide, see CRE, 1989, 1991), this research reflects the experiences of white groups. SIRAJ BLATCHFORD (1991) provides an important account of black students' experiences of teacher training.

2.   PE ITE institutions were obliged to accept coeducational cohorts as a result of the European Law of Equal Treatment in 1976. However, the speed with which the institutions have become truly coeducational has varied considerably. During the fieldwork of the initial research (academic year 1989/90), Brickhill, the former women's PE college, still recruited twice as many women as men students. At Heydonfield, the former men's PE college, the cohorts had become balanced much more quickly, perhaps reflecting the differing valuing of women's and men's activities and institutions.

3.   The term "girlie" was used by male students to describe and control women students in the same kinds of ways that terms like "slag" and "drag" are used by boys in school contexts (HALSON, 1991; LEES, 1987). The term "girlie" had two connotations; on one hand it was used to describe women who were worth "pursuing" sexually, on the other it was used to describe women's "inferior" physical abilities. It is

significant to note the resilience of such a term within PE ITE: it was in common usage at both institutions, and it is a term which is commonly used amongst students in other ITE institutions, including the one in which I work.

4. As KELLY ((1988) notes, sexual violence is best conceived as a continuum, ranging from jokes and sexually appraising looks, to acts of physical violence and rape. Not surprisingly, I did not observe actual incidences of physical violence. However, at Heydonfield, I was told by the recently appointed Equal Opportunities Officer (an academic member of staff who worked part-time in this capacity) that ongoing work on the production of an equal opportunities policy for the institution had originated partly as a consequence of a recent incident of alleged rape of a woman student by a male lecturer.

5. I was obviously limited by my gender in the extent to which I was able to observe 'male only' environments. As CURRY (1991) and DUNNING (1973) have shown, these are important contexts for such male identity work, and an area of research where much remains to be done.

6. The gender regime (KESSLER, ASHENDEN, CONNELL and DOWSETT, 1987) at Brickhill was very different to that at Heydonfield. Unlike the majority of teacher education institutions, the gender profile of the staff and students at Brickhill was skewed in favour of the women, reflecting its history as a women's PE college. This had significant implications, not just for the nature of the curriculum, but also for the ways in which gender identities were negotiated and constructed within the institution (see FLINTOFF, 1993a, 1993b).

7. The fieldwork for my research was carried out in the academic year 1989/90, prior to the effects of the governments' more recent, radical reforms (DFE, 1992a, 1992b) to teacher education. The latter part of the paper focuses on some aspects of how those reforms might be impacting on gender equity work.

8. In England and Wales, students can become specialist teachers of PE through two key routes: taking a one year Post Graduate Certificate of Education (PGCE) after a three year degree in Sports Studies or similar, or through a four year, concurrent Bachelor of Education degree. The latter remains the most popular route into PE teaching, although the balance is changing. The governments' ongoing policy initiatives for ITE may exacerbate this trend.

9. This section draws on more recent research which focused on students'

experiences on the new school-based PGCE at my own institution in the 1993/4 academic year, when I was the tutor in charge of the PE students. The research included the use of two questionnaires – one after the students' first teaching practice block, and a second, more in-depth questionnaire at the end of the course, together with in-depth, individual interviews. The interviews were held at the end of the students' year, after they had all passed their course – a significant factor, I suspect, in their open and often critical comments about their experiences.

10. The fact that some students had only taught same-sex groups is itself an equal opportunity issue.

References

ARNOT, M., DAVID, M. and WEINER, G. (1996) *Educational Reforms and Gender Equality in Schools*. Manchester, Equal Opportunities Commission.

ASKEW, S. and ROSS, C. (1988) *Boys Don't Cry: Boys and Sexism in Education*. Milton Keynes, Open University.

BRITTAN, A. (1989) *Masculinity and Power*. Oxford, Basil Blackwell.

BURGESS, R. (1989) Something you learn to live with? Gender and inequality in a comprehensive school. *Gender and Education*, 1, 2, 155-164.

CARRIGAN, T., CONNELL, R.W. and LEE, J. (1985) Towards a new sociology of masculinity. *Theory and Society: Renewal and Critique in Social Theory,* 14, 5, 551-603.

CLARKE, G. (1994) A hidden agenda: lesbian Physical Education students and concealment of sexuality. Paper presented at the BSA Annual Conference, University of Central Lancashire, England, March 28-31.

CLARKE, G. (1997) Playing a part: the lives of lesbian Physical Education teachers. In G. CLARKE and B. HUMBERSTONE (Eds) *Critically Researching Women. Physical Activity and Physical Education*. Basingstoke, Macmillan, pp.36-49.

COMMISSION FOR RACIAL EQUALITY (1989) Evidence submitted to the Education, Science, and Arts Committee of House of Commons. *The Supply of Teachers for the 1990's*. London, CRE.

COMMISSION FOR RACIAL EQUALITY (1991) *Ethnic Minority Teachers: a supplementary survey of eight local educational authorities.* London, CRE.

CONNELL, R.W. (1987) *Gender and Power.* Cambridge, Polity Press.

CUNNISON, E. (1989) Gender joking in the staffroom. In S. ACKER (Ed) *Teachers, Gender and Careers.* London, Falmer.

COVENEY, L. et al (1984) *The Sexuality Papers.* London, Hutchinson.

CURRY, T.J. (1991) Fraternal bonding in the locker room; a profeminist analysis of talk about competition and women. *Sociology of Sport,* 8, 119-135.

DEEM. R. (1980) Women, school and work; some conclusions. In R. DEEM (Ed) *Schooling for Women's Work.* London, RKP, pp.177-183.

DEEM, R. (1991) Feminist interventions in education, 1975-1990. In A. RATTANSI and D. REEDER (Eds) *Radicalism and Education.* London, Lawrence and Wishart.

DENSCOMBE, M. (1982) The hidden pedagogy and its implications for teacher training. *British Journal of Sociology of Education,* 3, 3, 249-265.

DEPARTMENT OF EDUCATION AND SCIENCE (1989) *Initial Teacher Training: Approval of Courses.* Circular 24/89, London, DES.

DEPARTMENT FOR EDUCATION (1992a) *Initial Teacher Training (Secondary Phase).* Circular 9/92. London, HMSO.

DEPARTMENT FOR EDUCATION (1992b) *The accreditation of initial teacher education under circular 9/92.* London, HMSO.

DEWAR, A. (1987) The social construction of gender in Physical Education. *Women's Studies International Forum,* 10, 4, 453-465.

DEWAR, A. (1990) Oppression and privilege in physical education: struggles in the negotiation of gender in a university programme. In D. KIRK and R. TINNING (Eds) *Physical Education, Curriculum and Culture: critical issues in the contemporary crisis.* Basingstoke, Falmer.

DEWAR, A. and INGRAM, A. (1987) Really useful knowledge; professional interests, critical discourse, student responses. Paper presented at the Annual Conference for the Sociology of Sport, Helsinki.

DUNNING, E. (1973) The football club as a type of 'male preserve'; some sociological notes. *International Review for the Sociology of Sport,* 8, 3/4, 5-21.

EQUAL OPPORTUNITIES COMMISSION (1989) *Formal Investigation Report: Initial Teacher Education in England and Wales.* Manchester, EOC.

FLETCHER, S. (1984) *Women First: The Female Tradition in English Physical Education 1880-1980.* London, Athlone.

FLINTOFF, A. (1991) Dance, masculinity and teacher education. *British Journal of Physical Education,* 22, 4, 31-35.

FLINTOFF, A. (1993a) *One of the Boys?: An ethnographic study of Gender relations. Co-education and Initial Teacher Education in Physical Education.* Unpublished PhD, School of Education, Open University.

FLINTOFF, A. (1993b) Gender, Physical Education and Initial Teacher Education. In J. EVANS (Ed) *Equality, Education and Physical Education.* London, Falmer, pp.184-204.

FLINTOFF, A. (1993c) One of the Boys?: Gender Identities in Physical Education Initial Teacher Education. In I. SIRAJ-BLATCHFORD (Ed) *'Race', Gender and the Education of Teachers.* Milton Keynes, Open University Press, pp.74-93.

FLINTOFF, A. (1995) Anti-sexist practice in secondary physical education. In L. Milosevic (Ed) *Fairplay: Gender and Physical Education.* Leeds Education Authority, Leeds.

FURLONG, J. (1992) Reconstructing professionalism: ideological struggle in initial teacher education. In M. ARNTO and L. BARTON (Eds) *Voicing Concerns: Sociological Perspectives on Contemporary Educational Reforms.* Wallingford, Triangle Books.

GRIFFIN, P. (1989a) Homophobia in Physical Education. *CAHPER,* 55, 2, 21-31.

GRIFFIN, P. (1989b) Gender as a socialising agent in Physical Education. In T. TEMPLIN and P. SCHEMP (Eds) *Socialisation into Physical Education: learning to teach.* Indianapolis, Benchmark Press, pp.219-233.

GRIFFIN, P. (1992) Changing the Game; homophobia, sexism and lesbians in sport. *Quest,* 44,2, 251-265.

GRIFFIN, P. and GENASCI, J. (1990) Addressing homophobia in Physical

Education; responsibilities for teachers and researchers. In M.A. MESSNER and D.F. SABO (Eds) *Sport, Men and the Gender Order: critical feminist perspectives*. Leeds, Human Kinetics.

HALSON, J. (1989) The sexual harassment of young women. In L. HOLLY (Ed) *Girls and Sexuality*. Milton Keynes, Open University.

HALSON, J. (1991) Young women, sexual harassment and heterosexuality: violence, power relations and mixed schooling. In P. ABBOTT and C. WALLACE (Eds) *Gender, Power and Sexuality*. London, Macmillan.

HOLLY, L. (Ed) (1989) *Girls and Sexuality: teaching and learning*. Milton Keynes, Open University Press.

JACKSON, D. (1990) *Unmasking masculinity*. London, Unwin Hyman.

KELLY, L. (1988) *Surviving Sexual Violence*. Cambridge, Polity Press.

KELLY, L. (1992) Not in front of the children; responding to right wing agenda on sexuality and education. In M. ARNOT and L. BARTON (Ed) *Voicing Concerns: sociological perspectives on contemporary educational reforms*. Wallingford, Triangle Books.

KESSLER, S., ASHENDEN, D., CONNELL, B. and DOWSETT, G. (1987) Gender relations in secondary schooling. In M. ARNOT and G. WEINER (Eds) *Gender and the politics of schooling*. Milton Keynes, Open University Press.

LEES, S. (1987) The structure of sexual relations in school. In M. ARNOT and G. WEINER (Eds) *Gender and the politics of schooling*. Milton Keynes, Open University Press.

LEONARD, D. (1989) Gender and initial teacher training. In H. DE LYON and F. WIDDOWSON MIGNIUOLO (Eds) *Women Teachers: issues and experiences*. Milton Keynes, Open University Press, pp.23-36.

MAGUIRE, M. and BALL, S.J. (1993) *Teacher education and education policy*. Unpublished paper, Kings College, London.

MAHONY, P. (1985) *School for the Boys? Coeducation reassessed*. London, Hutchinson.

MAHONY, P. (1989) Sexual violence and mixed schools. In C. JONES and P. MAHONY (Eds) *Learning our lines: sexuality and social control*. London, The Women's Press.

MCKAY, J., GORE, J., and KIRK, D. (1990) Beyond the limits of technocratic PE. *Quest*, 42, 1, 40-51.

MENTER, I. (1989) Teaching practice stasis: racism, sexism and school experience in initial teacher education. *British Journal of Sociology of Education*, 10, 4, 459-473.

MESSNER, M. (1987) The life of a man's seasons; male identity in the life course of the jock. In. M.S. KIMMELL (Ed) *Changing men: New directions in research on men and masculinity.* London, Sage.

MILOSEVIC, L. (Ed) (1995) *Fairplay: Gender and Physical Education.* Leeds Education Authority, Leeds.

SCRATON, S. (1985) *Losing ground: the implications for girls of mixed Physical Education.* Paper presented at the British Educational Research Association, Sheffield.

SCRATON, S. (1987) Gender and physical education: ideologies of the physical and the politics of sexuality. In S. WALKER and L. BARTON (Eds) *Changing Policies, Changing Teachers: New directions for schooling?* Milton Keynes, Open University Press.

SCRATON, S. (1992) *Shaping up to Womanhood: Gender and Girls Physical Education.* Milton Keynes, Open University Press.

SCRATON, S. (1993) Equality, Co-education and Physical Education. In J. EVANS (Ed) *Equality, Education and Physical Education.* London, Falmer Press, pp.139-153.

SHEPPARD, D. (1989) Organisations, power and sexuality; the image and self image of women managers. In J. HEARN et al (Ed) *The Sexuality of Organisation.* London, Sage.

SIRAJ-BLATCHFORD, I. (1991) A study of Black students' perceptions of initial teacher education. *British Educational Research Journal*, 17, 1, 35-50.

SKELTON, A. (1993) On becoming a male Physical Education teacher: the informal culture of students and the construction of hegemonic masculinity. *Gender and Education*, 5, 3, 288-303.

SKELTON, C. and HANSON, J. (1989) Schooling the teachers: gender and initial teacher education. In S. ACKER (Ed) *Teachers, Gender and Careers.* London, Falmer, pp.109-122.

STANWORTH, M. (1983) *Gender and Schooling: a study of sexual divisions in the classroom.* London, Hutchinson.

TINNING, R. (1988) Student teaching and the pedagogy of necessity. *Journal of Teaching in Physical Education,* 7, 82-89.

WHITBREAD, A. (1980) Female teachers are women first: sexual harassment at work. In D. SPENDER and E. SARAH (Eds) *Learning to Lose: sexism and education.* London, Women's Press.

WOOD, J. (1984) Groping towards sexism; boys sex talk. In A. MCROBBIE and M. NAVA (Eds) *Gender and Generation.* London, Macmillan.

WOODS, S. (1992) Describing the experience of lesbian physical educators: a phenomenological study. In A. SPARKES (Ed) *Research in Physical Education and Sport: Exploring alternative visions.* London, Falmer, pp.90-117.

Chapter 15

Multicultural Education and Equal Opportunities in Physical Education: Conflicts and Dilemmas

Bob Carroll

Introduction

Whilst there has been a spate of literature and research on multi-cultural education, cultural diversity and racist and anti-racist practices and policies in education, there has been very little mention of physical education. Yet, with the growing number of ethnic minority pupils in schools, both physical education (PE) teachers and their pupils face difficulties arising from different cultural backgrounds and traditions. There is a need for research which examines these difficulties, and particularly for research which takes the teachers' and pupils' views as the focal point, and follows a social action perspective (see SILVERMAN, 1971; ALMOND, 1986). The need for an understanding from the point of view of the participants and the need to inform and possibly change practice also called for a case-study approach. Research along these lines was carried out by CARROLL and HOLLINSHEAD (1993) and the results are presented here.

Policies in Education

It is impossible to do justice to the vast amount of literature on multicultural education and equal opportunities in education, but it is necessary to set this research in context. At the risk of oversimplifying and overgeneralising, broad comment will be made on general approaches and policies for both multi-cultural education and equal opportunities in education. From the 1960s to the 1990s, there have been changes in policies from assimilation to integration, from integration to multicultural education, and then from multicultural to anti-racist education and they have been discussed and researched at both the general and more local and specific levels (e.g. BRANDT, 1986; CARRINGTON and SHORT, 1989; VERMA, 1989; FOSTER, 1990). It is suggested that, in summary, policies have failed or partially failed to:

a)   totally assimilate or integrate ethnic minority groups into traditional white British society;

b)   provide a satisfactory pluralist orientation to multicultural education;

c)   deal adequately with the low attainment of pupils in specific ethnic minority groups;

d)   prevent racism in schools at either the personal or institutional level.

This apparent failure is perhaps not surprising when one considers the lack of coherence of policies and the underlying assumptions and ideological basis of many of these policies. There has been a confusion in the terms and concepts used, such as 'multicultural', 'racism' and 'anti-racist', and a vagueness and generality of many of the policies at the operational level. In addition, teacher awareness, knowledge and understanding of cultural and religious issues has often been limited, whilst teacher training (at least until recently) in multicultural education has been inadequate and even non-existent for many older teachers. It is therefore not surprising that contradictions and inconsistencies have existed in practice and ethnocentric curriculum policies and practices have persisted. This failure has been aided and abetted by the fact that policies and solutions to problems have been framed within various contexts which have ignored the wider political debate (TROYNA and WILLIAMS, 1986). These contexts are:

•   educationist context (it's just ignorance, education will solve it);

- moral context (justice, equality of opportunity);

- behavioural context (individual cases as they arise).

The wider political, structural and ideological roots and bases are neglected, and racism and white domination are reproduced and perpetuated in various forms outside and within the school institution (BRANDT, 1986; TROYNA and WILLIAMS, 1986).

Despite the *Swann Report* (DES, 1985), education authorities have been left to produce their own policies, and some Local Education Authorities (LEAs) have left it to the schools. Thus it has often been seen as only appropriate to schools where there are large numbers of ethnic minority children, and not to 'all white' schools. This situation has been exacerbated by the *Education Reform Act* (ERA) of 1988, with opting out and local management of schools (LMS).

The effect of all this is that school policies have come in for considerable criticism from both the political left and right. For example, both multicultural and anti-racist policies have been accused of being mere tokenism, pandering to ethnic minority group demands and interests, neglecting white majority views, discriminating against the white population, perpetuating the existing inequalities and ignoring the political issues (MODGIL, VERMA, MALLICK and MODGIL, 1986; SARUP, 1986).

It appears that multi-cultural education and racist issues have developed separately from gender and sexist issues (GERWITZ, 1991). However, their central concerns over inequalities in society and equal opportunities suggest they have similarities. Although they have their different histories located in their different contexts of development, there is a parallel in the focus of their strands of development.

Gender and sexist issues have led to feminist approaches which are well documented (ARNOT, 1985; WEINER, 1985, 1990; DELAMONT, 1990). Two main strands have been noted, the 'equal opportunities', and the 'anti-sexist' (WEINER, 1990; GERWITZ, 1991). The first stance, equal opportunities, tends to advocate change within the system, such as greater opportunity of access and representation and changing stereotypical images, whilst the second stance attacks the unequal power relations in society between men and women. The former has led to policies of accountability and entitlement, whilst the latter has led to policies of empowerment, which are deemed to deal with causes, not symptoms. In practice the differences are often blurred (WEINER, 1990). It can readily be seen that the two stances are also present in multi-cultural education and anti-racist policies. The first stance can also be called 'equal opportunities' and seeks to change and improve access, entitlement and representation, whilst the second stance is a stronger anti-racist stance which seeks positive action and empowerment to tackle white domination in society (GERWITZ, 1991).

There can be a real dilemma in accepting both equal opportunities for the two sexes and anti-sexist policies at the same time as accepting the cultural norms and values of certain ethnic minority groups (e.g. Muslim) because they are in conflict (from the Eurocentric view). (This is debated by WALKLING and BRANNIGAN, 1987; TROYNA and CARRINGTON, 1987; and HAW, 1991) At a simplistic level, it throws up the conflict between individual rights and freedom as against maintaining cultural traditions and the culture of a group, and taking a moral stance within a political context. This dilemma does occur within the research quoted in this paper.

BRAH and MINHAS (1985) argue for the need to show how race, gender and class inequalities are reproduced through the education system and the wider society. They suggest that the structural context is neglected in studies which show a 'cultural clash', and that there is a need to get away from the Eurocentric mode of thinking.

Policies and Research in PE

There is very little mention of physical education in the literature on multicultural policies in education. The *Swann Report* (DES, 1985) does mention that conflicts can occur because of pupils' religious beliefs, but this lacked empirical evidence from systematic research. Some LEAs did produce guidelines and policies for teachers, e.g. COVENTRY LEA (1980), and ROTHERHAM LEA (1986). MULLARD (1982) suggests that these responses were merely assimilation policies aimed at ensuring harmony and do not meet the real needs of ethnic minority groups.

There has been little research into PE and ethnic minority groups. The work of IKULAYO (1983), CARRINGTON and WOOD (1983), and CASHMORE (1982) points to the colonisation of school teams by West Indian pupils and the channelling of West Indians into sport and sporting careers. Although these processes may occur through equal opportunities policies and anti-racist policies, which are aimed at helping individuals, they often perpetuate stereotypes and myths of the 'black sportsman', depress academic attainment and motivation and narrow career routes. They are a form of racism which does a disservice to the black community (CASHMORE, 1982; HARGREAVES, 1986).

The research of CARRINGTON, CHIVERS and WILLIAMS (1987) and CARRINGTON and WILLIAMS (1988) (with South Asian Muslim samples) shows that ethnicity heightens gender differences with girls facing problems more than boys. These problems are associated with religious and cultural traditions which assign particular roles to men and women, and which contain moral codes controlling behaviour. This may result in a restriction of PE, sport and leisure opportunities. They show that, without taking into consideration these cultural traditions, equal opportunities cannot be a realistic policy. RAVAL (1989) criticises this research as a Eurocentric view which fails to grasp the experience of Asian girls and women and fails to address racist practices.

Sport and PE are often regarded as areas where equal opportunity and racial harmony exists. However, BAYLISS (1989) shows the use of stereotypes and assumptions which can unintentionally foster racism. FLEMING (1981) shows the existence of racism in a case study of one school, focusing on Asian boys. This racism is hardly likely to be an isolated example, judging from reports in the media of racism more generally. There is no real evidence to suppose that, in this respect, PE or sport are different from the society of which they are a part.

A Case Study

A case study was undertaken in one school, which shall be called Borin High School, to examine the perceptions of PE by ethnic minority pupils and their teachers. This school was chosen because of the increase in the numbers of Bangladeshi and Pakistani children in the school, which meant that staff faced issues and problems not hitherto faced. The number of children from South Asian descent had grown steadily from 20% of the total school population in 1983 to approximately 50% in 1989 with a first year intake of around 70%. The prediction was that this would rise to 90% in the near future. The borough council in which the school was situated had produced figures to show that 75% of the ethnic minority group population live in 4 of their 20 wards and that South Asian families have approximately three times the percentage of children under 4 years of age as has the population generally (HOLLINSHEAD, 1989). Most of these South Asians are devout Muslims. The first multicultural education policy was developed by the LEA in 1982, followed by a school policy in 1988. However, these were very general guidelines such as "the need to combat racism and to give equal opportunities", and did not give specific guidance for the practical difficulties faced by the PE staff.

There were separate PE lessons at Borin High School for boys and girls. There was a common core programme for boys and girls in the first three years (years 7-9) with more choice in years 10 and 11. However, the programme consisted of different activities for boys and girls, for example soccer, rugby, basketball, cricket for the boys and netball, hockey, dance and rounders for the girls. Both boys' and girls' programmes included gymnastics, athletics, volleyball, badminton and swimming. All pupils are expected to wear the school kit. For boys this is white vest and shorts for indoor lessons, and long sleeved jersey for outdoor work with appropriate footwear. Girls wear a plain white blouse and navy blue skirt for indoor and outdoor games, knickers for indoor gymnastics. The policy now allows tracksuit trousers and shalwars to be worn by the girls. Pupils are expected to shower after a lesson for hygiene reasons.

The approach adopted was a social action (SILVERMAN, 1971) and action research approach (see ALMOND, 1986). The main method of gathering the data was through in-depth tape recorded interviews. The pupil interviews consisted of groups of five pupils, boys and girls separately, from years 10 and 11 in school time. PE staff were interviewed both individually and as a group. Further details and justification for the approach are given in CARROLL and HOLLINSHEAD (1993), and in HOLLINSHEAD (1989). The main features were that they were semi-structured, open-ended questions with the opportunity for the respondents to talk about their perceptions at length, whilst the interviewer listened and prompted and probed in the traditions of good qualitative research (see JONES, 1985). The tapes were transcribed, and analysed according to the issues raised by the respondents.

Areas of Conflict

Both pupils and teachers perceived there were problems and specific areas of conflict in PE. These areas centred on PE kit, showers, Ramadan, and extra-curricular activities. These conflict areas are associated with the fact that the children are Muslims, and most of them come from a devout Muslim family background. All the evidence and the quotations used in this section come from the data published by CARROLL and HOLLINSHEAD (1993).

PE Kit

Before the teachers allowed the pupils to wear shalwars and tracksuits, there had been a real problem for the girls wearing skirts, as these did not adequately cover their bodies. As Naweeda explains, for Muslim children, the arms and legs should be completely covered,

> The only thing is that you have to cover your body. As long as you are in purdah you can do anything, as long as you are covered from top to bottom.

However, some of the teachers had not appreciated this fact and, in the early days, had compelled children to wear the correct kit. For example,

> I actually had to wear a very short skirt and not wear anything to cover my legs. And that's what I really felt bad about but couldn't say anything. (Morien)

> I felt the same ... (Naweeda)

> ... and when I came in and kept my shalwar on and went to the lesson, I had to be forced back to change and take it off. (Reza)

The teachers often saw the pupils' response as "mere embarrassment", whilst the devout Muslims actually felt shame and guilt at exposing their bodies, and public humiliation at being forced to change. The problem was not confined to the girls, as some devout Muslim boys also felt they should keep their arms and legs covered.

The problem is accentuated by having games on playing fields accessible to public viewing. The pupils can be seen by members of their community. Both teachers and pupils confirmed that word soon got around to parents and religious leaders about the children's dress at games, and that complaints had been received at the school and parents had reprimanded children. So the pupils felt parental and community pressure to conform to their religious code, but were required to meet the school's rules, whilst some wanted to dress according to the school rules to be like their white English peers. Some of the girls were further pressured by the boys. As one boy said,

> I don't feel that's right (refers to wearing skirts) 'cause in Islam it says that you have got to cover the bottom part of your legs, especially girls and most Muslim families apply that rule at home and they wish to apply it at school. Personally, my sister, she does not wear a shalwar underneath and I have seen her once or twice and I have complained to my dad.

Showers

The PE teachers felt strongly that children should shower at the end of PE lessons for hygiene reasons and that it was a proper part of health education. In view of the Muslim position on exposing and covering the body and the fact there were only communal changing rooms and showers, it was not surprising that this was an area for potential conflict between pupils and teachers. As Javid explains,

> In Islam, it says you are not supposed to have a shower with other people. You are supposed to have it on your own.

Both male and female teachers felt many children, including the white English population, did not like having showers, and that some children felt temporary embarrassment which they would get over.

They therefore saw the Muslim children in the same way and failed to see the shame and guilt felt by devout Muslim pupils.

> I felt really upset... it is strictly against the rules. (Foysin)

> We have this sense of shame. Really I don't think it is right. (Atia)

> We feel guilty because we are exposing ourselves in front of other girls. (Humera)

They said that, if their parents got to know, they would be "furious". Many pupils try to avoid showers. As Javid explains:

> we just stick our heads in, get out quickly and get changed, so it looks as if we've had a shower.

Some go much further and are willing to miss not only PE but other lessons as well. Zakia illustrates this:

> You tried to avoid it – not come to school on those days – you know, miss school for one day, for 10 minutes.

Ramadan

Ramadan, which lasts for approximately one month, is a major festival in the Muslim calendar. During this period Muslim families fast from sunrise to sunset, which means youngsters do without food and water for the whole of the school day. Clearly pupils get tired, and strenuous exercise can cause discomfort and be distressing. Ramadan has fallen during the summer term over the last few years and athletics has been taught during this period. As the activity demands strenuous activity and effort, pupils find it tiring and distressing during Ramadan. The pupils state that their teachers demand that they continue to put in their full physical effort during Ramadan and they found it difficult to do so. Abdul illustrates the pupils' dilemma and annoyance:

> he (the teacher) kept saying, 'you can do better than that. Why don't you?' And I kept telling him I was fasting but I could not run that fast, but he said that I had to try hard

'cause I was going to be in sports day... and I got mad about it but he wouldn't stop.

Swimming also created problems during Ramadan because water must not enter the mouth, and clearly this is difficult to avoid.

There is a real dilemma here for pupils. They feel guilty if they break their fast, and they will also incur parental wrath if they do so and their parents find out. If they do not put in much effort they do not do well and often feel disappointed in themselves and even guilty for not making the effort, and they feel the annoyance of the teachers. If they make the full effort, they get very tired and sometimes distressed, and they have the rest of the day to get through. Sipia captures something of this dilemma:

You feel guilty really because the teachers have difficulty understanding it but if we break the fast we feel guilty towards our parents.

To avoid the conflict and the temptation of the pupils' breaking the fast, some parents have encouraged their children to miss school on games days. As Morien admitted, "My parents tell me not to go to school if I have games".

Extra-Curricular Activities

Taking part in after-school, extra-curricular activities proved to be an area for potential conflict. It was more likely to affect the girls than boys, because girls had more restrictions placed upon them than boys. However, some boys said that they "had to attend the Mosque after the school to read the Quran". Many would have preferred to play games as one explained:

Yes, we wanted to play games but then we are forced by our parents to go to the Mosque because we have to learn our religion. It's the only way we can pass it forward.

Very few of the girls interviewed had taken part in extra-curricular activities, though many would have liked to have done so. The girls said that their parents were concerned about their safety, coming home alone, and developing social relationships with boys. These could damage their marriage prospects. Atia stated that she had had to stop netball after school, and Naweeda explained the situation:

> Staying after school would be a problem 'cause it's not usual for a Muslim girl to go out on her own. She would have to go with her parents or with a brother and sister. When you go out on your own then people start talking about you and you get a bad name. It's a cultural thing, and it's against your religion 'cos you shouldn't go somewhere you don't really need to.

The pressure from the family and community is very strong and difficult for the teachers to appreciate. Amreen illustrates this pressure: "the family are sort of branded for the rest of their lives. People would keep saying, 'do you remember when your daughter did this?' So parents are afraid of letting their daughters do what they want."

The Muslim girls are often envious of the freedom which their non-Muslim friends and Muslim boys seem to have. Whilst they appreciate the parental concern, they also feel frustrated and bitter, and even rebellious. So the issue of teenage freedom is a real source of potential conflict which links directly to religious and cultural values. Zakia and Sameena illustrated their feelings and dilemmas:

> Sometimes we rebel against it because my brothers are always going out doing this and that and I rebel against it sometimes.

> Sometimes, we feel angry when you see your friends going out and you want to join them but you can't because of your parents restrictions on you.

Extra-curricular activities are only part of the wider problem of freedom, access and equal opportunities, all exacerbated by exposure to a more liberal education and culture. Naweeda explains the problem:

> I don't think it is right at all. The boys can do almost anything that they want. I think it should be the same for both boys and girls but then again I've been taught to do certain things and I have to do them. I try not to question

some things that I have to do but it leads me to conflicts so I just accept what I can and cannot do. I am beginning to have more problems now because some of my cultural traditions are against what I want to do, which is to stay on at school and get a job. My brother can go to university – boys just go and parents encourage them but I never get any encouragement. This would be the same for anyone outstanding at games and probably more so. I have enough trouble with education. If I was brilliant at games as well, I would have an awful lot more problems at home.

Both boys and girls have to learn their roles within their culture, and extra-curricular activities and sport are not important in that context. Humera explains:

You are grown up and you've got other work to do rather than sports. When I was small, then I was allowed to do things, now I've grown up you have got housework to do.

The boys' view is put by Foysin:

Like a girl at the end of school comes home, she can't go out 'cos it's strictly against their religion. When she gets married it's up to her husband if she can go out and she should be covered up.

These comments raise issues of individual freedom and rights and cultural traditions, and male domination. These are discussed in the following section.

'Cultural Clash': Conflicts and Dilemmas

The data presented above within areas of conflict clearly show a clash in values between the teachers and the pupils. The teachers were trying to maintain many of the traditional values in PE, such as changing into suitable PE kit, showering after lessons, developing ability and offering extra-curricular activities, and making a full effort all the time. Not fully understanding the Muslim and South Asian culture, they had expected the Bangladeshi and Pakistani children to conform to their value system. It was in fact a simple integrationist policy. After all, they had met resistance before from many white English working class children and the pupils had been made to conform. As the number of ethnic minority children grew this policy brought increasing pupil embarrassment, anger and hostility and eventual conflict. Gradually the teachers realised they needed to change their policies and did so, allowing the wearing of tracksuit trousers and shalwars and the introduction of less strenuous activities such as table tennis during Ramadan. The changes did indicate a shift in the willingness of the staff to see the pupils' point of view. However, the practices themselves are basically integrationist, and a satisfactory multicultural and anti-racist policy had not been developed. In spite of the changes the children still felt that the teachers did not understand the importance of their religion nor the problems and dilemmas that PE policies had presented to them. This is reflected in the comments throughout the interviews, only a few of which have been presented here. The children see themselves very often as the 'victims', and this has resulted in conflicts both with teachers and their own parents.

Certainly the teachers admit to not knowing enough about Muslim beliefs and values, and the children's perceptions of PE practices. Clearly this is something which the teachers can do something about. That, however, may be the easy part for the teachers. It will be a lot more difficult for them to formulate policies and practices which remain honest to their traditional values and to equality of opportunity principles, whilst at the same time reconciling them with multicultural and anti-racist policies and practices which satisfy everyone. It will be even harder for teachers to challenge those traditional values, as they cannot be divorced from their biographies and their cultural values. Dealing with solutions in the educationist context is both necessary and possible but the moral context will be more difficult because, as we have seen in the data, it brings cultural dilemmas and clashes. Whilst the effects of the political context cannot be ignored, the PE teachers cannot deal with this context in isolation, and this is certainly a problem for a whole school approach and the wider community and society. These difficulties can be exemplified by the two issues of racist practices and equality of opportunity.

Whilst the pupils thought the teachers were being racist and grossly unfair in effect, though not necessarily by intention, the teachers believed they were not being racist and thought they were being fair to all groups. They also felt that 'giving way' to religious beliefs would be anti-racist but also positive discrimination, which would be seen as grossly unfair by other groups and would make the teachers' job harder in the future. Making changes to policy and practice in this case was clearly a delicate task and posed a moral dilemma.

Most of the teachers felt they were operating a policy of equal opportunities though two of the teachers did acknowledge that this must take into consideration the children's Islamic cultural traditions. Clearly the access to leisure opportunities offered to all pupils for the present and future was presented within a framework not acceptable to the Muslim community. Muslim boys and girls can only express themselves freely within the confines of the Islamic moral and cultural codes. Like many other aspects of the English education system which provide educational, religious, career and leisure opportunities, the teachers' practices offered a potential threat to the cultural values and differentiated roles of men and women of another culture. What the Eurocentric view sees as a sexist core in this cultural tradition, or as a restriction on equal opportunities, the Muslim view sees as a positive moral code to guide their community and as an essential part of the community structure. This is exemplified by the debate between TROYNA and CARRINGTON (1987) and WALKLING and BRANNIGAN (1987). It poses the moral dilemma of individual freedom, equality of opportunity and life chances against the rights of the group to maintain its cultural traditions and control over its members in the political context of Christian domination. It poses the further dilemma of how far parental rights, choice and control should go. It is complicated by the juxtaposition of male domination and the rights to equal opportunities of women in non-Muslim societies. As CARROLL and HOLLINSHEAD (1993) suggest, the teachers are caught in the middle of a complex political problem, where they may be accused of being sexist or racist depending on the action they take. They are in danger of being sexist if they accept cultural tradition, and racist if they operate equal opportunities policies and do not accept traditional cultural roles.

This study supports the 'cultural clash' and 'inter-generation' conflict theories, which have been criticised by BRAH and MINHAS (1985). The data show that children are often caught between the school values and their cultural values. Some of these children have clearly begun to question their cultural traditions and this had led to conflicts at home. Thus some children saw their parents' views as sexist and restrictive and unfair. For some children there was a clear identity crisis, as Zakia shows:

> and that's just it because we have to play two roles – one as a Muslim child and one as being in the host community and joining in with them.

This often leads to confusion and conflict, as Humera admits:

> We are confused and we can't communicate with them (parents).

Morien and Naweeda stated that their parents had lived most of their lives in Bangladesh, and suggested that they are too traditionalist and do not understand when children find it difficult to accept their parents' ways and values.

It is not uncommon, of course, to find these type of conflicts in non-Muslim households. Inter-generational conflict on questions of restrictions, religious practices and values are frequent. However, in this case the focus for the clash is within school practices and the acculturation process. It is this type of conflict situation which triggers and fuels the movement towards separate Muslim schools. It may also result in the community and parents putting even more restrictions on their children, and a stronger desire for separate activities and leisure opportunities. This illustrates that what may appear to be relatively insignificant conflicts in the PE situation may raise much broader issues.

SHAIKH and KELLY (1989) in a study in schools revealed fewer disputes than those in this study, and suggested that the "pupils task is to mix and match the two cultures to create their own design". Whilst this may be possible for less devout Muslim families, it is suggested that, for the more devout, their life is more like a game of hopscotch where they hop from one culture to another whilst trying to maintain their balance and 'not fall over'. 'Falling over' results in conflicts.

Conclusion

The existence of anti-racist and anti-sexist policies, when phrased in general and vague terms (which they often are) will not ensure that racist and sexist practices do not exist. The operation of equal opportunities policies and practices is clearly not a simple matter when cultural traditions and values are involved. This research has shown that there are potential dilemmas and conflicts which require very sensitive handling. Teachers have not had adequate training to gain: a) the required knowledge of cultural values and beliefs; b) expertise in the formulation of multicultural, anti-racist and equal opportunity policies; c) expertise at dealing with sensitive areas. Nor have they had enough support at the school or community level to counteract these problems. Greater school-community links would obviously be of value here. Whilst there appeared to be an improvement in the awareness of the need for multicultural and anti-racist and equal opportunity training at the initial teacher training and the inservice training levels during the 1980s, this seems to have been pushed to the background after the 1988 *Education Reform Act* with the focus on the National Curriculum content and assessment, and the organisational changes such as Local Management of Schools. Individual schools may have to do more themselves. By taking the action research perspective, CARROLL and HOLLINSHEAD (1993) have been able to influence school policy and practice. This type of approach might be fruitful elsewhere.

References

ALMOND, L. (1986) Research based teaching in games. In J. EVANS (Ed) *Physical Education, Sport and Schooling*. London, Falmer Press.

ARNOT, M. (1985) *Race and Gender. Equal Opportunities Policies in Education*. Oxford, Pergamon.

BAYLISS, T. (1989) PE and racism: making changes. *Multicultural Teaching, 7*, 2, 19-22.

BOURDIEU, P. (1974) The school as a conservative force: scholastic and cultural inequalities. In S. EGGLESTON (Ed) *Contemporary Research in Sociology of Education*. London, Methuen.

BRAH, A. and MINHAS, R. (1985) Structural racism or cultural difference: schooling for Asian girl. In G. WEINER (Ed) *Just a Bunch of Girls*. Milton Keynes, Open University Press.

BRANDT, G.H. (1986) *The Realization of Anti-Racist Teaching*. Lewes, Falmer Press.

CARRINGTON, B., CHIVERS, T. and WILLIAMS, T. (1987) Gender, leisure and sport: a case-study of young people of south Asian descent. *Leisure Studies,* 63, 265-279.

CARRINGTON, B. and SHORT, G. (1989) *Race and the Primary School. Theory into Practice*. Windsor NFER – NELSON.

CARRINGTON, B. and WILLIAMS, T. (1988) Patriarchy and ethnicity: the link between school physical education and community leisure activities. In J. EVANS (Ed) *Teachers. Teaching and Control in Physical Education*. Lewes, Falmer Press.

CARRINGTON, B. and WOOD, E. (1983) Body-talk: images of sport in a multi-racial school. *Multi-Racial Education,* 11, 2, 29-38.

CARROLL, B. and HOLLINSHEAD, G. (1993) Ethnicity and Conflict in Physical Education, *British Educational Research Journal* 19, 1, 59-76.

CASHMORE, E. (1982) *Black Sportsmen*. London, Routledge and Kegan Paul.

COVENTRY LEA (1980) *Physical Education in a Multi-Cultural Society*. Coventry, Elmbank Teachers Centre.

DELAMONT, S. (1990) *Sex roles and the School*. (2nd Ed.). London, Routledge.

DES (1985) *Education for All*. Report of the Committee of Inquiry into the Education of Children from Ethnic Minority groups. London, HMSO.

FLEMING, S. (1991) Sport, schooling and Asian male youth culture. In G. Jarvie (Ed) *Sport, Racism and Ethnicity*. London, Falmer.

FOSTER, P. (1990) *Policy and Practice in Multicultural and Anti-Racist Education*. London, Routledge.

GERWITZ, D. (1991) Analyses of racism and sexism in education and strategies for change. *British Journal of Sociology of Education,* 12, 2, 183-201.

GHUMAN, P.A.S. (1991) Best or worst of two worlds? A study of Asian adolescents. *Educational Research,* 33, 2, 121-132.

HARGREAVES, J. (1986) *Sport, Power and Culture.* Cambridge, Polity Press.

HAW, K.F. (1991) Interactions of gender and race – a problem for teachers? A review of emerging literature? *Educational Research,* 33, 1, 12-21.

HOLLINSHEAD, G. (1989) *Problems affecting the participation of Muslim Asians in physical education.* MEd dissertation, University of Manchester.

IKULAYO, P.B. (1983) Attitudes of Girls towards PE. *Physical Education Review,* 6, 1, 24-25.

INNER LONDON EDUCATION AUTHORITY (1986) *Approaches to Equal Opportunities in Secondary Schools.* (C. Adams (Ed)) London, ILEA.

JONES, S. (1985) Depth interviewing. In R. Walker (Ed) *Applied Qualitative Research.* Aldershot, Gower.

LA (1990) Interim Report of the 1989 Census of Bangladeshis in... LA Research Department. (Name withheld to protect anonymity of school).

MANGAN, J.A. (1973) *Physical Education and Sport: sociological and cultural perspectives.* Oxford, Basil Blackwell.

MODGIL, S., VERMA, G.K., MALLICK, K. and MODGIL, C. (1986) *Multicultural Education: The interminable debate.* Lewes, Falmer Press.

MULLARD, C. (1982) From assimilation to cultural pluralism. In J. Tierney (Ed) *Race, Migration and Schooling.* London, Holt Rinehart and Winston.

RAVAL, S. (1989) Gender, leisure and sport: a case study of young people of South Asian descent – a response. *Leisure Studies,* 8, 237-240.

ROTHERHAM LEA (1986) *Physical education in a multicultural society.* Guidelines and general information leaflet. Rotherham MBC.

SARUP, M. (1986) *The Politics of Multiracial Education.* London, Routledge and Kegan Paul.

SHAIKH, S and KELLY, A. (1989) To mix or not mix. Pakistani girls in British schools. *Educational Research,* 31, 1, 10-19.

SILVERMAN, D. (1971) The action frame of reference. In K. THOMPSON and J. TUNSTALL (Eds) *Sociological perspectives*. Penguin Education and Open University Press.

TROYNA, B. and CARRINGTON, B. (1987) Anti-sexist/anti-racist education – a false dilemma: a reply to Walkling and Brannigan. *Journal of Moral Education,* 16, 1, 60-66.

TROYNA, B. and CARRINGTON, B. (1990) *Education, Racism and Reform.* London, Routledge.

TROYNA, B. and WILLIAMS, J. (1986) *Racism, Education and the State.* London, Croom Helm.

VERMA, G.K. (1989) *Education For All. A Landmark in Pluralism.* Lewes, Falmer Press.

WALKLING, P.H. and BRANNIGAN, C. (1987) Muslim Schools – Troyna and Carrington's Dilemma. *Journal of Moral Education,* 16, 1, 67-69.

WEINER, G. (1985) Equal opportunities, feminism and girls' education. In G. Weiner (Ed) *Just a Bunch of Girls*. Milton Keynes, Open University Press.

WEINER, G. (1990) *The Primary School and Equal Opportunities.* London, Cassell.

WILKINSON, S (1988) *Muslim beliefs and practices in a new Muslim country.* MEd dissertation, University of Manchester.

Reprinted with kind permission of the Centre for Research into Sport and Society, University of Leicester.

PART 7

ISSUES IN
PHYSICAL EDUCATION

Chapter 16

The Emergence and Growth of Examinations in Physical Education

Bob Carroll

Introduction

This is an appropriate time to be writing about and reviewing the development of examinations in physical education (PE), as new courses are starting in the General Certificate of Secondary Education (GCSE) and the General Certificate of Education (GCE) Advanced level (A level), and new vocational courses are being developed in schools for the first time after the DEARING review (1994). This chapter will review the development of examinations in PE at school and further education (FE) level, explain what now can be described as its phenomenal success (see table 1 for statistics), examine the current situation, and conclude with the value of examinations to PE teachers and pupils. This paper draws upon previously published research work, for example, CARROLL (1982, 1986, 1994a), but brings the development and explanations up to date as examinations are still evolving.

Phases of Development

CARROLL (1986, 1994a) has identified different phases and their characteristics in the development of examinations at school and further education levels. These phases are:

Table 1

Figures for CSE, GCSE,
A level PE & SS, and vocational awards
in leisure area for selected years.

	CSE PE	GCSE PE	A level	C&G	BTEC	GNVQ
1978	7578					
1980	9901					
1985	13109					
1988		18131				
1990		34529	639			
1992		42026	2600	3976	4110	
1994						2578
1996*		80645	9732			

NB. other syllabuses , e.g. Dance and Outdoor pursuits also exist.
* Provisional figures.

1. Early 1970s

This was the period of the first acceptance of mode 3 (school's syllabus, external moderation) within the Certificate of Secondary Education (CSE) by some of the thirteen regional examination boards. Approval was made difficult as examination boards initially used the Secondary Schools Examination Council (SSEC) statement that PE should not be an examination subject at CSE level (SSEC, 1963) as a reason for rejecting syllabuses. This was a period of innovation mainly by individual teachers who had to work hard to get their syllabuses accepted. At that time, neither the teachers nor the examination boards had experience of examinations in PE so it was a learning experience for both. There was a great deal of variety in the content and standard of syllabuses in spite of them conforming to guidelines issued by the boards. The main issues at the time were: establishing what should be taught, how the pupils should be assessed, and the relationship and weighting of theoretical and practical work.

2. Mid/Late 1970s

This was the period when CSE mode 3 schemes were accepted in all the remaining regions and there was a rapid expansion of schemes under a proliferation of titles. Teachers and examination boards saw what was acceptable elsewhere and the interest that examinations had created, and this provided the basis for the expansion. However, there were still heated discussions on the advantages and disadvantages of examinations in the subject and many influental people were against examinations in PE (for example, EVANS, 1976; SCHOOLS COUNCIL, 1977; WOOLLAM, 1978). The main issues were the same as the previous phase with a need to standardise and control syllabus construction, content and assessment. This period saw the introduction of City and Guilds (C&G) syllabuses in Recreation and Leisure in further education colleges. This was the start of a rapid growth in interest in vocational education in PE departments in this sector.

3. Early 1980s

This was the period of the introduction of CSE mode 1 syllabuses (examination boards' syllabii and assessments) in five regions and the overtaking of mode 1 entries over mode 3 in those regions. In other regions during this period some examination boards actively discouraged further developments such as the introduction of mode 1 because of pending negotiations on examination board amalgamations and the possibility of a new 16+ examination. It was a period of slower expansion and consolidation. Entries for C&G examinations in Recreation and Leisure continued to increase. These had a sporting bias and were mainly taught in those days by PE teachers rather than people from the recreation industry (ELLINGHAM, 1984).

4. Mid/Late 1980s

This period saw the introduction of the new 16+ examination, the GCSE, by all five of the recently formed examination boards, London and East Anglian Examining Group (LEAG) – later called University of London Examinations and Assessment Council (ULEAC), Midland Examining Group (MEG), Northern Examining Association (later named Northern Examinations and Assessment Board (NEAB),

Southern Examining Group (SEG), Welsh Joint Examination Committee (WJEC), and also in Northern Ireland by Northern Ireland Schools Examination and Assessment Council (NISEAC). The GCSE was introduced in 1986 with the first examination in 1988, and was a move away from the norm reference examination of the CSE to a criterion reference examination. This period saw the the piloting of two A level syllabuses, and Sport Studies, by the Associated Examining Board (AEB). The main difference between these two syllabuses was that PE contained a practical element whilst Sport Studies was wholly theoretical and contained a study. The GCSE examination built on the experiences of the CSE and produced more refined syllabuses and assessment procedures which were acceptable to a large majority of PE teachers. At the same time it was much more prestigious than the CSE as it incorporated the former GCE level and brightest pupils. This helped to overcome the low status image of examination PE as not being worthy of GCE status. All of these influences combined to give further impetus to the expansion of PE as an examination subject.

Phase 4, at the FE – vocational level, brought the entry of the Business and Technology Education Council (BTEC) into the recreation and leisure examination market, which provided more flexibility and more demanding academic courses, as colleges could submit their own syllabuses for approval under BTEC arrangements. This brought a surge in the expansion of vocational qualifications in this area at the FE level.

5. Early 1990s

This period has seen the continued expansion and acceptance of GCSE PE, and A levels emerging from their pilot status to satisfy a rapidly expanding market in 6th forms and FE colleges. A level PE and Sport Studies are now accepted as entry to universities on a par with other subjects (FRANCIS, 1992), and this has certainly improved the status of PE as an examination subject. It was a period of consolidation and refinement of syllabuses at GCSE and A levels.

On the vocational front at post 16 level, this phase saw the piloting of a radically new examination, General National Vocational Qualifications (GNVQ) in Leisure and Tourism, which incorporated sport and recreation, and the advent of the equally radical competence work based National Vocational Qualifications (NVQ) in the Sport and Recreation industries. Both GNVQs and NVQs have had their difficulties, for example, the combining of leisure and tourism in GNVQ, and the large number of assessments in NVQs (HUNTER-JONES, CARROLL and JONES 1995). However, they have opened up twin routes which are discussed further under the current situation. Although many of the courses in leisure and sport studies continued to exist, there had been a big shift to GNVQs as they emerged from their pilot status and became acceptable as a route into higher education.

It is now suggested that we have just entered phase 6.

6. Mid 1990s

This is the period of new and wider ranging syllabuses in GCSE, another PE syllabus at A level, and the introduction of vocational qualifications at school level after the DEARING recommendations (DEARING, 1994). The changes in GCSE have been undertaken to meet the National Curriculum requirements, and to meet the new subject criteria for PE produced by the Schools Curriculum and Assessment Authority (SCAA). It has allowed the introduction of the more specialised syllabus in Games and short courses in both PE and Games (table 2), but it should be noted that all of them still contain approximately the same balance of theoretical and practical work. Although there are differences between syllabuses of the different boards, they are not substantially different in content or assessment from each other. For a comparison of syllabuses see CARROLL (1994a) and HODGSON (1996). However, these new syllabuses should suit many schools, particularly those which are restricted in time or facilities and find that the requirements of the full courses are too difficult to fulfill. It is predicted that these developments will bring a further expansion in the total number of entries and may bring in most of the schools not currently involved in examination work.

The amalgamation of the two theoretical components in the two A level examinations which has occured was a logical step considering the general similarity of their discipline approach, but it has brought a further syllabus, almost identical to the previous PE one, by the University of Cambridge Local Examinations Syndicate (UCLES). There is likely to be a further expansion in A level entries, and possibly an extension to other examination boards.

At the vocational level, the GNVQ has continued to expand and appears likely to continue, and colleges are finding more ways of cooperating with employers to provide NVQ qualifications. The DEARING recommendations (1994) have opened up vocational qualifications at school level. With the relationship of sport, leisure and health to PE, we are now seeing the introduction of GNVQs, sport leadership and coaching awards into schools. It is likely that there will be an expansion of these type of courses and qualifications run through the PE departments.

Table 2

GCSE courses available for 1998 examination

| | Full Course | | Short Course | |
	PE	Games	PE	Games
MEG	Y	Y	N	Y
NEAB	Y	N	Y	N
SEG	Y	Y	N	Y
ULEAC	Y	Y	Y	Y
WJEC	Y	N	N	N

Y = Yes   N = No.

Main Challenges in the Last Three Decades

In each of the last three decades, since the introduction of the CSE into schools in the 1960s, there have been many challenges for PE in relation to examinations. In 1966, there were no examinations in PE, and the main challenge was to get examination syllabuses accepted by the examination boards in the face of the SSEC's statement of 1963. As noted some PE teachers rose to and overcame this challenge.

By 1976 there were some 220 syllabuses in PE (SCHOOLS COUNCIL, 1977), and the main challenge was the standardisation of content and assessment in each region and the development of mode 1 syllabuses. As noted, PE teachers and examination boards combined to meet this challenge in some regions only. In the FE sector the challenge was to develop suitable vocational qualifications and courses in the sport and recreation fields, and this was tackled by some teachers and lecturers.

By 1986, GCSE syllabuses were published in all regions, and the main challenge was to convince hesitant PE teachers and headteachers that the GCSE in PE was a credible qualification. Many needed little convincing and this challenge was met rather more easily than the previous ones. A more difficult challenge faced post 16 education with the need to introduce a credible A level, but both Sport Studies and PE passed this test with flying colours. The main challenge facing FE was to prove that the C&G and new BTEC qualifications would be acceptable to both employers and higher education. This may have only been partially successful.

Now in 1997, GCSE and A levels in PE are well established and still expanding. Vocational qualifications including the new GNVQs and NVQs have also been shown to be acceptable to both industry and higher education and further expansion seems assured. The main challenge now appears to be how to cope with the growing number of academic and vocational qualifications at the same time, and for schools, how this can be related to the demands of the National Curriculum and demands for improving sporting opportunities for youngsters from Government directives, as in *Sport: Raising the Game* (DEPARTMENT OF NATIONAL HERITAGE (DNH), 1995).

Current Situation – Academic and Vocational Routes

Traditionally in this country, the academic and vocational routes have been entirely separate in 14-19 education. The school curriculum has been dominated by a general and academic tradition, whilst vocational courses and qualifications have been mainly reserved for further education colleges, and generally, for those who could not attain the A level route in sixth forms. Vocational qualifications generally have suffered from lower status in education.

In recent years there have been a number of government led initiatives at school level, such as, the introduction of the National Curriculum, the review of examinations at 16+ and the advent of the GCSE, all of which have strengthened academic education. There have also been initiatives on the vocational front, which have shown the government's intentions of valuing vocational qualifications and raising their status. These include the Technical and Vocational Education Initiative (TVEI) in schools, the establishment of the National Council for Vocational Qualifications (NCVQ) and the overhaul of qualifications with the development of NVQs and GNVQs. However, all of these initiatives have been introduced independently of each other and the opportunity of considering the relationship of these together in the school and 14-19 curriculum was missed. Now, with the DEARING review's (1994) recommendations that vocational qualifications be allowed to develop at Key Stage 4, there is clearly the opportunity to examine this relationship in a 14-19 education setting rather than be considered at 16 for the first time. Thus we are finding schools looking for appropriate vocational courses, and we may see a rapid uptake in areas where staff have expertise. Opportunities will arise through the recently developed vocational routes and a possible combination of the academic and vocational, such as travel and tourism GCSE, particularly when the GCSE and vocational boards either co-operate or amalgamate.

It would seem that there were two main thrusts to the development of the two vocational routes (NVQ, GNVQ). Firstly, a need for a coherent structure to the growing number of qualifications, and secondly, a criticism that they were too educationally based and divorced from the workplace, and so were not relevant. To meet these needs and criticisms, NCVQ was established to set up a structure and standards, and this they did. The NVQ route was competence based assessment in the workplace, each industry's standards being clearly laid to a national framework through its own industry leadbody (ILB) consisting of representatives from the industry. The education training system, mainly with college based work, could not realistically meet these demands so the GNVQ route was established which was skill outcomes and knowledge based. GNVQs included general and transferable skills such as communication and more specific outcomes and knowledge related to the industry. Clearly, then, there are now three distinct routes to qualifications (table 3). Route one is the traditional academic knowledge based route in education. Routes two and three are the vocational paths of the skills outcomes based GNVQs followed in colleges and the competence workbased assessed NVQs.

The structure not only established levels for these qualifications but, for the first time, offered a parity of levels across the two vocational routes and the academic. It is a crude attempt to attack the academic-vocational divide, and to raise the status of vocational qualifications. Whether it is successful or whether the very different structures strengthen the divide and the distinctiveness of the routes remains to be seen. Perhaps the movement of vocational qualifications into schools, at this time, will help to erode the status differential of these qualifications.

Table 3

National qualification framework
(adapted from NCVQ 1991)

Academic route Knowledge	Vocational route 1 Skills & Knowlege	Vocational route 2 Competence
Higher degree	GNVQ 5	NVQ 5
First degree	GNVQ 4	NVQ 4
A level	Advanced GNVQ	NVQ 3
	Intermediate GNVQ	NVQ 2
GCSE	Foundation GNVQ	NVQ 1

In recent years, sport and leisure have offered increased opportunities in the the job market and on the career front due to the increasing professionalisation and commercialisation of sport, health and leisure. There are now more full- and part-time jobs in coaching, administration and management in these industries, and the PE teacher appears to be in a unique position to offer units or modules for vocational courses related to sport which will not conflict with the recreational and academic work in the subject or the traditional role of the PE teacher. It would, of course, widen the role and make increasing demands on the teacher. A move in this direction will encourage closer links with work going on in further and higher education, such as, courses in sports science, health care and health promotion, leisure and tourism and leisure management. Quite clearly it is easier for schools, like colleges, to take the GNVQ or similar route rather than the NVQ, but units in sport and recreation which are a small part of a qualification are possible with links with other organisations, for example, governing bodies of sport. Types of accreditation, functions and possible career directions are shown in table 4. MACCONACHIE-SMITH (1996) also shows selection of courses for Key Stage 4 related to career routes.

Table 4

Types of accreditation with functions and career route.

		Accreditation		Function & Route
Academic	->	GCSE PE, Dance A level PE, SS	->	general qualification to employment and to FE and HE. also basis for study in same subjects.
Vocational	->	NVQ in Sports GNVQ in L & T	->	employment employment and to HE in same subject.

An issue which has been noted by CARROLL (1995) is the gender differential in examination entries. CARROLL showed that there were twice as many males as females entered for GCSE and A level PE examinations consistently over the years and across all examination boards. This discrepancy also existed in vocational examinations prior to the introduction of GNVQs. It would appear that examinations reflect and reinforce gender-stereotyping in PE. CARROLL (1995) treated the issue as problematic and analysed subject choice and advice received from significant others. However, this study did suggest, perhaps surprisingly, that girls thought it was a good idea for PE to be an examination subject, and that it was not a male subject. Less surprisingly, this study suggested that the explanation lay in a combination of, (a) personal preferences and perceptions, which gave rise to constraints, such as, perceptions of ability and status of the subject, and (b) mediating influences, such as school and parents, which gave rise to institutional constraints, for example, option blocks and teacher selection processes. This issue clearly needs further work in view of the increasing importance of examination subjects in relation to career routes, and PE's value in terms of leisure opportunities.

Accounting for the Success of Examinations in PE

As CARROLL (1982) points out the introduction of examinations was initially a 'grass roots' development as the impetus came from the teachers themselves through CSE mode 3 schemes. From the innovation point of view, it was individual teacher led, a 'bottom up' model, and it was not until the development of mode 1s, and particularly the GCSE with its 'cascade' model of diffusion, that it became a 'top down' institutional model of innovation. To explain why this innovation took place and took off in the way that it did, and to explain why it has been sustained, it is necessary to examine the prevailing ideologies in both PE and education at the time and more recently (CARROLL, 1994b).

In the late 1960s and early 1970s the stongest ideology in upper secondary school PE was recreational. A main aim of PE was activities or education for leisure, but the emphasis was on the playing of games (see KANE, 1974). Where possible a programme of a wide range of options had been developed, but very often without any real teaching going on (CARROLL, 1982). Very often too, extra-curricular activities, and in particular inter-school sport, received more attention than curriculum PE from significant others, such as the Headteacher and colleagues, and this was an area where the PE teacher could gain much needed prestige. The role as coach and manager in extra-curricular activities was often more clear cut and satisfying than that of the one in curriculum time, which was more diffuse and marginal (HENDRY, 1975). The raising of the school leaving age (ROSLA), the introduction of comprehensive education and the CSE, together brought the focus on education to the 14-16 age group and the 16+ examinations.

There was a rapid growth in the number of subjects available for examination at 16+, and a large increase in the number of pupils entered for those examinations. In order to prove themselves, the comprehensive schools tried to 'ape' the grammar schools in terms of GCE results at the same time as getting a larger section of the school population into the examination orbit. In this climate, the school was not supportive enough of the socialisation role or education for leisure, and PE teachers began to feel their marginal status. In addition, many teachers found the avenues for promotion into lecturing and advising more difficult to follow, and had to remain in their PE posts for longer periods of time and needed a stimulus. Many PE teachers became dissatisfied with their role as recreationalists and agents of socialisation and with their marginal status. At the same time, the CSE gave an opportunity for a real educational purpose, re-established the role of transmitter of knowledge and skills at this level, and provided motivation for both pupils and the teachers themselves. Paradoxically the CSE provided a better education for leisure than the non-examination recreational programme (CARROLL, 1984). It was easily justified on the educational grounds of pupils gaining knowledge and understanding and providing depth to the programme and covering areas neglected in the recreational programme. It brought PE into the central functions of the selection and allocative mechanisms of the school (table 5).

In FE a similar change took place. In the 1960s and 1970s, the main ideology in PE was recreational. PE departments were normally servicing other courses, providing the opportunity for students to exercise and participate in sports (ELLINGHAM, 1984; JONES, 1980; RYAN, 1986). Indeed, very often, the PE lecturer was reduced to merely giving out equipment and providing a supervisory role. The main purpose of FE was vocational training, and therefore PE was optional and marginal, providing little satisfaction for the majority of PE lecturers. The growth of sport in the leisure industry and the increase in the provision of facilities provided an opportunity for jobs in this area, and gave impetus to vocational courses and qualifications in recreation and leisure. The movement into vocational courses brought PE teachers and lecturers into a central role in FE colleges, just as CSE had done for PE teachers (ELLINGHAM, 1984; RYAN, 1986) (see table 5).

Major developments within the academic stream which have powered

Table 5

Changes in direction on the introduction of examinations
(adapted from Carroll 1994)

	Pre Examination and NC	National Curriculum	CSE, GCSE, A level	Vocational
Ideology	Recreational	Academic	Academic	Vocational
Knowledge	Practical. Knowing how. Physical experience narrow, activity related.	Practical. Knowing how. Narrow	Practical and theoretical. Knowing how and that, Broad, activity, science, social science.	Theoretical (GNVQ) Practical (NVQ) General industry Work (NVQ)
Assessment	Participation, effort performance in PE, school, club teams.	Participation and performance in practical. Report end Key Stage.	Performance in practical and knowledge, understand-ing. Examination results.	Skills outcomes and knowledge (GNVQ) Competence (NVQ)
Role	Recreationalist, official. organiser, coach,	Educator. Practical skills.	Educator. Knowledge, skills. Assessor, examiner	Educator, Examiner Vocational trainer
Status	Marginal	Marginal without exams	Central	Central
Function	Supporting	Supporting	Part of selective and allocative system	Part of selective and allocative system. Economic.

the rapid expansion and success of examinations in PE have been the advent of GCSE, the introduction of the National Curriculum and the development of A levels. The GCSE and A levels are both prestigious examinations, and GCSE became the means of assessing Key Stage 4 of the National Curriculum, which put a squeeze on non examination subjects. A levels in PE and Sports Studies provided the same function and incentive for the change of role as CSE and vocational quaifications had done for schools and FE respectively. The new range of GCSE and A level courses which have just been introduced should ensure the continued expansion and success of examinations in the subject. On the vocational route, the major developments which have powered the same sort of expansion and success as the academic route have been the entry of BTEC into the recreation and leisure market and, more recently, the advent of GNVQ and NVQ, mainly because of the standardisation and prestige of the new qualifications.

However, what has particularly fuelled the interest and support from those who need to be persuaded of the value of those examinations, such as headteachers and colleagues, has been the prevailing ideology of the 1990s, that of market forces (BALL, 1990; HATCHER, 1994). This has manifested itself in increased competition between schools, an emphasis on assessment and examinations as performance indicators and, finally, league tables (CARROLL, 1994b). This has resulted in an internal market within schools and resources linked to the performance indicators (PENNEY and EVANS, 1994). League tables have ensured that PE teachers cannot stay out of the competition whether they like examinations or not. It is a case of, 'if you can't beat 'em, join 'em'. This argument applies equally to post 16 education, where A levels in PE and Sports Studies and vocational qualifications in Sports Science and Leisure and Tourism feature strongly for many colleges in their league table standings. Not only this, but they are proving to be one of the most popular options, and ones where jobs are seen to exist.

In summary, across all 14-19 education and over many years, examinations in the subject have not only been of educational benefit for many pupils and students and provided the first step in gaining a career route, they have also been a mechanism for teachers' role satisfaction and survival, professional development and redefining status. This argument is supported by research over time (CARROLL, 1982, 1986, 1994a; SCHOOLS COUNCIL, 1981).

Conclusion

What have been the benefits of examinations for PE, teachers and pupils? The answer to this revolves round the explanations for the development and success of examinations. It has already been noted that the redefinition of PE's marginal role and status was a major explanation for the introduction and success of examinations. This has manifested itself within schools and colleges, at the 14-19 level, in a parity with some other foundation subjects in terms of resources (staffing, time, equipment), and outside the school, in the way that it is used as a selective mechanism for further and higher education and employment, just like most other subjects. Looking back, it is fortunate now that the early pioneers of CSE PE and C&G Recreation and Leisure did such a good job in establishing PE and Sport as an examination subject, as it could have been very difficult to become a successful GCSE and vocational subject if it had not been first established as a CSE mode 1 or C&G subject. I say fortunate because it is crucial in the climate of today to be part of school and college league tables. PE's survival would have been in doubt at this level if it had been regarded as a recreational subject. The examination initiative established PE and Recreation as an educational and vocational subject with a knowledge base which had previously been underplayed in its presentation as a practical and recreational subject. It extended the boundaries of the subject at these levels and alters what Bernstein calls the "classification and framing" of educational knowledge in the subject (BERNSTEIN, 1972). This has helped in the formation of the basis for the National Curriculum at school level and vocational education at FE level. Examinations have helped teachers to clarify the objectives, content and assessment criteria and become more precise in their use in the teaching situation. Examinations have helped to set high standards and achieve quality in the subject. In addition, they have offered teachers an opportunity for classroom teaching and examination work in their own subject rather than change to other subjects as they had done previously. However, they did not only bring satisfaction and professional development for the PE teacher, they also provided knowledge, understanding, qualifications and satisfaction for their pupils, which may be useful for leisure or careers. These benefits will continue on all these fronts whilst teachers take up the mantle of teacher/examiner and vocational trainer.

In 1982 I concluded my paper in the *Physical Education Review* with:

If PE does become firmly established in the new system
then this will take up a good deal of the PE teacher's time,
and this may well affect the amount of time available for
extra curricular activities. The PE teacher may well feel
more colleagues ought to help in after school activities,
and may well suffer from intra and inter role conflict. It
therefore remains to be seen whether the PE teacher can
retain a foot in both recreational and examination camps,
and whether he can retain the role satisfaction which he
has been seeking.

(CARROLL, 1982, p.34)

Well, PE did become firmly established in the new system (GCSE),
and examination work has taken up a good deal of time. However, it
can not be solely blamed for the decline in extra-curricular activities
(SHA, 1990). Now there is increasing pressure on schools' recreational
and sporting provision stemming from the Government's initiatives
(DNH, 1995), so, whilst it is good to see the Government's interest in
school and college sport, this puts an additional burden on PE teachers
without additional resources. Recreation looks as if it could become a
source of prestige once again for the PE teacher. However, there is
even less chance of help today from other than PE colleagues in extra
curricular work. Now, with the latest developments in examinations
and qualifications, it remains to be seen whether the PE teachers can
retain a footing in the three camps, recreational, academic
examinations and vocational, or, whether they will trip up trying to
meet too many demands.

References

BALL, S.T. (1990) *Politics and Policy Making in Education.* London,
Routledge.

BERNSTEIN, B. (1972) On Classification and Framing of Educational
Knowledge. In M.F.D. YOUNG (Ed) *Knowledge and Control.* London. Collier-
MacMillan.

CARROLL, B. (1982) Examinations and Curriculum Change in Physical
Education. *Physical Education Review*, 5, 1, 26-36.

CARROLL, B. (1984) Developments in CSE and the Leisure Paradox. *British Journal of Physical Education*. 15, 1, 25-26.

CARROLL, B. (1986) Examinations in Physical Education: an Analysis of Trends and Developments. In G.M. DONALD (Ed) *Trends and Developments in Physical Education*. London, E&F.N. Spon.

CARROLL, B. (1994a) *Assessment in Physical Education: a Teacher's Guide to the Issues*. London, Falmer Press.

CARROLL, B. (1994b) *On Becoming a 'Proper' Subject. The Role of Assessment and Accountability in Defining the Status of a Subject: The Case of Physical Education*. Paper at British Educational Research Association (BERA) annual conference. Oxford.

CARROLL, B. (1995) Examinations in Physical Education and Sport: Gender Differences and Influences on Subject Choice. In L. LAWRENCE, E. MURDOCH, and S. PARKER (Eds) *Professional and Development Issues in Leisure, Sport and Education*. Brighton. LSA Publications, pp.59-71.

DEARING, R. (1994) *The National Curriculum and its Assessment*. London, SCAA.

DEPARTMENT OF NATIONAL HERITAGE (1995) *Sport: Raising the Game*. London. DNH.

ELLINGHAM, K. (1984) *Developments of Physical Education and Recreation in Selected Colleges of Further Education*. M.Ed. dissertation. University of Manchester.

EVANS, J. (1976) An Argument Against Examinations. *British Journal of Physical Education*. 7, 1, 110.

FRANCIS, J. (1992) The Growth, Development and Future of PE and Sport Studies at Advanced Level. *British Journal of Physical Education*, 23, 1, 35-7.

HATCHER, R. (1994) Market Relationships and the Management of Teachers *British Journal of Sociology of Education,* 15, 41-61.

HENDRY, L.B. (1975) Survival in a Marginal Role: The Professional Identity of the PE teacher. *British Journal of Sociology,* 26, 4, 465-476.

HODGSON, B. (1996) 'Which Exam?' *British Journal of Physical Education*, 27, 2, 23-26.

HUNTER-JONES, J., CARROLL, B. and JONES, B. (1995) Knowledge or Competence? The Changing Face of Qualifications in the Leisure industry. In L. LAWRENCE, E. MURDOCH and S. PARKER (Eds) *Professional and Development Issues in Leisure, Sport and Education*. Brighton, LSA Publications, pp.231-250.

JONES, D.W. (1980) *The Role of Physical Education in Three Colleges of Further Education*. M.Ed. thesis. University of Manchester.

KANE, J.E. (1974) *Physical Education in Secondary Schools*. London, MacMillan.

MACCONACHIE-SMITH, J. (1996) Physical Education at Key Stage 4. In N. ARMSTRONG (Ed) *New Directions in Physical Education: Change and Innovation*. London, Cassell, pp.82-93.

PENNEY, D. and EVANS, J. (1994) *Controlling Management and Managing Control; Autonomy and Control in an Imperfect Market*. Paper at BERA annual conference. Oxford.

RYAN, B. (1986) *Curriculum Innovation in PE in Colleges in FE in the Eastern Region*. M.Phil. Thesis. University of Manchester.

SCHOOLS COUNCIL (1977) *Examinations in Physical Education. A Report of the Working Party of the Schools Council PE Committee*. London, Schools Council.

SCHOOLS COUNCIL (1981) *Examinations in Physical Education and Related Areas*. London, Schools Council.

SSEC (1963) *The Certificate of Secondary Education: Some Suggestions for Teachers and Examiners*. London, SSEC.

SHA (1990) *Enquiry into Provision of Physical Education in Secondary Schools*. London, SHA.

WOLF, A. (1995) *Competence Based Assessment*. Buckingham. Open University Press.

WOOLLAM, S. (1978) *The Case Against Examinations*. British Council of Physical Education Conference Proceedings. Assessment of Physical Education in Schools and Colleges. BCPE.

Chapter 17

To Be or Not to Be?
The Present and Future of School
Physical Education in International Context

Ken Hardman

Introduction

Throughout history, physical activity in diverse ways has been a significant element in all cultures. Nowadays, this significance is demonstrated in sporting spectacles such as the Olympic Games and World Soccer Championships, which attract audiences from all parts of the globe measured in millions. Within the academic domain, undergraduate, graduate and post-graduate Physical Education and/or Sports Science programmes in Institutions of Higher Education, a plethora of journal, text-book, electronic data-base publications and the increasing number of 'learned' societies are further testimony to its world-wide importance. Indeed, the preceding chapters of this *Reader* bear witness to the broad-scale scholarly interest and research endeavour in the area as well as to the apparent healthy state of this sphere of human endeavour.

One institutional form of physical activity, physical education, has long been considered an important component of the educational process, enjoying a sustained presence largely grounded in the Aristotelian concept of 'harmonious balance' and variously linked with a range of instrumental outcomes. However, as the next millennium draws near, despite this historical and, in some proponents' quarters essentially regarded presence, school physical education seems to be under threat in countries in all continental regions of the world. The

Swedish Education Minister's suggestion in 1990 that physical education should lose its compulsory subject status in secondary schools is one illustrative example of the serious nature of this threat. It did not happen, but the mere fact of its consideration in such a country with a distinguished record of school physical education was an alarming development.

Currently, there are numerous examples of the strains and tensions that physical education and physical educators are experiencing. The tensions are perhaps epitomised in Canadian Association of Health, Physical Education, Recreation and Dance (CAHPERD) immediate past-President, Mo MACKENDRICK's assertion (1996) that in Canada,

> physical education is not seen as a priority ... It is under severe attack and faces competition for time within the school curriculum. Often physical education is being taught by generalist teachers with little or no preparation in physical education methods. Additionally, budget cutbacks are impacting negatively on the time and resources required to teach a quality physical education programme. (p.2)

MACKENDRICK's assertion is reinforced by TREMBLAY, PELLA and TAYLOR (1996), who observe that,

> physical education programmes in many areas of Canada ... are being disproportionately cut as government departments try and cope with reduced funding. In New Brunswick, and likely in many other parts of Canada, both the quantity and quality of elementary physical education programs are being severely reduced. (p.5)

Generally, physical educators are being called upon to justify the inclusion of physical education within the school curriculum. The strong arguments proffered have met with only limited success: in many countries physical education is not accepted on par with seemingly superior academic subjects concerned with developing a child's intellect. A plethora of commentators (ANTALA, SYKORA and SEDLACEK, 1992; BONHOMME, 1992; FASTING, 1992; GRAHAM, 1990; HARDMAN, 1993, 1994, 1995, 1996; JANZEN, 1995; JOHNS, 1995; KARHUS, 1992; MOORE, 1994; NIELSEN, 1992; PULIS, 1994; RASHID, 1994; RILEY, 1992; TUOHIMAA, 1993; WAMUKOYA and HARDMAN, 1992) have argued that physical education has been pushed into a defensive position, that it is suffering from decreasing curriculum time allocation, budgetary controls with inadequate financial, material and personnel resources, and instability because of influences and pressure from groups with vested interests in sport and fitness, has low subject status and esteem, and is being ever more marginalised and undervalued by authorities. Against such a background, it is of little wonder that there has been widespread considerable concern amongst physical educationists. The concern is manifested, for example, in a conference in Geelong, Australia in 1991, devoted to the theme of 'Crisis in Physical Education' (ALEXANDER and SANDS, 1991), a special theme within the 1995 winter edition of the *Bulletin of IAPESGW* (International Association of Physical Education and Sport for Girls and Women) devoted to the status of physical education and reduction in curriculum time allocation and a fear amongst some European Physical Education Association's representatives that if present trends continue then physical education will have disappeared from the school curriculum within a decade. Clearly, a hitherto 'essentially' regarded school curriculum subject is at a crisis point in its history.

The intention here is to demonstrate the magnitude of the concerns about the current state of physical education with illustrations drawn from selected countries in various continental regions of the world and to present suggestions as to how school physical education might be sustained for the future through both a re-appraisal of concepts and practices and institutional intervention strategies.

State and Status of Physical Education

1. Europe

Some recent developments in Sweden, where there are reports of a curriculum time allocation reduction of 20% over the pre-1994 figure of 500 hours allocation, have been a cause for some alarm in Norway. Here, amongst some Norwegian physical educationists, there is a fear of the 'Swedish Ghost'. This is a fear which may have further dire consequences if the latest (1996) Swedish Education Ministry's deliberations on whether to drop physical education from the school curriculum at upper Secondary Stage come to fruition. In Finland, a new curriculum has led to a decrease in the amount of mandatory physical education (schools are bound only by stipulated minima) and an increase in options.

In the Scandinavian context, many teachers have suffered problems in the legitimization of the subject. It is argued that the number of lessons physical education teachers have to teach is a status indicator and generally in Scandinavia, this is greater than for so-called theoretical subjects (FASTING, 1992, p.46). Moreover, despite its status as a core subject, Norwegian physical educators believe it is seen to be inferior to other subjects, with head teachers rarely involved pedagogically: "Headmasters ... hardly know what is happening ... 'it is gym, the pupils like it, you fix it'" (KARHUS, 1992, p.2). The Finnish curriculum reforms have reduced state guidance and vested responsibility for curricular matters in schools. This is a recipe for potential local variations. Sceptical physical educators fear that a cheapened, 'babysitting' format, in which principles "... go to the dogs so long as the kids have a good time" (TUOHIMAA, 1993, p.41), will prevail in the future.

Reforms in Austria have produced a reduction in hours allocated to physical education. In Belgium, according to SMULDERS (1992), there is a trend, especially in Catholic denominational schools, of diminution of time-tabled physical education lessons. Moreover, curriculum reorganisation has seen physical education placed within the area of fine arts, where expression, cooperation and creativity rule, and sport and competition have been phased out.

Physical education in the three cycles of the primary phase of French schools, is officially allocated five 'hours' per week. However, BONHOMME (1992) asserts that the official requirement is not implemented in a majority of schools, citing insufficient human and physical resources as being responsible. He indicates that 72% of Primary (Elementary) schools have less than two hours physical education per week and 50% of children are taught by a sports coach. The application of official policy is but a "beautiful dream". Similarly, documentary indication of compulsory physical education lessons in the secondary phase colleges and lycees is to some extent at odds with some research findings (MALLALIEU and HARDMAN, 1986), that in some schools distanced from Paris, up to 90% of pupils had no compulsory physical education, though some 30% did engage in voluntary sporting activity. There are also reports of inadequacies in quality of facility provision in schools. The intellectually demanding education curriculum in France has resulted in, within some circles, physical education being merely seen as a diversion or even as a burden to be borne in order to pass examinations. The obligation, after 1974, on schools to form 'Association Sportives' to offer voluntary sport was viewed by the physical education teachers' union as undermining the broadly based curriculum. Government policies favouring a sports elite at the expense of a genuine physical education programme for all children in schools have facilitated the development of a sub-standard situation.

In the Netherlands, it is reported (VAN OUDENAARDE, 1995) that the number of lessons in primary schools has decreased to two per week and "school swimming has been cancelled" (p.9). Reductions in timetable allocation from three to two lessons each week in secondary schools are at least better than the situation in vocational schools, where physical education no longer features.

In Scotland a recent editorial in the weekly newspaper *Scotland on Sunday* (1997) recording disappointment with national teams' performances on the soccer and rugby fields, cites a Scottish Sports Council investigation into the organisation and funding of sport, in which a picture is painted "... of schools bereft of the physical education specialists who could spot and nurture ... athletic talents ...", functioning in a "culture that has relegated PE to an optional extra rather than a fundamental part of every child's development" (p.21). The editorial emphasises the essential role of physical education as the 'womb' of sport and as such echoes a central message of the English/Welsh Department of National Heritage's (1995) *Sport – Raising the Game*: physical education is identified as having an important role in perpetuating sport (especially team games) to achieve the ascribed outcomes such as "... fair play, self-discipline, respect for others, learning to live by laws and understanding one's obligations to others" (p.7). Research by JESS (1992) indicates that in many Scottish primary schools, there is inadequate provision of facilities for physical education classes: 70% rely on a multi-purpose hall, which is also used for school lunches, assemblies, concerts, drama and so on (a scenario not untypical of England and Wales), that radio broadcasts account for a large proportion of physical education time in Infant programmes, and that there is a problem of curriculum continuity because of the number of class teachers involved, the majority of whom do not share information. Primary school teachers in Scotland perceive physical education concerned essentially with functional activities such as games, gymnastics and swimming, and only marginally with expressiveness. This is ironic given that the Scottish Education Department has placed it alongside art, drama, and music within an 'Expressive Arts' area, despite opposition from the professionals. Hence, there has been conflict between teachers and the Education Department. The conflict is seen in credibility gaps between official 'Guidelines' and teachers' perceptions.

In England and Wales, after over a century of state-provided education, a government sponsored national curriculum was imposed in 1989 with physical education introduced as a statutorily required school subject for children aged 5-16 for the first time in its history. Even as the new physical education national curriculum was being implemented in schools, widespread professional and teacher unions' reaction to a grossly overloaded initial curriculum caused Government to set up an enquiry commission (the Dearing Commission). The result has been a revised national curriculum introduced in 1995, in which allocation of curriculum time to physical education has been reduced from a notional $7^{1}/_{2}\%$ to 5%! Even in the phased planning stages, the Secretary of State for Education had made it clear to the Physical Education National Curriculum Working Party that physical education curriculum time was a non-negotiable issue – resource implications and economic feasibility were set as markers for proposals. In effect, the Working Group was being directed to construct a curriculum based on economic viability and not educational desirability. This feature is reminiscent of the Newcastle Commission remit of 1861, which was required to make recommendations for a sound, but economically cheap system of 'popular' education.

Recent surveys suggest that since the introduction of the national curriculum, the amount of time actually given to physical education in state secondary schools is on the decline with 75% of schools "... providing less than two hours a week for pupils aged 14 and over" (THE DAILY TELEGRAPH, 22nd March, 1995, p.6). A major reason for the claimed reduction in allocated physical education curriculum time is increasing marginalisation due to priority accorded to the 'main' national curriculum subjects; it is particularly squeezed by the requirements of the three core subjects (English, mathematics and science) and technology studies.

The plight of physical education appears even worse in Greece, where, despite its compulsory status and position as an assessed graded subject, it "is not effective" (ASTERI, 1995, p.6). Many schools have minimal, if any, physical education facilities. Physical education teachers are a rarity in primary schools, in which "... P.E. lessons are non-existent" (ASTERI, 1995, p.7). In recent years, teachers have been reported as being unable to understand curricula because they were written in such obscure language, with statements so vague that presumptions regarding meaning had to be made. The curricula presented contradictory guidance: recommendation of freedom in movement was followed by prescription of static tasks. There was also a recommendation in the curriculum that during inclement weather, physical education should take place in the classroom, where simple ball games could be practised; spatial inadequacies for such activity meant that many lessons were cancelled. On the specific area swimming, the activity was to be included where possible but no further guidance was provided – no doubt the dearth of facilities and the issue whether public school teachers were actually qualified to teach swimming contributed to the lack of advice.

In the (re-)unified Germany, it is somewhat ironic that the five new eastern Länder (former German Democratic Republic – GDR) have been obliged, through 'partnerships', to base their respective school systems and curricula on suspect western Länder models, themselves needful of evaluation. The former GDR had already undertaken curriculum reform (1989-90), which has been completely overlooked by many west German sport pedagogues. In the present eastern part of Germany, physical education has been largely seen as a socialist relic of the former GDR competitive sport system. Many teachers have let pupils do what they want rather than intervening, for risk of being accused of being "an authoritarian ex-socialist" (NAUL, 1992, p.18). The 'open' instructional strategies and fun-oriented teaching methods (the dominant ideals) introduced by some west Germans as "missionaries of democracy", have caused some east German counterpart physical educators and sport pedagogues to have understandable doubts in accepting all the *new* teaching approaches when discipline and performance orientation are neglected (PORSCHUTZ, 1991). As in the western part of Germany, the subject is now regarded as of only minor significance in school education (NAUL, 1992).

Some aspects of the problems in Germany are also evidenced in the Czech and Slovak Republics, where the re-orientation of the concept of school physical education (ideas on humanism, democracy and freedom) has brought elements of liberalisation. This re-orientation is based only on pupils' interests and neglects knowledge of young people's needs, as well as scientific research. Thus, somewhat negative outcomes are witnessed in several schools, where pupils only want to engage in activities in which they are specifically interested, and many pupils see the physical education teacher solely as an activity organiser. ANTALA, SYKORA and SEDLACEK (1992) cite low participation rates in leisure activities in and out of school in support of their contention that recent changes in theoretical conceptions designed to create more positive attitudes towards physical activity engagement have not been realised in practice. School physical education in the two Republics is now undervalued as a subject: school senior management shows little interest in it and its contribution to the general development of pupils is not adequately appreciated; and physical education teachers are considered inferior, less capable and less skilful (ANTALA, SEDLACEK and SYKORA, 1992).

In Hungary, the "grim reality of little or no physical education in ... schools" is partially attributed to lack of facilities: "... seventy-five percent of schools do not have gymnasia or physical education programs" (ANDERSEN, 1996, p.41), known elsewhere. No wonder it is claimed that the "... majority of school children know little of values and practice of physical education" and that Hungarian males suffer poor general health "because they have received no physical fitness instruction during their formative years" (ANDERSEN, 1996, p.41).

Similar negative phenomena are also extant in Malta, where physical education has inferior status when compared with academic subjects. PULIS (1994) argues that the physical educator's "... work is not scrutinised with the same seriousness as in other 'academic' subjects", resulting "... in the lowering of standards and status" (p.1) and that the standard of physical education has reached a particularly "low ebb in the primary schools" (p.10). In addition, and mirroring the situation in Norway, "Heads of Schools ... do not bother much about what is happening in P.E." (p.40). The subject's presence in the curriculum is more of a convenience than one of educational conviction. In secondary schools, time allocation for physical education is 4.7% of the total curriculum in the first two years, reducing to 2.95% in years 3 to 5. This inadequate figure is exacerbated by deficiencies in facilities, substandard maintenance, disruption by adverse weather conditions and other school activities in halls designated for physical activity. The low budget allocation for physical education poses a serious limiting factor on its proper development. In initial teacher training courses, some teachers graduate without having attended a basic unit on physical education (PULIS, 1994, p.130). In short: physical education and its teachers have low status; attitudes of parents, colleagues, head-teachers and higher authorities are negative towards it; and there is a general lack of support services – funds, facilities and equipment are in short supply.

2. The Middle East

Inferior subject status is evident in the State of Kuwait: it no longer features on the Final School Certificate; and lessons are generally cancelled as examinations draw near. In new schools during adverse weather conditions, there are no physical education lessons because of lack of indoor facilities (BEHBEHANI, 1992). A reduction in curriculum hours is also evident in this small country, where physical education has decreased in importance: allocation of curriculum time has been reduced from three to two lessons in Year 4 and to one lesson in Year 9 (third year of High School).

Elsewhere in the Arabian Gulf region, in Saudi Arabia, there is no physical education in schools for Muslim girls and constraints on the development of physical education in and out of schools are variously evidenced in a number of other Gulf countries including Iraq, Iran, the Emirates and Yemen.

3. Africa

In some African countries, some of the above reported problems pale into relative insignificance, especially where Islam is the dominant religion practised. Physical education and sport are associated with the evils of gambling and alcohol especially by some Fundamentalist Muslim scholars. Pre-conditions have been stated for participation: development of strength, health and fitness for Islamic Jihad (Holy War) if necessary; skill and technique for self-defence; non-interference with prayer; and women's exercise to be performed with all parts of the body covered and unobserved by men. Several countries adhere to these conditions with the consequences that physical education does not feature in some curricula, (e.g. Chad, Libya, Mali and Niger). In some other countries, (e.g. Uganda), where teachers are female muslims, physical education might not be taught even when it is on the curriculum. Elsewhere, there is no physical education during 'Ramadan'; and physical educators are regarded as satanic agents indulging in play rather than in prayer and worship (KAMIYOLE, 1993, pp.29-31).

In Nigeria, there have been efforts to improve the delivery of physical education. SHEHU (1996) reports that there are obstacles to implementation: logistic inadequacies such as facilities and equipment; shortage of qualified physical educators and low moral and motivation of teaching personnel; a narrowly focused choice of curriculum activity; inferior role and esteem of the physical educator; student perception of physical education as lacking in intellectual and vocational substance; and financial constraints which inhibit curriculum development and delivery.

The situation is less dire in South Africa, but there are continuing problems which reflect discriminatory policies of immediate past times. In many 'black' schools, there is a large gap between policy of time allocation and syllabus content and implementation: physical education is prescribed but its practice depends on the head-teacher; there is an acute shortage of trained physical education specialists; and facilities are generally poor or non-existent. In 'Indian' schools, around 40% of teachers are non-specialists, hence the range of physical activity is narrow; amongst specialists, there are many whose promotion prospects are constrained and who seek to opt out of physical education classes to avoid exposure to sun and related skin problems as well as burdensome extra-curricular duties. Even in 'white' and 'coloured' schools, there are problems of inadequate supplies of specialist teachers. In some provinces physical education for grades 10-12 is allocated "only 30 minutes each week and often there is no P.E. for pupils in Grade 12 where time is taken for the academic subjects in preparation for the final school examinations" (KATZENELLENBOGEN, 1995, p.10).

In Kenya, familiar symptoms of physical education's malaise are to be found. In immediate post-Independence Kenya, physical education suffered low esteem and status, and lacked trained personnel, facilities and equipment. It was "... a subject without academic significance" (WAMUKOYA and HARDMAN, 1992, p.30). Even after a presidential directive making physical education a compulsory subject and an associated campaign to raise its level and profile, some head-teachers had physical education lessons timetabled only for inspection purposes. With only two Inspectors to oversee physical education in the whole of the country, such lessons are a rarity. School education continues to be regarded as a means of selecting and socialising members of an intellectual elite to maintain standards of cultural excellence. Thus, for the general populace, physical education is a non-intellectual sphere of activity, serving as a means of social training or as a means of compensating for the rigours of academic work (WAMUKOYA and HARDMAN, 1992). The physical education teaching and learning environment is faced with enormous problems. In schools, complaints are raised concerning lack of adequate facilities, lack of adequate equipment, lack of reading materials, negative attitude by the school head-teachers, teachers, students and parents, incompetent teachers of physical education, indifferent teachers, poor supervision of physical education teaching, boring and repetitive curriculum, inadequate content coverage, lack of continuity in syllabus coverage, lack of lesson preparation, teacher-master role conflict, too much work load, lack of time on the time-table for physical education, lack of finance, large class sizes, disinterested students, lack of individual attention and a poorly formulated syllabus (NJORORAI, 1990).

4. Asia

'Subsidiarity' of physical education to academic subjects is a feature of the curriculum in Malaysia. Here, as in some other countries, there is a difference between government policy and school practice. In aiming for holistic development of students, physical education notionally has

7-10% of total curriculum time, *but* during 5 years of secondary schooling, it is actually allocated less than 4% (134 hours, 44 of which are devoted to 'health education', in comparison with 300 hours for 'arts' and 'aesthetic education' and 4,000 hours for 'intellectual' components such as languages, science and mathematics). The government's attempt to integrate physical and health aspects of physical education has further reduced the academic significance of physical education. Lack of facilities exacerbates the situation, which is made even worse when lessons are cancelled during hot or rainy weather, endemic in such tropical climate countries. The physical education syllabus content is heavily weighted towards 'fitness' (again contrary to the concept of holistic development) and is regularly delivered by teachers, untrained in physical education, especially in Elementary and lower Secondary schools. Such teachers are designated (RASHID, 1994) "... remote control" teachers, who provide a ball, "... sit by a tree or stay in the staff room ... (At) the end of the lesson, the teacher blows the whistle and the pupils return to the classroom" (p.10). Contrasting the present situation with the "'Golden Age' for P.E. in Malaysia ...", RASHID (1994) comments that "... Malaysia is facing a 'Dark Age' in contributions to pupils' holistic development" (p.10).

In Hong Kong timetable organisation prioritises "... English, Chinese Putonghua, mathematics, computer literacy and science" which "are allocated the lion's share" (JOHNS, 1996, p.12). Subjects such as art, drama and physical education are considered peripheral. As a so-called 'cultural' subject, physical education is poorly placed in the hierarchy of esteem and so is starved for resources:

> Offerings in the timetable for cultural subjects often fall short of the minimum recommended by the Education Department. It is also not uncommon for physical education ... teachers to be asked to give over their classes in order that other subject teachers may use the time for extra preparation at examination time. In such an arrangement physical education teachers express frustration as they occupy positions of low status (JOHNS, 1996, p.13).

The marginalisation of physical education is manifested in several ways: one or two (at most) 35 minute lessons per week on concrete playgrounds on the ground floor of the school or on adjacent courts surrounding a school; no grass fields are available because of shortage of land; poor equipment, insufficient/inappropriate small apparatus because of inadequate budgets for such expenditures (JOHNS, 1996, p.13). At best it seems that "... school physical education is tolerated but not promoted sufficiently to be considered as a serious and beneficial contribution to the development and health of Hong Kong children" (JOHNS, 1996, p.14). Perhaps, this neglect of due consideration is the root cause of Hong Kong children's reported low activity levels, an increasing trend to obesity and signs of deteriorating health (JOHNS, 1996, p.14).

5. Australia

Threats to the status of school physical education are also endemic in Australia, where in the State of New South Wales, the curriculum reforms introduced by government in 1988 (as in other States and with similar consequences), placed physical education within the area of 'Personal Development, Health and Physical Education' (comprising health, physical education, life and career studies and home science). Outcomes reported include lowering of physical education status and perhaps loss of time, no support system, no in-service teaching, and no teacher training courses to prepare intending teachers for this Area (WILLIAMS P., WILLIAMS M., BERTRAM, MCCORMACK, GURAY and BRENTON, 1993). In the State of Victoria, RILEY (1992), argues that physical education declined after 1981, when the government tightened the 'economic belt': the Physical Education Branch of the Ministry of Education was closed; revamped teaching and curriculum strategies were introduced in schools with devolved powers; suddenly specialist physical education teachers found career pathways ended; and teachers' morale deteriorated as higher expectations were coupled with less support. Marginal developments sponsored by outside agencies producing exciting packages emerged to fill a void in schools with Sports Development Officers giving 'one-off' motivational lessons, which were "more like talent identification sessions" (RILEY, 1992, p.12). Two conferences in 1991, 'Australian Physical Education in Crisis' (Geelong) and 'Junior Sport – Time to Deliver' (Canberra), drew attention to the problems and concerns about the state of school physical education and sport. The issues raised by these two conferences prompted federal government to set up a Senate Enquiry. Its findings on *Physical Education and Sport Education* were published in December, 1992. The conclusion drawn was that "physical education and sport was in an unhealthy position" (RILEY and DONALD, 1995, p.178), for which key causes were cited: financial cuts; an over-crowded curriculum; the inclusion of physical education under the broad umbrella of health education; a lack of a coherent physical education policy in all States; reduction in trained specialist teachers and limited preparation of generalist teachers for physical education; lack of State Education Departments' support for teachers supervising physical education; devolution of decision-making to local school councils; and the introduction of sports programmes such as 'Aussie Sport' to justify the withdrawal of physical education from schools.

At State level, the immediate aftermath of the Inquiry Report was a number of policies designed to remedy the situation. In Victoria, for example, the newly elected (1992) Liberal Government established its own Committee, chaired by ex-teacher and internationally renowned athlete Steve Monaghetti, to examine physical education and sport in Victorian schools (RILEY and DONALD, 1995). This 'U-turn' in Victorian State policy represented a significant shift in government thinking in relation to physical education, but whether the Monanghetti *Physical and Sport Education* report's (1993) 19 recommendations will be fully implemented and sustained is open to speculation as are action programmes in other Australian States. Two years on from the Senate Inquiry Report, several initiatives have been stifled by minimal state financial investment: the programme in Victoria is seen to be a 'stop-gap' measures, which "when funding runs out after three years ... may be 'Custer's Last Stand' ... in PE and Sport" (TURNBULL, 1994, p.24); in South Australia, a survey investigating participation patterns found that many year 8 students have no physical education at all and 34% of year 10 girls are non-participants (TURNBULL, 1994, p.24). Perhaps, it is that great god, 'sport' (in its highly competitive form), which has concentrated the political mind: at federal level in Australia, a $289 million investment in preparation for 80 medals in the Sydney Olympic Games in 2000 has accompanied the virtual "shutdown of physical education" (NAURIGHT, 1995, p.5) in South Australia. This observation on the plight of physical education linked with investment for medals is shared by GRIER (1995), who expresses fears that such funding for sport "may be at the expense of basic physical education programmes" (p.5). Evidently, the Senate Inquiry on *Physical and*

Sport Education conclusion that the importance of physical education was not in dispute has become lost in the euphoria of 'Sydney 2000':

> Medals, medals, medals ... the system is a factory for producing elite athletes ... So much tax payers' money being spent on a few at the expense of the majority. But the 'system' produces winners – and 'winners in sport' within Australia typify the country's identity. (BUTLER, 1996)

6. North America

Problems also abound in physical education in North America. In the United States, the 'erosion' of physical education has been seen in a crisis of identity in Higher Education as demonstrated by the proliferation of different nomenclature descriptors and the separation of academic disciplines from practice (teaching in schools) – perhaps this is a way for scholars to avoid the stigma of being thought of as 'gym teachers'! In schools, the degree of autonomy in individual States and local School Boards together with educational priorities established by these agencies and the level of funding are significant determinants in the delivery of physical education. Thus, physical education is neither a compulsory nor is it a standardised curriculum subject throughout the country and hence, not all children necessarily participate in physical education programmes. Daily quality physical education in some schools contrasts with inadequate programme provision in others. Over 50% of the states have either no requirement for physical education in the High School or require only one semester or one year for graduation. GRAHAM (1990) reported on the dire situation in numerous high schools, commenting that in several states, the amount of time allocated to physical education had been reduced in recent years and that the curriculum is narrowly focused. He also pointed to pressurized physical education teachers turning to teaching driver education, supervising study and detention rooms or moving to teaching positions in middle or elementary schools. Research (KROTEE, 1992) conducted in the State of Minnesota, revealed that 45% of sample respondents listed lack of motivation and negative attitude of students towards physical education, and lack of respect towards the teacher. This introduces another dimension – that of quality of the physical education service being delivered – and one that is not peculiar to Minnesota. The President of the Fédération Internationale d'Éducation Physique (FIEP) has expressed the view that teaching in some European schools does not inspire confidence that children will enter adulthood with knowledge, skills attitudes and habits for the hoped-for active life-styles adopted (ANDREWS, 1993). Concern for the state and status of physical education in American schools is diverse in pattern as illustrated in attempts to find remedies to the situation by professional bodies such as American Alliance of Health, Physical Education, Recreation and Dance (AAHPERD), and by the U.S. Senate resolution to encourage state and local governments to provide a quality daily school physical education programme. The recent initiative by Human Kinetics Ltd., in sponsoring the formation of the United States Physical Education Association, was a response to the frustrations of physical educators there.

Concern has been expressed for physical education in Canada. From the so termed 'Golden Years' of the 1970s decade of daily physical education, "it is evident that physical education has been unable to maintain a position of priority in the school curriculum" (JANZEN, 1995, p.5). Indeed, CAHPERD's *Physical Education 2000* (1993) document indicated that "quality physical education is not seen as a priority in most Canadian schools" (p.17). The position was considered so serious that a 'Special Task Force on Canadian Physical Education' was formed in 1992 to promote the essential aspects of quality physical education and how it could contribute to the educational process. The perceived threats to the status of physical education, competition for curriculum time and the continued existence of the subject itself (NIELSEN, 1992) have continued unabated up to the present time. The threats have been exacerbated by a 1995 National Debt of $550 million and rising, a phenomenon which has stimulated educational reforms based in economic realities: Alberta's reform initiative excluded physical education from its 'basic education' programme; in Manitoba, the Minister for Education suggested that despite massive investment in physical education "the attitudes of society had not been positively affected by their physical education experience within the school system" (JANZEN, 1995, p.8). In his subsequent 'blue-print' for curriculum changes, the Minister posed a further threat to physical education by reducing the subject in Senior 1-4 level to a "supplementary or optional status, thus marginalising and weakening its ability to function in the school" (JOHNS, 1995, p.15). The 'blue-print' served to reinforce the view that in the province of Manitoba, as in many other Canadian provinces, "... physical education as a school subject has never been regarded as a significant contribution to the development of the individual" (JOHNS, 1995, p.15). In the province of New Brunswick the number of full-time equivalent physical education specialists for anglophone elementary schools was reduced by 60% between 1992 and 1995, a reduction which was accompanied by the elimination of the only consultancy position for physical and health education (TREMBLAY, PELLA and TAYLOR, 1996, p.5). New Brunswick offers an excellent illustration of the gap between officially stated policy and actual practice: a survey of elementary schools in the province revealed that curriculum delivery time for physical education averaged 55.9 minutes per week, which represents just over one half of the provincial guidelines (100 minutes) and about one third of the national recommendation (150 minutes). The same survey found that the major barriers to quality physical education were "insufficient training", "no access to expertise" and "lack of in-service" programmes (TREMBLAY et al, 1996, pp.5-6).

The conceptual development of physical education in Quebec Province has experienced a significant period of inactivity since the late 1970s. A divided profession with numerous splinter groups often in conflict has exacerbated the situation. The conceptual situation is typically restricted to fostering the 'biological machine', with teachers merely acting as 'movement technicians' and narrowly concerned with development of technical skills and physical qualities (sport practice and physical fitness).

The economic crises of 1982 and 1990 have led to government savings in expenditure on educational programmes: physical education has not been spared from the financial cut-backs. There has been a tendency for several years to reduce the amount of time allocated to physical education at all levels of the school system. Moreover, the contribution and course content of compulsory physical education courses is being seriously questioned. At elementary level, 75% of school boards do not observe the minimum standard of 120 minutes per week due to time constraints and competition from other subjects. Schools' physical education programmes are under attack with pressure to abolish compulsory physical education (BOILEAU, CHAISSON, DEMERS, GUAY, LAROUCHE, ROY and MARCOTTE, 1994, p.9). BOILEAU et al. (1994) also refer to a tarnished professional image amongst physical educators, caused by lack of ethics on the part of some who exploit physical education and 'entertain' rather than 'educate', and silence on the part of others (pp.12-13). Such behaviours are not unknown in other regions of the world.

Present and Future Directions

It could be argued that the various 'snap-shot' country scenarios presented above provide a somewhat distorted global picture of physical education in schools. The 'truth of fact' probably lies in a less negative direction. What *is* the reality? Without doubt, there are examples of positively implemented programmes and good practices in physical education. Equally, idealised documentary statements and sometimes politically inspired rhetoric can, and do, mask the truth: in spite of official documentation on principles, policies and aims, actual implementation into practice exposes the realities of situations, which are often far removed from national political ideologies. Clearly, whatever the situation, there are widespread common concerns.

If physical education is to sustain a school curricular presence, then issues have to be confronted, and rigidity and resistance to change overcome. Status, however, will not be freely granted by those who hold a perception of a 'superior' position. If significant others are to be persuaded of the real importance of physical education, commitment to an essential enterprise and delivery of a quality curriculum will in themselves be insufficient. Application of political skills and argument of the case at local, through national to international levels will be required. Policy makers, decision takers, committees, administrators, other subject colleagues and 'clients' need to be lobbied and convinced that physical education is "an authentic educational activity" (KIRK, 1987, p.147).

To this end, perhaps the better interests of children will be served by closer partnerships of parents and schools. It is desirable that gaps in understanding between parents, teachers and pupils be bridged. Material, cultural and psychological factors relating to the home exercise a powerful influence on children's development and progress at school. But factors at school (organisation, policy, curriculum and general climate) interact with home factors and may compensate to some extent for adverse features in the family environment. The resilience of children may also be important – success despite social disadvantages. The message here is the desirability of bridging any gaps in understanding between parents, teachers and pupils.

1. Role and Reconstruction of Physical Education

It is widely acknowledged that physical activity can positively influence physical and psycho-social health at *all* stages in the life-cycle from infancy to old age. Hence, it seems reasonable to suggest that physical education should have a role to play over the full life-span, i.e. 'from cradle to grave'. However, if physical education is to have a relevant and significant role in education, health and quality of life in a range of life-span programmes, then the frame of reference should be widened. The individual as a whole as well as the environmental socio-cultural complexity of which the individual is a product should be taken more fully into account (BOILEAU et al, 1994, p.7).

For the process of socialisation into, in and through life-span physical activity engagement, the school physical education curriculum is in need of re-appraisal both with regard to its fundamental purposes in view of social and peer culture and other projected and hidden changes, and to the pedagogic processes that might best bring these about. There is a need to recognise the importance of contemporary youth culture in structuring a relevant curriculum. Research studies around the world indicate changing activity patterns of adolescents with gender distinctions blurring, sport culture and sport settings becoming more differentiated, traditional activities in decline and greater awareness of what is being sought (BRETTSCHNEIDER and BRÄUTIGAM, 1991; KROTEE, BLAIR, NAUL, NEUHAUS, HARDMAN, KOMUKU, MATSUMURA, NUMMINEN and JWO, 1994). Generally, a body concept revolution is occurring. The body culture is expanding to incorporate body-building, yoga, tai chi chuan, budo, dance, therapeutic exercises, martial arts, jazz gymnastics etc., health practices, and sports tourism amongst others, and involving a range of social groups and sub-groups (EICHBERG, 1993). Increasing numbers of new groups (women, senior citizens, ethnic minorities, members of different socio-economic strata, people with disabilities etc.) with different abilities and interests have become more physically active in both formal and informal settings.

Trends in changing activity patterns and body concepts have implications for the future of planned physical education curriculum development. At the very least, any reconstruction of physical education should include strategies to foster body/self-concepts, promote healthy well-being and moral education, which together will contribute to the enrichment of quality of life, and stimulate socialisation into habitual regular practice in the pursuit of those values. Any reshaping, however, should recognise local and cultural diversities, as well as traditions and different social and economic conditions; it should also incorporate a range of aspects related to the all-round and harmonious development of the individual within society.

a) Body/Self-Concepts

Body/self-concepts have to be seen in a multi-dimensional context, in which pervading societal values and cultural sub-groups have some part. Thus, ascribed characteristics may be dominant in some cultures but subsidiary in others. One clear implication for physical education is that the pervasive value systems of young people have to be taken into account. However, physical educationists will need to be selective in the values they attempt to promote and those they decide to challenge. Therefore, it is essential to foster acceptance of limitations alongside motivation retention with 'self-improvement' as a measure of success: many with disabilities seem to have accepted their limitations and yet still take on the challenge of personal improvement!

Several researchers (SONSTROEM, 1984; SONSTROEM and MORGAN, 1989; GRUBER, 1986) have reported positive outcomes of engagement in physical exercise programmes on self-esteem. Physical education can contribute by assisting children to develop an inner, stable core of self-esteem that is independent of talents and inadequacies. The problem here for physical educators is to identify mechanisms and evolve strategies for its attainment, rather than rely on optimistic belief in enhancement through exposure. It is critical that the efficacy of teaching styles and interpersonal relationships, methods and curriculum content in fostering self-esteem be better understood. The processes involved with self-esteem are incomplete without other significant support 'systems': peers, friends, parents, teachers, family, and quality of competence information.

b) Healthy Well-Being

The increased interest especially in economically developed nations in health-related exercise and fitness has produced greater attention to the body and its physical condition. As body image and concepts are increasingly likely to play a greater role in the psychology of personal stability, for healthy well-being, an appropriate rationale and capacity for establishing the foundation of self-care of the functioning body should be developed.

If health-related exercise programmes are to be effective, perceptions of young people on health, fitness and exercise issues need to be understood. The need for understanding people's attitudes, views and beliefs from the outset is essential as is assistance in "relating perceptions and experiences to their everyday lives" (HARRIS, 1994, p.149). Individuals should be helped to adopt a 'fitness for life' or 'active life-style' philosophy with a concomitant focus on understanding, relevance and individuality.

Any emphasis on healthy well-being and fitness education, however, should not be regarded as a substitute for an integrated programme of physical education, which has, or ought to have, wider and more intrinsic purposes. Young people need to acquire fundamental motor skills and competency in movement to enjoy an active lifestyle – it is "where self-efficacy begins" (DENNY, 1996, p.34). They should be initiated into life-style management skills that keep them reflecting and acting upon their needs for activity. These skills will need to be reinforced with links into post-school lifelong participation.

c) Moral Education

In his prefatory comments on the UNESCO International Commission on 'Education for the Twenty-First Century', Jacques DELORES (1993) referred to a weakening of societal value systems and called on education to contribute to the evolution of common values as well as to a better understanding of others. Moral value is characterised by the embodiment of concern for the promotion of at least certain human interests and avoidance of at least certain types of human harm and by ethical and social morality, a reciprocal acknowledgement of rights and duties and concern for human interests (STRAWSON, 1970).

Moral education (the fostering of knowledge and understanding and emotional development, which are necessary conditions for critical thinking on moral issues and making rational moral judgements, which then translate into appropriate intentional behaviour), has long been associated with physical education. It could be argued that physical activity is uniquely placed to inculcate many of the related and desirable moral virtues (such as fair play, honesty, losing or winning gracefully and the like). Physical education teachers can make or break on moral education. A focal core for consideration should include: discussion of moral values; commendation of morally praiseworthy behaviour; condemnation of gross breaches of moral values; embodiment of morally sound behaviour in activities engaged in; and reflection on attitudes to pupils and style of communication. Sustained efforts and greater resources, however, are needed to increase the impacts. To these should be added research to assist in identifying the best pedagogic methods by which to achieve greater success, for pedagogical methodology is the crucial factor rather than the subject matter itself.

d) Enriched Quality of Life

In all communities, education is a means of achieving enriched quality of life. Physical education in schools can make a contribution to the education of young people. An initiation into purposeful physical activity transmits practices which can bring understanding of its significance within the culture, its transformative power in developing an enhanced appreciation, and contributing to the development, of the culture. It can, through engagement in purposeful activities, produce understanding and, thereby, more informed choice about 'What' and 'How' to do in life as well as facilitate understanding about the promotion of an individual's welfare and well-being. Physical education should be utilised to attract people to the joy and pleasure of physical activity as in the traditional Japanese philosophy of engagement in exercise for its own sake, and to achieve development through 'instrumental' body and self concepts which, in turn from acquired competence, will affect behavioural perceptions of self-adequacy, self-assurance, self-esteem and self-fulfilment and foster self-actualization.

2. Institutional Collaborative Initiatives

A coordinated concerted effort is required at all levels to promote physical education and enhance its profile not only in schools, but also over the full life-span. To this end a number of collaborative initiatives should be seriously considered.

A truly international lobby for the cause of physical education, comprising coordinated representations from world agencies, such as the International Council of Sport Science and Physical Education (ICSSPE), the International Council on Health, Physical Education, Sport and Dance (ICHPER•SD), the Fédération Internationale d'Éducation Physique (FIEP), the International Society for Comparative Physical Education and Sport (ISCPES), International Federation of Adapted Physical Activity (IFAPA), the International Association of Physical Education and Sports for Girls and Women (IAPESGW), and including powerful groups such as medical, health and related associations, would provide a powerful forum, which could not be ignored by politicians. At regional continental level, the Declaration of Intent made by the Forum of European Physical Education Associations (EUPEA) at its Madrid meeting (1991) serves as one example of the way forward. The Declaration embraced the following aims:

1.   to have no education without physical education; physical education is to be promoted as a core curriculum subject;

2.   to promote the study and practice of physical education as an important discipline in its own right;

3.   to exchange information on physical education as a basis for lobbying national governments and European agencies;

4.   to explore a minimum European curriculum and secure resources to implement it;

5.   to promote in-service training courses for teachers, supported by Governments and Institutions;

6.   to develop links with influential European bodies with vested interests in physical education.

A second initiative was the inauguration of the Commonwealth Presidents of Physical Education Associations at Victoria, Canada, in August 1994. Optimistically, this body, if it is proactive, might produce a geographically wider forum for concerted international lobbying, for physical education has to be rethought in a broad and global context. There is a role here also for a number of other national, regional and international agencies. One example of which was seen in the World Forum which gathered in Quebec City in 1995, and brought together physical educators and sports personnel on a common platform to share ideas and ideals. The Forum culminated in the formulation of a series of agreed recommendations, featured in which was the promotion of the cause of physical education world-wide in a sense of shared and mutually beneficial interests.

The UNESCO International Commission on Education for the 21st Century provides a potential international vehicle to promote the essential contribution of physical education within tomorrow's education and is another initiative.

Concluding Comments

Physical education delivery systems are unique to any one country. There are similarities, differences and variations in process and product orientation based in politico-ideological, socio-cultural, economic values and norms and ecological settings. Thus, policy and practice are, more often than not, 'localised' and not 'globalised'. Nevertheless, whatever the context, the promotion of the cause of physical education is a task for *all* physical educators and research pedagogues. The redefinition of concepts of physical education together with a reconstruction of physical education presents challenges, which can only serve to improve the status, state and quality of the service to be delivered. Additionally, they will contribute to extend opportunities for engagement in physical activity to all cultural and sub-cultural groups over the full life span as well as in all institutional and wider societal communities over the four points of the compass. They are challenges which should not ignore relevant scholarly research in the social and pedagogical sciences, which, in recent years have made significant progress in unravelling some of the 'mysteries' of learning and socialisation processes in different and various cultural and cross-cultural contexts. They are also challenges which, to paraphrase the United States Surgeon General's 1994 Report on Physical Activity and Health, should be taken up to accord physical education the same level of attention given to other public policies and practices that affect the population at large: this review is more than a summary of the present state and status of physical education, it is an international call to international action.

References

ANDERSEN, D. (1996) Health and physical education in Hungary: a status report. *ICHPER•SD Journal*, Vol.XXXII, 2, 40-42.

ALEXANDER, K. and SANDS, R.A. (1991) Report of the recent conference at Deakin University on the crisis in physical education in Australia. Victoria College, November.

ANDREWS, J.A. (1993) The work of the Fédération Internationale d'Education Physique (FIEP) and its contributions to world-wide developments in physical education and sport. In HARDMAN, K. (Ed) *Proceedings, International Sports Science Summit: Towards a Richer and Healthier World through Sports Science.* Nafferton, Studies in Education.

ANTALA, B., SYKORA, F. and SEDLACEK, J. (1992) Topical problems of physical education in schools in Czechoslovakia. *British Journal of Physical Education,* 23, 4, 20-22.

ASPERI, D. (1995) News from the nations. Greece. *Bulletin of IAPESGW,* 5, 1, 6-7.

BEHBEHANI, K. (1992) Physical education in the State of Kuwait. *British Journal of Physical Education,* 23, 4, 33-35.

BOILEAU, R., CHAISSON, L., DEMERS, P., GUAY, D., LAROUCHE, R., ROY, R. and MARCOTTE, G. (Eds) (1994) *The future of physical education. A time for commitment.* Report prepared by the CÉÉPQ Steering Committee. Quebec, CÉÉPQ.

BONHOMME, G. (1992) The training of physical education teachers in France. Paper, SCOPE Conference, *The Training of Physical Education Teachers – The European Dimension.* University of Warwick, 27-29 November.

BRETTSCHNEIDER, W.-D. and BRÄUTIGAM, M. (1991) *Sport in der*

Alltagswelt von Jugendlichen. Frechen, Rittersbach.

BUTLER, M. (1996) Personal Communication.

CAHPERD (1993) Physical Education 2000 - Foundations for achieving balance in education 1992-1993. *CAHPERD Journal,* 59, 1, 14-23.

DELORES, J. (1993) *International commission on education for the twenty-first century.* UNESCO. 15th February.

DENNY, C. (1996) Physical activity or physical education? *CAHPERD Journal,* 62, 1, 34.

EDITORIAL (1997) Scots can be sporting heroes. *Scotland on Sunday,* 16th February, 21.

EICHBERG, H. (1993) Problems and future research in sports sociology: a revolution of body culture. In Hardman, K. (Ed) *Proceedings, International Sports Science Summit: Towards a richer and healthier world.* Nafferton, Studies in Education.

FASTING, K. (1992) The Prince Phillip Fellows Lecture – The European tradition and current practice in physical education. *British Journal of Physical Education,* 23, 4, 44-48.

GRAHAM, G. (1990) Physical education in U.S. schools, K-12. *Journal of Physical Education, Recreation and Dance,* 61, 2, 35-39.

GRIER, J. (1995) News from the nations. Australia. *Bulletin of IAPESGW,* 5, 1, 5.

GRUBER, J.J. (1986) Physical activity and self-esteem development in children: a meta-analysis. *American Academy of Physical Education Papers,* 19, 30-48.

HARDMAN, K. (1989) Students' and teachers' attitudes to interscholastic sports competition – a trans-national comparison. In FU, F., NG, M.L. and SPEAK, M. (Eds) *Comparative physical education and sport,* ISCPES, 6. Hong Kong, Chinese University of Hong Kong, pp.183-192.

HARDMAN, K. (1993) Physical education within the school curriculum; MESTER, J. (Ed) *Sport sciences in Europe 1993 – current and future perspectives.* Aachen, Meyer and Meyer Verlag, 544-560.

HARDMAN, K. (1994) Physical education in schools. In BELL, F.I. and VAN

GLYN, G.H. (Eds) *Access to active living*. Proceedings of the 10th Commonwealth and Scientific Congress. Victoria, Canada, University of Victoria, 71-76.

HARDMAN, K. (1995) World crisis in physical education: a bird's eye view in international context. In VARNES, J.W., GAMBLE, D. and HORODYSKI, M.B. (Eds) *Scientific and pragmatic aspects of HPER•SD*. Gainsville, FL, University of Florida, pp.78-81.

HARDMAN, K. (1996) The fall and rise of physical education in international context. Symposium Paper, Pre-Olympic and International Scientific Congress. Dallas, Texas, 9-14 July.

HARDMAN, K., KROTEE, M.L. and CHRISSANTHOPOULOS, A. (1988) A comparative study of interschool competition in England, Greece and the United States. In BROOM, E.F., CLUMPNER, R., PENDLETON, B. and POOLEY, C.A. (Eds) *Comparative physical education and sport*. ISCPES, 5. Champaign IL, Human Kinetics Publishers Inc., pp.91-102.

HARRIS, J. (1994) Young people's perception of health, fitness and exercise: implications for the teaching of health-related exercise. *Physical Education Review*, 17, 2, 143-151.

JANZEN, H. (1995) The status of physical education in Canadian public schools. *CAHPERD Journal*, 61, 3, 5-9.

JESS, M.C. (1992) *The provision and perception of physical education by primary class teachers: report of a survey carried out in Fife Region. February 1991*. Manchester Metropolitan University.

JOHNS, D. (1995) Moving to the margins: physical education another disposable program? *CAHPERD/ACSEPLD Journal*, 61, 2, 15-19.

JOHNS, D. (1996) Hong Kong children at risk: the challenge to school physical education. *CAHPERD/ACSEPLD Journal*, 62, 3, 12-14.

KAMIYOLE, T.O. (1993) Physical educators' albatross in African societies. *International Journal of Physical Education*, XXX, 2, 29-31.

KARHUS, S. (1992) The Norwegian school system – its role in Norwegian society – and physical education in the national curriculum guidelines in the secondary school. Paper, SCOPE Conference, *The Training of Physical Education Teachers – The European Dimension*. University of Warwick, 27th-29th November.

KATZENELLENBOGEN, E. (1995) News from the nations. South Africa. *Bulletin of IAPESGW*, 5, 1, 9-10.

KIRK, D. (1987) *The Orthodoxy of rational-technocracy and the research practice gap: a critique of an alternative view.* Unpublished Paper, Department of Human Movement Studies, University of Queensland.

KROTEE, M.L. (1992) Physical education in the United States: overview, issues and problems. *British Journal of Physical Education*, 23, 4, 7-10.

KROTEE, M.L., BLAIR, P.F., NAUL, R., NEUHAUS, H-W., HARDMAN, K., KOMUKU, H., MATSUMURA, K., NUMMINEN, P. and JWO, C. (1994) A six-nation study concerning attitudes and participation patterns of youth toward competitive sport. In WILCOX, R. (Ed) *Sport in the global village.* Morgantown, WV, Fitness Information Technology Inc., pp.467-476.

MACKENDRICK, M. (1996) Active living + quality daily physical education = the perfect solution. *CAHPERD Journal*, 62, 1, 2.

MALLALIEU, A. and HARDMAN, K. (1988) Autonomy versus centralism: a comparative study of physical education in England and France. In BROOM, E.F., CLUMPNER, R., PENDLETON, B. and POOLEY, C.A. (Eds) *Comparative Physical Education and Sport*, 5. Champaign, Il, Human Kinetics Books, pp.225-232.

NAUL, R. (1992) German unification: curriculum development and physical education at school in East Germany. *British Journal of Physical Education*, 23, 4, 14-19.

NAURIGHT, J. (1995) *Aussie 2000 – policies for medals.* Unpublished Paper, Kuwait Olympic Centre, Kuwait, May.

NIELSEN, A.B. (1992) Quality daily physical education: Reaching for the dream. *CAHPERD Journal*, 58, 4, 33.

PORSCHUTZ, W. (1991) Selbständigkeit, Leistungsstreben, Ordnung. Diskussion der notwendigen Komponenten im motorischen Lern- und Übungsprozess. *Sportunterricht*, 40, 377-381.

PULIS, P.L. (1994) *The structural organisation of physical education in Maltese state secondary schools.* Unpublished M.Ed. Dissertation, University of Malta, Malta.

RASHID, S. (1994) *The physical education curriculum in Malaysia.*

Unpublished Paper, University of Manchester.

RILEY, C. (1992) The rise and fall of physical education in Victoria, Australia. *British Journal of Physical Education,* 23, 4, 11-13.

RILEY, C. and DONALD, M. (1995) Changes in state government policy in Victoria, Australia: its effects on physical education in schools. *ICHPER•SD Proceedings Scientific and Pragmatic Aspects of HPER•SD.* 38th World Congress, Gainsville, Florida, 9-16 July, 178-179.

SHEHU, J. (1996) Implementation of Nigerian secondary school physical education curriculum: observations and suggestions. *ICHPER•SD Journal,* XXXII, 2, 17-20.

SMULDERS, H. (1992) *Physical education and sport in Belgium.* Unpublished manuscript.

SONSTROEM, J. (1984) Exercise and self-esteem. *Exercise and Sport Sciences,* 12, 123-155.

SONSTROEM, J.J. and MORGAN, W.P. (1989) Exercise and self-esteem: rationale and model. *Medicine and Science in Sports and Exercise,* 21, 329-337.

STRAWSON, P.F. (1970) Social morality and individual ideal. In WALLACE, G., and WALKER, A.D.M. (Eds) *The definition of morality.* London, Methuen.

THE DAILY TELEGRAPH, (1995). *PE takes a back seat, say heads.* 22nd March.

TREMBLAY, M., PELLA, T. and TAYLOR, K. (1996) The quality and quantity of school-based physical education: a growing concern. *CAHPERD Journal,* 62, 4, 4-7.

TURNBULL, J. (1994) Still a state of crisis. *The ACHPER Healthy Lifestyles Journal,* Summer, 24.

TUOHIMAA, O. (1993) Finnish physical education. At the crossroads? Motion. *Sport in Finland,* 2, 40-42.

VAN OUDENAARDE, E. (1995) News from the nations. *Bulletin of IAPESGW,* 5, 1, 9.

WAMUKOYA, E.K. and HARDMAN, K. (1992) Physical education in Kenyan Secondary Schools. *British Journal of Physical Education,* 23, 4, 30-33.

WILLIAMS, P., WILLIAMS, M., BERTRAM, A., McCORMACK, A., GURAY, C. and BRENTON, R. (1993). Implementing a new integrated curriculum in Australia: the views of head teachers, physical education. *Physical Education Review*, 16, 1, 31-40.